ECONOMIC AND SOCIAL COMMISSION
FOR WESTERN ASIA (ESCWA)

اللجنة الاقتصادية والاجتماعية
لغربي آسيا (الإسكوا)

نشرة التجارة الخارجية
للمنطقة العربية

EXTERNAL TRADE BULLETIN
OF THE ARAB REGION

العدد الرابع والعشرون
Twenty-fourth Issue

الأمم المتحدة
نيويورك، 2016

United Nations
New York, 2016

UNITED NATIONS PUBLICATION
E/ESCWA/SD/2015/7
ISBN: 978-92-1-128384-6
e-ISBN: 978-92-1-057860-8
ISSN. 0258-4948
Sales No. B.16.II.L.5
16-00023

	Page الصفحة	

List of graphs / قائمة الرسوم البيانية

		الصفحة *Page*	
Graph 9	Iraq imports and exports, 1980-2014	28	الرسم البياني ٩ واردات وصادرات العراق، ١٩٨٠-٢٠١٤
Graph 10	Jordan imports and exports, 1980-2014	29	الرسم البياني ١٠ واردات وصادرات الأردن، ١٩٨٠-٢٠١٤
Graph 11	Kuwait imports and exports, 1980-2014	30	الرسم البياني ١١ واردات وصادرات الكويت، ١٩٨٠-٢٠١٤
Graph 12	Lebanon imports and exports, 1980-2014	31	الرسم البياني ١٢ واردات وصادرات لبنان، ١٩٨٠-٢٠١٤
Graph 13	Libya imports and exports, 1980-2014	32	الرسم البياني 13 واردات وصادرات ليبيا، ١٩٨٠-٢٠١٤
Graph 14	Morocco imports and exports, 1980-2014	33	الرسم البياني 14 واردات وصادرات المغرب، ١٩٨٠-٢٠١٤
Graph 15	Oman imports and exports, 1980-2014	34	الرسم البياني 15 واردات وصادرات عمان، ١٩٨٠-٢٠١٤
Graph 16	Palestine imports and exports, 1995-٢٠١٤	35	الرسم البياني 16 واردات وصادرات فلسطين، ١٩٩٥-٢٠١٤
Graph 17	Qatar imports and exports, 1980-2014	36	الرسم البياني 17 واردات وصادرات قطر، ١٩٨٠-٢٠١٤
Graph 18	Saudi Arabia imports and exports, 1980-2014	37	الرسم البياني 18 واردات وصادرات المملكة العربية السعودية، ١٩٨٠-٢٠١٤
Graph 19	The Sudan imports and exports, 1980-2014	38	الرسم البياني 19 واردات وصادرات السودان، ١٩٨٠-٢٠١٤
Graph 20	Syrian Arab Republic imports and exports, 1980-2014	39	الرسم البياني 20 واردات وصادرات الجمهورية العربية السورية، ١٩٨٠-٢٠١٤
Graph 21	Tunisia imports and exports, 1980-2014	40	الرسم البياني 21 واردات وصادرات تونس، ١٩٨٠-٢٠١٤
Graph 22	United Arab Emirates imports and exports, 1980-2014	41	الرسم البياني 22 واردات وصادرات الإمارات العربية المتحدة، ١٩٨٠-٢٠١٤
Graph 23	Yemen imports and exports, 1991-2014	42	الرسم البياني 23 واردات وصادرات اليمن، ١٩٩١-٢٠١٤

Foreword

The secretariat of the Economic and Social Commission for Western Asia (ESCWA) is pleased to present the twenty-fourth issue of the *External Trade Bulletin of the Arab Region*.

The Bulletin includes data and statistical indicators on the international trade in goods of ESCWA member countries, based primarily on national sources and on secondary sources where needed.

The *External Trade Bulletin of the Arab Region* aims to provide complete detailed international merchandise trade data on ESCWA member countries for the users of such statistics, including planners and researchers at the national, regional and international levels.

The Bulletin is divided into three parts:

Part I includes summary tables on the trends of overall trade in the region, its annual growth and its share of total world trade. It also includes a set of indicators on the share of external trade in the gross domestic product (GDP) of ESCWA member countries, and itemizes total imports, exports and the trade balance of these countries.

Part II presents the values of intraregional trade in ESCWA member countries in a series of tables. These tables underline the importance of intraregional trade as part of total world trade, identify the trade network within the region and provide a concise reflection of the structure of intraregional trade according to the main sections of the Harmonized Commodity Description and Coding System (HS). Trade in crude oil has been excluded from the data in this part in order to show the structure of intraregional trade in non-oil merchandise.

تمهيد

يسر الأمانة التنفيذية للجنة الاقتصادية والاجتماعية لغربي آسيا (الإسكوا) أن تقدم العدد الرابع والعشرين من نشرة التجارة الخارجية للمنطقة العربية.

وتحتوي النشرة على بيانات ومؤشرات إحصائية حول التجارة الخارجية للسلع في البلدان الأعضاء في الإسكوا، مستمدّة من المصادر الوطنية بالدرجة الأولى، إضافة إلى مصادر ثانوية.

وتهدف نشرة التجارة الخارجية للمنطقة العربية إلى تقديم الإحصاءات الإجمالية والتفصيلية حول التجارة الخارجية للبضائع في البلدان الأعضاء في الإسكوا لمستخدمي هذا النوع من الإحصاءات، بمن فيهم المخططون والباحثون على المستوى الوطني والإقليمي والعالمي.

وتتضمّن النشرة ثلاثة أجزاء:

يتضمن الجزء الأول جداول تلخيصيّة تبيّن اتجاهات التجارة الإجمالية في المنطقة ومعدل نموها السنوي، وحصتها من مجموع التجارة العالمية. وهو يشمل مجموعة من المؤشرات الإحصائية حول نسبة التجارة الخارجية من الناتج المحلي الإجمالي للبلدان الأعضاء في الإسكوا، ويبيّن أيضاً إجمالي الواردات والصادرات والميزان التجاري لهذه البلدان.

ويبيّن الجزء الثاني قيمة التجارة البينية للبلدان الأعضاء في الإسكوا، ويتضمن مجموعة من الجداول تبرز أهمية التجارة ضمن المنطقة باعتبارها جزءاً من إجمالي التجارة العالمية، وتحدد شبكة التبادل التجاري داخل المنطقة، وتعطي صورة موجزة عن هيكلية التجارة البينية حسب المجموعات الرئيسية للنظام المنسق لتوصيف السلع الأساسية وترميزها (النظام المنسق). وقد استثنيت تجارة النفط الخام من بيانات هذا الجزء لإظهار هيكلية التجارة البينية للسلع غير النفطية.

Part III provides data on the trends of foreign trade of ESCWA member countries, disaggregated by country and region, for the period 2010-2014. Tables, however, do not include Iraq due to the lack of detailed data on foreign trade. Data cover the value of imports and exports of ESCWA member countries by major countries and economic groupings, in line with the practices of the United Nations Statistics Division and other international organizations.

ويتضمن الجزء الثالث بيانات عن اتجاه التجارة الخارجية للبلدان الأعضاء في الإسكوا، موزعة حسب البلدان والمناطق، في الفترة ٢٠١٠-٢٠١٤. وتستثنى بيانات العراق من هذه الجداول، لعدم توفّر إحصاءات مفصّلة عن اتجاه التجارة الخارجية فيه. وتتضمن بيانات هذا الجزء قيمة الواردات والصادرات في البلدان الأعضاء في الإسكوا، حسب أهم البلدان والمجموعات الاقتصادية، على النحو المعتمد في الشعبة الإحصائية في الأمم المتحدة وغيرها من المنظمات الدولية.

General notes

Part I. Summary of the external trade statistics of ESCWA member countries

Tables I.1 to I.8 touch upon trade in crude oil and oil products.

Tables I.1 and I.2 show the share of ESCWA member countries in total world trade and their annual trade growth rates, respectively. In both tables, ESCWA member countries are divided into two groups: major oil-exporting countries (Iraq, Kuwait, Libya, Oman, Qatar, Saudi Arabia and United Arab Emirates) and other countries.

In the light of the definitions in relevant international sources, total world trade is defined in this bulletin as the arithmetic average of exports and imports of all countries in the world. Identified in this manner, world exports would theoretically equal world imports after the deduction of shipping and insurance charges. However, import values, which are usually more accurate than export values, do not reflect alone the reality of merchandise trade due to the said difference of trade in services. Therefore the arithmetic average is used for more accurate figures.

Tables I.3 and I.4 include a set of indicators related to the value of imports and exports of ESCWA member countries, the share of their external trade in GDP and total trade per capita.

Trade annual growth rates for the periods 1991-2001 and 2001-2014 are calculated using exponential trend functions.

Tables I.7 and I.8 show the percentage share of imports and exports for each ESCWA member country in the total value of world imports and exports, by HS Section.

ملاحظات عامة

الجزء ١: ملخص إحصاءات التجارة الخارجية للبلدان الأعضاء في الإسكوا

تتناول الجداول من ١-١ إلى ١-٨ تجارة النفط الخام والمشتقات النفطية.

يبيّن الجدولان ١-١ و١-٢ حصة البلدان الأعضاء في الإسكوا من مجموع التجارة العالمية، ومعدلات النمو السنوي للتجارة في هذه البلدان. وتتوزّع البلدان في هذين الجدولين إلى مجموعتين هما البلدان الرئيسية المصدرة للنفط (الإمارات العربية المتحدة والعراق وعُمان وقطر والكويت وليبيا والمملكة العربية السعودية) والبلدان الأخرى.

واستمدّ تعريف إجمالي التجارة العالمية في هذه النشرة من المصادر الدولية ذات الصلة، ويقصد به المتوسط الحسابي لمجموع صادرات جميع البلدان في العالم مضافاً إليه مجموع وارداتها. وحيث أن مجموع صادرات جميع بلدان العالم يعادل نظرياً مجموع وارداتها بعد طرح قيمة رسوم الشحن والتأمين، فإنه ثبت أن بيانات الواردات أدقّ، إلا أن الاكتفاء بالواردات لا يعكس واقع تجارة السلع لوجود الفارق المذكور لتجارة الخدمات. ولهذا فإن استخدام المتوسط الحسابي المذكور يوفّر أرقاماً أكثر دقة.

ويشمل الجدولان ١-٣ و١-٤ مجموعة من المؤشرات المتعلقة بقيمة واردات البلدان الأعضاء في الإسكوا وصادراتها، ومساهمة تجارتها الخارجية في الناتج المحلي الإجمالي، ونصيب الفرد من إجمالي التجارة.

وحُسب معدل النمو السنوي للتجارة للفترتين ١٩٩١-٢٠٠١ و٢٠٠١-٢٠١٤ على أساس الدالة الأسّية.

ويتضمّن الجدولان ١-٧ و١-٨ النسبة المئوية لواردات البلدان الأعضاء في الإسكوا وصادراتها من إجمالي واردات وصادرات العالم، حسب أقسام النظام المنسق.

Part II. Intraregional trade of ESCWA member countries

All tables in part II exclude crude oil unless otherwise indicated in the footnotes.

Table II.3 and II.4 show matrices of intraregional imports and exports of ESCWA member countries, by country and partner, for countries on which data are available.

Table II.7 should be interpreted with care when used to obtain trade balances between ESCWA member countries, as the available statistics may not reflect the true situation. Certain member countries use the general trade system to record their international trade statistics, while others use a special system.

Part III. Trends of the foreign trade of ESCWA member countries

The partners of ESCWA member countries in foreign trade in goods are classified as "developed" and "developing" economies, distributed over the five continents (Africa, America, Asia, Europe and Oceania).

Crude oil data are presented as a separate item in the world aggregate, in order to reflect the share of oil in the imports and exports of ESCWA member countries. This is due to the fact that, very often, detailed data on this commodity are not available.

Some differences may be found between statistics on the value of overall imports and exports in tables I.5 and I.6, and statistics contained in tables I.7, I.8 and III.1 to III.13. This may be attributed to the non-distribution of crude oil import/export values or re-export values by HS section to different countries and economic blocs; to the non-distribution of import/export values of free zones and non-monetary gold; or simply to differences in approximation.

الجزء ٢: التجارة البينية للبلدان الأعضاء في الإسكوا

يُستثنى النفط الخام من جميع الجداول في هذا الجزء، باستثناء الحالات التي يشار فيها إلى عكس ذلك في الحاشية.

ويبين الجدولان ٢-٣ و٢-٤ مصفوفات قيم الواردات والصادرات البينية للبلدان الأعضاء في الإسكوا، حسب البلدان والجهات الشريكة التي تتوفر عنها البيانات.

ويجدر الحذر عند استخدام بيانات الجدول ٢-٧ للحصول على الميزان التجاري بين البلدان الأعضاء في الإسكوا، نظراً إلى أن الإحصاءات قد لا تعطي صورة حقيقية للموازين بسبب اختلاف الأنظمة التجارية المستعملة. فبعض البلدان تتبع نظام التجارة العام في تدوين إحصاءات التجارة الخارجية، بينما يتبع البعض الآخر نظاماً خاصاً.

الجزء ٣: اتجاه التجارة الخارجية للبلدان الأعضاء في الإسكوا

صنفت البلدان التي تتعامل معها البلدان الأعضاء في الإسكوا في مجال التجارة الخارجية بالسلع في مجموعتين هما البلدان المتقدّمة والبلدان النامية؛ ووُزّعت حسب القارات الخمس: أفريقيا وأمريكا وآسيا وأوروبا وأوقيانيا.

وترد بيانات النفط الخام في بند منفصل لتبيان مساهمة واردات وصادرات النفط الخام في التجارة الخارجية للبلدان الأعضاء في الإسكوا؛ ففي أغلب الأحيان لا تتوفر بيانات تفصيلية عن هذه السلعة.

وقد تظهر بعض الفوارق بين إحصاءات إجمالي قيمة الواردات والصادرات في الجدولين ١-٥ و١-٦ والبيانات التي تتضمنها الجداول ١-٧ و١-٨ و٣-١ إلى ٣-١٣. وقد تعود هذه الفوارق إلى عدم توزيع قيم واردات وصادرات النفط الخام أو قيم إعادة التصدير على البلدان والكتل الاقتصادية المختلفة حسب أقسام النظام المنسق؛ أو إلى عدم توزيع قيم واردات وصادرات المناطق الحرة والذهب غير النقدي؛ أو إلى الفوارق الناتجة من القيمة التقريبية للأعداد.

Abbreviations and symbols
المختصرات والرموز

Abbreviations		المختصرات
c.i.f	Including cost, insurance and freight	يتضمن عناصر الكلفة والتأمين والشحن (سيف)
f.o.b.	Free on board	تسليم على ظهر السفينة (فوب)
ASEAN	Association of Southeast Asian Nations	رابطة أمم جنوب شرق آسيا
CACEU	Central African Customs and Economic Union	الاتحاد الجمركي والاقتصادي لوسط أفريقيا
ECOWAS	Economic Community of West African States	المجموعة الاقتصادية لدول غرب أفريقيا
EFTA	European Free Trade Association	الرابطة الأوروبية للتجارة الحرّة
ESCWA	Economic and Social Commission for Western Asia	الإسكوا: اللجنة الاقتصادية والاجتماعية لغربي آسيا (الإسكوا)
EU	European Union	الاتحاد الأوروبي
HS	Harmonized Commodity Description and Coding System	النظام المنسق لتوصيف السلع الأساسية وترميزها (النظام المنسق)
LAIA	Latin American Integration Association	رابطة تكامل أمريكا اللاتينية
SITC	Standard International Trade Classification	التصنيف الموحّد للتجارة الدولية

Symbols		الرموز	
*	Preliminary estimates	تقديرات أولية	*
..	Data not available	بيانات غير متوفر	..
—	Negligible or zero	ضئيل أو صفر	—

معدلات التحويل التجارية للدولار الأمريكي بالعملات المحلية[1]

Trade conversion factors in national currencies per US dollar[1]

		2005	2006	2007	2008	2009	2010	2011	2012	2013	2014		
Bahrain	Import	0.3760	0.3760	0.3760	0.3760	0.3760	0.3760	2.6490	0.3760	0.3775	0.3775	استيراد	**البحرين**
(Dinar)	Export	0.3760	0.3760	0.3760	0.3760	0.3760	0.3760	2.6490	0.3760	0.3775	0.3775	تصدير	***(دينار)***
Eygpt	Import	5.7889	5.7383	5.6892	5.3236	5.5855	5.6807	5.9324	6.0683	6.0683	7.0765	استيراد	**مصر**
(Pound)	Export	5.7885	5.7380	5.3492	5.3492	5.6134	5.7096	5.9323	6.0683	6.0683	7.0765	تصدير	***(جنيه)***
Iraq	Import	..	..	..	..	..	1181.8491	1194.2572	1169.5685	..	..	استيراد	**العراق**
(Dinar)	Export	..	..	1267.0001	1200.0003	1170.0994	1170.1153	1170.0574	1169.9987	..	..	تصدير	***(دينار)***
Jordan	Import	0.7090	0.7090	0.7090	0.7097	0.7100	0.7100	0.7100	0.7100	0.7100	0.7100	استيراد	**الأردن**
(Dinar)	Export	0.7090	0.7090	0.7090	0.7097	0.7100	0.7100	0.7100	0.7100	0.7100	0.7100	تصدير	***(دينار)***
Kuwait	Import	0.2920	0.2900	0.2837	0.2689	0.2878	0.2867	0.2759	0.2799	0.2839	0.2839	استيراد	**الكويت**
(Dinar)	Export	0.2920	0.2901	0.2834	0.2682	0.2876	0.2862	0.2759	0.2799	0.2839	0.2839	تصدير	***(دينار)***
Lebanon	Import	1508.00	1508.00	1508.00	1508.00	1508.00	1508.00	1508.00	1508.00	1508.00	1508.00	استيراد	**لبنان**
(Pound)	Export	1508.00	1508.00	1508.00	1508.00	1508.00	1508.00	1508.00	1508.00	1508.00	1508.00	تصدير	***(ليرة)***
Libya	Import	..	..	1.2589	1.2281	1.2489	1.2660	..	..	..	..	استيراد	**ليبيا**
(Dinar)	Export	..	..	1.2605	1.2245	1.2501	1.2677	..	..	..	..	تصدير	***(دينار)***
Morocco	Import	8.8621	8.7815	8.1598	8.4207	7.7027	8.1598	8.0820	8.6208	8.4050	8.4073	استيراد	**المغرب**
(dirham)	Export	8.8750	8.7867	8.1790	8.4202	7.6698	8.1790	8.0829	8.6216	8.4064	8.4080	تصدير	***(درهم)***
Oman	Import	0.3845	0.3845	0.3845	0.3845	0.3845	0.3845	0.3845	0.3845	0.3845	0.3845	استيراد	**عمان**
(Rial)	Export	0.3845	0.3845	0.3845	0.3845	0.3845	0.3845	0.3845	0.3845	0.3845	0.3845	تصدير	***(ريال)***
Qatar	Import	3.6399	3.6399	3.6399	3.6399	3.6399	3.6399	3.6399	3.6400	3.6400	3.6400	استيراد	**قطر**
(Rial)	Export	3.6399	3.6399	3.6399	3.6399	3.6399	3.6399	3.6399	3.6400	3.6400	3.6400	تصدير	***(ريال)***
Saudi Arabia	Import	3.7478	3.7450	3.7467	3.7500	3.7500	3.7500	3.7500	3.7500	3.7500	3.7500	استيراد	**المملكة العربية السعودية**
(Rial)	Export	3.7466	3.7450	3.7467	3.7500	3.7500	3.7500	3.7500	3.7500	3.7500	3.7500	تصدير	***(ريال)***
The Sudan	Import	..	..	..	..	..	..	..	..	..	..	استيراد	**السودان**
(Dinar)	Export	..	..	..	..	..	..	..	..	..	..	تصدير	***(دينار)***
Syrian Arab Republic	Import	50.0000	50.0000	50.000	46.650	46.810	46.700	48.560	48.560(2)	..	..	استيراد	**الجمهورية العربية السورية**
(Pound)	Export	50.0000	50.0000	50.000	46.470	46.610	46.500	48.100	48.100(2)	..	..	تصدير	***(ليرة)***
Tunisia	Import	1.2978	1.3297	1.279	1.229	1.346	1.432	1.407	1.562	1.625	..	استيراد	**تونس**
(Dinar)	Export	1.2968	1.3304	1.280	1.223	1.348	1.432	1.406	1.561	1.624	..	تصدير	***(دينار)***
United Arab Emirates	Import	3.6726(3)	3.6725	3.6725	3.6725	3.6725	3.6725	3.6725	3.6725	3.6725	3.6725	استيراد	**الإمارات العربية المتحدة**
(Dirham)	Export	3.6726(3)	3.6725	3.6725	3.6725	3.6725	3.6725	3.6725	3.6725	3.6725	3.6725	تصدير	***(درهم)***
Yemen	Import	183.49(4)	197.05	198.89	200.08	207.32	218.53	213.81	214.27	214.87	214.87	استيراد	**اليمن**
(Rial)	Export	183.49(4)	197.05	198.97	200.08	207.32	219.68	213.81	214.36	214.87	214.87	تصدير	***(ريال)***

(1)Trade conversion factors are derived from: Monthly Bulletin of Statistics, UNSD, available at: http://unstats.un.org/unsd/mbs and from the national statistical abstracts of ESCWA member countries.

(2) Conversion factor for 2011 was derived.

(3) Conversion factor for 2002 was derived.

(4) Conversion factor for 2003 was derived.

(1) أخذت معدلات التحويل التجارية من موقع النشرة الإحصائية الشهرية لشعبة الإحصاءات في الأمم المتحدة، المتاح على http://unstats.un.org/unsd/mbs. ومن المجموعات الإحصائية للبلدان الأعضاء في الإسكوا.

(2) أخذ معدل التحويل لعام 2011.

(3) أخذ معدل التحويل لعام 2002.

(4) أخذ معدل التحويل لعام 2003.

الجزء الأول

ملخص إحصاءات التجارة الخارجية للبلدان الأعضاء في الإسكوا

Part I

SUMMARY OF THE EXTERNAL TRADE STATISTICS OF ESCWA MEMBER COUNTRIES

Introduction

World trade continued to grow at a slow pace for a third year in a row. Its weak growth rate of 1 per cent in 2014 is even lower than the 2.2 per cent recorded in the two previous years. According to the World Trade Organization's data, growth in the volume of world trade reached 2.5 per cent which better matches the growth in world output during 2014. Among the factors responsible for this continued slow growth of world trade is the sudden and sustained decline of oil prices since August 2014, slow growth of the emerging economies and the slow and uneven recovery of the developed countries. In value terms, world exports reached US$ 18.4 billion in 2014. Germany and Canada achieved 4 per cent growth rates in their exports in 2014 while growth rate of USA exports settled around 3 per cent. Major developed countries witnessed negative growth rates of their exports during 2014 among them Britain which suffered a 7 per cent drop of their exports and Japan 4 per cent. The scene in the developing world was slightly similar with the exception of China and Mexico having 6 per cent and 5 per cent growth of their exports respectively. Negative growth rates of exports generally speaking characterized the rest of the developing regions that averaged 8 per cent in Africa and 6 per cent in Latin America.

The falling oil prices, that started deteriorating since August 2014 through the end of the year, had negative effects on the exports of the Arab region of which oil exports constitute around 70 per cent. Oil prices declined by 47 per cent from the level of US$ ١١٠ per barrel in June 2014 to less than US$ 58 by the end of the year. Thus, for the first time in many years, ESCWA's oil-rich countries suffered in 2014 a considerable retraction of their oil revenues and the region's total trade decreased to US$ 2.07 trillion compared to US$ 2.16 trillion in 2013. In addition, trade surpluses realized by the region's oil-rich countries decreased by 23.9 per cent from about US$ 465.4 billion in 2013 to about US$ 354.1 billion in 2014. The share of the ESCWA region of world trade declined to 5.6 per cent in 2014.

مقدمة

تميّزت التجارة العالمية، وللعام الثالث على التوالي، بتراخي الأداء وتحقيق معدلات نمو متواضعة فيما يمكن وصفه بحالة من الركود الاقتصادي حيث نمت قيمة الصادرات العالمية بمعدل ١ في المئة فقط خلال عام ٢٠١٤ وهو ما يمثل تراجعاً حتى بالقياس الى المعدل المتباطيء المتحقق في العامين السابقين والبالغ حوالي ٢،٢ في المئة. الا أنه وحسب بيانات منظمة التجارة العالمية فإن نمو التجارة العالمية بالنظر الى الحجم قد بلغ ٢،٥ في المئة. ويمكن النظر الى جملة من الأسباب وراء هذا الأداء المتواصل في في معدلات نمو التجارة الدولية حيث يأتي في مقدمتها الهبوط المفاجيء والمتواصل في أسعار النفط العالمية منذ منتصف العام، يضاف الى ذلك تراجع معدلات نمو الناتج القومي في الاقتصادات الناشئة وعدم تعافي البلدان المتقدمة بشكل متساوي. فقد بلغت الصادرات العالمية ١٨،٤ تريليون دولار أمريكي بالأسعار الجارية في عام ٢٠١٤. أهم البلدان المتقدمة التي حققت نمواً ايجابياً في صادراتها خلال عام ٢٠١٤ كانت ألمانيا وكندا اللتان حققتا معدل ٤ في المئة زيادة تلتها الولايات المتحدة الأمريكية بواقع ٣ في المئة. وكانت بلدان متقدمة عديدة قد حققت هذا العام معدلات نمو سالبة مثل بريطانيا التي حققت معدل ٧ في المئة واليابان ٤ في المئة. أما في جانب البلدان النامية فقد حققت الصين زيادة في صادراتها بلغت ٦ في المئة تلتها المكسيك بمعدل ٥ في المئة في حين سجلت معظم الدول الأخرى معدلات نمو سالبة تراوحت في المعدل بين ٨ في المئة في القارة الأفريقية و٦ في المئة في بلدان أمريكا الجنوبية.

كان لانخفاض أسعار النفط في النصف الثاني من العام ٢٠١٤ وحتى نهاية العام أثر سلبي على حصيلة الصادرات من المنطقة العربية التي يشكل النفط أكثر من ٧٠ في المئة. فقد انخفضت أسعار النفط من ١١٠ دولار أمريكي للبرميل في شهر حزيران من ذات العام الى أقل من ٥٨ دولار في نهايته أي بنسبة ٤٧ في المئة. وهكذا فإنها المرة الأولى منذ سنوات عديدة التي تعاني فيها بلدان الإسكوا خاصة الغنية بالنفط من تراجع العوائد النفطية بشكل ملموس. وقد تسبّب هذا الانخفاض في أسعار النفط الى تراجع قيمة التجارة الكلية لمنطقة الاسكوا الى ٢،٠٧ تريليون دولار عام ٢٠١٤ بالمقارنة مع ٢،١٦ تريليون دولار عام ٢٠١٣. بالاضافة الى ذلك، فقد تركت أثراً مباشراً على الفوائض التجارية المتحققة لبلدان الاسكوا الغنية بالنفط والتي انخفضت الى حوالي 354,1 مليار دولار عام ٢٠١٤ بالمقارنة مع حوالي ٤٦٥،٤ مليار دولار عام ٢٠١٣ اي أنها تراجعت بواقع ٢٣،٩ في المئة. أما حصة منطقة الاسكوا من التجارة العالمية فقد انخفضت الى ٥،٦ في المائة عام ٢٠١٤.

For the first time since 2009, ESCWA region exports shrank by 7.5 per cent in 2014 while their imports continued to rise but at a modest rate of 1.7 per cent. The region's oil-rich exporting countries[1] realized the largest share of the region's total exports that was amounted to 90.7 per cent in 2014 while their share of imports was 72.6 per cent. It is worth noting that this group of countries depends to a large degree on the export of crude oil and its derivatives but to varying degrees within a range from 53.3 per cent in the United Arab Emirates to the percentage of 93.5 per cent in Kuwait.

وللمرة الأولى منذ عام ٢٠٠٩، شهدت صادرات بلدان منطقة الإسكوا ككل خلال عام ٢٠١٤ انخفاضاً بلغ 7,5 في المئة بينما واصلت واردات منطقة الاسكوا الكلية ارتفاعها وبنسبة ١،٧ في المئة خلال العام نفسه. ولا زالت البلدان الرئيسية المصدرة للنفط في منطقة الاسكوا[١] تتمتع بالنصيب الأكبر من التجارة الخارجية للمنطقة حيث بلغت نسبة صادراتها الى مجموع صادرات الاسكوا حوالي ٩٠،٧ في المئة بينما استأثرت بنسبة 72,6 في المئة من واردات المنطقة. ويتميز الأداء التجاري لهذه المجموعة من البلدان بالاعتماد المطلق على التجارة الدولية في النفط ومشتقاته والتي تتدرج من مستوى ٥٣،٣ في المئة من مجموع صادرات الأمارات العربية المتحدة وصولاً الى نسبة ٩٣،٥ في المئة من الصادرات الكلية للكويت.

At the level of countries, most countries in the ESCWA region suffered declining exports during 2014 except Morocco and Jordan whose exports had risen by 8.4 per cent and 6 per cent respectively. The largest declines occurred in the countries hit by political instability in particular Yemen and Libya where exports declined sharply by 66 per cent and 51 per cent during 2014 respectively. As for the oil-rich countries, Saudi Arabia suffered the largest loss of exports in 2014 where its exports declined by US$ 33 billion or by 8.9 per cent, US$ 13 billion loss in Kuwait while the least decline was felt by UAE whose exports fell only by US$ 3 billion constituting less than 1 per cent of its total exports.

أما على المستوى القطري، فقد انخفضت صادرات معظم بلدان الاسكوا باستثناء المغرب الذي ارتفعت صادراته بنسبة ٨،٤ في المئة والأردن بنسبة ٦ في المئة عام ٢٠١٤. وكان أكبر الانخفاض من نصيب البلدان العربية التي تمر في حالات من عدم الاستقرار السياسي وهي اليمن وليبيا والتي تراجعت صادراتها بشكل كبير تجاوز ٦٦ في المئة في اليمن و٥١ في المئة في ليبيا خلال هذا العام. أما بالنسبة للدول العربية الغنية بالنفط، فقد خسرت السعودية أكثر من ٣٣ مليار دولار أمريكي هذا العام بما شكل حوالي ٨،٩ في المئة من صادراتها تلتها الكويت بتراجع مقداره ١٣ مليار دولار بينما شهدت الامارات العربية المتحدة أقل تراجع في صادرات هذه المجموعة بواقع ٣ مليار دولار أوأقل من ١ في المئة من مجموع صادراتها.

Despite the fact that the imports of many countries in the ESCWA region increased, the total imports of the region declined by 1.7 per cent in 2014. UAE claimed the largest increase of its imports which amounted to US$ 11.8 billion, followed by US$ 5 billion for Saudi Arabia and US$ 3.9 billion dollars for Egypt. With respect to countries of the region whose imports declined during 2014, Libya experienced the largest decline of its imports that fell by US$ 8 billion, followed Oman and Iraq whose imports fell by US$ 5 and US$ 2 billion respectively.

أما في جانب الواردات فقد كان الاتجاه متباين بين بلدان الاسكوا بين الزيادة والتراجع خلال عام ٢٠١٤ الا أن الواردات الكلية للمنطقة ارتفعت بنسبة ١،٧ في المئة. حققت الأمارات العربية المتحدة أعلى زيادة في حجم الواردات في منطقة الاسكوا وبلغت ١١،٨ مليار دولار أمريكي، تلتها السعودية بواقع ٥ مليار ومصر بزيادة قدرها ٣،٩ مليار دولار. أما بالنسبة للبلدان التي انخفضت وارداتها خلال عام ٢٠١٤ فقد حققت ليبيا أعلى تراجع في وارداتها في منطقة الاسكوا خلال عام ٢٠١٤ حيث بلغ حجم التراجع حوالي ٨ مليار دولار أمريكي تلتها سلطنة عمان بتراجع وقدره ٥ مليار دولار، تلاها العراق بقيمة ٢ مليار دولار.

(1) Iraq, Kuwait, Libya, Omar, Qatar, Saudi Arabia and United Arab Emirates.

(١) العراق وليبيا وعُمان والكويت وقطر والسعودية والإمارات العربية المتحدة.

As for the ESCWA region's more diversified economies[2], their combined exports constituted about 9.3 per cent of total exports while the share of their imports was 27.4 per cent of the region's total imports in 2014. While trade surpluses realized by the region's oil-rich countries fell sharply during 2014, the combined trade deficit realized for the region's more diversified countries rose to US$ 123 billion after it actually declined to US$ 107 billion in 2013. Having a closer look at the trade deficit figures of the latter group, it is expected that those countries will narrow their deficits in 2015 with the falling oil prices and decreasing oil bill. However, their continuous and chronic trade deficit will not be affected substantially in the long run.

With respect to trade openness and dependency for which the indicators are explained in the previous issue, ESCWA member countries depend highly on foreign markets to sell their products and secure the products they need. Trade dependence for the ESCWA region as a whole scored 80.0 per cent in 2014 which shows the region's high degree of dependency. It rises to the level of 92.4 per cent for the region's oil-rich countries and diminishes to 48.1 per cent for the more diversified economies. On the level of countries, the most dependent/open country in the ESCWA region was UAE where its trade dependence ratio reached 163.5 per cent, followed by Bahrain 128.3 per cent, Oman 102.9 per cent and Jordan 86.8 per cent. On the other hand, the least trade dependent/open country in the ESCWA region in 2014 was Sudan that scored a ratio of 18.1 per cent, followed by Syria 29.2 per cent, Egypt 33.2 per cent and Yemen scoring 33.4 per cent dependency ratio. A ratio that exceeds 100 per cent can be explained within the context of the ESCWA region by extensive re-exporting.

(2) Bahrain, Jordan, Lebanon, Morocco, Palestine, Sudan, Syria, Tunisia and Yemen.

أما بالنسبة لمجموعات بلدان منطقة الاسكوا الأخرى ذات الاقتصادات الأكثر تنوعاً[٢] فقد شكلت نسبة صادراتها ما نسبته ٩،٣ في المئة من إجمالي صادرات المنطقة بينما بلغت حصة وارداتها حوالي ٢٧،٤ في المئة من إجمالي واردات المنطقة عام ٢٠١٤. واذا كانت بلدان منطقة الاسكوا الغنية بالنفط قد شهدت فوائضها التجارية تراجعاً كبيراً بنسبة 24 في المئة خلال هذا العام، فإن العجز التجاري الكلي لمجموعة بلدان منطقة الاسكوا ذات الاقتصادات الأكثر تنوعاً ارتفع ليبلغ ١٢٣ مليار دولار بعد أن انخفض في عام ٢٠١٣ الى حوالي ١٠٧ مليار دولار. وبالنظر الى تطور أرقام فجوة العجز التجاري لهذه المجموعة من الدول فإنه يؤمل في عام ٢٠١٥ أن تنخفض نتيجة لانخفاض فاتورة النفط المستورد لديها الا أنه في المدى الطويل لن يؤثر ذلك على اتجاهات العجز التجاري المستمر والمزمن لهذه البلدان.

أما فيما يتعلق بالانفتاح التجاري على العالم الخارجي الذي تم شرح المؤشرات الخاصة بها في العدد الماضي، فإن بلدان منطقة الاسكوا تعتمد الى درجة كبيرة على الأسواق الخارجية في تأمين أسواق لمنتجاتها وكذلك الأمر شراء احتياجاتها المختلفة. بلغ معدل الاعتماد التجاري في منطقة الاسكوا ككل 80 في المئة في عام ٢٠١٤ بينما ارتفع للبلدان الغنية بالنفط الى ٩٢،٤ في المئة واخفض الى 48,1 في المئة في البلدان ذات الاقتصادات الأكثر تنوعاً. أما على المستوى القطري، فإن أكثر بلدان منطقة الاسكوا انفتاحاً على الخارج خلال عام ٢٠١٤ كانت الامارات العربية المتحدة التي بلغت نسبة انفتاحها التجاري حوالي ١٦٣،٥ في المئة، تلتها البحرين بنسبة ١٢٨،٣ في المئة، فسلطنة عمان بنسبة ١٠٢،٩ في المئة، ثم الأردن بنسبة 86,8 في المائة. في حين كانت أقل بلدان منطقة الاسكوا انفتاحاً تجارياً في عام ٢٠١٤ كان السودان حيث بلغت نسبة انفتاحه التجاري على الخارج حوالي ١٨،١ في المئة، تلته الجمهورية العربية السورية بنسبة ٢٩،٢ في المئة، تلتها جمهورية مصر العربية بنسبة ٣٣،٢ في المئة، ثم اليمن بنسبة انفتاح تجاري بلغت ٣٣،٤ في المئة. وتفسّر النسبة التي تتجاوز ١٠٠ في المئة في بعض بلدان المنطقة بارتفاع عمليات اعادة التصدير الى جانب الصادرات الوطنية.

(٢) البحرين، الأردن، لبنان، المغرب، فلسطين، السودان، الجمهورية العربية السورية، تونس واليمن.

الجدول 1-1- حصة البلدان الأعضاء في الإسكوا من مجموع التجارة العالمية[1]

Table I.1. Share of ESCWA member countries in total world trade[1]
2005-2014

(Millions of US dollars) (مليون دولار أمريكي)

	2005	2006	2007	2008	2009	2010	2011	2012	2013	2014	
Total value of world trade[2]	10 559 100	12 157 450	14 094 200	16 263 626	12 548 684	15 112 305	18 070 674	18 150 691	18 445 090	18 646 300	القيمة الإجمالية للتجارة العالمية[2]
Total ESCWA imports	306 234	351 036	471 962	641 907	541 438	606 795	716 996	771 854	847 203	861 640	مجموع واردات الإسكوا
ESCWA share (percentage)	2.9	2.9	3.3	3.9	4.3	4.0	4.0	4.3	4.6	4.6	حصة الإسكوا (نسبة مئوية)
Of which: Major oil exporters[3]	1.9	1.9	2.3	2.6	2.9	2.7	2.7	3.0	3.3	3.4	ومنها: البلدان الرئيسية المصدرة للنفط[3]
Other countries	1.0	1.0	1.1	1.4	1.4	1.3	1.3	1.3	1.2	1.3	باقي البلدان
Total ESCWA exports	504 468	589 815	686 231	969 381	681 992	847 510	1 144 748	1 311 578	1 312 631	1 214 632	مجموع صادرات الإسكوا
ESCWA share (percentage)	4.8	4.9	4.9	6.0	5.4	5.6	6.3	7.2	7.1	6.5	حصة الإسكوا (نسبة مئوية)
Of which: Major oil exporters[3]	4.1	4.2	4.2	5.2	4.6	4.8	5.6	6.6	6.5	5.9	ومنها: البلدان الرئيسية المصدرة للنفط[3]
Other countries	0.7	0.7	0.7	0.8	0.8	0.8	0.7	0.7	0.7	0.6	باقي البلدان
Total value of ESCWA Trade[4]	810 702	940 851	1 158 194	1 611 288	1 223 430	1 454 305	1 861 744	2 083 432	2 159 833	2 076 271	القيمة الإجمالية للتجارة في منطقة الإسكوا[4]
ESCWA share of world trade (percentage)[4]	3.8	3.9	4.1	5.0	4.9	4.8	5.2	5.7	5.9	5.6	حصة الإسكوا من التجارة العالمية (نسبة مئوية)[4]
Of which: Major oil exporters[3]	3.0	3.1	3.2	3.9	3.8	3.7	4.2	4.8	4.9	4.6	ومنها: البلدان الرئيسية المصدرة للنفط[3]
Other countries	0.8	0.8	0.9	1.1	1.1	1.1	1.0	1.0	1.0	0.9	باقي البلدان

(1) Crude oil and oil products are included in this table.
(2) International Monetary Fund, *Direction of trade statisics*, http://www.imf.org.
The total value of world trade is calculated as the arithmetic average of total world exports and the total world imports,
(3) Iraq, Kuwait, Libya, Oman, Qatar, Saudi Arabia and United Arab Emirates.
(4) The total value of the share of ESCWA member countries is calculated as the arithmetic average of the region total exports and total imports divided by the total value of world trade.

(1) يشمل هذا الجدول تجارة النفط الخام ومنتجاته.
(2) صندوق النقد الدولي، http://www.imf.org.
وتم احتساب القيمة الإجمالية على أساس المتوسط الحسابي للواردات والصادرات العالمية.
(3) الإمارات العربية المتحدة والعراق وعُمان وقطر والكويت وليبيا والمملكة العربية السعودية.
(4) تم احتساب حصة البلدان الأعضاء في الإسكوا على أساس المتوسط الحسابي لوارداتها وصادراتها مقسوما على القيمة الإجمالية للتجارة العالمية.

الرسم البياني 1- القيمة الإجمالية لواردات العالم ومنطقة الإسكوا (المقياس اللوغاريثمي)، 1980-2014

Graph 1: Total imports, world and ESCWA region (logarithmic scale), 1980-2014

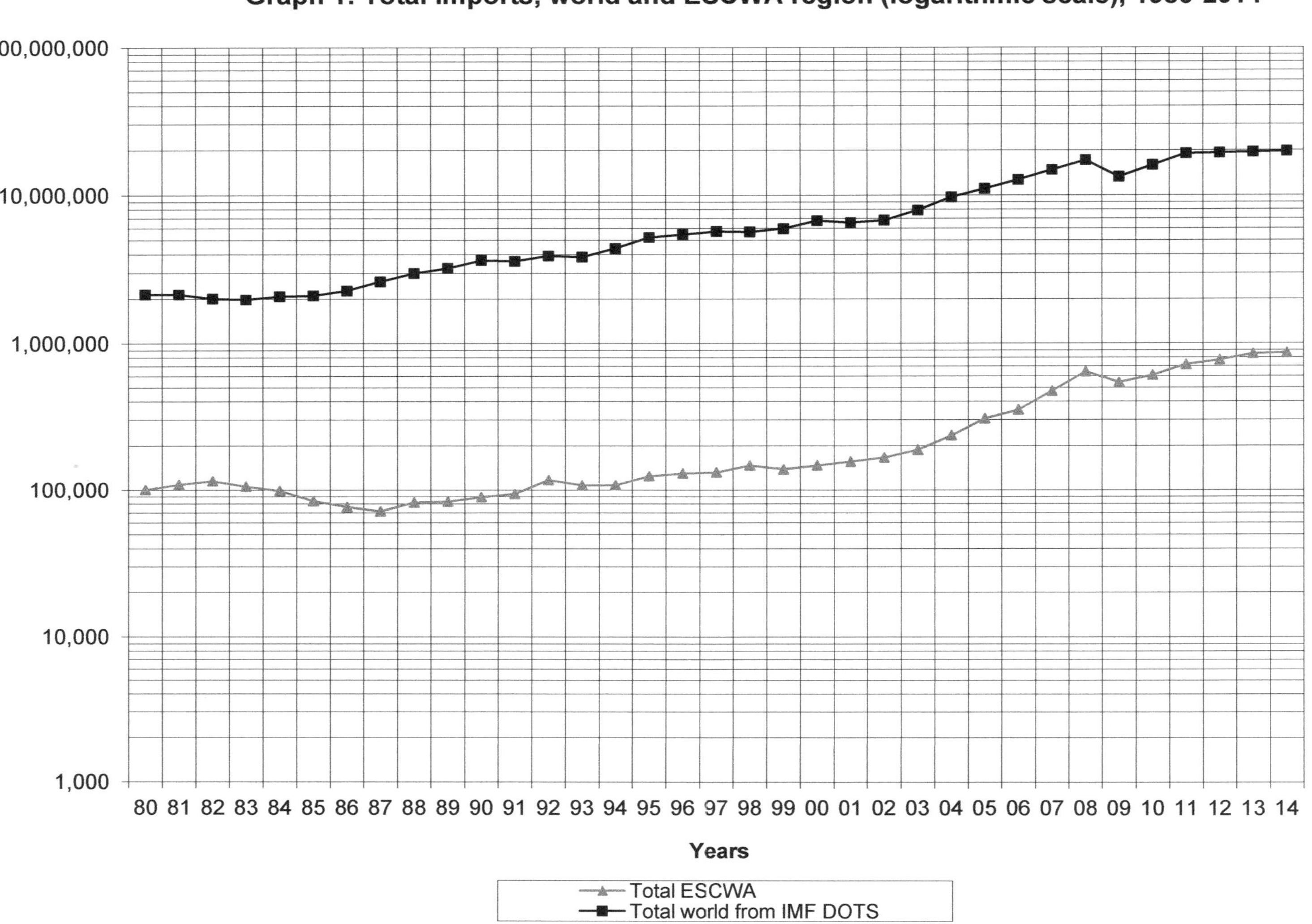

الرسم البياني 2- القيمة الإجمالية لصادرات العالم ومنطقة الإسكوا (المقياس اللوغاريثمي)، 1980-2014

Graph 2: Total exports, world and ESCWA region (logarithmic scale), 1980-2014

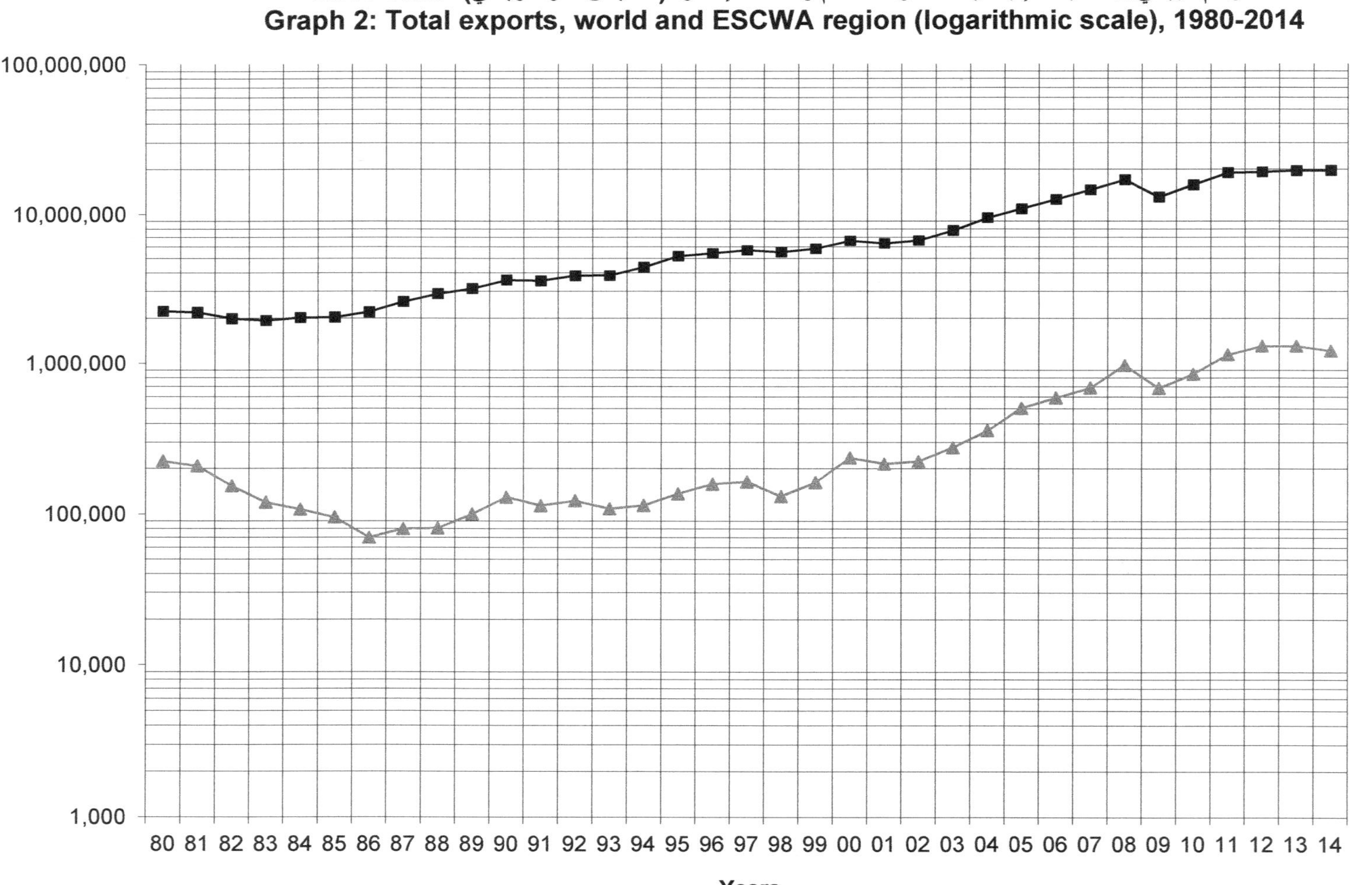

الرسم البياني 3- واردات البلدان الأعضاء في الإسكوا، 1980-2014

Graph 3. Imports of ESCWA member countries, 1980-2014

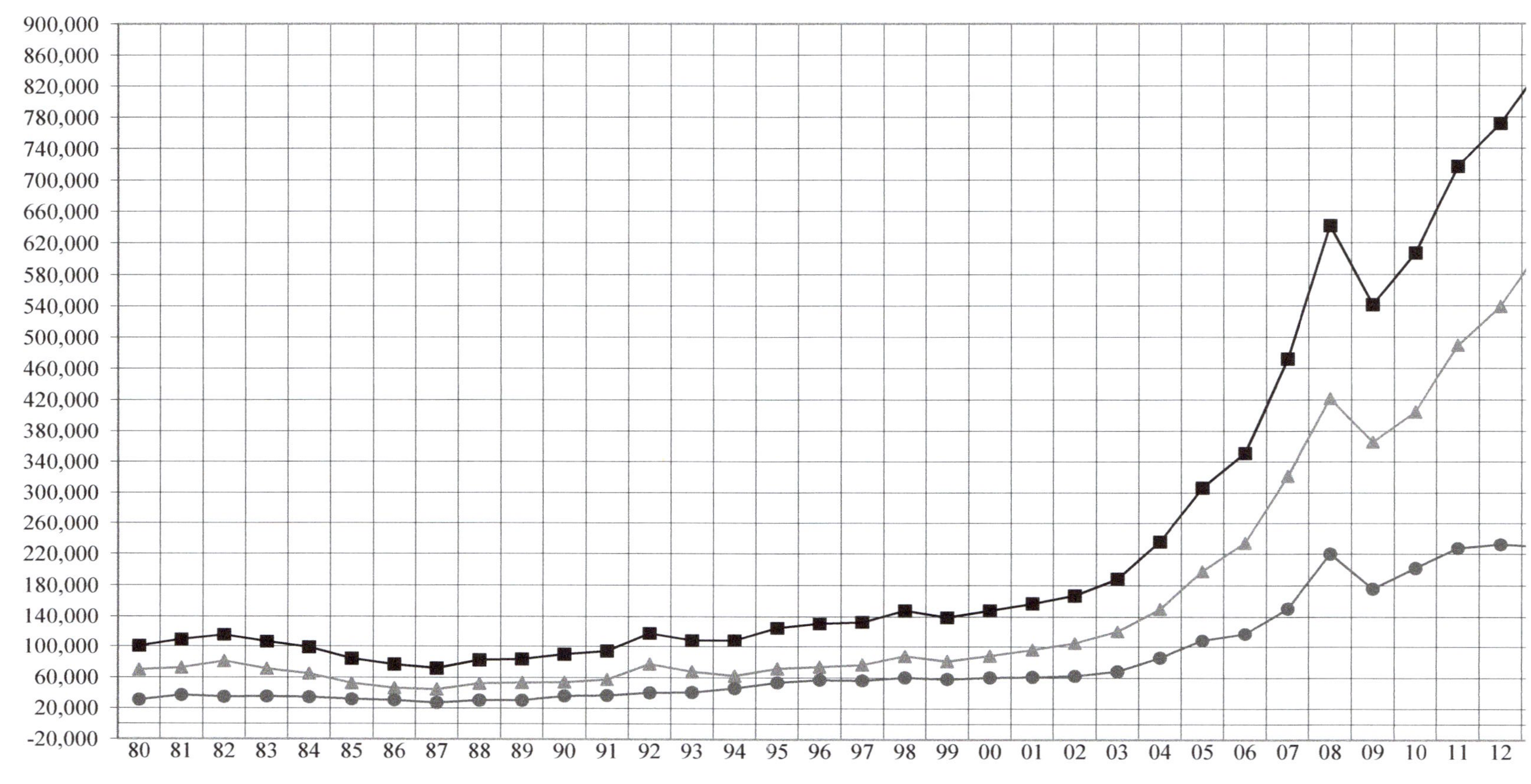

الرسم البياني 4- واردات البلدان الأعضاء في الإسكوا، المقياس اللوغاريثمي، 1980 -2014

Graph 4. Imports of ESCWA member countries, logarithmic scale, 1980-2014

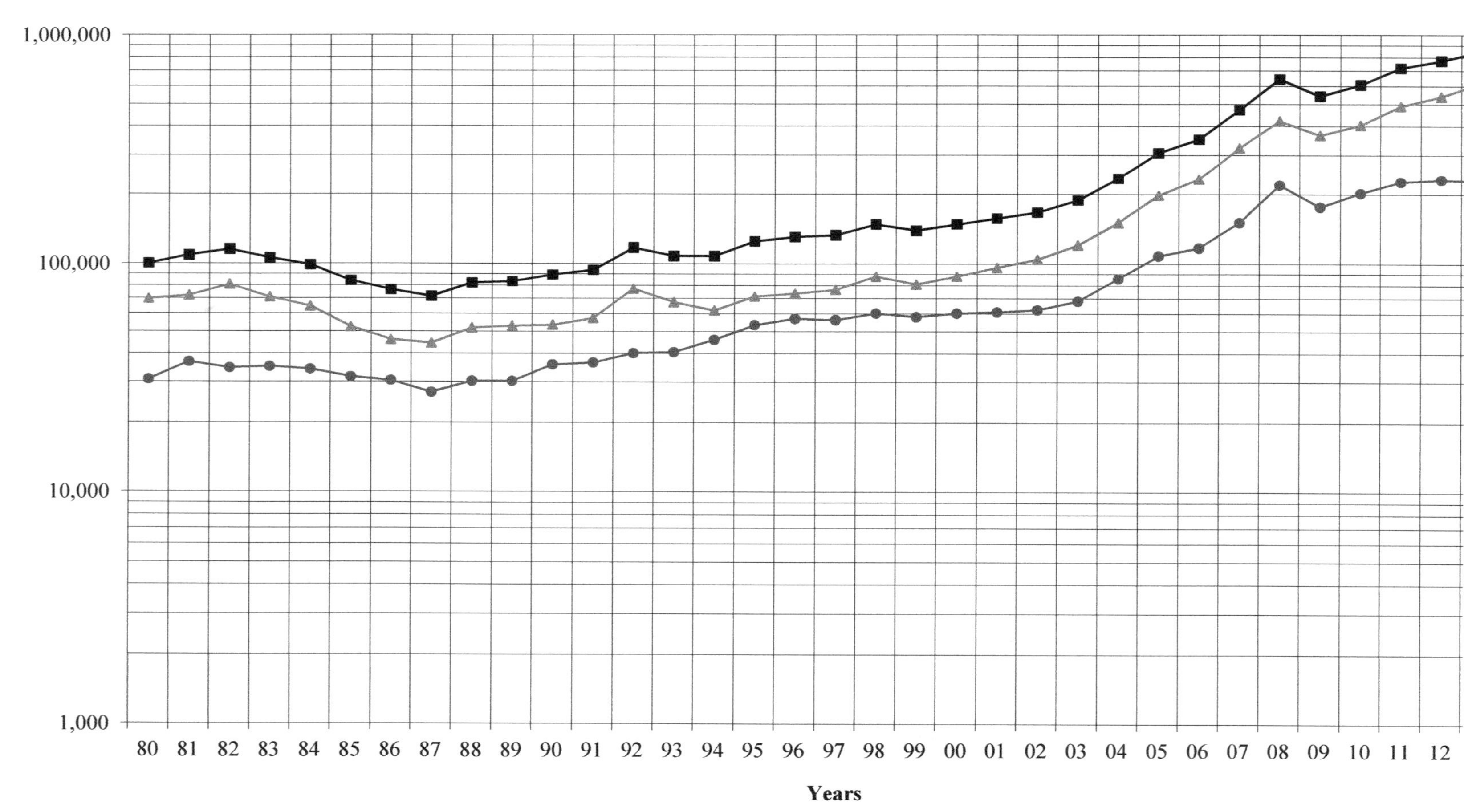

الرسم البياني 5 - صادرات البلدان الأعضاء في الإسكوا، 1980 -2014
Graph 5. Exports of ESCWA member countries, 1980-2014

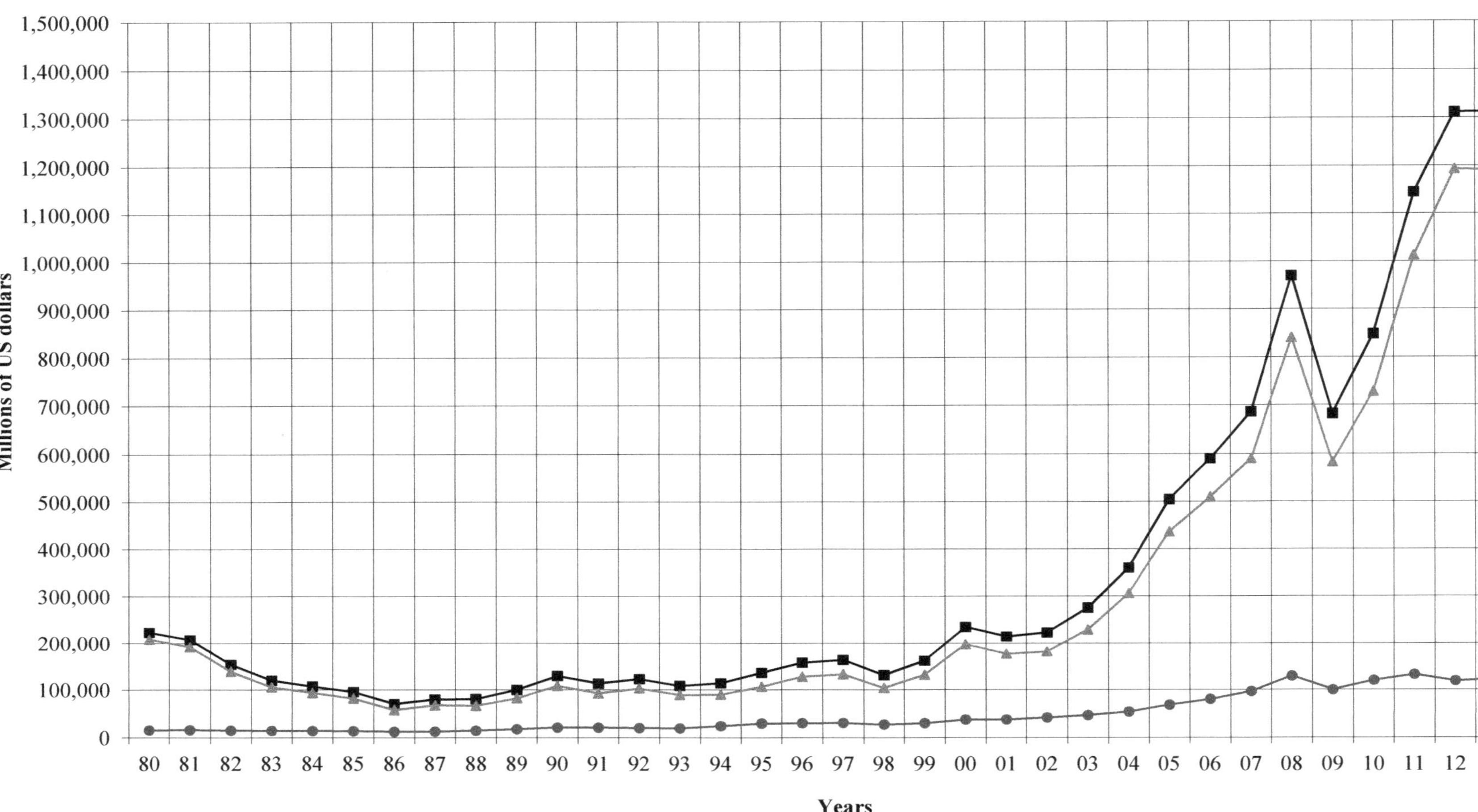

Total ESCWA — Major oil exporters — Other ESCWA countries

الرسم البياني 6: 6- صادرات البلدان الأعضاء في الإسكوا، المقياس اللوغاريتمي، 1980- 2014

Graph 6. Exports of ESCWA member countries, logarithmic scale, 1980-2014

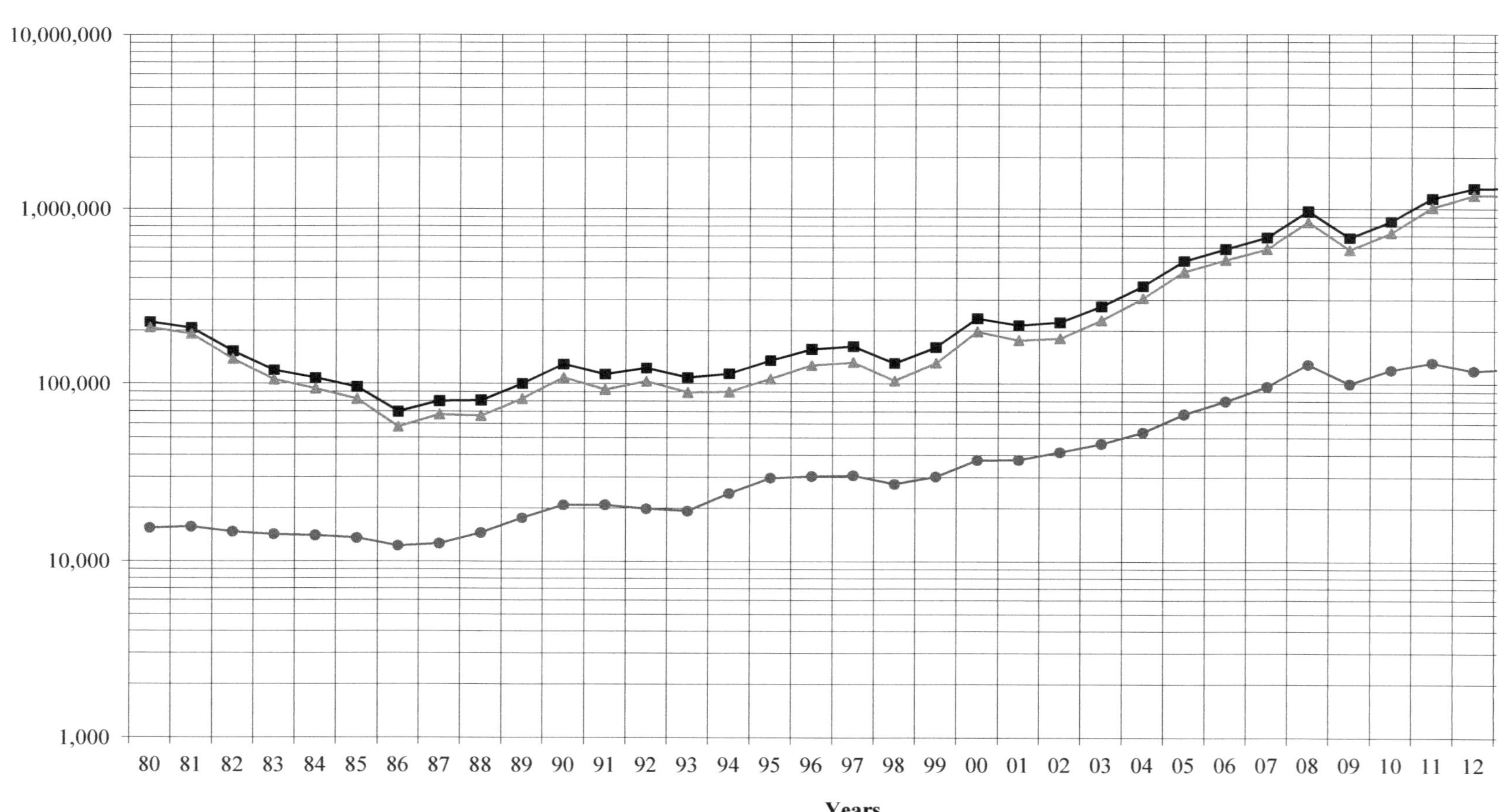

الجدول 1-2- معدل النمو السنوي للتجارة في البلدان الأعضاء في الإسكوا[1]

Table I.2. Annual trade growth rates in ESCWA member countries[1]

2005-2014

(*Percentage*) (نسبة مئوية)

	2005-2006	2006-2007	2007-2008	2008-2009	2009-2010	2010-2011	2011-2012	2012-2013	2013-2014	1991-2001	2001-2014	
Imports:												الواردات:
World	14.8	16.0	15.5	-22.9	20.3	19.6	0.6	1.0	1.3	6.5	8.8	العالم
ESCWA	14.6	34.4	36.0	-15.7	12.1	18.2	7.7	9.8	1.7	4.5	14.4	الإسكوا
Of which:												ومنها:
Major oil exporters[2]	18.1	37.4	31.2	-13.3	10.7	21.0	10.2	14.5	1.2	4.0	15.6	البلدان الرئيسية المصدرة للنفط[2]
Other countries	8.2	28.6	46.3	-20.1	14.9	12.5	2.2	-1.3	3.0	5.3	12.0	باقي البلدان
Exports:												الصادرات:
World	15.5	15.9	15.3	-22.8	20.5	19.5	0.3	2.2	0.8	6.3	8.9	العالم
ESCWA	16.9	16.3	41.3	-29.6	24.3	35.1	14.6	0.1	-7.5	6.8	14.9	الإسكوا
Of which:												ومنها:
Major oil exporters[2]	16.8	15.7	42.5	-30.7	25.0	39.1	17.8	-0.2	-7.4	6.8	15.6	البلدان الرئيسية المصدرة للنفط[2]
Other countries	17.9	20.4	33.7	-22.6	20.0	10.3	-10.1	3.2	-8.4	6.5	9.8	باقي البلدان
Total trade:												القيمة الإجمالية للتجارة:
World	15.1	15.9	15.4	-22.8	20.4	19.6	0.4	1.6	1.1	6.4	6.8	العالم
ESCWA	16.1	23.1	39.1	-24.1	18.9	28.0	11.9	3.7	-3.9	5.8	14.5	الإسكوا
Of which:												ومنها:
Major oil exporters[2]	17.2	22.5	38.5	-24.9	19.5	32.7	15.3	4.4	-4.4	5.8	15.6	البلدان الرئيسية المصدرة للنفط[2]
Other countries	11.9	25.3	41.4	-21.0	16.8	11.7	-2.3	0.2	-1.0	5.7	10.9	باقي البلدان

(1) Including crude oil and oil products.

(2) Iraq, Kuwait, Libya, Oman, Qatar, Saudi Arabia and United Arab Emirates.

(1) بما في ذلك تجارة النفط الخام ومنتجاته.

(2) الإمارات العربية المتحدة والعراق وعُمان وقطر والكويت وليبيا والمملكة العربية السعودية.

الجدول 1-3- مؤشرات مختارة للتجارة الخارجية في البلدان الأعضاء في الإسكوا

Table I.3. Selected foreign trade indicators of ESCWA member countries
2005-2014

	2005	2006	2007	2008	2009	2010	2011	2012	2013	2014	
Bahrain											**البحرين**
Foreign trade coverage ratio (exports/imports*100)	109.0	130.2	118.2	102.7	95.5	100.4	127.6	110.6	137.2	116.8	معدّل التغطية في قطاع التجارة الخارجية (الصادرات/الواردات *100)
Imports to GDP ratio (percentage)	58.8	48.4	54.9	69.1	54.4	62.2	60.5	64.4	56.5	59.2	نسبة الواردات من الناتج المحلي الإجمالي
Exports to GDP ratio (percentage)	64.1	63.0	64.8	71.0	51.9	62.5	77.2	71.3	77.5	69.1	نسبة الصادرات من الناتج المحلي الإجمالي
Trade balance to GDP ratio (percentage)	5.3	14.6	10.0	1.9	-2.4	0.2	16.7	6.8	21.0	9.9	نسبة الميزان التجاري من الناتج المحلي الإجمالي
Trade to GDP ratio (percentage)	122.9	111.4	119.7	140.1	106.3	124.7	137.7	135.7	134.0	128.3	نسبة القيمة الإجمالية للتجارة من الناتج المحلي الإجمالي
Trade per capita (thousands of US dollars)	22.3	21.7	25.2	32.3	20.5	25.6	30.9	31.7	33.1	32.3	نصيب الفرد من القيمة الإجمالية للتجارة (ألف دولار أمريكي)
Trade as percentage of ESCWA total trade	2.4	2.2	2.2	2.2	2.0	2.2	2.1	2.0	2.0	2.2	نسبة إجمالي التجارة من إجمالي تجارة الإسكوا
Export market share (percentage): exports/ESCWA total exports	2.0	2.0	2.1	1.9	1.7	1.9	2.0	1.7	1.9	1.9	حصة الصادرات من السوق: نسبة الصادرات إلى إجمالي صادرات الإسكوا
Egypt											**مصر**
Foreign trade coverage ratio (exports/imports*100)	53.7	66.6	59.6	49.5	51.1	51.3	51.9	43.1	44.7	39.3	معدّل التغطية في قطاع التجارة الخارجية (الصادرات/الواردات *100)
Imports to GDP ratio (percentage)	21.0	19.1	20.3	32.8	23.8	24.6	25.6	27.5	25.2	23.8	نسبة الواردات من الناتج المحلي الإجمالي
Exports to GDP ratio (percentage)	11.3	12.7	12.1	16.2	12.2	12.6	13.3	11.8	11.3	9.4	نسبة الصادرات من الناتج المحلي الإجمالي
Trade balance to GDP ratio (percentage)	-9.7	-6.4	-8.2	-16.6	-11.6	-12.0	-12.3	-15.6	-13.9	-14.5	نسبة الميزان التجاري من الناتج المحلي الإجمالي
Trade to GDP ratio (percentage)	32.2	31.9	32.4	49.0	36.0	37.3	39.0	39.3	36.5	33.2	نسبة القيمة الإجمالية للتجارة من الناتج المحلي الإجمالي
Trade per capita (thousands of US dollars)	0.4	0.5	0.6	1.1	0.9	1.0	1.1	1.3	1.1	1.1	نصيب الفرد من القيمة الإجمالية للتجارة (ألف دولار أمريكي)
Trade as percentage of ESCWA total trade	3.8	3.6	3.7	5.0	5.5	5.5	4.8	4.9	4.3	4.8	نسبة إجمالي التجارة من إجمالي تجارة الإسكوا
Export market share (percentage): exports/ESCWA total exports	2.1	2.3	2.3	2.8	3.4	3.2	2.7	2.3	2.2	2.2	حصة الصادرات من السوق: نسبة الصادرات إلى إجمالي صادرات الإسكوا
Iraq											**العراق**
Foreign trade coverage ratio (exports/imports*100)	135.3	175.5	193.4	285.5	175.1	191.5	169.4	386.2	147.1	143.4	معدّل التغطية في قطاع التجارة الخارجية (الصادرات/الواردات *100)
Imports to GDP ratio (percentage)	36.0	24.8	20.2	20.9	21.8	23.4	31.2	13.3	31.2	26.4	نسبة الواردات من الناتج المحلي الإجمالي
Exports to GDP ratio (percentage)	48.7	43.6	39.2	59.6	38.1	44.8	52.8	51.3	45.9	37.9	نسبة الصادرات من الناتج المحلي الإجمالي
Trade balance to GDP ratio (percentage)	12.7	18.7	18.9	38.7	16.4	21.4	21.6	38.0	14.7	11.5	نسبة الميزان التجاري من الناتج المحلي الإجمالي
Trade to GDP ratio (percentage)	84.6	68.4	59.4	80.4	59.9	68.2	84.0	64.5	77.1	64.3	نسبة القيمة الإجمالية للتجارة من الناتج المحلي الإجمالي
Trade per capita (thousands of US dollars)	1.1	1.3	1.5	2.8	2.2	2.6	4.2	3.6	4.5	4.1	نصيب الفرد من القيمة الإجمالية للتجارة (ألف دولار أمريكي)
Trade as percentage of ESCWA total trade	3.8	4.0	3.8	5.1	5.4	5.5	7.1	5.7	7.0	7.2	نسبة إجمالي التجارة من إجمالي تجارة الإسكوا
Export market share (percentage): exports/ESCWA total exports	3.5	4.0	4.3	6.3	6.1	6.2	7.3	7.2	6.8	7.0	حصة الصادرات من السوق: نسبة الصادرات إلى إجمالي صادرات الإسكوا

الجدول 1-3- مؤشرات مختارة للتجارة الخارجية في البلدان الأعضاء في الإسكوا

Table I.3. Selected foreign trade indicators of ESCWA member countries
2005-2014

	2005	2006	2007	2008	2009	2010	2011	2012	2013	2014	
Jordan											الأردن
Foreign trade coverage ratio (exports/imports*100)	41.0	45.1	41.7	46.1	45.2	46.0	42.3	38.0	35.9	36.9	معدّل التغطية في قطاع التجارة الخارجية (الصادرات/الواردات *100)
Imports to GDP ratio (percentage)	83.4	76.7	80.4	76.8	59.1	57.8	65.6	67.1	65.7	63.4	نسبة الواردات من الناتج المحلي الإجمالي
Exports to GDP ratio (percentage)	34.2	34.6	33.5	35.4	26.7	26.6	27.8	25.5	23.6	23.4	نسبة الصادرات من الناتج المحلي الإجمالي
Trade balance to GDP ratio (percentage)	-49.2	-42.1	-46.9	-41.4	-32.4	-31.2	-37.9	-41.6	-42.1	-40.0	نسبة الميزان التجاري من الناتج المحلي الإجمالي
Trade to GDP ratio (percentage)	117.6	111.3	113.9	112.2	85.8	84.3	93.4	92.6	89.2	86.8	نسبة القيمة الإجمالية للتجارة من الناتج المحلي الإجمالي
Trade per capita (thousands of US dollars)	2.8	3.1	3.4	4.2	3.3	3.5	4.0	4.1	4.1	4.1	نصيب الفرد من القيمة الإجمالية للتجارة (ألف دولار أمريكي)
Trade as percentage of ESCWA total trade	1.8	1.8	1.7	1.5	1.7	1.5	1.4	1.4	1.4	1.5	نسبة إجمالي التجارة من إجمالي تجارة الإسكوا
Export market share (percentage): exports/ESCWA total exports	0.9	0.9	0.8	0.8	0.9	0.8	0.7	0.6	0.6	0.7	حصة الصادرات من السوق: نسبة الصادرات إلى إجمالي صادرات الإسكوا
Kuwait											الكويت
Foreign trade coverage ratio (exports/imports*100)	283.9	324.8	293.5	352.1	255.4	276.8	408.5	420.0	385.9	321.2	معدّل التغطية في قطاع التجارة الخارجية (الصادرات/الواردات *100)
Imports to GDP ratio (percentage)	19.7	17.0	18.6	16.9	19.2	19.6	16.3	15.7	16.9	18.2	نسبة الواردات من الناتج المحلي الإجمالي
Exports to GDP ratio (percentage)	55.9	55.1	54.7	59.3	49.0	54.4	66.7	65.8	65.1	58.6	نسبة الصادرات من الناتج المحلي الإجمالي
Trade balance to GDP ratio (percentage)	36.2	38.2	36.1	42.5	29.8	34.7	50.4	50.1	48.2	40.3	نسبة الميزان التجاري من الناتج المحلي الإجمالي
Trade to GDP ratio (percentage)	75.6	72.1	73.3	76.2	68.2	74.0	83.0	81.5	81.9	76.8	نسبة القيمة الإجمالية للتجارة من الناتج المحلي الإجمالي
Trade per capita (thousands of US dollars)	26.6	30.3	32.9	41.6	25.4	28.6	40.9	43.6	42.8	38.1	نصيب الفرد من القيمة الإجمالية للتجارة (ألف دولار أمريكي)
Trade as percentage of ESCWA total trade	7.5	7.8	7.3	7.0	5.9	5.9	6.9	6.8	6.7	6.7	نسبة إجمالي التجارة من إجمالي تجارة الإسكوا
Export market share (percentage): exports/ESCWA	9.0	9.5	9.1	9.0	7.6	7.4	9.0	8.7	8.7	8.3	حصة الصادرات من السوق: نسبة الصادرات إلى إجمالي صادرات الإسكوا
Lebanon											لبنان
Foreign trade coverage ratio (exports/imports*100)	20.1	24.3	23.8	21.6	21.5	23.7	21.2	21.1	18.5	16.2	معدّل التغطية في قطاع التجارة الخارجية (الصادرات/الواردات *100)
Imports to GDP ratio (percentage)	43.5	42.6	47.5	55.2	45.8	46.8	50.3	48.3	45.0	41.0	نسبة الواردات من الناتج المحلي الإجمالي
Exports to GDP ratio (percentage)	8.7	10.4	11.3	11.9	9.8	11.1	10.6	10.2	8.3	6.6	نسبة الصادرات من الناتج المحلي الإجمالي
Trade balance to GDP ratio (percentage)	-34.7	-32.3	-36.2	-43.3	-36.0	-35.7	-39.7	-38.1	-36.6	-34.3	نسبة الميزان التجاري من الناتج المحلي الإجمالي
Trade to GDP ratio (percentage)	52.2	53.0	58.8	67.1	55.6	57.8	60.9	58.4	53.3	47.6	نسبة القيمة الإجمالية للتجارة من الناتج المحلي الإجمالي
Trade per capita (thousands of US dollars)	2.8	2.9	3.5	4.7	4.6	5.1	5.5	5.5	5.2	4.8	نصيب الفرد من القيمة الإجمالية للتجارة (ألف دولار أمريكي)
Trade as percentage of ESCWA total trade	1.4	1.2	1.3	1.2	1.6	1.5	1.3	1.2	1.2	1.2	نسبة إجمالي التجارة من إجمالي تجارة الإسكوا
Export market share (percentage): exports/ESCWA total exports	0.4	0.4	0.4	0.4	0.5	0.5	0.4	0.3	0.3	0.3	حصة الصادرات من السوق: نسبة الصادرات إلى إجمالي صادرات الإسكوا

الجدول 1-3- مؤشرات مختارة للتجارة الخارجية في البلدان الأعضاء في الإسكوا

Table I.3. Selected foreign trade indicators of ESCWA member countries 2005-2014

	2005	2006	2007	2008	2009	2010	2011	2012	2013	2014	
Libya											ليبيا
Foreign trade coverage ratio (exports/imports*100)	515.8	666.5	697.6	490.3	212.0	206.2	237.5	277.0	161.1	110.5	معدّل التغطية في قطاع التجارة الخارجية (الصادرات/الواردات *100)
Imports to GDP ratio (percentage)	13.4	11.0	10.7	9.6	18.7	21.8	19.7	23.0	36.2	46.2	نسبة الواردات من الناتج المحلي الإجمالي
Exports to GDP ratio (percentage)	69.0	73.1	75.0	46.9	39.6	45.0	46.8	63.6	58.3	51.0	نسبة الصادرات من الناتج المحلي الإجمالي
Trade balance to GDP ratio (percentage)	55.6	62.1	64.2	37.3	20.9	23.2	27.1	40.7	22.1	4.9	نسبة الميزان التجاري من الناتج المحلي الإجمالي
Trade to GDP ratio (percentage)	82.4	84.1	85.7	56.5	58.3	66.9	66.5	86.6	94.5	97.2	نسبة القيمة الإجمالية للتجارة من الناتج المحلي الإجمالي
Trade per capita (thousands of US dollars)	6.7	8.1	9.3	9.2	6.7	9.0	4.4	13.5	11.4	6.4	نصيب الفرد من القيمة الإجمالية للتجارة (ألف دولار أمريكي)
Trade as percentage of ESCWA total trade	4.6	4.9	4.6	3.3	3.3	3.7	1.5	4.0	3.3	2.0	نسبة إجمالي التجارة من إجمالي تجارة الإسكوا
Export market share (percentage): exports/ESCWA total exports	6.2	6.8	6.8	4.6	4.0	4.3	1.7	4.6	3.3	1.7	حصة الصادرات من السوق: نسبة الصادرات إلى إجمالي صادرات الإسكوا
Morocco											المغرب
Foreign trade coverage ratio (exports/imports*100)	53.8	53.1	47.9	48.0	42.8	50.2	48.9	47.8	48.6	51.6	معدّل التغطية في قطاع التجارة الخارجية (الصادرات/الواردات *100)
Imports to GDP ratio (percentage)	34.9	36.5	42.6	47.6	36.2	39.0	44.6	46.7	43.5	42.0	نسبة الواردات من الناتج المحلي الإجمالي
Exports to GDP ratio (percentage)	18.8	19.4	20.4	22.8	15.5	19.6	21.8	22.3	21.2	21.6	نسبة الصادرات من الناتج المحلي الإجمالي
Trade balance to GDP ratio (percentage)	-16.1	-17.1	-22.2	-24.8	-20.7	-19.4	-22.8	-24.4	-22.4	-20.3	نسبة الميزان التجاري من الناتج المحلي الإجمالي
Trade to GDP ratio (percentage)	53.7	55.9	62.9	70.5	51.6	58.5	66.4	69.0	64.7	63.6	نسبة القيمة الإجمالية للتجارة من الناتج المحلي الإجمالي
Trade per capita (thousands of US dollars)	1.1	1.2	1.5	2.0	1.5	1.7	2.1	2.0	2.0	2.1	نصيب الفرد من القيمة الإجمالية للتجارة (ألف دولار أمريكي)
Trade as percentage of ESCWA total trade	3.9	3.9	4.1	3.9	3.8	3.7	3.5	3.2	3.1	3.5	نسبة إجمالي التجارة من إجمالي تجارة الإسكوا
Export market share (percentage): exports/ESCWA total exports	2.2	2.2	2.2	2.1	2.1	2.1	1.9	1.6	1.7	2.0	حصة الصادرات من السوق: نسبة الصادرات إلى إجمالي صادرات الإسكوا
Oman											عُمان
Foreign trade coverage ratio (exports/imports*100)	211.8	198.1	154.5	164.5	154.9	185.1	199.4	185.4	161.7	173.1	معدّل التغطية في قطاع التجارة الخارجية (الصادرات/الواردات *100)
Imports to GDP ratio (percentage)	28.4	29.3	38.0	37.6	36.9	33.7	34.0	36.3	43.1	37.7	نسبة الواردات من الناتج المحلي الإجمالي
Exports to GDP ratio (percentage)	60.1	58.0	58.7	61.9	57.1	62.4	67.7	67.3	69.7	65.2	نسبة الصادرات من الناتج المحلي الإجمالي
Trade balance to GDP ratio (percentage)	31.7	28.7	20.7	24.3	20.3	28.7	33.8	31.0	26.6	27.5	نسبة الميزان التجاري من الناتج المحلي الإجمالي
Trade to GDP ratio (percentage)	88.5	87.3	96.6	99.6	94.0	96.1	101.7	103.6	112.8	102.9	نسبة القيمة الإجمالية للتجارة من الناتج المحلي الإجمالي
Trade per capita (thousands of US dollars)	10.9	12.7	15.8	23.4	17.1	20.1	23.4	24.2	24.7	20.4	نصيب الفرد من القيمة الإجمالية للتجارة (ألف دولار أمريكي)
Trade as percentage of ESCWA total trade	3.4	3.5	3.5	3.8	3.7	3.9	3.8	3.9	4.2	4.0	نسبة إجمالي التجارة من إجمالي تجارة الإسكوا
Export market share (percentage): exports/ESCWA total exports	3.7	3.7	3.6	3.9	4.1	4.3	4.1	4.0	4.2	4.2	حصة الصادرات من السوق: نسبة الصادرات إلى إجمالي صادرات الإسكوا

الجدول 1-3- مؤشرات مختارة للتجارة الخارجية في البلدان الأعضاء في الإسكوا

Table I.3. Selected foreign trade indicators of ESCWA member countries
2005-2014

	2005	2006	2007	2008	2009	2010	2011	2012	2013	2014	
Palestine											**فلسطين**
Foreign trade coverage ratio (exports/imports*100)	12.6	13.3	16.3	15.6	14.4	14.5	17.0	16.7	22.6	16.6	معدّل التغطية في قطاع التجارة الخارجية (الصادرات/الواردات *100)
Imports to GDP ratio (percentage)	57.5	59.7	60.6	57.1	53.6	47.5	43.2	45.8	48.0	50.4	نسبة الواردات من الناتج المحلي الإجمالي
Exports to GDP ratio (percentage)	7.2	7.9	9.9	8.9	7.7	6.9	7.4	7.6	10.8	8.4	نسبة الصادرات من الناتج المحلي الإجمالي
Trade balance to GDP ratio (percentage)	-50.3	-51.8	-50.7	-48.2	-45.9	-40.6	-35.8	-38.2	-37.2	-42.0	نسبة الميزان التجاري من الناتج المحلي الإجمالي
Trade to GDP ratio (percentage)	64.8	67.7	70.5	66.1	61.3	54.4	50.5	53.4	58.8	58.7	نسبة القيمة الإجمالية للتجارة من الناتج المحلي الإجمالي
Trade per capita (thousands of US dollars)	0.8	0.9	1.0	1.1	1.1	1.1	1.2	1.3	1.5	1.5	نصيب الفرد من القيمة الإجمالية للتجارة (ألف دولار أمريكي)
Trade as percentage of ESCWA total trade	0.4	0.3	0.3	0.3	0.3	0.3	0.3	0.3	0.3	0.3	نسبة إجمالي التجارة من إجمالي تجارة الإسكوا
Export market share (percentage): exports/ESCWA total exports	0.1	0.1	0.1	0.1	0.1	0.1	0.1	0.1	0.1	0.1	حصة الصادرات من السوق: نسبة الصادرات إلى إجمالي صادرات الإسكوا
Qatar											**قطر**
Foreign trade coverage ratio (exports/imports*100)	256.1	207.1	191.0	202.8	198.5	321.9	511.9	509.8	506.2	432.3	معدّل التغطية في قطاع التجارة الخارجية (الصادرات/الواردات *100)
Imports to GDP ratio (percentage)	22.6	27.0	27.6	24.2	25.5	18.6	13.2	13.7	13.4	14.5	نسبة الواردات من الناتج المحلي الإجمالي
Exports to GDP ratio (percentage)	57.9	55.9	52.7	49.1	50.6	59.8	67.3	70.0	67.6	62.6	نسبة الصادرات من الناتج المحلي الإجمالي
Trade balance to GDP ratio (percentage)	35.3	28.9	25.1	24.9	25.1	41.2	54.2	56.3	54.2	48.1	نسبة الميزان التجاري من الناتج المحلي الإجمالي
Trade to GDP ratio (percentage)	80.4	82.9	80.3	73.3	76.1	78.4	80.5	83.7	81.0	77.1	نسبة القيمة الإجمالية للتجارة من الناتج المحلي الإجمالي
Trade per capita (thousands of US dollars)	1.1	1.6	1.9	2.5	2.1	2.8	3.8	4.3	4.3	4.2	نصيب الفرد من القيمة الإجمالية للتجارة (ألف دولار أمريكي)
Trade as percentage of ESCWA total trade	4.4	5.4	5.5	5.2	6.1	6.7	7.3	7.6	7.6	8.2	نسبة إجمالي التجارة من إجمالي تجارة الإسكوا
Export market share (percentage): exports/ESCWA total exports	5.1	5.8	6.1	5.8	7.3	8.8	10.0	10.1	10.4	10.8	حصة الصادرات من السوق: نسبة الصادرات إلى إجمالي صادرات الإسكوا
Saudi Arabia											**المملكة العربية السعودية**
Foreign trade coverage ratio (exports/imports*100)	303.8	270.0	228.0	272.3	201.3	235.0	277.2	249.6	223.5	197.0	معدّل التغطية في قطاع التجارة الخارجية (الصادرات/الواردات *100)
Imports to GDP ratio (percentage)	18.9	22.1	28.5	36.5	30.3	33.9	41.7	49.3	53.3	23.3	نسبة الواردات من الناتج المحلي الإجمالي
Exports to GDP ratio (percentage)	57.3	59.7	65.1	99.3	60.9	79.6	115.6	123.1	119.1	45.9	نسبة الصادرات من الناتج المحلي الإجمالي
Trade balance to GDP ratio (percentage)	38.4	37.6	36.6	62.9	30.7	45.7	73.9	73.8	65.8	22.6	نسبة الميزان التجاري من الناتج المحلي الإجمالي
Trade to GDP ratio (percentage)	76.1	81.8	93.7	135.8	91.2	113.4	157.3	172.4	172.4	69.2	نسبة القيمة الإجمالية للتجارة من الناتج المحلي الإجمالي
Trade per capita (thousands of US dollars)	9.7	10.2	11.4	16.3	10.7	13.1	17.9	19.2	18.9	17.6	نصيب الفرد من القيمة الإجمالية للتجارة (ألف دولار أمريكي)
Trade as percentage of ESCWA total trade	29.6	27.5	25.5	26.6	23.5	24.6	26.7	26.1	25.2	26.0	نسبة إجمالي التجارة من إجمالي تجارة الإسكوا
Export market share (percentage): exports/ESCWA total exports	35.8	32.0	29.9	32.3	28.2	29.6	31.9	29.6	28.6	28.2	حصة الصادرات من السوق: نسبة الصادرات إلى إجمالي صادرات الإسكوا

الجدول 1-3- مؤشرات مختارة للتجارة الخارجية في البلدان الأعضاء في الإسكوا

Table I.3. Selected foreign trade indicators of ESCWA member countries
2005-2014

	2005	2006	2007	2008	2009	2010	2011	2012	2013	2014	
Sudan											**السودان**
Foreign trade coverage ratio (exports/imports*100)	61.2	61.9	90.0	57.9	105.7	95.2	94.1	51.4	71.4	47.2	معدّل التغطية في قطاع التجارة الخارجية (الصادرات/الواردات *100)
Imports to GDP ratio (percentage)	27.8	25.2	21.7	33.9	17.8	22.0	17.3	12.7	18.2	12.3	نسبة الواردات من الناتج المحلي الإجمالي
Exports to GDP ratio (percentage)	17.0	15.6	19.5	19.6	18.8	20.9	16.2	6.5	13.0	5.8	نسبة الصادرات من الناتج المحلي الإجمالي
Trade balance to GDP ratio (percentage)	-10.8	-9.6	-2.2	-14.3	1.0	-1.1	-1.0	-6.2	-5.2	-6.5	نسبة الميزان التجاري من الناتج المحلي الإجمالي
Trade to GDP ratio (percentage)	44.8	40.7	41.2	53.5	36.6	42.9	33.5	19.2	31.1	18.1	نسبة القيمة الإجمالية للتجارة من الناتج المحلي الإجمالي
Trade per capita (thousands of US dollars)	0.4	0.4	0.6	0.8	0.5	0.6	0.5	0.3	0.4	0.3	نصيب الفرد من القيمة الإجمالية للتجارة (ألف دولار أمريكي)
Trade as percentage of ESCWA total trade	1.5	1.5	1.6	1.6	1.4	1.6	1.0	0.5	0.8	0.7	نسبة إجمالي التجارة من إجمالي تجارة الإسكوا
Export market share (percentage): exports/ESCWA total exports	0.9	0.9	1.3	1.0	1.3	1.3	0.8	0.3	0.5	0.4	حصة الصادرات من السوق: نسبة الصادرات إلى إجمالي صادرات الإسكوا
Syrian Arab Republic											**الجمهورية العربية السورية**
Foreign trade coverage ratio (exports/imports*100)	86.3	96.6	85.7	85.7	71.3	73.6	52.8	54.8	37.0	29.9	معدّل التغطية في قطاع التجارة الخارجية (الصادرات/الواردات *100)
Imports to GDP ratio (percentage)	35.4	32.1	33.7	34.2	28.2	28.8	37.0	17.6	15.4	22.5	نسبة الواردات من الناتج المحلي الإجمالي
Exports to GDP ratio (percentage)	30.5	31.0	28.9	29.3	20.1	21.2	19.6	9.6	5.7	6.7	نسبة الصادرات من الناتج المحلي الإجمالي
Trade balance to GDP ratio (percentage)	-4.9	-1.1	-4.8	-4.9	-8.1	-7.6	-17.5	-8.0	-9.7	-15.8	نسبة الميزان التجاري من الناتج المحلي الإجمالي
Trade to GDP ratio (percentage)	65.9	63.1	62.5	63.6	48.3	49.9	56.6	27.2	21.0	29.2	نسبة القيمة الإجمالية للتجارة من الناتج المحلي الإجمالي
Trade per capita (thousands of US dollars)	1.0	1.1	1.3	1.6	1.2	1.4	1.4	0.5	0.3	0.4	نصيب الفرد من القيمة الإجمالية للتجارة (ألف دولار أمريكي)
Trade as percentage of ESCWA total trade	2.3	2.2	2.2	2.1	2.1	2.1	1.6	0.5	0.3	0.4	نسبة إجمالي التجارة من إجمالي تجارة الإسكوا
Export market share (percentage): exports/ESCWA total exports	1.7	1.7	1.7	1.6	1.6	1.5	0.9	0.3	0.2	0.2	حصة الصادرات من السوق: نسبة الصادرات إلى إجمالي صادرات الإسكوا
Tunisia											**تونس**
Foreign trade coverage ratio (exports/imports*100)	79.6	77.9	79.4	78.4	75.6	73.9	74.5	69.5	70.3	67.5	معدّل التغطية في قطاع التجارة الخارجية (الصادرات/الواردات *100)
Imports to GDP ratio (percentage)	40.8	43.7	49.1	54.9	43.9	50.4	52.2	54.2	51.8	51.1	نسبة الواردات من الناتج المحلي الإجمالي
Exports to GDP ratio (percentage)	32.5	34.0	39.0	43.1	33.2	37.3	38.9	37.7	36.4	34.5	نسبة الصادرات من الناتج المحلي الإجمالي
Trade balance to GDP ratio (percentage)	-8.3	-9.6	-10.1	-11.9	-10.7	-13.1	-13.3	-16.5	-15.4	-16.6	نسبة الميزان التجاري من الناتج المحلي الإجمالي
Trade to GDP ratio (percentage)	73.3	77.7	88.1	98.0	77.2	87.7	91.1	91.9	88.1	85.5	نسبة القيمة الإجمالية للتجارة من الناتج المحلي الإجمالي
Trade per capita (thousands of US dollars)	2.4	2.6	3.3	4.2	3.2	3.6	3.9	3.8	3.8	3.7	نصيب الفرد من القيمة الإجمالية للتجارة (ألف دولار أمريكي)
Trade as percentage of ESCWA total trade	2.9	2.8	3.0	2.7	2.7	2.7	2.2	2.0	1.9	2.1	نسبة إجمالي التجارة من إجمالي تجارة الإسكوا
Export market share (percentage): exports/ESCWA total exports	2.1	2.0	2.2	2.0	2.1	1.9	1.6	1.3	1.3	1.4	حصة الصادرات من السوق: نسبة الصادرات إلى إجمالي صادرات الإسكوا

الجدول 1-3- مؤشرات مختارة للتجارة الخارجية في البلدان الأعضاء في الإسكوا

Table I.3. Selected foreign trade indicators of ESCWA member countries
2005-2014

	2005	2006	2007	2008	2009	2010	2011	2012	2013	2014	
United Arab Emirates											**الإمارات العربية المتحدة**
Foreign trade coverage ratio (exports/imports*100)	138.4	145.5	119.0	119.4	112.7	114.2	122.6	136.6	138.3	131.4	معدّل التغطية في قطاع التجارة الخارجية (الصادرات/الواردات *100)
Imports to GDP ratio (percentage)	46.9	45.0	58.2	63.5	67.1	65.4	66.1	68.7	67.3	70.7	نسبة الواردات من الناتج المحلي الإجمالي
Exports to GDP ratio (percentage)	64.9	65.5	69.3	75.8	75.6	74.7	81.1	93.9	93.0	92.9	نسبة الصادرات من الناتج المحلي الإجمالي
Trade balance to GDP ratio (percentage)	18.0	20.5	11.1	12.3	8.6	9.3	14.9	25.1	25.8	22.2	نسبة الميزان التجاري من الناتج المحلي الإجمالي
Trade to GDP ratio (percentage)	111.8	110.6	127.5	139.3	142.7	140.0	147.2	162.6	160.3	163.5	نسبة القيمة الإجمالية للتجارة من الناتج المحلي الإجمالي
Trade per capita (thousands of US dollars)	48.6	50.4	56.7	64.7	46.9	47.4	57.3	65.8	69.0	69.2	نصيب الفرد من القيمة الإجمالية للتجارة (ألف دولار أمريكي)
Trade as percentage of ESCWA total trade	24.9	26.1	28.4	27.3	29.6	27.5	27.5	29.1	29.9	31.4	نسبة إجمالي التجارة من إجمالي تجارة الإسكوا
Export market share (percentage): exports/ESCWA total exports	23.2	24.7	26.0	24.7	28.1	25.2	24.6	26.6	28.5	30.5	حصة الصادرات من السوق: نسبة الصادرات إلى إجمالي صادرات الإسكوا
Yemen											**اليمن**
Foreign trade coverage ratio (exports/imports*100)	111.7	126.2	74.1	72.8	68.3	69.5	71.4	62.5	53.7	20.1	معدّل التغطية في قطاع التجارة الخارجية (الصادرات/الواردات *100)
Imports to GDP ratio (percentage)	26.7	23.2	33.2	34.3	31.5	30.0	31.2	35.2	38.2	27.9	نسبة الواردات من الناتج المحلي الإجمالي
Exports to GDP ratio (percentage)	29.8	29.3	24.6	25.0	21.5	20.8	22.3	22.0	20.5	5.6	نسبة الصادرات من الناتج المحلي الإجمالي
Trade balance to GDP ratio (percentage)	3.1	6.1	-8.6	-9.4	-10.0	-9.1	-8.9	-13.2	-17.7	-22.3	نسبة الميزان التجاري من الناتج المحلي الإجمالي
Trade to GDP ratio (percentage)	56.5	52.5	57.9	59.3	53.0	50.8	53.4	57.3	58.8	33.4	نسبة القيمة الإجمالية للتجارة من الناتج المحلي الإجمالي
Trade per capita (thousands of US dollars)	0.5	0.6	0.7	0.8	0.7	0.7	0.7	0.8	0.8	0.6	نصيب الفرد من القيمة الإجمالية للتجارة (ألف دولار أمريكي)
Trade as percentage of ESCWA total trade	1.3	1.3	1.3	1.1	1.2	1.1	0.9	0.9	0.9	0.7	نسبة إجمالي التجارة من إجمالي تجارة الإسكوا
Export market share (percentage): exports/ESCWA total exports	1.1	1.1	0.9	0.8	0.9	0.8	0.6	0.5	0.5	0.2	حصة الصادرات من السوق: نسبة الصادرات إلى إجمالي صادرات الإسكوا

الجدول 1-3- مؤشرات مختارة للتجارة الخارجية في البلدان الأعضاء في الإسكوا

Table I.3. Selected foreign trade indicators of ESCWA member countries 2005-2014

	2005	2006	2007	2008	2009	2010	2011	2012	2013	2014	
Total, (ESCWA member countries)											**القيمة الإجمالية (البلدان الأعضاء في الإسكوا)**
Foreign trade coverage ratio (exports/imports*100)	164.7	168.0	145.4	151.0	126.0	139.7	159.7	169.9	154.9	141.0	معدّل التغطية في قطاع التجارة الخارجية (الصادرات/الواردات *100)
Imports to GDP ratio (percentage)	29.2	29.1	34.3	38.5	35.1	35.9	38.2	37.6	40.3	33.2	نسبة الواردات من الناتج المحلي الإجمالي
Exports to GDP ratio (percentage)	48.1	48.9	49.9	58.2	44.2	50.1	60.9	63.9	62.5	46.8	نسبة الصادرات من الناتج المحلي الإجمالي
Trade balance to GDP ratio (percentage)	18.9	19.8	15.6	19.7	9.1	14.2	22.8	26.3	22.2	13.6	نسبة الميزان التجاري من الناتج المحلي الإجمالي
Trade to GDP ratio (percentage)	77.3	78.0	84.3	96.7	79.3	85.9	99.1	101.5	102.8	80.0	نسبة القيمة الإجمالية للتجارة من الناتج المحلي الإجمالي
Trade per capita (thousands of US dollars)	3.1	3.5	4.2	5.7	4.2	4.9	6.1	6.7	6.8	6.5	نصيب الفرد من القيمة الإجمالية للتجارة (ألف دولار أمريكي)
Trade as percentage of ESCWA total trade	100.0	100.0	100.0	100.0	100.0	100.0	100.0	100.0	100.0	100.0	نسبة إجمالي التجارة من إجمالي تجارة الإسكوا
Export market share (percentage): exports/ESCWA total exports	100.0	100.0	100.0	100.0	100.0	100.0	100.0	100.0	100.0	100.0	حصة الصادرات من السوق: نسبة الصادرات إلى إجمالي صادرات الإسكوا
Major oil exporters(*)											**البلدان الرئيسية المصدرة للنفط(*)**
Foreign trade coverage ratio (exports/imports*100)	220.4	217.8	183.5	199.3	159.3	179.9	206.9	221.1	192.6	176.3	معدّل التغطية في قطاع التجارة الخارجية (الصادرات/الواردات *100)
Imports to GDP ratio (percentage)	27.0	27.6	33.9	36.6	36.6	36.8	39.0	38.3	42.7	33.4	نسبة الواردات من الناتج المحلي الإجمالي
Exports to GDP ratio (percentage)	59.4	60.2	62.2	72.9	58.2	66.2	80.7	84.6	82.3	58.9	نسبة الصادرات من الناتج المحلي الإجمالي
Trade balance to GDP ratio (percentage)	32.5	32.6	28.3	36.3	21.7	29.4	41.7	46.4	39.6	25.5	نسبة الميزان التجاري من الناتج المحلي الإجمالي
Trade to GDP ratio (percentage)	86.4	87.8	96.2	109.5	94.8	103.1	119.7	122.9	125.0	92.4	نسبة القيمة الإجمالية للتجارة من الناتج المحلي الإجمالي
Trade per capita (thousands of US dollars)	9.4	10.6	12.6	16.8	12.2	14.1	18.2	20.4	20.7	19.3	نصيب الفرد من القيمة الإجمالية للتجارة (ألف دولار أمريكي)
Trade as percentage of ESCWA total trade	78.3	79.0	78.7	78.3	77.5	77.9	80.7	83.1	83.7	83.2	نسبة إجمالي التجارة من إجمالي تجارة الإسكوا
Export market share (percentage): exports/ESCWA total exports	86.5	86.4	85.9	86.7	85.4	85.9	88.5	90.9	90.7	90.7	حصة الصادرات من السوق: نسبة الصادرات إلى إجمالي صادرات الإسكوا
Other countries											**البلدان الأخرى**
Foreign trade coverage ratio (exports/imports*100)	62.8	68.4	64.1	58.6	56.7	59.2	58.1	51.1	53.4	47.5	معدّل التغطية في قطاع التجارة الخارجية (الصادرات/الواردات *100)
Imports to GDP ratio (percentage)	34.4	32.6	35.3	42.9	32.5	34.1	36.5	36.2	35.0	32.6	نسبة الواردات من الناتج المحلي الإجمالي
Exports to GDP ratio (percentage)	21.6	22.3	22.6	25.1	18.4	20.2	21.2	18.5	18.7	15.5	نسبة الصادرات من الناتج المحلي الإجمالي
Trade balance to GDP ratio (percentage)	-12.8	-10.3	-12.7	-17.8	-14.0	-13.9	-15.3	-17.7	-16.3	-17.1	نسبة الميزان التجاري من الناتج المحلي الإجمالي
Trade to GDP ratio (percentage)	55.9	54.9	57.9	68.0	50.9	54.2	57.6	54.7	53.8	48.1	نسبة القيمة الإجمالية للتجارة من الناتج المحلي الإجمالي
Trade per capita (thousands of US dollars)	0.9	1.0	1.2	1.7	1.3	1.5	1.6	1.6	1.5	1.5	نصيب الفرد من القيمة الإجمالية للتجارة (ألف دولار أمريكي)
Trade as percentage of ESCWA total trade	21.7	21.0	21.3	21.7	22.5	22.1	19.3	16.9	16.3	16.8	نسبة إجمالي التجارة من إجمالي تجارة الإسكوا
Export market share (percentage): exports/ESCWA total exports	13.5	13.6	14.1	13.3	14.6	14.1	11.5	9.1	9.3	9.2	حصة الصادرات من السوق: نسبة الصادرات إلى إجمالي صادرات الإسكوا

(*) Iraq, Kuwait,Libya, Oman, Qatar, Saudi Arabia and United Arab

(*) الإمارات العربية المتحدة والعراق وليبيا وعُمان وقطر والكويت والمملكة العربية السعودية.

الجدول 1-4- إجمالي قيمة الواردات والصادرات والميزان التجاري للبلدان الأعضاء في الإسكوا

Table I.4. Total value of imports, exports and balance of trade of ESCWA member countries
2005-2014

(Millions of US dollars) (مليون دولار أمريكي)

	2005	2006	2007	2008	2009	2010	2011	2012	2013	2014	
Bahrain											البحرين
Imports (c.i.f)	9 393	8 957	11 925	17 768	12 469	16 002	17 573	19 822	18 584	20 044	الواردات (سيف)
Exports and re-exports (f.o.b)	10 240	11 662	14 092	18 246	11 909	16 059	22 417	21 928	25 500	23 405	الصادرات وإعادة التصدير (فوب)
Balance of trade	847	2 705	2 167	478	- 560	57	4 843	2 106	6 916	3 360	الميزان التجاري
Egypt											مصر
Imports (c.i.f)	19 812	20 613	26 820	54 046	44 752	52 871	59 269	71 469	64 368	68 294	الواردات (سيف)
Exports and re-exports (f.o.b)	10 646	13 720	15 989	26 738	22 890	27 121	30 782	30 778	28 789	26 812	الصادرات وإعادة التصدير (فوب)
Balance of trade	-9 166	-6 893	-10 831	-27 308	-21 862	-25 750	-28 487	-40 691	-35 580	-41 482	الميزان التجاري
Iraq											العراق
Imports (c.i.f)	13 041 (1)	13 535 (1)	15 167 (1)	21 465 (1)	23 862 (1)	27 411	49 142	24 443	61 000 (2)	59 000 (2)	الواردات (سيف)
Exports (f.o.b)	17 645 (1)	23 760 (1)	29 329 (1)	61 273	41 792	52 483	83 226	94 392	89 742 (2)	84 630 (2)	الصادرات (فوب)
Balance of trade	4 605	10 225	14 162	39 808	17 930	25 072	34 084	69 948	28 742	25 630	الميزان التجاري
Jordan											الأردن
Imports (c.i.f)	10 497	11 548	13 756	16 872	14 075	15 262	18 930	20 752	22 068	22 740	الواردات (سيف)
Exports and re-exports (f.o.b)	4 301	5 204	5 730	7 782	6 366	7 023	8 006	7 887	7 913	8 385	الصادرات وإعادة التصدير (فوب)
Balance of trade	-6 196	-6 344	-8 027	-9 090	-7 710	-8 239	-10 923	-12 865	-14 155	-14 355	الميزان التجاري
Kuwait											الكويت
Imports (c.i.f)	15 907 (2)	17 240	21 363	24 840	20 334	22 670	25 144	27 267	29 646	31 489	الواردات (سيف)
Exports and re-exports (f.o.b)	45 155 (2)	56 003	62 691	87 457	51 937	62 749	102 704	114 516	114 404	101 132	الصادرات وإعادة التصدير (فوب)
Balance of trade	29 247	38 763	41 329	62 617	31 602	40 079	77 560	87 249	84 758	69 643	الميزان التجاري

الجدول 1-4- إجمالي قيمة الواردات والصادرات والميزان التجاري للبلدان الأعضاء في الإسكوا

Table I.4. Total value of imports, exports and balance of trade of ESCWA member countries 2005-2014

(Millions of US dollars) (مليون دولار أمريكي)

	2005	2006	2007	2008	2009	2010	2011	2012	2013	2014	
Lebanon											لبنان
Imports (c.i.f)	9 340	9 398	11 815	16 137	16 242	17 964	20 158	21 280	21 228	20 494	الواردات (سيف)
Exports and re-exports (f.o.b)	1 880	2 283	2 816	3 478	3 484	4 253	4 265	4 483	3 936	3 313	الصادرات وإعادة التصدير (فوب)
Balance of trade	-7 460	-7 115	-8 999	-12 658	-12 757	-13 711	-15 893	-16 797	-17 293	-17 181	الميزان التجاري
Libya											ليبيا
Imports (c.i.f)	6 079 (2)	6 041 (2)	6 733 (2)	9 116	12 859	17 674	8 000 (2)	22 000 (2)	27 000 (2)	19 000 (2)	الواردات (سيف)
Exports and re-exports (f.o.b)	31 358 (2)	40 260 (2)	46 970 (2)	44 696	27 256	36 440	18 996 (2)	60 946 (2)	43 500 (2)	21 000 (2)	الصادرات وإعادة التصدير (فوب)
Balance of trade	25 279	34 220	40 237	35 580	14 396	18 766	10 996	38 946	16 500	2 000	الميزان التجاري
Morocco											المغرب
Imports (c.i.f)	20 790 (2)	23 980 (2)	32 010 (2)	42 322	32 882	35 379	44 263	44 790	45 186	46 192	الواردات (سيف)
Exports and re-exports (f.o.b)	11 190 (2)	12 744 (2)	15 340 (2)	20 306	14 069	17 765	21 650	21 417	21 965	23 816	الصادرات وإعادة التصدير (فوب)
Balance of trade	-9 600	-11 236	-16 670	-22 016	-18 813	-17 614	-22 613	-23 373	-23 221	-22 376	الميزان التجاري
Oman											عُمان
Imports (c.i.f)	8 827	10 898	15 980	22 925	17 852	19 778	23 620	28 118	34 331	29 303	الواردات (سيف)
Exports and re-exports (f.o.b)	18 692	21 585	24 692	37 719	27 652	36 601	47 092	52 138	55 497	50 718	الصادرات وإعادة التصدير (فوب)
Balance of trade	9 865	10 687	8 712	14 794	9 799	16 824	23 472	24 021	21 166	21 415	الميزان التجاري
Palestine											فلسطين
Imports (c.i.f)	2 667	2 759	3 141	3 569	3 601	3 959	4 221	4 697	5 164	5 683	الواردات (سيف)
Exports and re-exports (f.o.b)	335	367	513	558	518	576	720	782	1 165	944	الصادرات وإعادة التصدير (فوب)
Balance of trade	-2 331	-2 392	-2 628	-3 010	-3 082	-3 383	-3 502	-3 915	-3 999	-4 739	الميزان التجاري
Qatar											قطر
Imports (c.i.f)	10 061	16 440	22 005	27 901	24 922	23 240	22 330	26 083	27 038	30 443	الواردات (سيف)
Exports and re-exports (f.o.b)	25 762	34 051	42 020	56 594	49 474	74 812	114 301	132 968	136 858	131 592	الصادرات وإعادة التصدير (فوب)
Balance of trade	15 702	17 611	20 015	28 693	24 552	51 571	91 971	106 885	109 819	101 149	الميزان التجاري
Saudi Arabia											المملكة العربية السعودية
Imports (c.i.f)	59 498	69 799	90 098	115 135	95 552	106 864	131 588	155 595	168 153	173 835	الواردات (سيف)
Exports and re-exports (f.o.b)	180 737	188 467 (1)	205 452 (1)	313 487	192 315	251 147	364 703	388 404	375 871	342 437	الصادرات وإعادة التصدير (فوب)
Balance of trade	121 239	118 668	115 354	198 352	96 763	144 282	233 115	232 810	207 718	168 602	الميزان التجاري

الجدول 1-4- إجمالي قيمة الواردات والصادرات والميزان التجاري للبلدان الأعضاء في الإسكوا

Table I.4. Total value of imports, exports and balance of trade of ESCWA member countries

2005-2014

(Millions of US dollars) (مليون دولار أمريكي)

	2005	2006	2007	2008	2009	2010	2011	2012	2013	2014	
Sudan											السودان
Imports (c.i.f)	7 367	8 844	9 854	16 417	8 590	11 855	9 546	6 581	9 918	9 211 (2)	الواردات (سيف)
Exports and re-exports (f.o.b)	4 506	5 479	8 867 (1)	9 501	9 080	11 284	8 982	3 384	7 086	4 350 (2)	الصادرات وإعادة التصدير (فوب)
Balance of trade	-2 861	-3 366	- 986	-6 916	490	- 571	- 565	-3 197	-2 832	-4 861	الميزان التجاري
Syrian Arab Republic											الجمهورية العربية السورية
Imports (c.i.f)	10 047	10 626	13 556	17 994	15 258	17 392	19 871	7 300 (2)	5 400 (2)	6 700 (2)	الواردات (سيف)
Exports and re-exports (f.o.b)	8 669	10 269	11 619	15 419	10 878	12 796	10 501	4 000 (2)	2 000 (2)	2 000 (2)	الصادرات وإعادة التصدير (فوب)
Balance of trade	-1 379	- 357	-1 937	-2 575	-4 380	-4 596	-9 370	-3 300	-3 400	-4 700	الميزان التجاري
Tunisia											تونس
Imports (c.i.f)	13 177	15 007	19 099	24 638	19 096	22 215	23 952	24 476	24 266	24 828 (1)	الواردات (سيف)
Exports and re-exports (f.o.b)	10 494	11 694	15 165	19 320	14 445	16 427	17 847	17 008	17 060	16 755 (1)	الصادرات وإعادة التصدير (فوب)
Balance of trade	-2 683	-3 313	-3 934	-5 318	-4 651	-5 789	-6 105	-7 468	-7 206	-8 073	الميزان التجاري
United Arab Emirates											الإمارات العربية المتحدة
Imports (c.i.f)	84 654	100 057	150 123	200 327	170 121	187 001	229 709	255 882	270 579	282 343	الواردات (سيف)
Exports and re-exports (f.o.b)	117 188	145 586	178 630	239 213	191 802	213 539	281 640	349 482	374 214	370 926	الصادرات وإعادة التصدير (فوب)
Balance of trade	32 534	45 529	28 507	38 886	21 681	26 538	51 931	93 601	103 635	88 583	الميزان التجاري
Yemen											اليمن
Imports (c.i.f)	5 077	5 294	8 517	10 435	8 969	9 257	9 681	11 301	13 273	12 042	الواردات (سيف)
Exports and re-exports (f.o.b)	5 672	6 680	6 315	7 593	6 126	6 437	6 917	7 065	7 130	2 417	الصادرات وإعادة التصدير (فوب)
Balance of trade	594	1 386	-2 202	-2 842	-2 842	-2 820	-2 765	-4 235	-6 143	-9 625	الميزان التجاري
ESCWA region											منطقة الإسكوا
Imports (c.i.f)	306 234	351 036	471 962	641 907	541 438	606 795	716 996	771 854	847 203	861 640	الواردات (سيف)
Exports and re-exports (f.o.b)	504 468	589 815	686 231	969 381	681 992	847 510	1144 748	1311 578	1312 631	1214 632	الصادرات وإعادة التصدير (فوب)
Balance of trade	198 234	238 778	214 269	327 474	140 554	240 715	427 752	539 724	465 428	352 992	الميزان التجاري

(1) International Monetary Fund, Direction of trade statisics, 2008, http://www.imf.org.

(2) United Nations Conference on Trade and Development , http://unctad.org.

(1) صندوق النقد الدولي، إحصاءات التجارة: الاتجاهات السائدة، 2008، http://imf.org (بالإنكليزية).

(2) مؤتمر الأمم المتحدة للتجارة والتنمية، http://unctad.org.

الجدول 1-5- إجمالي قيمة واردات البلدان الأعضاء في الإسكوا[1]

Table I.5. Total value of imports of ESCWA member countries[1]

2004-2013

(Millions of US dollars) (مليون دولار أمريكي)

Country	2005	2006	2007	2008	2009	2010	2011	2012	2013	2014	Growth Rate (%) معدّل النمو 1991-2001	2001-2014	البلد
Bahrain	9 393	8 957	11 925	17 768	12 469	16 002	17 573	19 822	18 584	20 044	0.4	12.3	البحرين
Egypt	19 812	20 613	26 820	54 046	44 752	52 871	59 269	71 469	64 368	68 294	7.0	16.6	مصر
Iraq	13 041	13 535	15 167	21 465	23 862	27 411	49 142	24 443	61 000	59 000	24.4	19.3	العراق
Jordan	10 497	11 548	13 756	16 872	14 075	15 262	18 930	20 752	22 068	22 740	4.7	12.4	الأردن
Kuwait	15 907	17 240	21 363	24 840	20 334	22 670	25 144	27 267	29 646	31 489	4.4	10.2	الكويت
Lebanon	9 340	9 398	11 815	16 137	16 242	17 964	20 158	21 280	21 228	20 494	5.5	10.3	لبنان
Libya	6 079	6 041	6 733	9 116	12 859	17 674	8 000	22 000	27 000	19 000	-2.3	13.9	ليبيا
Morocco	20 790	23 980	32 010	42 322	32 882	35 379	44 263	44 790	45 186	46 192	5.2	11.8	المغرب
Oman	8 827	10 898	15 980	22 925	17 852	19 778	23 620	28 118	34 331	29 303	4.9	14.6	عمان
Palestine	2 667	2 759	3 141	3 569	3 601	3 959	4 221	4 697	5 164	5 683	4.4 (2)	9.3	فلسطين
Qatar	10 061	16 440	22 005	27 901	24 922	23 240	22 330	26 083	27 038	30 443	6.7	17.1	قطر
Saudi Arabia	59 498	69 799	90 098	115 135	95 552	106 864	131 588	155 595	168 153	173 835	0.0	14.3	المملكة العربية السعودية
Sudan	7 367	8 844	9 854	16 417	8 590	11 855	9 546	6 581	9 918	9 211	3.3	11.3	السودان
Syrian Arab Republic	10 047	10 626	13 556	17 994	15 258	17 392	19 871	7 300	5 400	6 700	2.0	4.4	الجمهورية العربية السورية
Tunisia	13 177	15 007	19 099	24 638	19 096	22 215	23 952	24 476	24 266	24 828	5.1	8.3	تونس
United Arab Emirates	84 654	100 057	150 123	200 327	170 121	187 001	229 709	255 882	270 579	282 343	8.7	16.7	الإمارات العربية المتحدة
Yemen	5 077	5 294	8 517	10 435	8 969	9 257	9 681	11 301	13 273	12 042	3.0	12.9	اليمن
Total (ESCWA region)	306 234	351 036	471 962	641 907	541 438	606 795	716 996	771 854	847 203	861 640	4. 5	14.4	القيمة الإجمالية (منطقة الإسكوا)

(1) Including crude oil and oil products.

(2) For the period 1995-2001.

(1) بما في ذلك النفط الخام والمنتجات النفطية.

(2) للفترة 1995-2001.

الجدول 1-6- إجمالي قيمة صادرات البلدان الأعضاء في الإسكوا[1]

Table I.6. Total value of exports of ESCWA member countries[1]

2005-2014

(Millions of US dollars) (مليون دولار أمريكي)

Country	2005	2006	2007	2008	2009	2010	2011	2012	2013	2014	Growth Rate (%) معدّل النمو 1991-2001	2001-2014	البلد
Bahrain	10 240	11 662	14 092	18 246	11 909	16 059	22 417	21 928	25 500	23 405	4.7	12.3	البحرين
Egypt	10 646	13 720	15 989	26 738	22 890	27 121	30 782	30 778	28 789	26 812	2.4	16.5	مصر
Iraq	17 645	23 760	29 329	61 273	41 792	52 483	83 226	94 392	89 742	84 630	42.6	20.4	العراق
Jordan	4 301	5 204	5 730	7 782	6 366	7 023	8 006	7 887	7 913	8 385	7.3	10.0	الأردن
Kuwait	45 155	56 003	62 691	87 457	51 937	62 749	102 704	114 516	114 404	101 132	18.5	15.8	الكويت
Lebanon	1 880	2 283	2 816	3 478	3 484	4 253	4 265	4 483	3 936	3 313	4.3	11.7	لبنان
Libya	31 358	40 260	46 970	44 696	27 256	36 440	18 996	60 946	43 500	21 000	0.5	8.1	ليبيا
Morocco	11 190	12 744	15 340	20 306	14 069	17 765	21 650	21 417	21 965	23 816	7.2	9.5	المغرب
Oman	18 692	21 585	24 692	37 719	27 652	36 601	47 092	52 138	55 497	50 718	7.4	14.1	عمان
Palestine	335	367	513	558	518	576	720	782	1 165	944	-2.2 (2)	11.4	فلسطين
Qatar	25 762	34 051	42 020	56 594	49 474	74 812	114 301	132 968	136 858	131 592	12.6	22.0	قطر
Saudi Arabia	180 737	188 467	205 452	313 487	192 315	251 147	364 703	388 404	375 871	342 437	3.6	13.5	المملكة العربية السعودية
Sudan	4 506	5 479	8 867	9 501	9 080	11 284	8 982	3 384	7 086	4 350	13.8	8.9	السودان
Syrian Arab Republic	8 669	10 269	11 619	15 419	10 878	12 796	10 501	4 000	2 000	2 000	3.8	-5.0	الجمهورية العربية السورية
Tunisia	10 494	11 694	15 165	19 320	14 445	16 427	17 847	17 008	17 060	16 755	5.6	8.0	تونس
United Arab Emirates	117 188	145 586	178 630	239 213	191 802	213 539	281 640	349 482	374 214	370 926	8.7	16.6	الإمارات العربية المتحدة
Yemen	5 672	6 680	6 315	7 593	6 126	6 437	6 917	7 065	7 130	2 417	25.5	3.2	اليمن
Total (ESCWA region)	504 468	589 815	686 231	969 381	681 992	847 510	1144 748	1311 578	1312 631	1214 632	6. 8	14.9	القيمة الإجمالية (منطقة الإسكوا)

(1) Including crude oil and oil products.

(2) For the period 1995-2001.

(1) بما في ذلك النفط الخام والمنتجات النفطية.

(2) للفترة 1995-2001.

الرسم البياني 7 - واردات وصادرات البحرين، 1980- 2014
Graph 7. Bahrain imports and exports, 1980-2014

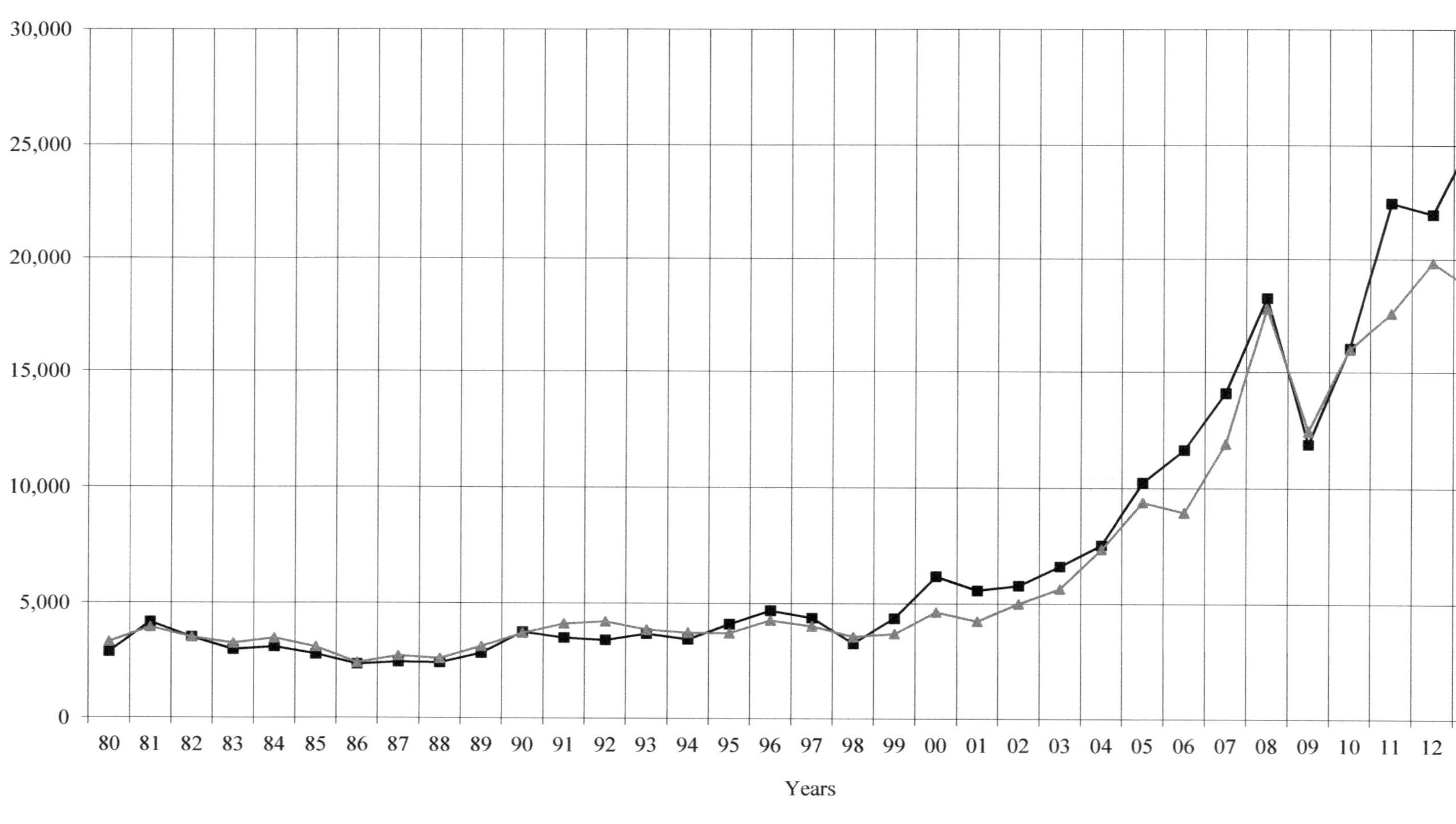

الرسم البياني 8: واردات وصادرات مصر، 1980- 2014
Graph 8. Egypt imports and exports, 1980-2014

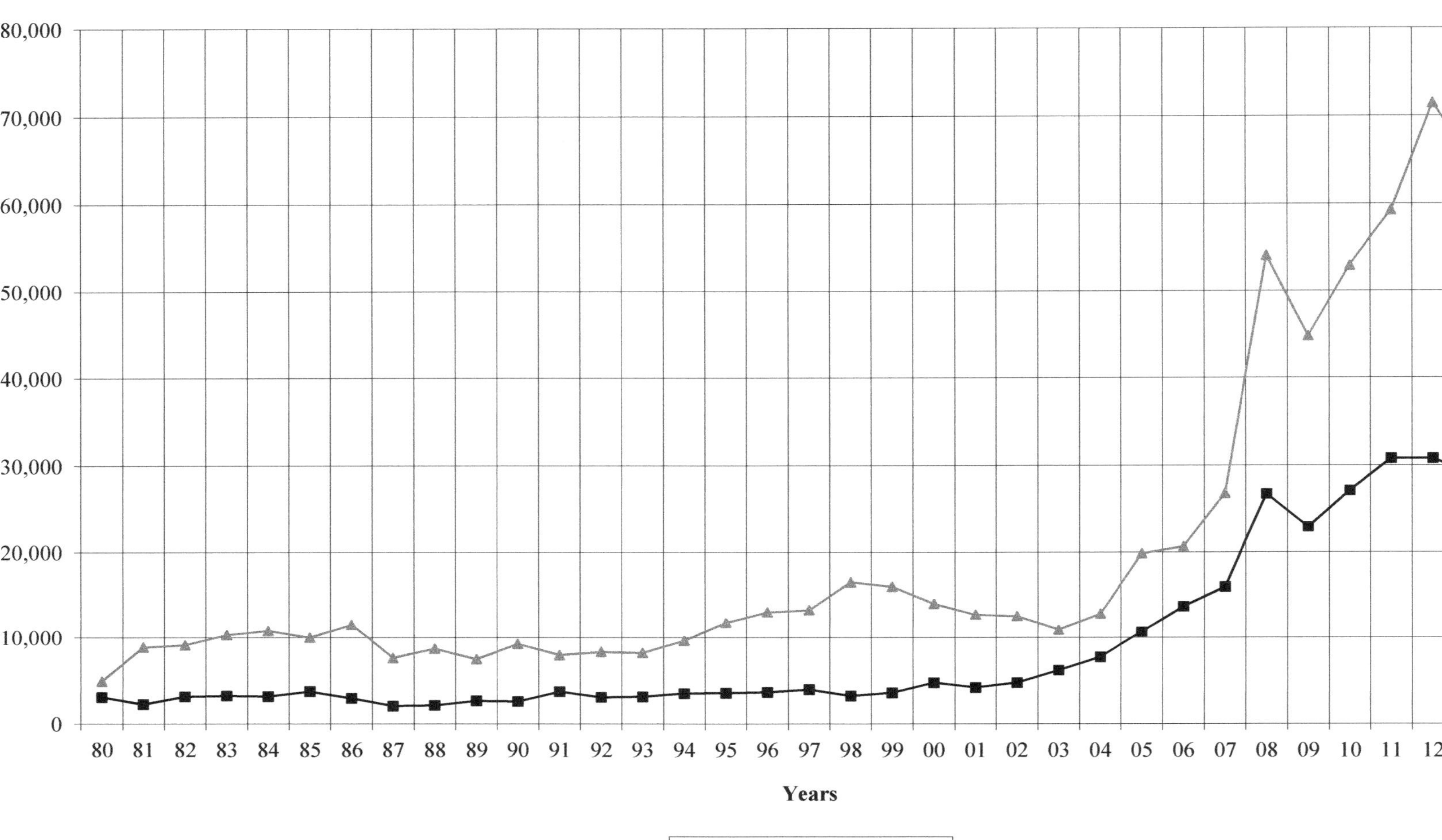

الرسم البياني 9- واردات وصادرات العراق، 1980- 2014
Graph 9. Iraq imports and exports, 1980-2014

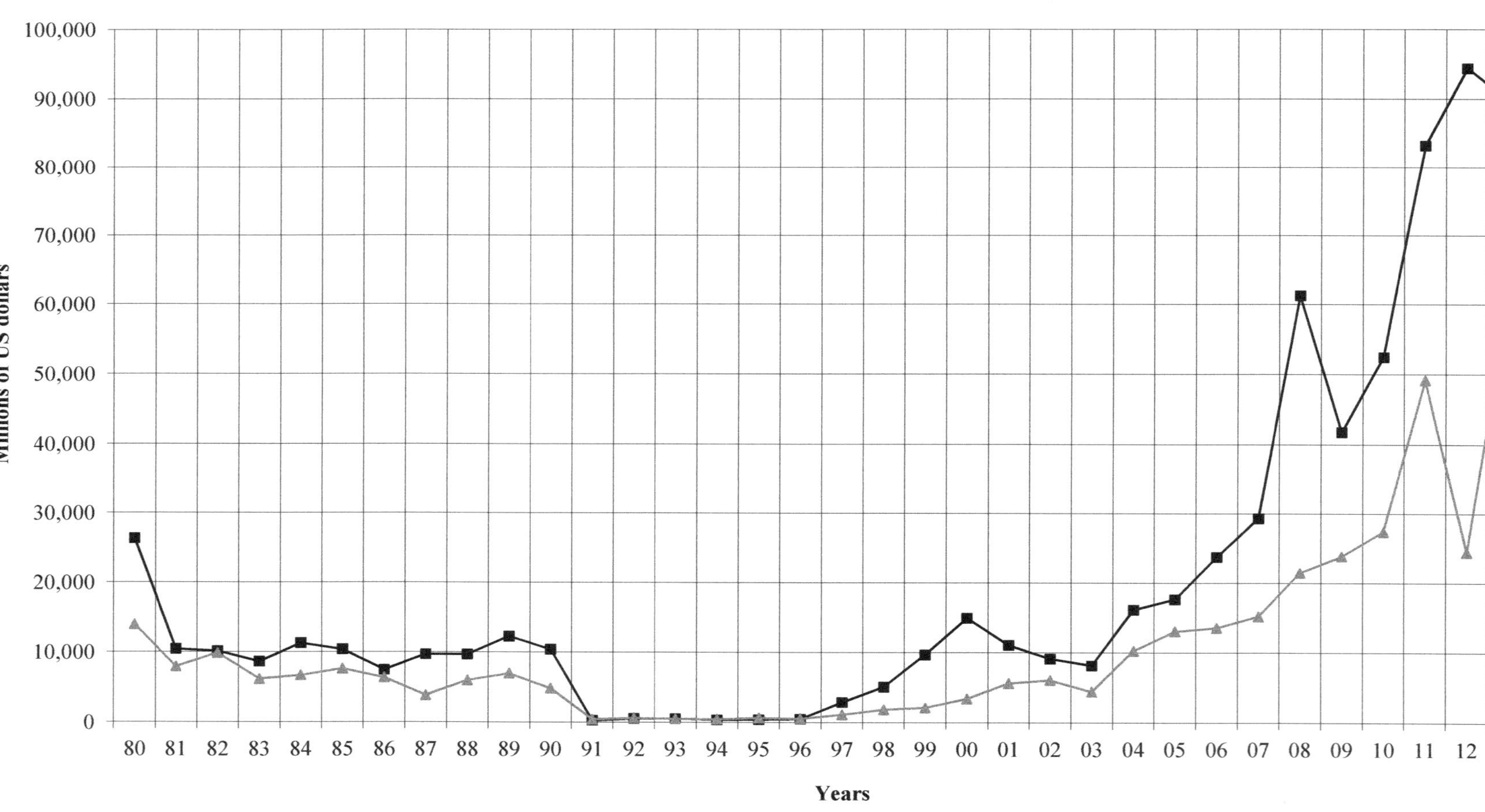

الرسم البياني 10 - واردات وصادرات الأردن، 1980- 2014

Graph 10. Jordan imports and exports, 1980-2014

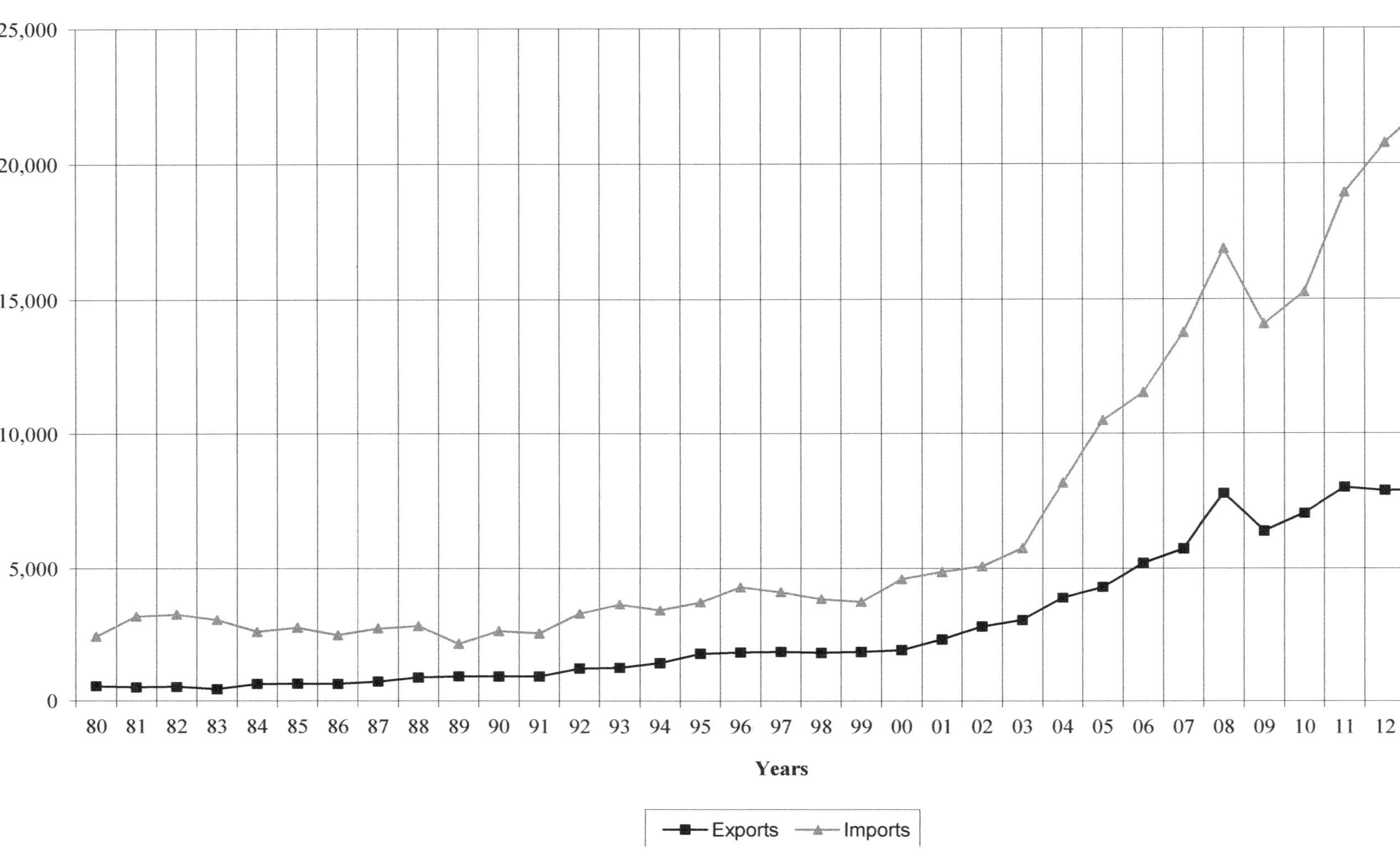

الرسم البياني 11- واردات وصادرات الكويت، 1980- 2014

Graph 11. Kuwait imports and exports, 1980-2014

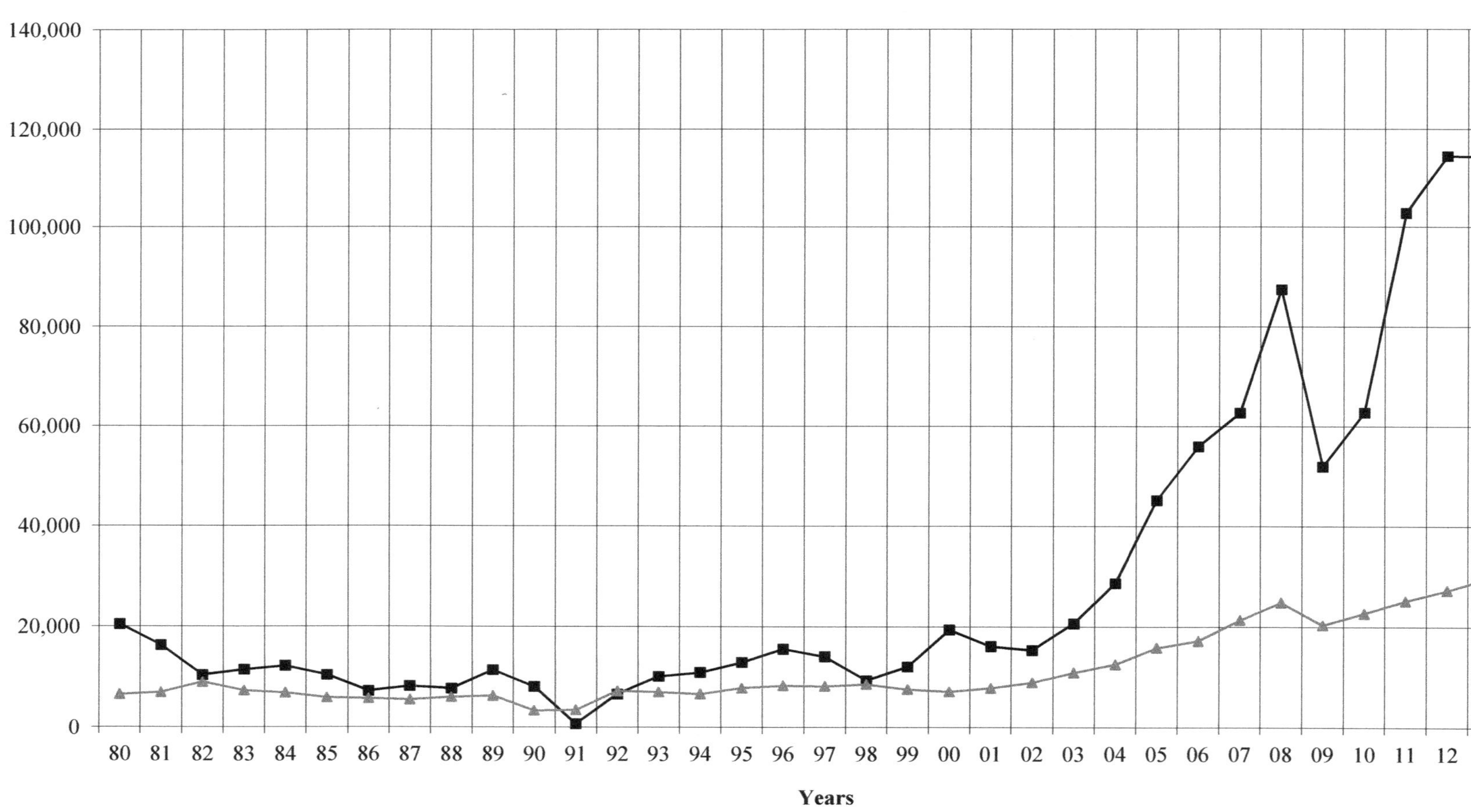

الرسم البياني 12- واردات وصادرات لبنان، 1980- 2014
Graph 12. Lebanon imports and exports, 1980- 2014

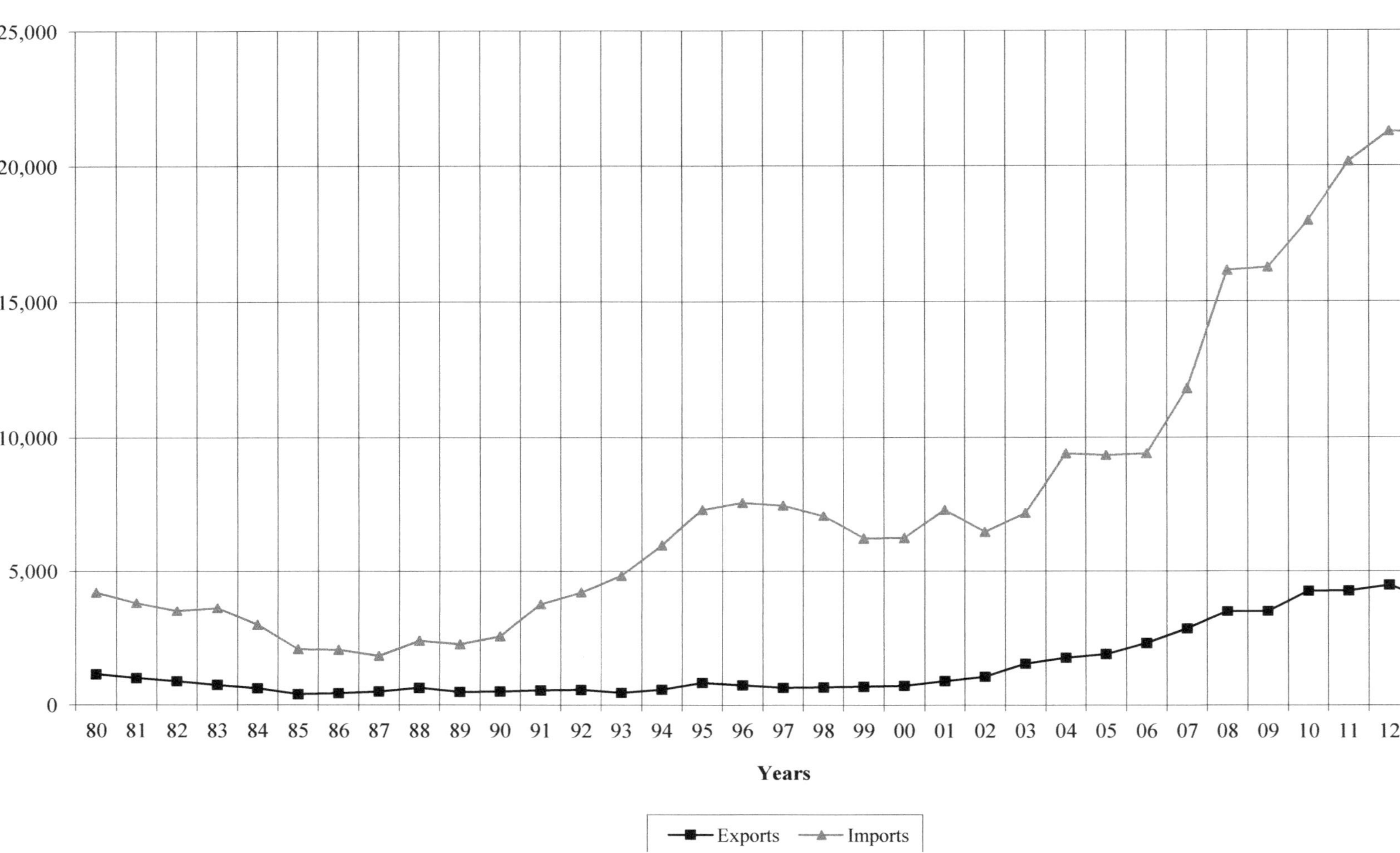

الرسم البياني 13 -واردات وصادرات ليبيا، 1980- 2014

Graph 13. Libya imports and exports, 1980-2014

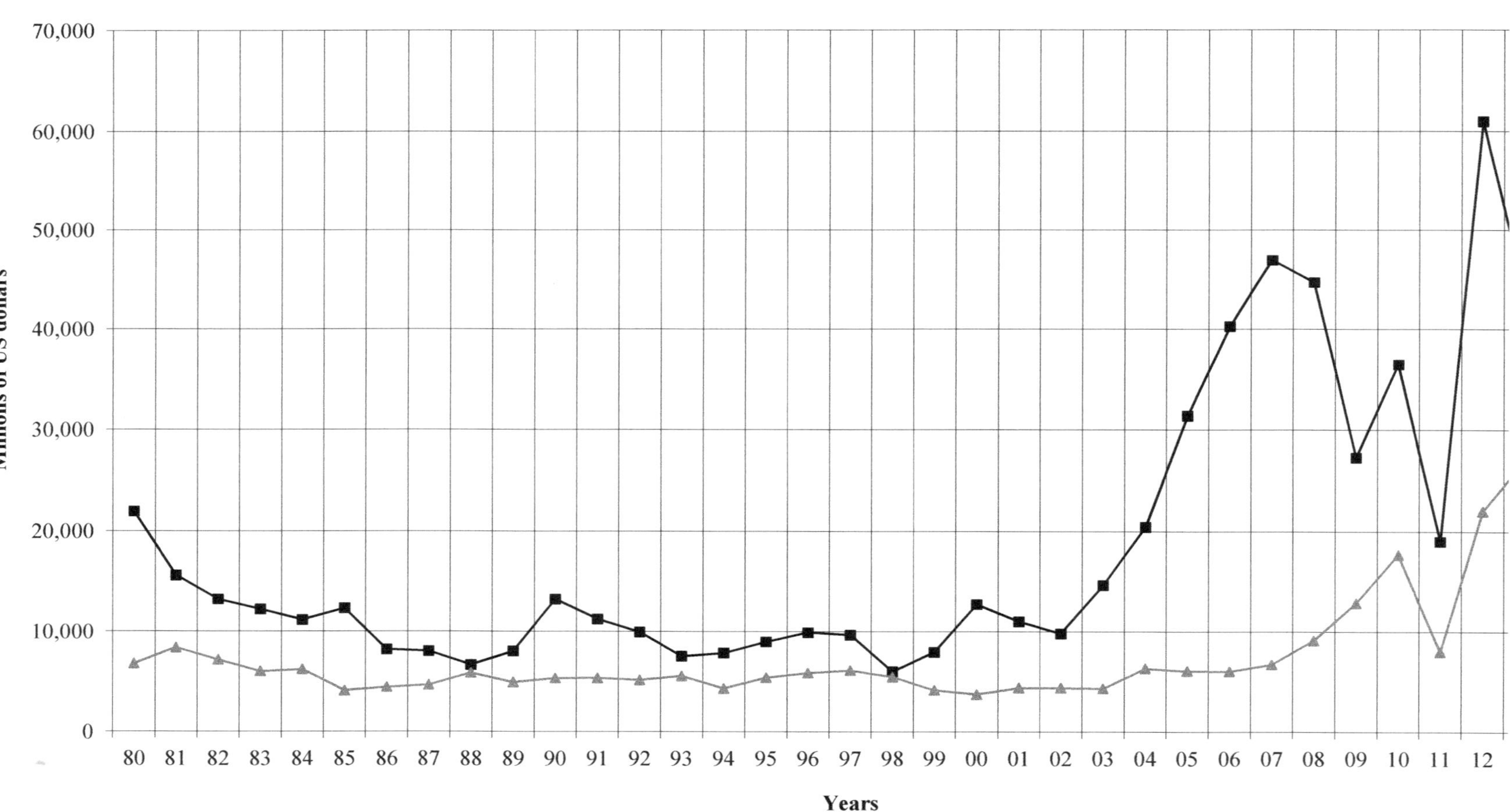

الرسم البياني 14 - واردات وصادرات المغرب، 1980- 2014

Graph 14. Morocco imports and exports, 1980-2014

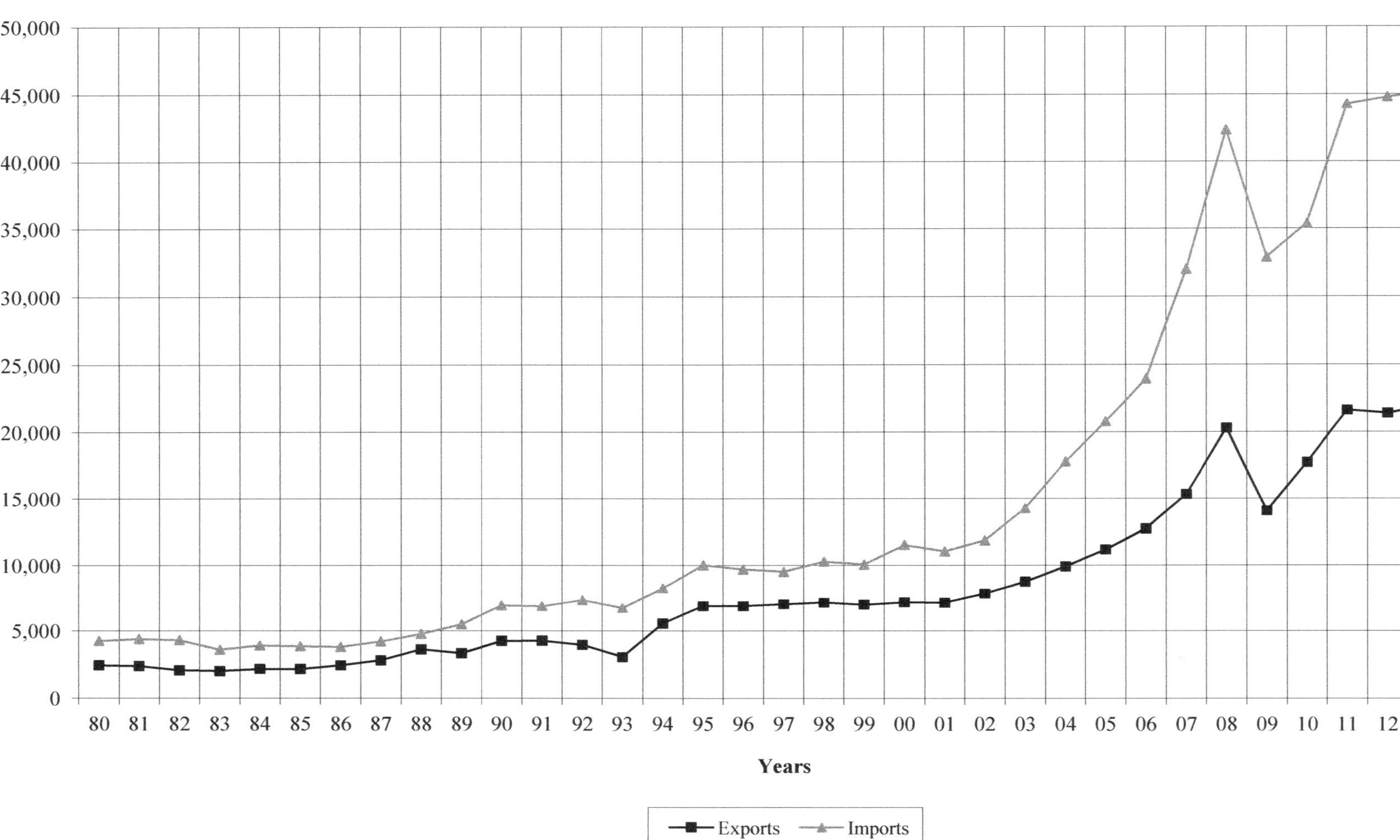

الرسم البياني 15 - واردات وصادرات عمان، 1980- 2014
Graph 15. Oman imports and exports, 1980-2014

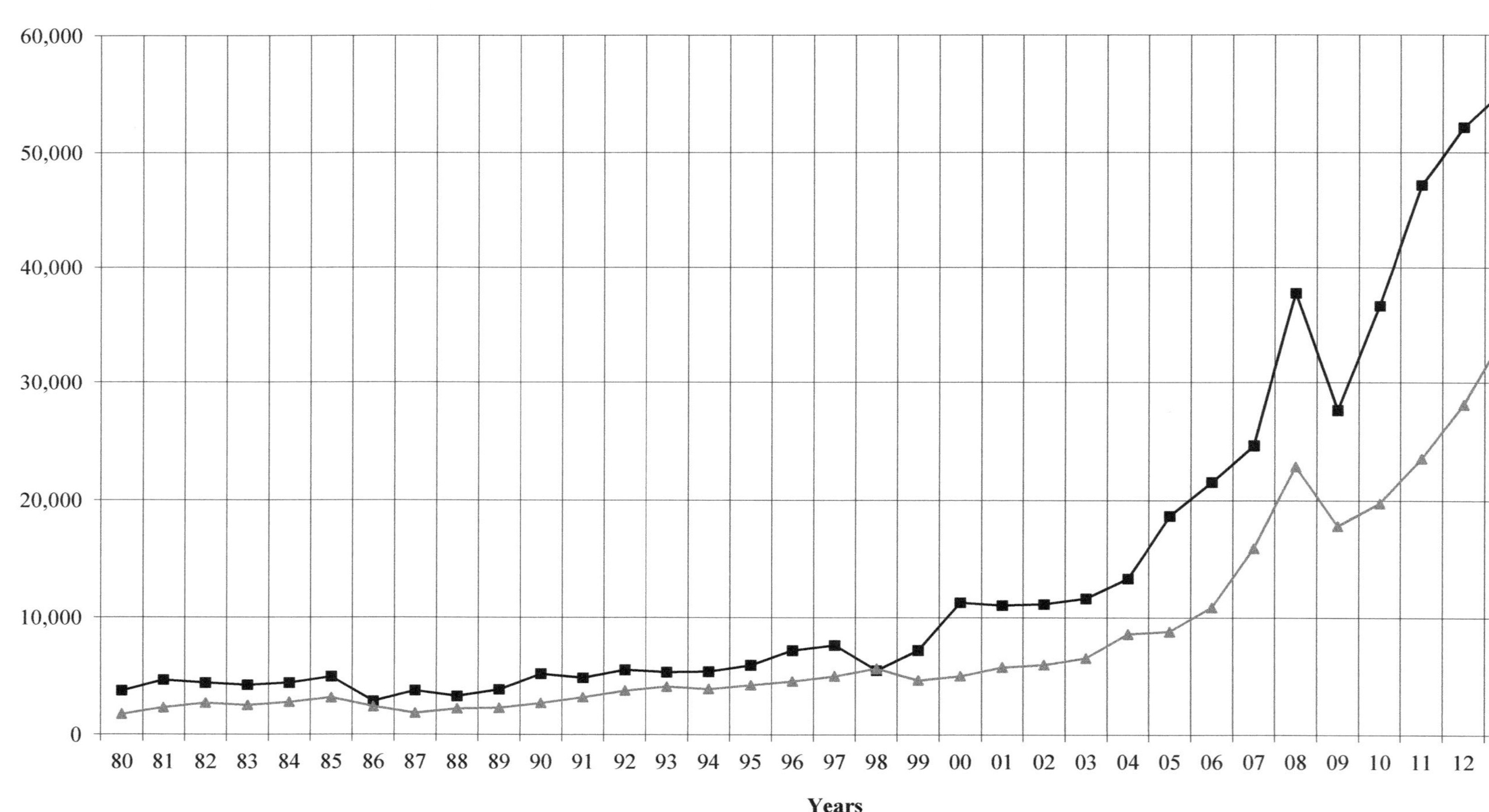

الرسم البياني 16 - واردات وصادرات فلسطين، 1995- 2014
Graph 16. Palestine imports and exports, 1995-2014

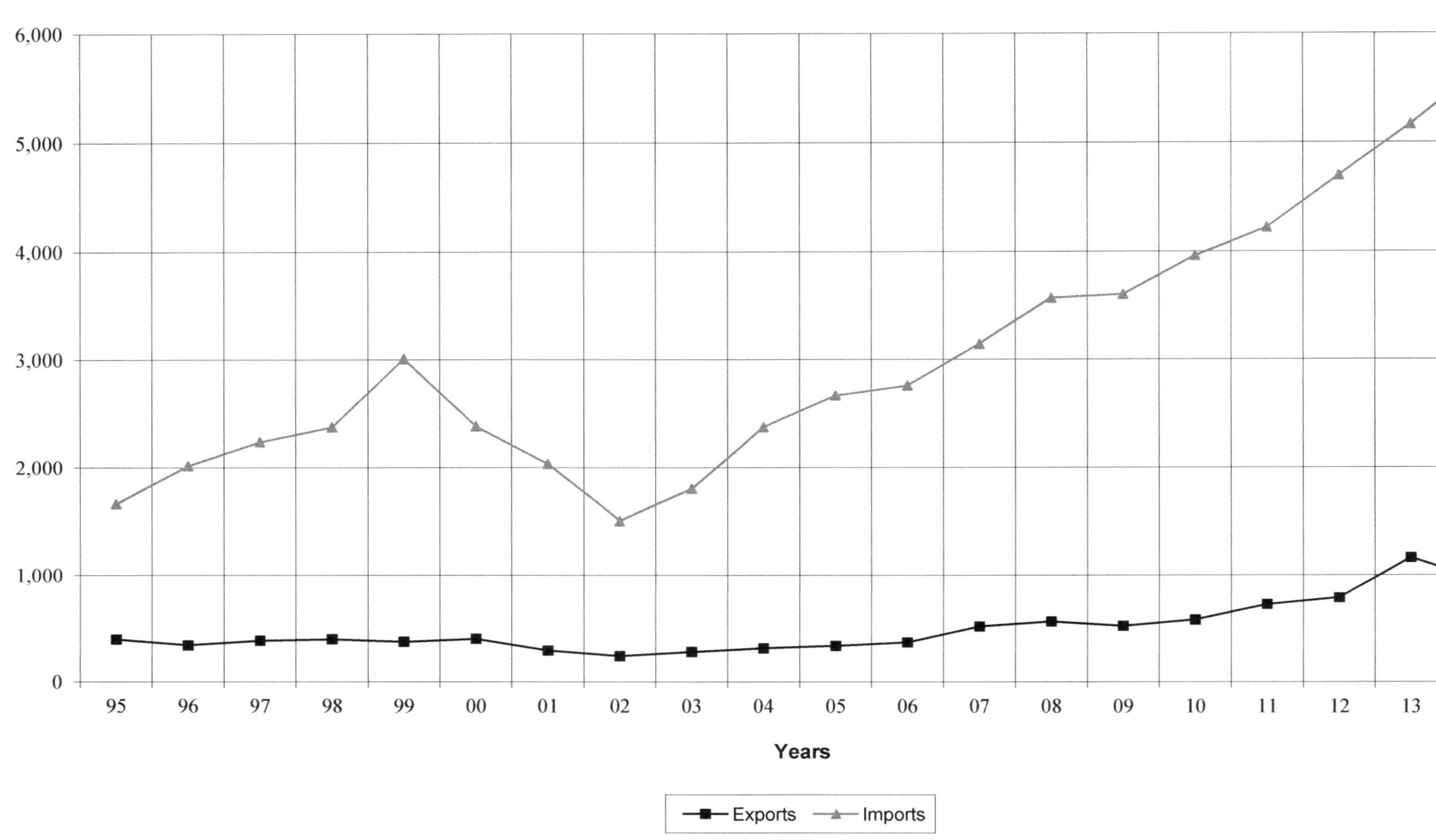

الرسم البياني 17 - واردات وصادرات قطر، 1980- 2014
Graph 17. Qatar imports and exports, 1980-2014

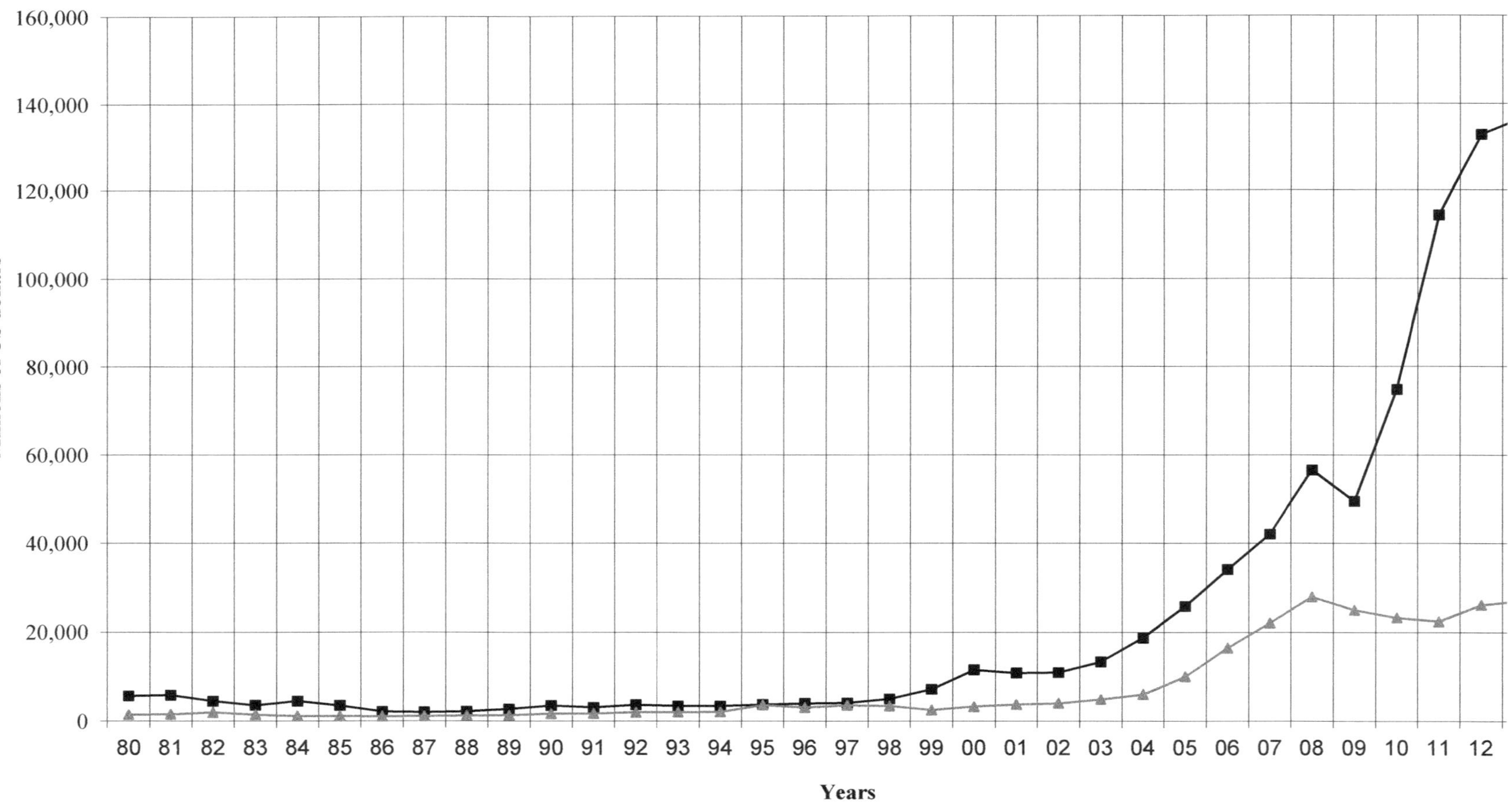

الرسم البياني 18 - واردات وصادرات المملكة العربية السعودية، 1980- 2014
Graph 18. Saudi Arabia imports and exports, 1980-2014

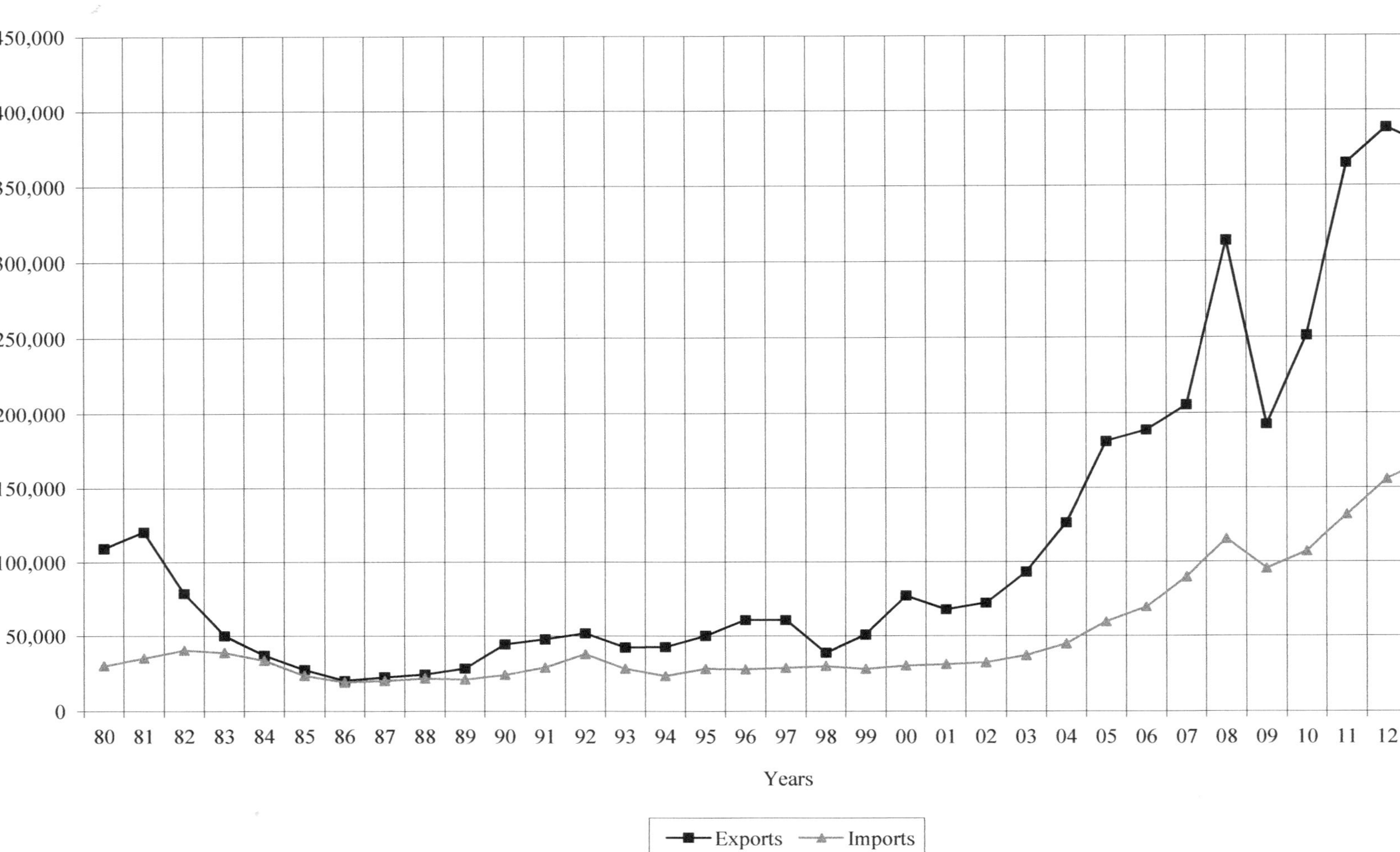

الرسم البياني 19 - واردات وصادرات السودان، 1980- 2014
Graph 19. The Sudan imports and exports, 1980-2014

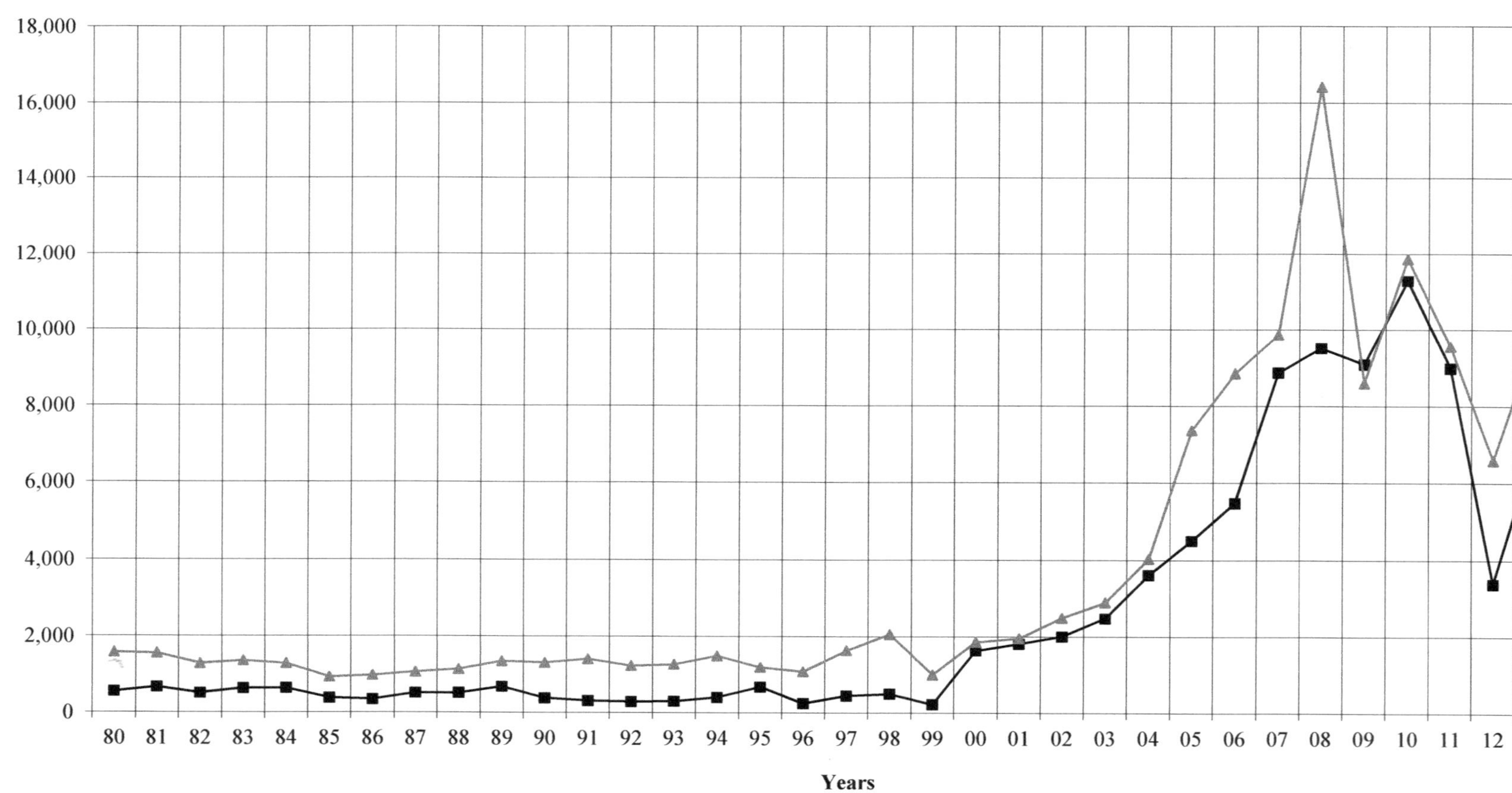

الرسم البياني 20 - واردات وصادرات الجمهورية العربية السورية، 1980- 2014

Graph 20. Syrian Arab Republic imports and exports, 1980-2014

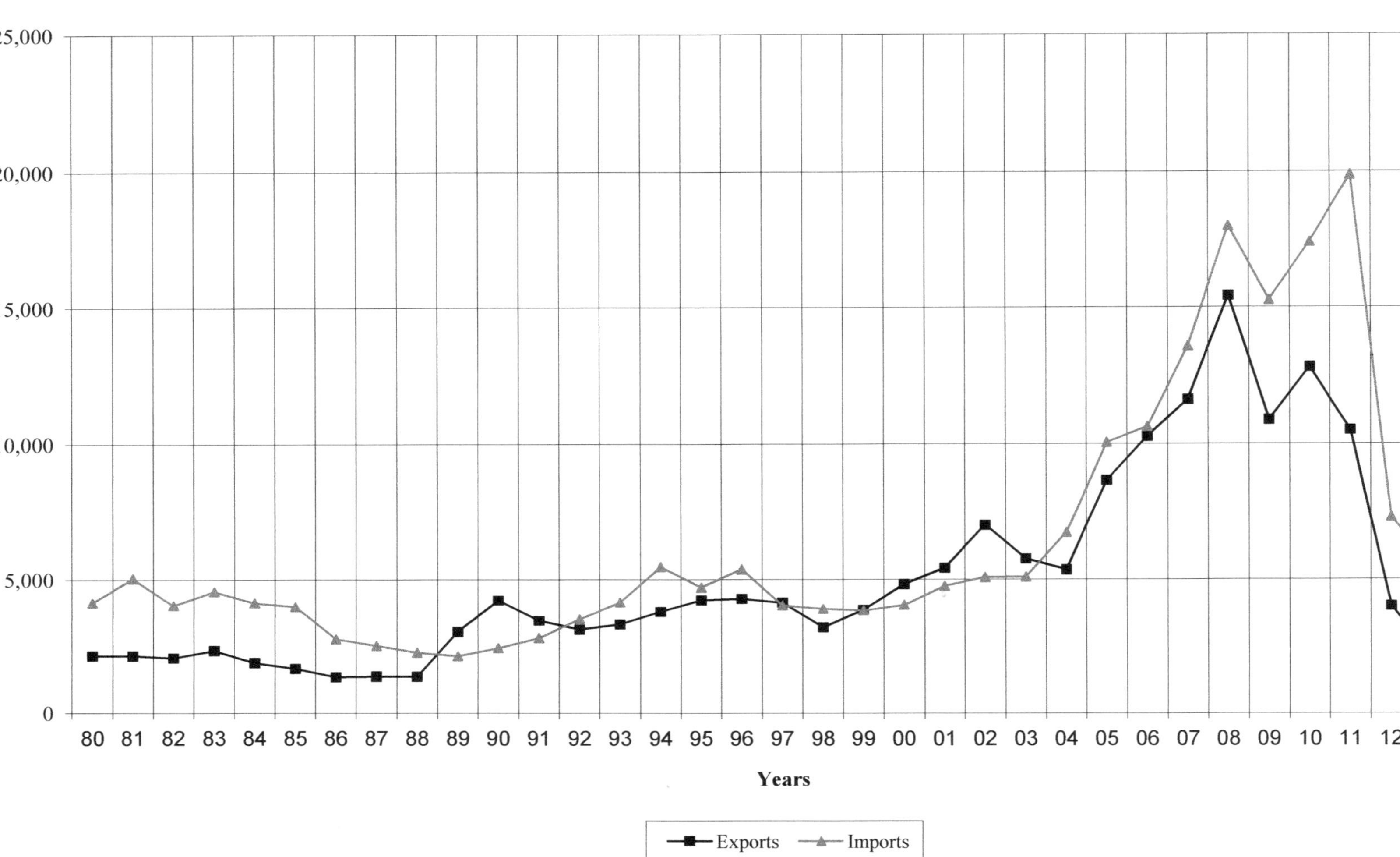

الرسم البياني 21 - واردات وصادرات تونس، 1980- 2014
Graph 21. Tunisia imports and exports, 1980-2014

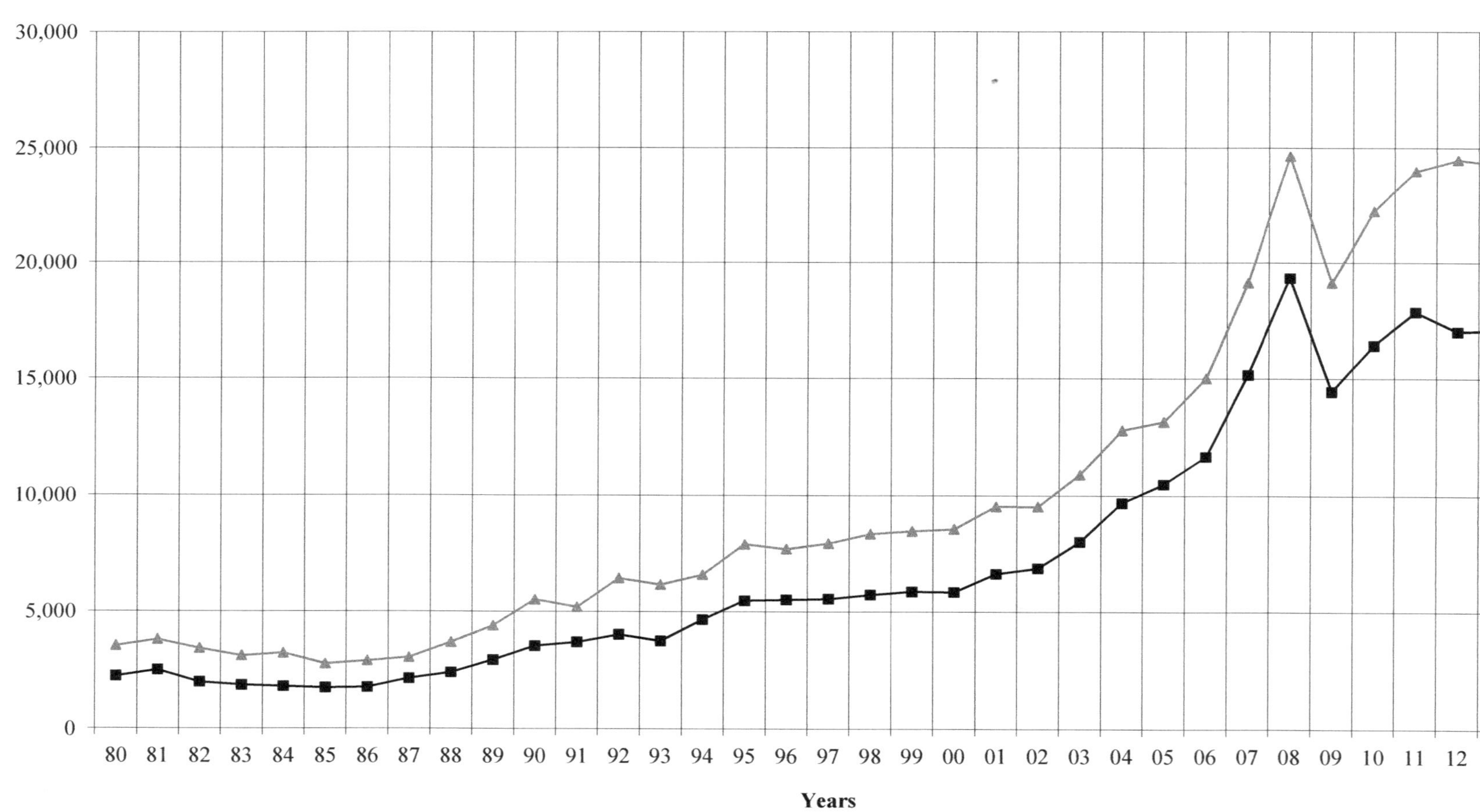

الرسم البياني 22 - واردات وصادرات الإمارات العربية المتحدة ، 1980- 2014
Graph 22. United Arab Emirates imports and exports, 1980-2014

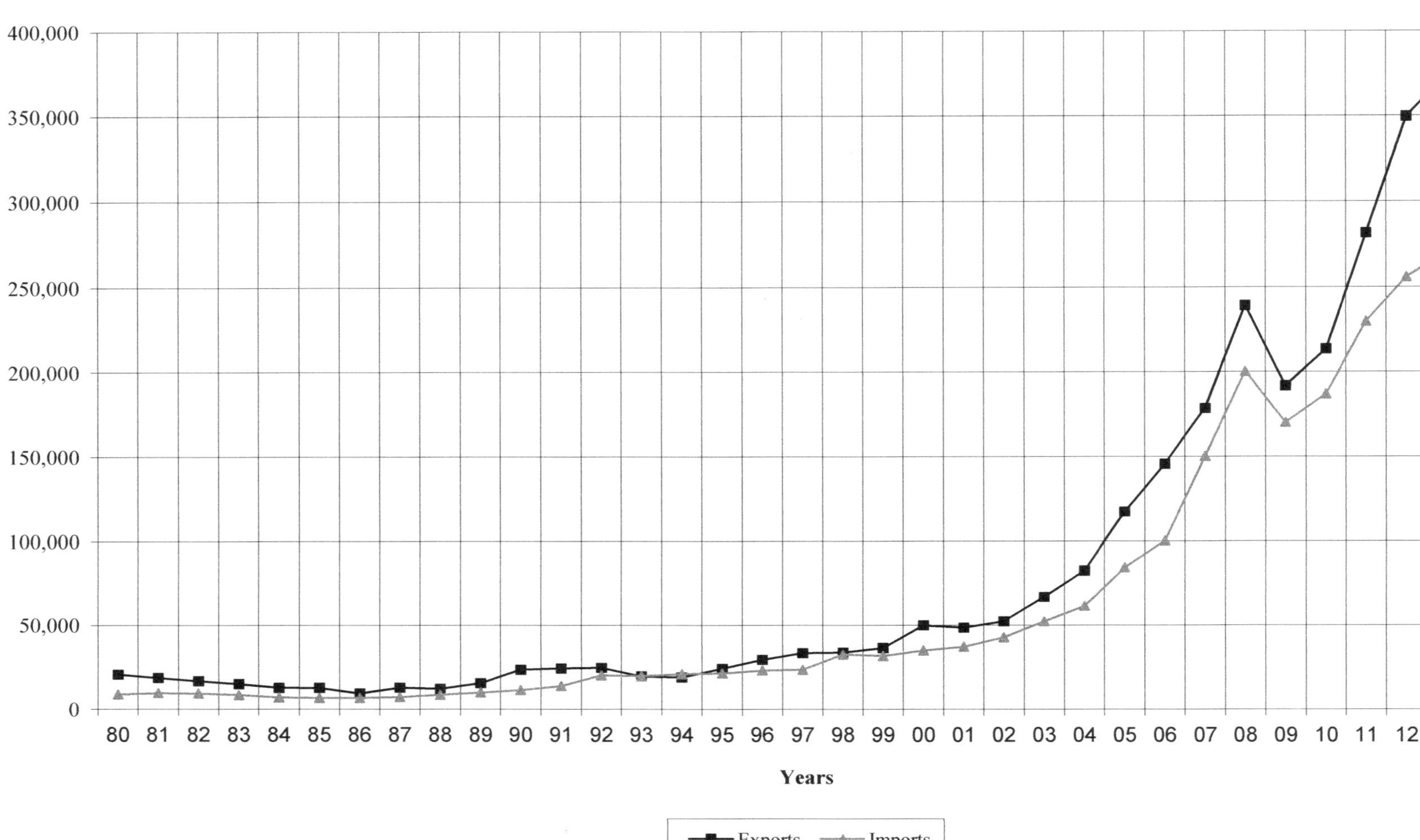

الرسم البياني 23 - واردات وصادرات اليمن ، 1991- 2014

Graph 23. Yemen imports and exports, 1991-2014

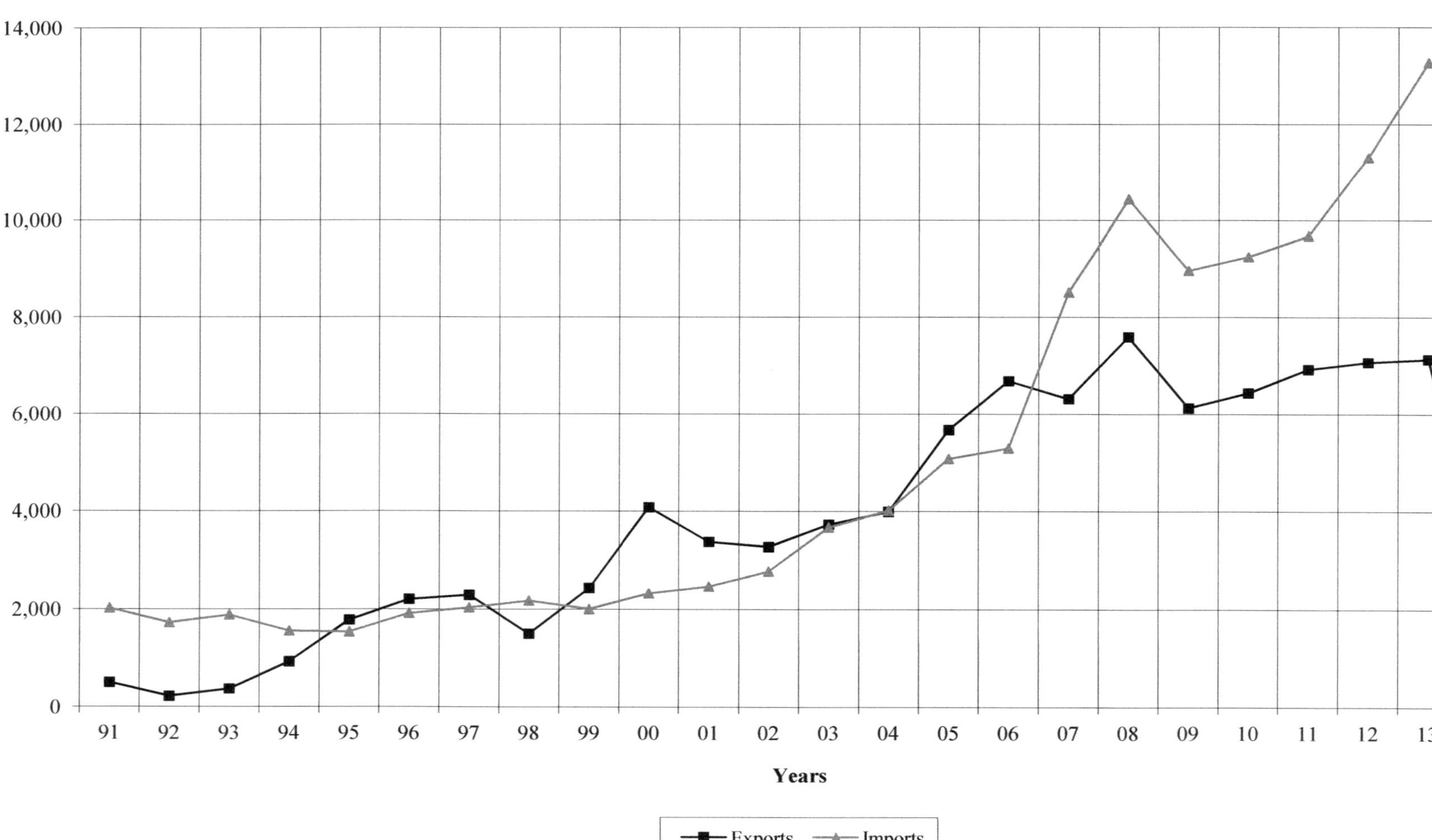

الجدول 1-7- النسبة المئوية لواردات البلدان الأعضاء في الإسكوا حسب أقسام النظام المنسق(*)

Table 1.7. Percentage of the imports of ESCWA member countries by HS section(*)

2010

(Percentage) (نسبة مئوية)

Section \ Country	البحرين Bahrain	مصر Egypt	العراق Iraq	الأردن Jordan	الكويت Kuwait	لبنان Lebanon	ليبيا Libya	المغرب Morocco	عُمان Oman	فلسطين Palestine	قطر Qatar	المملكة العربية السعودية Saudi Arabia	السودان Sudan	الجمهورية العربية السورية Syrian Arab Republic	تونس Tunisia	الإمارات العربية المتحدة United Arab Emirates	اليمن Yemen	البلد \ القسم
1. Live animals, animal products.	2.7	3.9	1.8	3.9	4.4	4.8	1.8	1.5	3.7	4.3	3.2	4.0	1.1	1.4	0.8	1.9	5.2	1. حيوانات حية ومنتجات حيوانية.
2. Vegetable products.	1.8	10.1	3.1	5.6	5.4	4.0	7.0	5.8	2.9	6.9	2.3	6.2	14.2	9.9	5.1	4.2	13.0	2. منتجات نباتية.
3. Animal or vegetable fats and oils.	0.2	1.9	0.4	0.9	0.5	0.7	0.4	1.3	0.8	0.5	0.3	0.7	4.7	1.0	1.2	0.4	3.4	3. شحوم ودهون وزيوت حيوانية أو نباتية.
4. Prepared foodstuffs, beverages, spirits, vinegar, tobacco…etc.	3.0	3.4	2.1	6.1	5.1	6.4	3.0	3.3	4.8	11.1	2.7	4.9	5.9	9.0	2.5	2.1	9.1	4. منتجات صناعة الأغذية، مشروبات، مشروبات روحية، خل، تبغ ... الخ.
5. Mineral products.	50.1	15.2	9.4	22.6	2.0	21.1	2.9	24.5	8.9	34.9	3.8	1.9	7.3	21.4	13.7	2.1	21.6	5. منتجات معدنية.
6. Chemical industry products.	6.2	8.3	1.8	8.4	8.6	8.6	4.1	7.2	7.9	6.6	7.2	8.7	6.5	7.3	7.2	5.6	5.6	6. منتجات الصناعات الكيميائية.
7. Plastics, rubber and related items.	1.5	5.6	0.7	4.1	3.1	3.6	3.0	4.4	3.7	2.9	2.8	3.6	4.9	6.7	5.4	3.2	3.6	7. اللدائن والمطاط ومصنوعاتها.
8. Raw hides and skins, leather…etc.	0.2	0.1	—	0.1	0.5	0.4	0.1	0.4	0.1	0.3	0.3	0.3	0.1	0.1	1.3	0.4	0.1	8. جلود خام ومدبوغة ...الخ.
9. Wood and wood products.	0.6	2.3	0.2	1.2	0.8	1.3	1.3	1.4	1.0	1.9	1.0	1.1	0.7	1.3	1.0	0.7	1.4	9. خشب ومصنوعات خشبية.
10. Pulp of wood or of other fibrous cellulosic material.	0.9	2.7	0.2	2.5	1.9	2.4	1.5	1.9	1.1	2.3	1.0	1.6	1.7	1.9	1.9	1.0	2.5	10. عجينة الخشب أو غيرها من عجائن المواد الليفية السليلوزية.
11. Textiles and textile articles.	1.7	5.5	0.8	5.6	4.5	3.9	1.4	7.0	1.6	2.2	2.2	3.3	4.2	3.8	11.3	3.7	1.5	11. مواد نسجية ومصنوعاتها.
12. Footwear, headgear and umbrellas.	0.1	0.3	0.2	0.4	0.8	0.7	0.4	0.3	0.4	0.4	0.5	0.5	0.9	0.1	0.8	0.6	0.3	12. أحذية، أغطية للرأس، مظلات للمطر.
13. Articles of stones, plaster, cement...etc.	1.1	0.7	0.7	1.6	1.4	2.1	3.1	1.1	1.4	4.1	3.2	1.4	1.7	1.3	0.9	1.4	0.9	13. مصنوعات من حجر أو جص أو إسمنت ...الخ.
14. Authentic and artificial peals, precious stones… etc.	0.4	0.2	—	1.2	1.9	6.5	0.1	0.1	1.2	0.1	1.9	1.2	—	—	0.3	28.7	0.2	14. لؤلؤ طبيعي أو مستنبت، أحجار كريمة ...الخ.
15. Base metals and related articles.	4.7	13.4	33.4	8.8	11.2	7.1	14.4	7.6	11.6	5.5	13.0	12.4	7.3	13.0	9.2	8.6	8.2	15. معادن متبلورة (فلزات) ومصنوعاتها.
16. Electrical machines and mechanical appliances.	14.8	17.0	15.5	14.4	28.1	12.1	32.0	19.2	20.7	8.5	32.8	24.7	20.6	13.2	25.6	19.4	10.9	16. آلات وأجهزة، معدات كهربائية.
17. Transportation vehicles.	7.7	7.4	23.0	8.6	15.0	10.8	17.1	9.7	25.6	5.1	15.7	18.4	14.3	7.2	9.4	12.4	11.1	17. مركبات النقل.
18. Optical, photographic, cinematographic…etc.	0.9	1.3	4.5	1.2	2.5	1.7	3.2	1.3	1.4	1.5	2.7	2.6	1.4	0.8	1.8	1.8	0.7	18. أدوات وأجهزة للبصريات أو التصوير الفوتوغرافي ...الخ.
19. Arms and ammunition: parts and accessories.	—	—	—	—	0.1	0.1	—	0.1	0.2	—	0.2	0.7	0.4	—	—	1.8	—	19. أسلحة وذخائر: أجزاؤها ولوازمها.
20. Miscellaneous manufactured articles.	1.3	0.8	2.1	1.2	2.3	1.7	3.0	1.6	1.3	1.1	3.0	1.8	1.9	0.5	0.8	0.1	0.7	20. سلع ومنتجات مصنعة أخرى.
21. Works of art, collectors' pieces.	—	—	—	1.6	—	0.1	—	—	—	—	0.1	—	0.3	—	—	0.1	—	21. تحف فنية وقطع أثرية.
Unspecified.	—	—	—	—	—	—	—	—	—	—	—	—	—	—	—	—	—	غير محدد.
Total (millions of US dollars)	16 002	52 871	27 411	15 262	22 670	17 964	17 674	35 379	19 775	3 959	23 240	106 863	11 855	17 392	22 215	132 175	9 257	المجموع (مليون دولار أمريكي)

(*) Including crude oil.

(*) بما في ذلك النفط الخام.

الجدول 1-7- النسبة المئوية لواردات البلدان الأعضاء في الإسكوا حسب أقسام النظام المنسق(*)

Table 1.7. Percentage of the imports of ESCWA member countries by HS section(*)

2011

(Percentage) (نسبة مئوية)

Section / Country	Bahrain البحرين	Egypt مصر	Iraq العراق	Jordan الأردن	Kuwait الكويت	Lebanon لبنان	Libya ليبيا	Morocco المغرب	Oman عُمان	Palestine فلسطين	Qatar قطر	Saudi Arabia المملكة العربية السعودية	Sudan السودان	Syrian Arab Republic الجمهورية العربية السورية	Tunisia تونس	United Arab Emirates الإمارات العربية المتحدة	Yemen اليمن	القسم / البلد
1. Live animals, animal products.	2.6	3.4	5.7	3.7	5.1	4.3	..	1.5	3.7	4.3	3.9	4.1	0.9	..	0.7	1.9	4.6	1. حيوانات حية ومنتجات حيوانية.
2. Vegetable products.	1.6	12.5	16.0	7.3	5.6	4.2	..	6.5	2.8	6.5	2.8	5.7	9.3	..	5.8	4.0	15.6	2. منتجات نباتية.
3. Animal or vegetable fats and oils.	0.2	2.8	0.4	1.1	0.8	0.9	..	1.6	1.1	0.6	0.4	0.9	1.2	..	2.1	0.5	2.0	3. شحوم ودهون وزيوت حيوانية أو نباتية.
4. Prepared foodstuffs, beverages, spirits, vinegar, tobacco…etc.	3.2	4.4	3.3	5.5	5.4	6.4	..	3.6	3.5	10.5	3.0	4.6	6.8	..	2.9	2.0	10.5	4. منتجات صناعة الأغذية، مشروبات، مشروبات روحية، خل، تبغ ... الخ.
5. Mineral products.	52.5	17.7	8.7	29.6	1.9	22.9	..	27.4	14.5	35.9	6.4	1.9	13.6	..	15.8	2.4	32.0	5. منتجات معدنية.
6. Chemical industry products.	5.5	8.3	2.3	7.8	8.9	8.6	..	7.1	7.3	6.3	8.3	8.5	8.7	..	7.0	5.5	5.1	6. منتجات الصناعات الكيميائية.
7. Plastics, rubber and related items.	2.4	6.2	1.1	4.0	3.6	3.5	..	4.7	3.7	3.3	3.1	3.8	6.2	..	5.7	2.9	3.1	7. اللدائن والمطاط ومصنوعاتها.
8. Raw hides and skins, leather…etc.	0.2	0.1	—	0.1	0.6	0.4	..	0.4	0.1	0.3	0.4	0.3	0.1	..	1.2	0.5	—	8. جلود خام ومدبوغة ...الخ.
9. Wood and wood products.	0.4	2.2	0.2	1.0	0.8	1.2	..	1.3	0.9	1.9	1.0	1.0	0.6	..	1.0	0.6	1.1	9. خشب ومصنوعات خشبية.
10. Pulp of wood or of other fibrous cellulosic material.	0.8	2.4	0.4	2.3	2.0	2.1	..	1.9	1.1	2.1	1.0	1.5	2.3	..	1.9	0.9	2.1	10. عجينة الخشب أو غيرها من عجائن المواد الليفية السليلوزية.
11. Textiles and textile articles.	1.9	4.7	0.4	5.2	4.9	3.5	..	6.9	1.6	2.1	2.5	3.4	3.6	..	11.4	3.4	1.2	11. مواد نسجية ومصنوعاتها.
12. Footwear, headgear and umbrellas.	0.3	0.2	0.1	0.3	0.8	0.7	..	0.4	0.3	0.4	0.5	0.5	0.8	..	0.8	0.5	0.3	12. أحذية، أغطية للرأس، مظلات للمطر.
13. Articles of stones, plaster, cement…etc.	1.1	0.6	1.6	1.4	1.6	2.0	..	1.2	1.4	4.1	2.9	1.4	1.1	..	0.8	1.2	0.6	13. مصنوعات من حجر أو جص أو إسمنت ...الخ.
14. Authentic and artificial peals, precious stones… etc.	0.5	0.1	—	1.1	3.1	10.6	..	0.1	1.0	0.1	2.5	1.9	—	..	—	31.3	—	14. لؤلؤ طبيعي أو مستنبت، أحجار كريمة ...الخ.
15. Base metals and related articles.	5.7	12.9	20.6	7.7	11.9	7.6	..	8.1	12.1	5.4	10.9	13.4	8.4	..	9.4	9.3	5.1	15. معادن متبلورة (فلزات) ومصنوعاتها.
16. Electrical machines and mechanical appliances.	12.2	14.6	21.4	12.1	23.6	10.6	..	17.1	21.4	8.9	27.6	26.7	19.4	..	24.1	17.6	8.0	16. آلات وأجهزة، معدات كهربائية.
17. Transportation vehicles.	6.4	5.3	15.9	5.9	14.1	7.3	..	7.6	20.7	5.0	16.1	15.6	13.4	..	7.1	12.0	7.5	17. مركبات النقل.
18. Optical, photographic, cinematographic…etc.	1.2	1.0	0.8	1.1	2.7	1.5	..	1.1	1.4	1.2	2.7	2.3	1.2	..	1.6	1.7	0.6	18. أدوات وأجهزة للبصريات أو التصوير الفوتوغرافي ...الخ.
19. Arms and ammunition: parts and accessories.	—	—	—	—	0.1	0.1	..	0.3	—	—	0.1	0.7	0.6	..	—	0.1	—	19. أسلحة وذخائر: أجزاؤها ولوازمها.
20. Miscellaneous manufactured articles.	1.0	0.6	1.0	1.2	2.5	1.5	..	1.4	1.3	1.1	3.3	1.8	1.6	..	0.8	1.6	0.4	20. سلع ومنتجات مصنعة أخرى.
21. Works of art, collectors' pieces.	—	—	—	1.4	—	0.1	..	—	—	—	0.6	—	—	..	—	—	—	21. تحف فنية وقطع أثرية.
Unspecified.	—	—	—	—	—	—	..	—	—	—	—	—	—	..	—	—	—	غير محدد.
Total (millions of US dollars)	17 573	59 269	49 142	18 930	25 144	20 158	..	44 263	23 620	4 221	22 329	131 588	9 546	..	23 952	164 127	9 681	المجموع (مليون دولار أمريكي)

(*) Including crude oil.

(*) بما في ذلك النفط الخام.

الجدول 1-7- النسبة المئوية لواردات البلدان الأعضاء في الإسكوا حسب أقسام النظام المنسق(*)

Table 1.7. Percentage of the imports of ESCWA member countries by HS section(*)

2012

(*Percentage*) (نسبة مئوية)

Section / Country	Bahrain البحرين	Egypt مصر	Iraq العراق	Jordan الأردن	Kuwait الكويت	Lebanon لبنان	Libya ليبيا	Morocco المغرب	Oman عُمان	Palestine فلسطين	Qatar قطر	Saudi Arabia المملكة العربية السعودية	Sudan السودان	Syrian Arab Republic الجمهورية العربية السورية	Tunisia تونس	United Arab Emirates الإمارات العربية المتحدة	Yemen اليمن	البلد / القسم
1. Live animals, animal products.	2.9	4.0	1.9	4.1	4.7	3.9	..	1.3	3.5	4.5	4.1	3.6	1.8	..	0.9	1.9	5.2	1. حيوانات حية ومنتجات حيوانية.
2. Vegetable products.	1.7	12.1	13.3	7.0	5.0	4.1	..	6.6	2.9	8.1	2.7	5.4	8.1	..	5.5	3.4	18.0	2. منتجات نباتية.
3. Animal or vegetable fats and oils.	0.2	2.3	0.3	1.0	0.7	0.9	..	1.4	0.8	0.6	0.3	0.7	0.5	..	1.5	0.4	2.3	3. شحوم ودهون وزيوت حيوانية أو نباتية.
4. Prepared foodstuffs, beverages, spirits, vinegar, tobacco…etc.	3.0	4.6	3.6	5.5	5.1	6.6	..	3.7	3.3	10.8	3.2	4.2	9.9	..	2.9	2.3	10.0	4. منتجات صناعة الأغذية، مشروبات، مشروبات روحية، خل، تبغ ... الخ.
5. Mineral products.	52.7	19.6	24.5	32.1	2.2	28.4	..	29.7	13.5	34.6	5.0	1.8	11.3	..	18.6	2.0	27.8	5. منتجات معدنية.
6. Chemical industry products.	4.1	8.3	3.0	7.4	8.5	8.2	..	6.6	7.9	6.0	8.1	8.3	9.2	..	7.6	5.2	5.7	6. منتجات الصناعات الكيميائية.
7. Plastics, rubber and related items.	1.9	5.9	1.3	4.2	3.4	3.6	..	4.7	3.3	3.5	3.0	3.6	6.2	..	5.4	2.8	3.5	7. اللدائن والمطاط ومصنوعاتها.
8. Raw hides and skins, leather…etc.	0.2	0.1	—	0.1	0.6	0.4	..	0.4	0.1	0.3	0.4	0.3	0.1	..	1.1	0.5	0.1	8. جلود خام ومدبوغة ...الخ.
9. Wood and wood products.	0.5	2.4	0.4	1.1	0.9	1.2	..	1.2	1.0	2.3	1.1	1.0	0.7	..	1.0	0.6	1.3	9. خشب ومصنوعات خشبية.
10. Pulp of wood or of other fibrous cellulosic material.	1.0	2.2	0.3	1.8	1.7	1.7	..	1.8	1.1	1.9	0.9	1.3	2.6	..	1.8	0.9	1.6	10. عجينة الخشب أو غيرها من عجائن المواد الليفية السليلوزية.
11. Textiles and textile articles.	1.5	4.2	0.3	5.1	5.1	3.5	..	6.6	1.4	2.1	2.5	3.1	4.5	..	9.4	3.4	1.7	11. مواد نسجية ومصنوعاتها.
12. Footwear, headgear and umbrellas.	0.2	0.2	0.1	0.3	0.9	0.7	..	0.4	0.3	0.4	0.5	0.5	0.9	..	0.7	0.6	0.4	12. أحذية، أغطية للرأس، مظلات للمطر.
13. Articles of stones, plaster, cement...etc.	1.0	0.6	1.2	1.5	1.5	1.9	..	1.3	1.6	3.8	2.6	1.4	1.4	..	0.8	1.0	0.9	13. مصنوعات من حجر أو جص أو إسمنت ...الخ.
14. Authentic and artificial peals, precious stones… etc.	1.2	0.2	—	1.1	3.0	7.4	..	0.1	1.3	0.1	3.3	1.9	—	..	0.2	31.8	0.1	14. لؤلؤ طبيعي أو مستنبت، أحجار كريمة ...الخ.
15. Base metals and related articles.	4.9	12.7	9.3	7.4	10.6	7.2	..	7.6	13.0	5.6	11.0	13.8	9.2	..	7.9	8.2	5.3	15. معادن متبلورة (فلزات) ومصنوعاتها.
16. Electrical machines and mechanical appliances.	12.2	13.4	20.9	10.6	22.9	9.7	..	15.6	18.4	8.2	25.7	26.4	18.4	..	21.7	17.4	6.4	16. آلات وأجهزة، معدات كهربائية.
17. Transportation vehicles.	8.7	5.5	18.4	5.8	17.6	7.1	..	8.5	0.7	4.2	19.1	17.7	12.0	..	10.2	14.3	8.3	17. مركبات النقل.
18. Optical, photographic, cinematographic…etc.	0.9	1.1	0.8	1.1	2.8	1.5	..	1.1	1.5	1.1	2.6	2.5	1.1	..	1.8	1.7	0.6	18. أدوات وأجهزة للبصريات أو التصوير الفوتوغرافي ...الخ.
19. Arms and ammunition: parts and accessories.	—	—	—	—	0.1	0.1	..	—	—	—	0.1	0.7	0.2	..	—	—	—	19. أسلحة وذخائر: أجزاؤها ولوازمها.
20. Miscellaneous manufactured articles.	1.1	0.6	0.3	1.3	2.6	1.8	..	1.5	1.2	1.3	3.6	1.9	1.4	..	0.9	1.5	0.8	20. سلع ومنتجات مصنعة أخرى.
21. Works of art, collectors' pieces.	—	—	—	1.5	—	0.2	..	—	—	—	0.4	—	—	..	—	—	—	21. تحف فنية وقطع أثرية.
Unspecified.	—	—	—	—	—	—	..	—	23.1	0.5	—	—	—	..	—	—	—	غير محدد.
Total (millions of US dollars)	19 822	71 469	24 443	20 752	27 267	21 280	..	44 790	28 118	4 697	26 083	155 595	6 581	..	24 476	181 762	11 301	المجموع (مليون دولار أمريكي)

(*) Including crude oil.

(*) بما في ذلك النفط الخام.

الجدول 1-7- النسبة المئوية لواردات البلدان الأعضاء في الإسكوا حسب أقسام النظام المنسق(*)

Table 1.7. Percentage of the imports of ESCWA member countries by HS section(*)

2013

(Percentage) (نسبة مئوية)

Section \ Country	Bahrain البحرين	Egypt مصر	Iraq العراق	Jordan الأردن	Kuwait الكويت	Lebanon لبنان	Libya ليبيا	Morocco المغرب	Oman عمان	Palestine فلسطين	Qatar قطر	Saudi Arabia المملكة العربية السعودية	Sudan السودان	Syrian Arab Republic الجمهورية العربية السورية	Tunisia تونس	United Arab Emirates الإمارات العربية المتحدة	Yemen اليمن	البلد \ القسم
1. Live animals, animal products.	2.9	3.8	..	4.3	4.6	4.2	..	1.5	3.3	4.4	3.6	3.6	..	..	0.9	2.0	4.7	1. حيوانات حية ومنتجات حيوانية.
2. Vegetable products.	1.9	11.3	..	6.9	5.0	4.3	..	5.0	2.5	9.5	2.6	5.7	..	..	6.1	3.5	13.4	2. منتجات نباتية.
3. Animal or vegetable fats and oils.	0.3	2.4	..	0.9	0.6	0.9	..	1.2	0.7	0.6	0.4	0.6	..	..	1.2	0.3	1.8	3. شحوم ودهون وزيوت حيوانية أو نباتية.
4. Prepared foodstuffs, beverages, spirits, vinegar, tobacco…etc.	4.2	4.1	..	5.4	4.9	6.6	..	3.5	2.9	10.8	3.3	4.5	..	..	2.6	2.2	8.8	4. منتجات صناعة الأغذية، مشروبات، مشروبات روحية، خل، تبغ ... الخ.
5. Mineral products.	50.0	15.5	..	26.6	2.1	24.1	..	28.2	27.5	34.3	4.8	2.5	..	..	18.8	0.5	2.1	5. منتجات معدنية.
6. Chemical industry products.	4.8	9.1	..	7.1	8.6	9.1	..	6.9	7.6	6.5	8.0	8.0	..	..	8.0	2.4	5.3	6. منتجات الصناعات الكيميائية.
7. Plastics, rubber and related items.	1.9	6.4	..	4.2	3.2	3.9	..	5.2	2.9	3.6	3.1	3.4	..	..	6.0	5.5	3.6	7. اللدائن والمطاط ومصنوعاتها.
8. Raw hides and skins, leather…etc.	0.2	0.1	..	0.1	0.7	0.4	..	0.4	0.1	0.3	0.4	0.3	..	..	1.1	2.7	0.1	8. جلود خام ومدبوغة ...الخ.
9. Wood and wood products.	0.5	2.2	..	1.1	0.8	1.1	..	1.1	0.7	2.2	1.0	0.9	..	..	0.8	0.6	1.3	9. خشب ومصنوعات خشبية.
10. Pulp of wood or of other fibrous cellulosic material.	0.9	2.4	..	1.8	1.7	1.8	..	1.9	0.7	2.3	0.9	1.2	..	..	1.9	0.8	1.6	10. عجينة الخشب أو غيرها من عجائن المواد الليفية السليلوزية.
11. Textiles and textile articles.	1.8	4.9	..	5.8	4.9	3.7	..	6.6	1.1	2.1	2.6	3.0	..	..	9.5	3.5	1.6	11. مواد نسجية ومصنوعاتها.
12. Footwear, headgear and umbrellas.	0.3	0.2	..	0.4	0.9	0.7	..	0.4	0.2	0.4	0.6	0.5	..	..	0.7	0.7	0.4	12. أحذية، أغطية للرأس، مظلات للمطر.
13. Articles of stones, plaster, cement...etc.	1.1	0.7	..	1.5	1.6	2.1	..	1.3	1.2	3.8	3.1	1.4	..	..	0.9	0.9	0.9	13. مصنوعات من حجر أو جص أو إسمنت ...الخ.
14. Authentic and artificial peals, precious stones… etc.	2.1	1.4	..	3.4	4.8	5.3	..	0.1	1.9	—	2.8	3.0	..	..	0.1	32.7	0.3	14. لؤلؤ طبيعي أو مستنبت، أحجار كريمة ...الخ.
15. Base metals and related articles.	4.8	12.6	..	8.4	10.2	7.4	..	8.0	10.4	5.4	9.5	12.4	..	..	8.1	—	5.7	15. معادن متبلورة (فلزات) ومصنوعاتها.
16. Electrical machines and mechanical appliances.	10.4	15.6	..	12.0	21.4	12.2	..	17.0	15.6	8.3	25.5	26.2	..	..	21.6	7.4	7.4	16. آلات وأجهزة، معدات كهربائية.
17. Transportation vehicles.	9.9	5.3	..	6.2	18.0	8.2	..	9.1	18.0	3.8	21.1	17.1	..	..	8.9	17.0	8.5	17. مركبات النقل.
18. Optical, photographic, cinematographic…etc.	0.9	1.2	..	1.2	3.2	1.6	..	1.1	1.4	1.0	2.8	2.6	..	..	1.9	13.8	0.6	18. أدوات وأجهزة للبصريات أو التصوير الفوتوغرافي ...الخ.
19. Arms and ammunition: parts and accessories.	—	—	..	—	0.1	0.1	..	—	—	—	0.2	1.2	..	..	—	1.7	—	19. أسلحة وذخائر: أجزاؤها ولوازمها.
20. Miscellaneous manufactured articles.	1.1	0.7	..	1.4	2.4	1.9	..	1.4	1.2	0.9	3.6	2.0	..	..	1.0	1.6	0.4	20. سلع ومنتجات مصنعة أخرى.
21. Works of art, collectors' pieces.	0.1	—	..	—	0.1	0.1	..	—	—	—	0.3	—	..	..	—	—	—	21. تحف فنية وقطع أثرية.
Unspecified.	—	—	..	1.5	—	—	..	—	0.1	—	—	—	..	..	—	—	31.4	غير محدد.
Total (millions of US dollars)	18 584	66 397	..	22 068	29 646	21 228	..	45 186	34 331	5 164	27 038	168 153	..	..	24 266	186 540	13 273	المجموع (مليون دولار أمريكي)

(*) Including crude oil.

(*) بما في ذلك النفط الخام.

الجدول 1-7- نسبة واردات بلدان الإسكوا حسب أقسام النظام المنسق(*)

Table 1.7. Percentage share of import value of ESCWA member countries by HS sections(*)

2014

(Percentage) (نسبة مئوية)

Section / Country	Bahrain البحرين	Egypt مصر	Iraq العراق	Jordan الأردن	Kuwait الكويت	Lebanon لبنان	Libya ليبيا	Morocco المغرب	Oman عُمان	Palestine فلسطين	Qatar قطر	Saudi Arabia المملكة العربية السعودية	Sudan السودان	Syrian Arab Republic الجمهورية العربية السورية	Tunisia تونس	United Arab Emirates الإمارات العربية المتحدة	Yemen اليمن	القسم / البلد
1. Live animals, animal products.	3.3	4.5	..	4.4	4.7	5.1	..	1.7	4.2	3.8	3.8	3.8	..	..	..	2.2	5.9	1. حيوانات حية ومنتجات حيوانية.
2. Vegetable products.	2.2	11.3	..	7.0	5.5	4.7	..	6.5	3.6	2.1	3.0	5.3	..	..	..	3.7	17.2	2. منتجات نباتية.
3. Animal or vegetable fats and oils.	0.3	1.6	..	0.8	0.6	0.9	..	1.2	0.9	2.2	0.3	0.6	..	..	..	0.3	3.0	3. شحوم ودهون وزيوت حيوانية أو نباتية.
4. Prepared foodstuffs, beverages, spirits, vinegar, tobacco…etc.	3.8	3.8	..	5.8	5.0	6.9	..	3.4	3.7	0.4	3.0	4.4	..	..	..	2.6	13.7	4. منتجات صناعة الأغذية، مشروبات، مشروبات روحية، خل، تبغ ... الخ.
5. Mineral products.	46.1	15.4	..	27.4	2.1	23.8	..	25.6	11.5	2.4	4.4	2.6	..	..	..	2.1	2.9	5. منتجات معدنية.
6. Chemical industry products.	5.6	8.8	..	6.9	8.8	9.8	..	7.1	8.8	—	7.7	8.6	..	..	..	6.2	6.9	6. منتجات الصناعات الكيميائية.
7. Plastics, rubber and related items.	2.2	6.0	..	4.4	3.2	4.0	..	5.4	3.7	5.4	3.3	3.4	..	..	..	3.0	4.5	7. اللدائن والمطاط ومصنوعاتها.
8. Raw hides and skins, leather…etc.	0.3	0.1	..	0.1	0.8	0.4	..	0.5	0.1	8.2	0.4	0.3	..	..	..	0.6	0.1	8. جلود خام ومدبوغة ...الخ.
9. Wood and wood products.	0.6	2.6	..	1.0	0.9	1.3	..	1.1	1.0	4.1	1.0	0.9	..	..	..	0.6	2.4	9. خشب ومصنوعات خشبية.
10. Pulp of wood or of other fibrous cellulosic material.	0.9	2.2	..	2.2	1.4	1.8	..	2.0	1.1	1.3	0.8	1.2	..	..	..	0.8	3.0	10. عجينة الخشب أو غيرها من عجائن المواد الليفية السليلوزية.
11. Textiles and textile articles.	2.9	5.1	..	5.5	4.8	4.0	..	6.9	1.3	8.7	2.7	3.1	..	..	..	3.8	2.6	11. مواد نسجية ومصنوعاتها.
12. Footwear, headgear and umbrellas.	0.3	0.2	..	0.3	1.0	0.8	..	0.4	0.3	1.0	0.6	0.5	..	..	..	0.8	0.5	12. أحذية، أغطية للرأس، مظلات للمطر.
13. Articles of stones, plaster, cement...etc.	1.0	0.6	..	1.6	1.7	2.3	..	1.6	2.3	—	2.8	1.3	..	..	..	1.0	1.2	13. مصنوعات من حجر أو جص أو إسمنت ...الخ.
14. Authentic and artificial peals, precious stones… etc.	2.3	1.3	..	3.2	4.7	4.8	..	0.3	1.5	0.6	2.6	2.9	..	..	..	26.1	1.7	14. لؤلؤ طبيعي أو مستنبت، أحجار كريمة ...الخ.
15. Base metals and related articles.	4.4	12.0	..	6.8	9.5	7.3	..	7.8	11.7	11.5	10.0	12.2	..	..	..	7.7	10.1	15. معادن متبلورة (فلزات) ومصنوعاتها.
16. Electrical machines and mechanical appliances.	10.3	14.7	..	10.7	22.7	10.7	..	16.9	17.2	36.1	26.1	26.2	..	..	..	19.8	12.0	16. آلات وأجهزة، معدات كهربائية.
17. Transportation vehicles.	11.1	7.6	..	7.6	16.6	7.4	..	8.8	22.8	6.1	20.9	16.7	..	..	..	14.9	9.7	17. مركبات النقل.
18. Optical, photographic, cinematographic…etc.	1.0	1.3	..	1.3	3.1	1.7	..	1.2	1.8	3.9	2.6	2.8	..	..	..	1.9	1.5	18. أدوات وأجهزة للبصريات أو التصوير الفوتوغرافي ...الخ.
19. Arms and ammunition: parts and accessories.	—	—	..	—	0.1	0.1	..	—	—	—	0.1	0.9	..	..	..	—	0.2	19. أسلحة وذخائر: أجزاؤها ولوازمها.
20. Miscellaneous manufactured articles.	1.4	0.7	..	1.2	2.8	2.0	..	1.6	2.3	0.3	3.4	2.2	..	..	..	1.8	0.9	20. سلع ومنتجات مصنعة أخرى.
21. Works of art, collectors' pieces.	—	—	..	—	—	0.1	..	—	—	2.0	0.6	—	..	..	..	0.1	—	21. تحف فنية وقطع أثرية.
Unspecified.	—	0.4	..	1.7	—	—	..	—	—	—	—	—	..	..	..	—	—	غير محدد.
Total (millions of US dollars)	20 044	71 338	..	22 740	31 489	20 494	..	46 192	29 303	5 683	30 443	173 835	..	..	..	189 762	12 042	المجموع (مليون دولار أمريكي)

(*) Including crude oil.

(*) بما في ذلك النفط الخام.

الجدول 1-8- النسبة المئوية لصادرات البلدان الأعضاء في الإسكوا حسب أقسام النظام المنسق[1]

Table I.8. Percentage of the exports of ESCWA member countries by HS section[1]

2010

(*Percentage*)

Section / Country	البحرين Bahrain	مصر Egypt	العراق Iraq	الأردن Jordan	الكويت Kuwait	لبنان Lebanon	ليبيا Libya	المغرب Morocco	عُمان Oman	فلسطين Palestine	قطر Qatar	المملكة العربية السعودية Saudi Arabia	السودان Sudan	الجمهورية العربية السورية[2] Syrian Arab Republic[2]	تونس Tunisia	الإمارات العربية المتحدة United Arab Emirates	اليمن Yemen	البلد / القسم
1. Live animals, animal products.	0.8	2.2	—	2.9	0.1	0.4	—	5.2	1.2	3.3	0.1	0.5	1.6	4.2	1.2	0.3	3.7	1. حيوانات حية ومنتجات حيوانية.
2. Vegetable products.	—	10.5	—	7.8	—	3.6	—	7.6	0.3	7.2	—	0.2	2.5	8.4	2.1	1.0	1.7	2. منتجات نباتية.
3. Animal or vegetable fats and oils.	—	0.6	—	0.2	—	0.5	—	0.8	0.4	2.7	—	0.1	—	0.8	2.9	0.1	0.1	3. شحوم ودهون وزيوت حيوانية أو نباتية.
4. Prepared foodstuffs, beverages, spirits, vinegar, tobacco...etc.	0.7	5.0	—	4.9	0.2	7.6	97.7	6.1	0.8	8.8	—	0.5	0.1	6.5	1.8	1.8	1.8	4. منتجات صناعة الأغذية، مشروبات، مشروبات روحية، خل، تبغ ... الخ.
5. Mineral products.	79.4	29.8	99.7	6.6	92.8	1.3	1.3	11.1	73.9	2.3	90.3	85.8	84.6	47.7	15.7	51.4	88.1	5. منتجات معدنية.
6. Chemical industry products.	2.9	11.6	0.2	32.4	1.6	7.3	0.3	19.4	5.1	5.5	3.1	4.3	—	4.5	10.1	1.1	0.4	6. منتجات الصناعات الكيميائية.
7. Plastics, rubber and related items.	0.7	3.6	—	2.7	2.7	2.8	—	0.9	1.9	8.0	2.0	4.5	—	3.0	2.4	2.0	0.2	7. اللدائن والمطاط ومصنوعاتها.
8. Raw hides and skins, leather...etc.	—	0.7	—	0.2	—	0.3	—	0.6	—	0.6	—	—	0.3	0.3	0.7	0.1	0.3	8. جلود خام ومدبوغة ...الخ.
9. Wood and wood products.	—	0.1	—	0.4	—	0.5	—	0.2	—	4.0	—	—	—	0.2	0.2	0.1	—	9. خشب ومصنوعات خشبية.
10. Pulp of wood or of other fibrous cellulosic material.	0.3	1.6	—	3.6	0.1	5.6	—	1.0	0.1	1.8	—	0.4	—	0.9	1.4	0.4	0.1	10. عجينة الخشب أو غيرها من عجائن المواد الليفية السليلوزية.
11. Textiles and textile articles.	0.7	11.3	—	13.7	0.1	2.5	—	18.8	0.3	1.5	—	0.2	0.3	9.7	21.5	2.0	0.1	11. مواد نسجية ومصنوعاتها.
12. Footwear, headgear and umbrellas.	—	0.1	—	0.1	—	0.5	—	2.0	—	4.5	—	—	—	0.9	3.5	0.2	—	12. أحذية، أغطية للرأس، مظلات للمطر.
13. Articles of stones, plaster, cement...etc.	0.1	3.3	—	0.7	0.2	1.0	—	0.4	0.5	20.8	—	0.2	—	0.5	0.9	0.8	—	13. مصنوعات من حجر أو جص أو إسمنت ...الخ.
14. Authentic and artificial peals, precious stones... etc.	0.1	3.8	—	4.7	0.2	26.1	0.8	2.1	0.3	0.3	—	0.2	10.2	—	0.4	21.4	0.6	14. لؤلؤ طبيعي أو مستنبت، أحجار كريمة ...الخ.
15. Base metals and related articles.	10.9	10.3	—	6.8	0.6	10.8	—	3.8	2.6	14.7	2.0	0.9	0.2	2.4	4.1	2.4	0.5	15. معادن متبلورة (فلزات) ومصنوعاتها.
16. Electrical machines and mechanical appliances.	1.6	3.9	—	8.0	0.6	17.4	—	16.3	2.0	4.4	1.0	1.0	—	1.8	25.7	7.1	1.6	16. آلات وأجهزة، معدات كهربائية.
17. Transportation vehicles.	1.3	0.4	—	2.6	0.8	8.5	—	2.7	10.3	1.3	1.3	0.9	—	0.2	2.7	6.5	0.7	17. مركبات النقل.
18. Optical, photographic, cinematographic...etc.	0.1	0.2	—	0.5	—	0.5	—	0.3	0.1	0.7	—	0.1	—	—	1.7	0.6	0.1	18. أدوات وأجهزة للبصريات أو التصوير الفوتوغرافي ...الخ.
19. Arms and ammunition: parts and accessories.	—	—	—	—	—	—	—	—	—	—	—	—	—	—	—	0.5	—	19. أسلحة وذخائر: أجزاؤها ولوازمها.
20. Miscellaneous manufactured articles.	0.3	1.0	—	1.1	0.1	2.4	—	0.7	0.1	7.6	—	0.1	—	0.3	1.1	—	—	20. سلع ومنتجات مصنعة أخرى.
21. Works of art, collectors' pieces.	—	—	—	0.1	—	0.2	—	—	—	—	—	—	—	—	—	0.1	—	21. تحف فنية وقطع أثرية.
Unspecified.	—	—	—	—	—	—	—	—	—	—	—	—	—	7.7	—	—	—	غير محدد.
Total (millions of US dollars)	18 246	27 121	52 483	7 023	62 749	4 253	36 440	17 765	36 601	576	74 812	251 147	11 284	12 238	16 427	148 303	6 437	المجموع (مليون دولار أمريكي)

(1) Including crude oil.

(2) Excluding re-exports.

(1) بما في ذلك النفط الخام.

(2) باستثناء إعادة التصدير.

الجدول 1-8- النسبة المئوية لصادرات البلدان الأعضاء في الإسكوا حسب أقسام النظام المنسق(*)

Table I.8. Percentage of the exports of ESCWA member countries by HS section(*)

2011

(Percentage) (نسبة مئوية)

Section / Country	Bahrain البحرين	Egypt مصر	Iraq العراق	Jordan الأردن	Kuwait الكويت	Lebanon لبنان	Libya ليبيا	Morocco المغرب	Oman عُمان	Palestine فلسطين	Qatar قطر	Saudi Arabia المملكة العربية السعودية	Sudan السودان	Syrian Arab Republic الجمهورية العربية السورية	Tunisia تونس	United Arab Emirates الإمارات العربية المتحدة	Yemen اليمن	البلد / القسم
1. Live animals, animal products.	1.0	1.8	—	3.0	0.1	0.4	..	4.8	1.0	3.0	—	0.4	3.3	..	1.6	0.2	3.9	1. حيوانات حية ومنتجات حيوانية.
2. Vegetable products.	—	8.9	—	8.0	—	3.8	..	7.8	0.2	7.4	—	0.1	3.6	..	2.6	0.8	2.1	2. منتجات نباتية.
3. Animal or vegetable fats and oils.	—	0.6	—	0.2	—	0.5	..	0.8	0.4	2.9	—	0.1	—	..	3.8	0.2	0.2	3. شحوم ودهون وزيوت حيوانية أو نباتية.
4. Prepared foodstuffs, beverages, spirits, vinegar, tobacco...etc.	1.0	4.2	—	4.5	0.1	8.9	..	4.5	0.7	9.2	—	0.4	0.1	..	2.3	1.4	1.5	4. منتجات صناعة الأغذية، مشروبات، مشروبات روحية، خل، تبغ ... الخ.
5. Mineral products.	79.9	31.9	99.8	9.0	94.8	0.8	..	13.2	76.0	0.8	92.1	87.2	82.6	..	15.4	56.7	88.4	5. منتجات معدنية.
6. Chemical industry products.	1.1	11.8	0.2	31.1	1.4	9.0	..	21.7	6.6	4.1	2.7	4.5	0.1	..	6.3	1.2	0.5	6. منتجات الصناعات الكيميائية.
7. Plastics, rubber and related items.	0.5	3.9	—	3.0	1.8	3.1	..	0.9	1.7	8.1	2.1	4.0	—	..	2.6	1.7	0.2	7. اللدائن والمطاط ومصنوعاتها.
8. Raw hides and skins, leather...etc.	—	0.5	—	0.2	—	0.3	..	0.6	—	0.4	—	—	0.4	..	0.8	0.1	0.3	8. جلود خام ومدبوغة ...الخ.
9. Wood and wood products.	0.2	0.2	—	0.4	—	0.4	..	0.2	—	3.8	—	—	—	..	0.1	0.1	—	9. خشب ومصنوعات خشبية.
10. Pulp of wood or of other fibrous cellulosic material.	0.8	1.6	—	3.0	0.1	5.1	..	0.7	0.1	1.9	—	0.3	—	..	1.2	0.3	0.1	10. عجينة الخشب أو غيرها من عجائن المواد الليفية السليلوزية.
11. Textiles and textile articles.	0.7	10.5	—	13.4	0.1	3.0	..	17.1	0.1	1.8	—	0.2	0.3	..	21.1	1.5	0.1	11. مواد نسجية ومصنوعاتها.
12. Footwear, headgear and umbrellas.	—	0.1	—	0.2	—	0.5	..	1.8	—	5.0	—	—	—	..	3.3	0.1	—	12. أحذية، أغطية للرأس، مظلات للمطر.
13. Articles of stones, plaster, cement...etc.	0.2	2.6	—	0.6	0.1	0.9	..	0.4	0.3	21.4	—	0.1	—	..	0.7	0.7	—	13. مصنوعات من حجر أو جص أو إسمنت ...الخ.
14. Authentic and artificial peals, precious stones... etc.	—	5.6	—	4.8	0.1	35.0	..	1.6	—	0.1	—	0.3	9.2	..	—	20.9	0.1	14. لؤلؤ طبيعي أو مستنبت، أحجار كريمة ...الخ.
15. Base metals and related articles.	10.8	9.7	—	6.4	0.4	12.3	..	4.5	3.1	16.9	1.8	0.7	0.3	..	3.9	2.5	0.8	15. معادن متبلورة (فلزات) ومصنوعاتها.
16. Electrical machines and mechanical appliances.	2.0	4.4	—	7.9	0.4	12.2	..	15.8	1.6	3.5	0.5	0.8	—	..	27.9	6.2	0.8	16. آلات وأجهزة، معدات كهربائية.
17. Transportation vehicles.	1.6	0.3	—	2.2	0.4	0.9	..	3.0	7.7	0.8	0.6	0.7	—	..	3.3	4.4	1.0	17. مركبات النقل.
18. Optical, photographic, cinematographic...etc.	—	0.2	—	0.8	—	0.5	..	0.1	0.1	0.4	—	0.1	—	..	1.8	0.3	0.1	18. أدوات وأجهزة للبصريات أو التصوير الفوتوغرافي ...الخ.
19. Arms and ammunition: parts and accessories.	—	—	—	—	—	—	..	—	—	—	—	—	—	..	—	—	—	19. أسلحة وذخائر: أجزاؤها ولوازمها.
20. Miscellaneous manufactured articles.	0.2	1.0	—	1.0	—	2.2	..	0.4	0.1	8.4	—	0.1	—	..	1.3	0.4	0.1	20. سلع ومنتجات مصنعة أخرى.
21. Works of art, collectors' pieces.	—	0.1	—	0.1	—	0.1	..	—	—	0.2	—	—	—	..	—	0.1	—	21. تحف فنية وقطع أثرية.
Unspecified.	—	—	—	—	—	—	..	—	—	—	—	—	—	..	—	—	—	غير محدد.
Total (millions of US dollars)	22 417	30 782	83 226	8 006	102 704	4 265	..	21 650	47 092	720	114 301	364 703	8 982	..	17 847	200 070	6 917	المجموع (مليون دولار أمريكي)

(*) Including crude oil.

(*) بما في ذلك النفط الخام.

الجدول 1-8- النسبة المئوية لصادرات البلدان الأعضاء في الإسكوا حسب أقسام النظام المنسق(*)

Table I.8. Percentage of the exports of ESCWA member countries by HS section(*)

2012

(*Percentage*) (نسبة مئوية)

Section / Country	Bahrain البحرين	Egypt مصر	Iraq العراق	Jordan الأردن	Kuwait الكويت	Lebanon لبنان	Libya ليبيا	Morocco المغرب	Oman عُمان	Palestine فلسطين	Qatar قطر	Saudi Arabia المملكة العربية السعودية	Sudan السودان	Syrian Arab Republic الجمهورية العربية السورية	Tunisia تونس	United Arab Emirates الإمارات العربية المتحدة	Yemen اليمن	القسم / البلد
1. Live animals, animal products.	1.0	1.5	—	3.4	0.1	0.4	..	5.0	0.9	2.4	—	0.4	12.1	..	1.3	0.2	3.2	1. حيوانات حية ومنتجات حيوانية.
2. Vegetable products.	0.1	8.2	—	8.9	—	3.8	..	7.0	0.3	8.9	—	0.1	9.6	..	2.1	0.7	2.0	2. منتجات نباتية.
3. Animal or vegetable fats and oils.	—	1.0	—	0.3	—	0.7	..	0.6	0.3	3.9	—	0.1	—	..	3.9	0.1	0.2	3. شحوم ودهون وزيوت حيوانية أو نباتية.
4. Prepared foodstuffs, beverages, spirits, vinegar, tobacco…etc.	1.2	4.1	—	4.9	0.1	8.7	..	5.2	0.7	10.3	—	0.4	1.4	..	2.4	1.3	1.1	4. منتجات صناعة الأغذية، مشروبات، مشروبات روحية، خل، تبغ ... الخ.
5. Mineral products.	75.8	31.8	99.7	8.7	94.8	2.9	..	15.0	77.5	2.7	88.3	86.9	7.7	..	17.6	54.1	89.6	5. منتجات معدنية.
6. Chemical industry products.	3.0	12.4	0.2	30.0	1.7	7.6	..	20.1	5.5	3.9	4.0	4.7	2.3	..	7.7	1.0	0.6	6. منتجات الصناعات الكيميائية.
7. Plastics, rubber and related items.	0.7	4.4	—	4.1	1.5	3.3	..	0.8	1.3	8.2	3.3	4.0	—	..	2.6	2.4	0.1	7. اللدائن والمطاط ومصنوعاتها.
8. Raw hides and skins, leather…etc.	—	0.4	—	0.2	—	0.3	..	0.6	—	0.4	—	—	1.1	..	0.8	0.1	0.2	8. جلود خام ومدبوغة ...الخ.
9. Wood and wood products.	0.1	0.1	—	1.1	—	0.5	..	0.2	—	3.7	—	—	0.1	..	0.1	0.1	—	9. خشب ومصنوعات خشبية.
10. Pulp of wood or of other fibrous cellulosic material.	0.5	1.6	—	2.9	0.1	4.1	..	0.6	0.1	2.0	—	0.3	—	..	0.9	0.4	—	10. عجينة الخشب أو غيرها من عجائن المواد الليفية السليلوزية.
11. Textiles and textile articles.	0.8	10.2	—	14.5	—	2.6	..	16.7	0.1	1.9	—	0.2	0.6	..	18.5	1.2	—	11. مواد نسجية ومصنوعاتها.
12. Footwear, headgear and umbrellas.	—	—	—	0.3	—	0.5	..	1.5	0.1	4.1	—	—	—	..	3.0	0.1	—	12. أحذية، أغطية للرأس، مظلات للمطر.
13. Articles of stones, plaster, cement...etc.	0.2	3.7	—	0.6	0.1	1.0	..	0.4	0.4	19.7	0.1	0.1	—	..	0.7	0.5	—	13. مصنوعات من حجر أو جص أو إسمنت ...الخ.
14. Authentic and artificial peals, precious stones… etc.	0.4	5.4	—	3.3	0.2	38.5	..	1.3	—	—	—	0.2	64.2	..	0.2	23.5	0.1	14. لؤلؤ طبيعي أو مستنبت، أحجار كريمة ...الخ.
15. Base metals and related articles.	10.8	8.6	—	5.1	0.3	10.5	..	3.4	3.5	13.7	3.4	0.7	0.6	..	4.0	3.1	0.6	15. معادن متبلورة (فلزات) ومصنوعاتها.
16. Electrical machines and mechanical appliances.	3.2	4.9	—	7.3	0.3	10.7	..	14.4	1.4	3.3	0.4	0.7	—	..	27.0	5.7	0.9	16. آلات وأجهزة، معدات كهربائية.
17. Transportation vehicles.	2.0	0.4	—	2.0	0.6	0.9	..	6.2	0.2	1.1	0.5	1.0	0.1	..	3.6	4.4	1.1	17. مركبات النقل.
18. Optical, photographic, cinematographic…etc.	0.1	0.3	—	0.6	—	0.4	..	0.1	0.1	0.3	—	—	—	..	2.0	0.3	0.1	18. أدوات وأجهزة للبصريات أو التصوير الفوتوغرافي ...الخ.
19. Arms and ammunition: parts and accessories.	—	—	—	—	—	—	..	—	—	—	—	—	—	..	—	—	—	19. أسلحة وذخائر: أجزاؤها ولوازمها.
20. Miscellaneous manufactured articles.	0.2	1.1	—	1.5	—	2.4	..	0.6	0.1	8.5	—	0.1	—	..	1.5	0.4	—	20 . سلع ومنتجات مصنعة أخرى.
21. Works of art, collectors' pieces.	—	—	—	0.2	—	0.1	..	—	—	—	—	—	—	..	—	0.1	—	21 . تحف فنية وقطع أثرية.
Unspecified.	—	—	—	—	—	—	..	0.1	7.7	1.1	—	—	—	..	—	—	—	غير محدد.
Total (millions of US dollars)	21 928	30 778	94 392	7 887	114 516	4 483	..	21 417	52 138	782	132 968	388 406	3 384	..	17 008	225 727	7 065	المجموع (مليون دولار أمريكي)

(*) Including crude oil.

(*) بما في ذلك النفط الخام.

الجدول 1-8- النسبة المئوية لصادرات البلدان الأعضاء في الإسكوا حسب أقسام النظام المنسق(*)

Table I.8. Percentage of the exports of ESCWA member countries by HS section(*)

2013

(Percentage) (نسبة مئوية)

Section / Country	Bahrain البحرين	Egypt مصر	Iraq العراق	Jordan الأردن	Kuwait الكويت	Lebanon لبنان	Libya ليبيا	Morocco المغرب	Oman عُمان	Palestine فلسطين	Qatar قطر	Saudi Arabia المملكة العربية السعودية	Sudan السودان	Syrian Arab Republic الجمهورية العربية السورية	Tunisia تونس	United Arab Emirates الإمارات العربية المتحدة	Yemen اليمن	البلد / القسم
1. Live animals, animal products.	1.1	1.6	..	4.6	0.1	0.6	..	5.3	0.9	2.9	—	0.4	..	..	1.3	0.3	3.4	1. حيوانات حية ومنتجات حيوانية.
2. Vegetable products.	—	9.7	..	9.1	0.1	5.5	..	8.2	0.5	14.3	—	0.1	..	..	2.4	0.7	1.9	2. منتجات نباتية.
3. Animal or vegetable fats and oils.	—	0.9	..	0.2	—	0.9	..	0.5	0.3	1.4	—	0.1	..	..	3.9	0.1	0.1	3. شحوم ودهون وزيوت حيوانية أو نباتية.
4. Prepared foodstuffs, beverages, spirits, vinegar, tobacco…etc.	2.1	4.9	..	5.6	0.2	11.5	..	5.5	0.8	12.3	—	0.4	..	..	2.3	1.5	0.9	4. منتجات صناعة الأغذية، مشروبات، مشروبات روحية، خل، تبغ ... الخ.
5. Mineral products.	63.8	28.5	..	5.9	94.3	9.1	..	14.4	77.6	2.8	87.9	85.7	..	..	16.1	54.4	83.7	5. منتجات معدنية.
6. Chemical industry products.	2.5	12.4	..	30.5	1.8	8.4	..	16.5	4.4	4.2	4.0	4.9	..	..	7.7	1.0	0.5	6. منتجات الصناعات الكيميائية.
7. Plastics, rubber and related items.	0.7	5.6	..	4.5	1.4	3.7	..	0.7	1.4	7.7	3.8	4.6	..	..	2.8	1.0	0.1	7. اللدائن والمطاط ومصنوعاتها.
8. Raw hides and skins, leather…etc.	—	0.6	..	0.1	—	0.5	..	0.6	—	0.5	—	—	..	..	0.8	2.0	0.3	8. جلود خام ومدبوغة ...الخ.
9. Wood and wood products.	0.2	0.1	..	0.6	—	0.5	..	0.2	—	3.4	—	—	..	..	0.1	0.1	—	9. خشب ومصنوعات خشبية.
10. Pulp of wood or of other fibrous cellulosic material.	0.5	1.4	..	2.6	0.1	4.5	..	0.5	0.1	1.9	—	0.2	..	..	1.5	0.6	—	10. عجينة الخشب أو غيرها من عجائن المواد الليفية السليلوزية.
11. Textiles and textile articles.	0.9	10.8	..	15.9	0.1	3.1	..	16.0	0.1	1.9	—	0.2	..	..	18.8	1.4	—	11. مواد نسجية ومصنوعاتها.
12. Footwear, headgear and umbrellas.	0.1	—	..	0.1	—	0.5	..	1.6	—	3.3	—	—	..	..	2.8	0.1	—	12. أحذية، أغطية للرأس، مظلات للمطر.
13. Articles of stones, plaster, cement...etc.	0.4	3.7	..	0.6	0.1	1.1	..	0.4	0.4	17.4	0.1	0.1	..	..	0.8	0.7	—	13. مصنوعات من حجر أو جص أو إسمنت ...الخ.
14. Authentic and artificial peals, precious stones… etc.	2.6	3.2	..	1.6	0.3	19.6	..	0.8	—	—	—	0.2	..	..	0.1	20.1	0.2	14. لؤلؤ طبيعي أو مستنبت، أحجار كريمة ...الخ.
15. Base metals and related articles.	15.2	9.0	..	5.7	0.4	13.4	..	2.7	3.5	11.5	3.1	0.9	..	..	3.8	—	0.7	15. معادن متبلورة (فلزات) ومصنوعاتها.
16. Electrical machines and mechanical appliances.	4.2	4.8	..	7.2	0.3	12.9	..	15.9	1.5	4.9	0.5	0.8	..	..	26.8	3.6	0.7	16. آلات وأجهزة، معدات كهربائية.
17. Transportation vehicles.	5.0	0.6	..	2.6	0.7	0.9	..	9.4	8.1	1.3	0.4	1.1	..	..	4.5	6.9	0.6	17. مركبات النقل.
18. Optical, photographic, cinematographic…etc.	0.2	0.2	..	0.6	—	0.5	..	0.1	0.1	0.3	—	—	..	..	2.2	4.7	—	18. أدوات وأجهزة للبصريات أو التصوير الفوتوغرافي ...الخ.
19. Arms and ammunition: parts and accessories.	—	—	..	—	—	—	..	—	—	—	—	—	..	..	—	0.3	—	19. أسلحة وذخائر: أجزاؤها ولوازمها.
20. Miscellaneous manufactured articles.	0.4	1.7	..	1.7	0.1	2.9	..	0.6	0.1	7.8	—	0.1	..	..	1.1	0.4	0.1	20 . سلع ومنتجات مصنعة أخرى.
21. Works of art, collectors' pieces.	—	—	..	—	—	0.2	..	—	—	—	—	—	..	..	—	0.1	—	21 . تحف فنية وقطع أثرية.
Unspecified.	—	—	..	0.3	—	—	..	—	—	—	—	—	..	..	—	—	6.8	غير محدد.
Total (millions of US dollars)	25 500	28 789	..	7 913	114 404	3 936	..	21 965	55 497	1 165	136 858	375 871	..	..	17 060	226 549	7 130	المجموع (مليون دولار أمريكي)

(*) Including crude oil.

(*) بما في ذلك النفط الخام.

الجدول 1-8- نسبة صادرات بلدان الإسكوا حسب أقسام النظام المنسق(*)

Table I.8. Percentage share of export value of ESCWA member countries by HS sections (*)

2014

(Percentage) (نسبة مئوية)

Section / Country	Bahrain البحرين	Egypt مصر	Iraq العراق	Jordan الأردن	Kuwait الكويت	Lebanon لبنان	Libya ليبيا	Morocco المغرب	Oman عُمان	Palestine فلسطين	Qatar قطر	Saudi Arabia المملكة العربية السعودية	Sudan السودان	Syrian Arab Republic الجمهورية العربية السورية	Tunisia تونس	United Arab Emirates الإمارات العربية المتحدة	Yemen اليمن	البلد / القسم
1. Live animals, animal products.	1.0	1.8	..	4.0	0.2	0.8	..	5.0	1.1	0.5	—	0.5	..	..	..	0.5	9.9	1. حيوانات حية ومنتجات حيوانية.
2. Vegetable products.	—	10.5	..	9.6	0.1	6.3	..	7.7	0.3	11.5	—	0.1	..	..	..	0.8	6.0	2. منتجات نباتية.
3. Animal or vegetable fats and oils.	—	0.7	..	0.2	—	1.0	..	0.8	0.4	3.1	—	0.1	..	..	..	0.2	0.5	3. شحوم ودهون وزيوت حيوانية أو نباتية.
4. Prepared foodstuffs, beverages, spirits, vinegar, tobacco…etc.	1.6	5.0	..	5.9	0.2	15.6	..	6.0	0.6	9.6	—	0.5	..	..	..	1.6	3.6	4. منتجات صناعة الأغذية، مشروبات، مشروبات روحية، خل، تبغ ... الخ.
5. Mineral products.	65.2	24.9	..	6.3	93.5	1.3	..	11.2	85.3	1.6	86.8	83.2	..	..	..	53.3	55.8	5. منتجات معدنية.
6. Chemical industry products.	3.4	11.6	..	29.5	2.2	11.5	..	16.3	4.9	3.3	4.1	5.8	..	..	..	1.2	1.5	6. منتجات الصناعات الكيميائية.
7. Plastics, rubber and related items.	1.1	6.6	..	4.6	1.1	4.1	..	0.8	1.8	7.9	4.0	5.5	..	..	..	2.2	0.2	7. اللدائن والمطاط ومصنوعاتها.
8. Raw hides and skins, leather…etc.	—	0.7	..	0.1	—	0.6	..	0.6	—	0.8	—	—	..	..	..	0.1	0.8	8. جلود خام ومدبوغة ...الخ.
9. Wood and wood products.	0.1	0.2	..	0.3	—	0.4	..	0.2	—	3.2	—	—	..	..	..	0.1	—	9. خشب ومصنوعات خشبية.
10. Pulp of wood or of other fibrous cellulosic material.	0.6	1.7	..	2.9	0.1	6.3	..	0.6	0.1	2.0	—	0.3	..	..	..	0.6	0.2	10. عجينة الخشب أو غيرها من عجائن المواد الليفية السليلوزية.
11. Textiles and textile articles.	1.2	11.2	..	16.5	0.1	3.7	..	15.6	0.1	1.3	—	0.2	..	..	..	1.5	0.1	11. مواد نسجية ومصنوعاتها.
12. Footwear, headgear and umbrellas.	—	—	..	0.1	—	0.8	..	1.5	—	4.5	—	—	..	..	..	0.1	—	12. أحذية، أغطية للرأس، مظلات للمطر.
13. Articles of stones, plaster, cement...etc.	0.3	3.9	..	0.9	0.2	1.1	..	0.5	0.5	23.2	—	0.2	..	..	..	0.6	0.1	13. مصنوعات من حجر أو جص أو إسمنت ...الخ.
14. Authentic and artificial peals, precious stones… etc.	2.0	2.5	..	1.7	0.2	16.4	..	0.9	—	—	—	0.2	..	..	..	17.4	0.7	14. لؤلؤ طبيعي أو مستنبت، أحجار كريمة ...الخ.
15. Base metals and related articles.	14.9	7.2	..	5.1	0.4	11.3	..	2.4	3.9	11.9	3.6	1.2	..	..	..	4.8	2.7	15. معادن متبلورة (فلزات) ومصنوعاتها.
16. Electrical machines and mechanical appliances.	4.1	8.2	..	7.8	0.5	13.4	..	17.2	0.8	2.8	0.4	0.8	..	..	..	7.9	3.2	16. آلات وأجهزة، معدات كهربائية.
17. Transportation vehicles.	3.5	0.5	..	2.3	1.0	1.0	..	12.0	0.1	1.2	0.7	1.3	..	..	..	6.1	14.3	17. مركبات النقل.
18. Optical, photographic, cinematographic…etc.	0.3	0.2	..	0.6	0.1	0.6	..	0.1	—	0.4	—	—	..	..	..	0.4	0.1	18. أدوات وأجهزة للبصريات أو التصوير الفوتوغرافي ...الخ.
19. Arms and ammunition: parts and accessories.	—	—	..	—	—	—	..	—	—	—	—	—	..	..	..	—	—	19. أسلحة وذخائر: أجزاؤها ولوازمها.
20. Miscellaneous manufactured articles.	0.4	1.4	..	1.4	0.1	3.5	..	0.6	0.1	11.2	—	0.1	..	..	..	0.4	0.1	20. سلع ومنتجات مصنعة أخرى.
21. Works of art, collectors' pieces.	0.2	—	..	—	—	0.2	..	—	—	—	—	—	..	..	..	0.2	—	21. تحف فنية وقطع أثرية.
Unspecified.	—	1.1	..	0.3	—	—	..	—	—	—	—	—	..	..	..	—	—	غير محدد.
Total (millions of US dollars)	23 405	26 812	..	8 385	101 132	3 313	..	23 816	50 718	944	131 592	342 437	..	..	..	214 074	2 417	المجموع (مليون دولار أمريكي)

(*) Including crude oil.

(*) بما في ذلك النفط الخام.

الجزء الثاني

التجارة البينية للبلدان الأعضاء في الإسكوا

Part II

Intraregional trade of ESCWA member countries

Introduction

This chapter presents analysis and statistics for ESCWA member countries for which data on intraregional trade in non-oil goods were available for 201٤. Available data show no common trend for intraregional exports but rather varying performance between the ESCWA countries ranging from slight increase, stable to decrease. The outcome for the region was a net decline of non-oil intraregional exports by US$ 1 billion compared to their level in 2013. Figures also highlight the increasing importance of the share of intraregional exports in the ESCWA region to total non-oil exports, which rose to 21.9 per cent in 2014 from 20.5 per cent in 2013.

Non-oil intraregional exports continued in 2014 to play a vital role in supporting the growth of trade in the ESCWA region through offsetting exports losses in foreign markets. Available data on the performance of ESCWA member countries in this chapter show that despite the decline of non-oil intraregional exports in 2014, a drop far smaller than the 7.8 per cent decline in the countries' total exports. The highest increase of non-oil intraregional exports in the region was claimed by UAE which increased their exports to the region by US$ 4.2 billion at a 16 per cent rate of increase. In the second place, Qatar raised their intraregional exports by US$ 569.8 million at a 5.9 per cent, and followed by Jordan with a US$ 113 million and 2.9 per cent percentage change. On the contrary, Oman suffered a huge decrease of their intraregional exports in 2014 that reached US$ 4.7 billion and recording a negative 51 per cent percentage rate, followed by Bahrain which lost US$ 801 million with 11.3 per cent and Yemen whose non-oil intraregional exports retracted by US$ 346.6 million with a negative percentage change of 30 per cent in 2014.

On the side of the non-oil intraregional imports for the countries in the ESCWA region where data was available we notice that imports dropped by US$ 2 billion at rate of 2.5 per cent in 2014. Despite the fact that intraregional imports increased in most of the mentioned countries, the large decline of the intraregional imports of Oman by US$ 2.6 billion with a

مقدمة

التحليل والاحصاءات الواردة في الفصل الحالي من هذه النشرة ينحصر في أداء بلدان منطقة الاسكوا بخصوص التجارة البينية في المنتجات غير النفطية التي توفرت البيانات عنها للعام ٢٠١٤. تباينت اتجاهات الصادرات البينية للبلدان التي توفرت عنها البيانات بين الزيادة الطفيفة والثبات والتراجع الا أن مجموع الصادرات البينية لتلك البلدان قد انخفض بمقدار مليار دولار أمريكي قياساً الى مستواها في عام ٢٠١٣. كما وتظهر البيانات التي توفرت عن البلدان الأعضاء في الاسكوا الأهمية المتزايدة للتجارة البينية في المنطقة العربية بالنسبة لاجمالي صادراتها غير النفطية حيث بلغت نسبتها في المتوسط حوالي ٢١،٩ في المئة في عام ٢٠١٤ بالقياس الى ٢٠،٥ في المئة في عام ٢٠١٣.

استمرت الصادرات البينية غير النفطية لبلدان منطقة الاسكوا في عام ٢٠١٤ في تشكيل رافعة لنمو التجارة تعمل على تعويض التراجع في التصدير الى الأسواق الأجنبية. فالبيانات التي توفرت عن بلدان الاسكوا في هذا الجزء تبيّن أنه وعلى الرغم من تراجع الصادرات البينية للمنتجات غير النفطية في منطقة الاسكوا خلال عام ٢٠١٤، الا أن هذا التراجع والذي بلغت نسبته 1,9 في المئة يعدّ أقل بكثير من النسبة التي انخفضت بها الصادرات الكلية غير النفطية للبلدان المذكورة والتي بلغت 7,8 في المئة في عام ٢٠١٤. أما أكبر معدلات الزيادة في الصادرات البينية غير النفطية خلال عام ٢٠١٤ كانت من نصيب الأمارات العربية المتحدة التي ارتفعت صادارتها البينية بقيمة ٤،٢ مليار دولار أمريكي أو ما نسبته ١٦ في المئة، تلتها قطر بزيادة مقدارها ٥٦٩،٨ مليون دولار وبنسبة ٥،٩ في المئة، تلاهما الأردن بحجم زيادة مقداره 113 مليون دولار أي بنسبة ارتفاع مقدارها 2,9 في المئة. بينما لوحظ التراجع الكبير للصادرات البينية لسلطنة عمان خلال عام ٢٠١٤ بحوالي ٤،٧ مليار دولار أمريكي وما نسبته ٥١ في المئة، والبحرين بواقع ٨٠١ مليون دولار أي ما نسبته ١١،٣ في المئة. كما تراجعت صادرات اليمن البينية بحوالي ٣٤٦،٦ مليون دولار اي بمعدل تراجع مقداره ٣٠ في المئة.

أما بالنسبة للواردات البينية غير النفطية في منطقة الاسكوا للبلدان التي توفرت عنها البيانات خلال عام ٢٠١٤ فقد انخفضت بمقدار ٢ مليار دولار أو ما نسبته ٢،٥ في المئة. وعلى الرغم من أن معظم البلدان التي توفرت عنها البيانات قد ارتفعت وارداتها البينية من بقية بلدان منطقة الاسكوا الا أن الانخفاض الكبير للورادات البينية لكل من سلطنة عمان بواقع ٢،٦ مليار

55

percentage change of 18 per cent, and Yemen that suffered a decline of US$ 2.3 billion that accounts for a decline of 54 per cent of its regional imports all contributed to the overall decline of intraregional imports in the ESCWA region in 2014.

With respect to the intraregional trade integration, available data in 2014 show that the most integrated ESCWA countries in terms of their non-oil intraregional exports were the most diversified economies. Bahrain and Yemen claimed the first ranks with about 70 per cent of their exports found their destination to the other countries in the ESCWA region, followed by 51.2 per cent for Lebanon, 47.1 per cent for Jordan, 36 per cent Egypt and 29.7 per cent for UAE. As for the least integrated countries in the region for which data were made available in 2014 were Morocco where only 3.7 per cent of its exports are destined the ESCWA countries, followed by both Kuwait and Qatar with about 9 per cent of their non-oil exports were destined to the other ESCWA countries.

In addition, the absolute value of intraregional exports is a significant element for a comprehensive analysis and to highlight the importance of intraregional trade. Available statistics on the values of intraregional non-oil exports for 2014 show that UAE was by far the largest exporter of non-oil goods to the rest of the region with US$30.4 billion that was US$ 4.2 billion increase, followed by Qatar with US$ 10.2 billion, Egypt with US$ 8.6 billion, and Bahrain with US$ 6.3 billion. The modest values of intraregional non-oil exports in 2014 were recorded in Palestine, whose intraregional exports reached US$ 112 million, followed by Morocco with US$ 693.7 million, and Lebanon with US$ 1.7 billion.

Unfortunately, and due to the unavailability of data on foreign and regional trade in all the Arab countries to date, it is difficult to provide a complete view of intraregional trade in the ESCWA region.

دولار أمريكي اي بنسبة تراجع قدرها ١٨ في المئة واليمن بمقدار ٢،٣ مليار دولار وذلك بتراجع نسبته ٥٤ في المئة ساهم في تدنّي الحجم الاجمالي للواردات البينية في منطقة الاسكوا عام ٢٠١٤.

وعلى صعيد التكامل التجاري الاقليمي، تبين بأن أكثر اقتصادات المنطقة ترابطاً مع بلدان المنطقة بالنسبة لصادراتها غير النفطية التي توفرت عنها البيانات في عام ٢٠١٤ كانت البلدان العربية ذات الاقتصادات الأكثر تنوعاً. فقد تبوأت البحرين واليمن المركز الأول حيث بلغت حصة صادراتها البينية من اجمالي صادراتها حوالي ٧٠ في المئة ، تلاهما لبنان بنسبة ٥١،٢ في المئة ثم الأردن بنسبة 47,1 في المئة، وجمهورية مصر العربية بنسبة ٣٦ في المئة والأمارات العربية المتحدة بنسبة ٢٩،٧ في المئة. في المقابل تبيّن البيانات عن بلدان المنطقة العربية التي توفرت عنها البيانات في عام ٢٠١٤، أن أقل بلدان المنطقة ارتباطاً اقتصادات المنطقة في هذا العام بالنسبة للصادرات البينية غير النفطية كانت المغرب بنسبة 3,7 في المئة والكويت وقطر التي بلغت نسبة صادراتها البينية الى اجمالي صادراتها من المنتجات غير النفطية حوالي ٩ في المئة.

أما فيما يتعلق بالقيمة النقدية للصادرات البينية في منطقة الاسكوا والتي تَبين الكثير من معالم التجارة البينية وأهميتها، فقد بلغت أعلى قيمة للصادرات البينية غير المشتملة على النفط في البلدان التي توفرت عنها البيانات في عام ٢٠١٤، في الامارات العربية المتحدة التي صدرت ما قيمته ٣٠،٤ مليار دولار أمريكي الى باقي بلدان منطقة الاسكوا وبزيادة مقدارها ٤،٢ مليار عن العام الذي سبق، تلتها قطر بقيمة ١٠،٢ مليار دولار ثم مصر بقيمة ٨،٦ مليار والبحرين ٦،٣ مليار دولار. أما أدنى قيم للصادرات البينية غير النفطية عام ٢٠١٤ فكانت من نصيب فلسطين التي صدرت ماقيمته ١١٢ مليون دولار أمريكي لبلدان المنطقة، تلاها المغرب ٦٩٣،٧ مليون دولار ثم لبنان بقيمة ١،٧ مليار دولار أمريكي.

ونظراً لعدم امكانية الحصول على جميع البيانات الخاصة بالتجارة الكلية وتلك البينية لجميع البلدان العربية وبشكل محدّث، فإنه من الصعوبة بمكان تقديم صورة شاملة ومتكاملة أكثر للتجارة البينية لبلدان منطقة الاسكوا.

الجدول 2-1- حصة الواردات البينية من إجمالي قيمة الواردات حسب البلدان

Table II.1. Intraregional imports as a share of the total value of imports by country

2005-2014

A: Intraregional imports excluding crude oil
B: Total imports excluding crude oil
C: Percentage share A/B
(Millions of US dollars)

أ- الواردات البينية باستثناء النفط الخام
ب- مجموع الواردات باستثناء النفط الخام
ج- النسبة المئوية أ/ب
(مليون دولار أمريكي)

Country		2005	2006	2007	2008 (1)	2009 (1)	2010 (1)	2011 (1)	2012 (2)	2013 (2)	2014 (2)		البلد
Bahrain	A	786.3	821.8 (3)	1 099.5 (3)	1 699.5 (3)	1 306.4 (3)	1 127.8 (3)	1 499.1 (3)	2 052.3 (3)	2 225.6 (3)	2 603.2 (3)	أ	البحرين
	B	5,223.4	4 055.5 (3)	6 060.5 (3)	10 563.9 (3)	8 114.6 (3)	10 143.4 (3)	10 133.5 (3)	10 891.4 (3)	10 131.6 (3)	12 633.7 (3)	ب	
	C	15.1	20.3	18.1	16.1	16.1	11.1	14.8	18.8	22.0	20.6	ج	
Egypt	A	1 472.6	2 083.8	2 926.1	5 080.0	3 256.9	4 000.5	5 378.7	5 923.4	6 316.9	6 734.1	أ	مصر
	B	19 009.6	19 570.1	25 638.4	52 411.9	43 677.7	51 553.5	57 559.7	68 535.9	64 368.5	68 293.7	ب	
	C	7.7	10.6	11.4	9.7	7.5	7.8	9.3	8.6	9.8	9.9	ج	
Iraq [4]	A	..	..	..	..	..	2 683.1	2 955.4	1 901.7	..	..	أ	العراق [4]
	B	..	..	..	..	..	25 483.3	45 724.6	19 123.5	..	..	ب	
	C	..	..	..	..	..	10.5	6.5	9.9	..	..	ج	
Jordan	A	1 784.3	2 081.1	2 465.6	2 839.0	2 899.1	3 422.7	4 320.6	4 644.9	4 194.5	4 543.1	أ	الأردن
	B	8 786.0	9 524.0	11 690.1	14 162.6	12 573.3	13 396.2	16 315.3	17 993.7	19 492.6	20 426.6	ب	
	C	20.3	21.9	21.1	20.0	23.1	25.5	26.5	25.8	21.5	22.2	ج	
Kuwait	A	..	3 034.2	2 762.3	3 216.9	2 818.3	3 062.0	4 261.4	4 571.7	5 580.9	6 183.2	أ	الكويت
	B	..	17 240.2	21 362.7	24 839.8	20 334.4	22 670.5	25 143.6	27 267.4	29 645.6	31 488.7	ب	
	C	..	17.6	12.9	13.0	13.9	13.5	16.9	16.8	18.8	19.6	ج	
Lebanon	A	1 210.8	1 334.1	1 632.7	2 056.1	1 767.5	2 201.6	3 129.7	3 100.9	2 507.7	2 148.4	أ	لبنان
	B	9 339.7	9 397.5	11 815.3	16 136.7	16 241.5	17 963.8	20 158.3	21 279.8	21 228.5	20 493.7	ب	
	C	13.0	14.2	13.8	12.7	10.9	12.3	15.5	14.6	11.8	10.5	ج	
Libya	A	..	..	..	..	..	..	..	..	..	..	أ	ليبيا
	B	..	..	..	..	..	..	..	..	..	..	ب	
	C	..	..	..	..	..	..	..	..	..	..	ج	
Morocco	A	..	..	..	..	..	..	..	2 148.7	1 930.0	2 256.9	أ	المغرب
	B	..	..	..	..	..	..	..	40 437.8	40 865.6	42 817.5	ب	
	C	..	..	..	..	..	..	..	5.3	4.7	5.3	ج	
Oman	A	2 852.2	3 403.2	4 916.1	6 713.0	5 169.4	6 606.0	8 224.2	8 743.2	14 406.9	11 826.6	أ	عُمان
	B	8 826.7	10 896.5	15 978.3	22 924.7	17 850.9	19 777.5	23 619.7	28 113.8	34 315.3	29 298.8	ب	
	C	32.3	31.2	30.8	29.3	29.0	33.4	34.8	31.1	42.0	40.4	ج	
Palestine	A	68.6	..	82.0	163.4	91.8	129.0	161.7	187.2	214.8	274.3	أ	فلسطين
	B	2 666.8	..	3141.3	3568.7	3600.8	3958.5	4221.1	4697.4	5163.9	5683.2	ب	
	C	2.6	..	2.6	4.6	2.5	3.3	3.8	4.0	4.2	4.8	ج	

الجدول 2-1- حصة الواردات البينية من إجمالي قيمة الواردات حسب البلدان

Table II.1. Intraregional imports as a share of the total value of imports by country
2005-2014

A: Intraregional imports excluding crude oil
B: Total imports excluding crude oil
C: Percentage share A/B
(Millions of US dollars)

أ- الواردات البينية باستثناء النفط الخام
ب- مجموع الواردات باستثناء النفط الخام
ج- النسبة المئوية أ/ب
(مليون دولار أمريكي)

Country		2005	2006	2007	2008 (1)	2009 (1)	2010 (1)	2011 (1)	2012 (2)	2013 (2)	2014 (2)		البلد
Qatar	A	1 561.2	2 404.2	3 420.1	4 446.0	4 426.8	4 254.4	4 313.2	4 639.0	4 546.3	5 448.9	أ	قطر
	B	10 060.9	16 440.1	22 005.1	27 900.6	24 922.4	23 240.2	22 328.7	26 082.6	27 038.3	30 442.7	ب	
	C	15.5	14.6	15.5	15.9	17.8	18.3	19.3	17.8	16.8	17.9	ج	
Saudi Arabia	A	4 608.3	5 147.6	6 194.6	7 884.8	7 508.2	9 492.2	12 606.8	14 789.5	17 557.9	17 512.0	أ	المملكة العربية السعودية
	B	59 498.3	69 799.5	90 097.6	115 133.7	95 552.0	106 864.0	131 588.3	155 594.7	168 152.7	173 835.0	ب	
	C	7.7	7.4	6.9	6.8	7.9	8.9	9.6	9.5	10.4	10.1	ج	
Sudan	A	..	..	..	5 214.9	1 992.8	3 150.6	2 449.8	1 592.1	..	..	أ	السودان
	B	..	..	..	16 416.1	8 567.0	11 837.5	9 516.4	6 545.3	9 918.1	..	ب	
	C	..	..	..	31.8	23.3	26.6	25.7	24.3	..	..	ج	
Syrian Arab Republic	A	1 163.8	1 752.2	2 436.7	2 533.1	2 296.3	2 351.8	2 494.4	..	..	..	أ	الجمهورية العربية السورية
	B	10 047.4	10 626.5	13 555.8	17 994.0	15 257.8	17 392.0	19 870.8	..	..	..	ب	
	C	11.6	16.5	18.0	14.1	15.0	13.5	12.6	..	..	..	ج	
Tunisia	A	..	..	..	..	..	..	..	906.0	1 049.5	..	أ	تونس
	B	..	..	..	..	..	..	..	23 616.1	22 352.0	..	ب	
	C	..	..	..	..	..	..	..	3.8	4.7	..	ج	
United Arab Emirates	A	3 802.7	6 094.9	6 185.1	8 782.2	9 075.5	10 334.5	12 589.3	17 139.3	13 489.5	13 754.6	أ	الإمارات العربية المتحدة
	B	67 417.2	79 250.9	105 747.3	154 042.2	121 822.7	132 175.3	164 127.2	181 761.8	186 540.0	189 761.9	ب	
	C	5.6	7.7	5.8	5.7	7.4	7.8	7.7	9.4	7.2	7.2	ج	
Yemen	A	1 978.5	2 265.3	3 376.8	3 358.3	2 041.2	3 363.8	3 515.6	2 489.1	4 128.0	1 898.9	أ	اليمن
	B	5 077.2	5 292.4	8 516.0	10 434.8	8 968.4	9 256.6	9 680.9	11 300.6	13 272.9	12 041.4	ب	
	C	39.0	42.8	39.7	32.2	22.8	36.3	36.3	22.0	31.1	15.8	ج	
Total intraregional imports		..	..	37 497.6	48 772.3	42 657.3	53 497.0	..	..	..	..		مجموع الواردات البينية
Total imports		..	..	335 608.4	470 114.0	388 916.1	440 229.3	..	..	..	..		مجموع الواردات
Percentage share		..	..	11.2	10.4	11.0	12.2	..	..	..	..		النسبة المئوية

(1) Including Sudan figures.
(2) Including Libya, Morocco,Sudan and Tunisia figures.
(3) Preliminary data.
(4) Excluding Oil Products.

(1) بما في ذلك بيانات السودان.
(2) بما في ذلك بيانات ليبيا، المغرب، السودان وتونس.
(3) بيانات أولية.
(4) لا تتضمن المنتجات النفطية.

الجدول 2-2- حصة الصادرات البينية من إجمالي قيمة الصادرات حسب البلدان

Table II.2. Intraregional exports as a share of the total value of exports by country

2005-2015

A: Intraregional exports excluc
B: Total exports excluding crude oil
C: Percentage share A/B

أ- الصادرات البينية باستثناء النفط الخام
ب- مجموع الصادرات باستثناء النفط الخام
ج- النسبة المئوية أ/ب

(Millions of US dollars) (مليون دولار أمريكي)

Country		2005	2006	2007	2008 (1)	2009 (1)	2010 (1)	2011 (1)	2012 (2)	2013 (2)	2014 (2)		البلد
Bahrain[3]	A	1 094.1	1 007.5 (4)	1 660.9 (4)	2 715.5 (4)	1 945.5 (4)	2 720.7 (4)	4 196.4 (4)	4 084.1 (4)	7 086.0 (4)	6 284.9 (4)	أ	البحرين[3]
	B	2 458.4	2 444.1 (4)	3 296.0 (4)	4 457.6 (4)	2 995.1 (4)	4 554.4 (4)	6 987.5 (4)	6 734.2 (4)	10 268.9 (4)	8 961.2 (4)	ب	
	C	44.5	41.2	50.4	60.9	65.0	59.7	60.1	60.6	69.0	70.1	ج	
Egypt	A	1 475.3	1 604.0	1 658.9	5 204.5	5 897.4	6 438.4	6 992.6	8 845.5	8 830.0	8 561.3	أ	مصر
	B	10 130.8	12 835.8	14 950.4	24 500.8	21 294.3	25 357.0	27 752.0	27 755.1	25 729.4	23 761.7	ب	
	C	14.6	12.5	11.1	21.2	27.7	25.4	25.2	31.9	34.3	36.0	ج	
Iraq[3]	A	..	..	..	..	115.2	157.5	171.1	227.0	..	..	أ	العراق[3]
	B	..	..	..	200.3	140.4	201.0	223.8	294.0	..	..	ب	
	C	..	..	..	..	82.0	78.4	76.5	77.2	..	..	ج	
Jordan	A	1 704.5	1 991.6	2 360.8	3 239.0	3 069.9	3 192.1	3 459.7	3 589.8	3 838.3	3 951.3	أ	الأردن
	B	4 300.8	5 204.4	5 729.6	7 781.9	6 365.7	7 023.1	8 006.4	7 886.6	7 912.7	8 385.3	ب	
	C	39.6	38.3	41.2	41.6	48.2	45.5	43.2	45.5	48.5	47.1	ج	
Kuwait	A	..	1 278.5	1 652.4	2 175.6	1 980.1	1 894.4	2 020.5	2 278.6	2 837.0	2 959.2	أ	الكويت
	B	..	19 351.3	24 080.2	29 702.6	22 277.7	25 866.4	33 887.5	36 107.4	35 363.2	31 833.8	ب	
	C	#VALUE!	6.6	6.9	7.3	8.9	7.3	6.0	6.3	8.0	9.3	ج	
Lebanon	A	947.2	947.8	1 231.2	1 564.1	1 482.4	1 672.7	1 462.9	1 711.8	1 982.6	1 697.6	أ	لبنان
	B	1 879.8	2 282.5	2 816.2	3 478.3	3 484.4	4 252.9	4 265.4	4 483.1	3 936.0	3 312.9	ب	
	C	50.4	41.5	43.7	45.0	42.5	39.3	34.3	38.2	50.4	51.2	ج	
Libya	A	..	..	..	..	..	..	..	..	..	..	أ	ليبيا
	B	..	..	..	..	..	..	..	..	..	..	ب	
	C	..	..	..	..	..	..	..	..	..	..	ج	
Morocco	A	..	..	..	..	..	..	..	742.1	658.8	693.7	أ	المغرب
	B	..	..	..	..	..	..	..	21 417.2	21 965.1	18 631.2	ب	
	C	..	..	..	..	..	..	..	3.5	3.0	3.7	ج	
Oman[3]	A	914.2 (5)	772 (5)(7)	1 883.4 (5)	2 815.0 (5)	2 186.5 (5)	2 546.9 (5)	2 627.9 (5)	4 408.6	9 227.9	4 514.6	أ	عُمان[3]
	B	1 444.3 (5)	5 166 (5)(7)	3 356.9 (5)	5 105.0 (5)	4 810.2 (5)	6 367.4 (5)	7 888.7 (5)	21 461.7	23 410.0	15 883.8	ب	
	C	63.3	15.0	56.1	55.1	45.5	40.0	33.3	20.5	39.4	28.4	ج	
Palestine	A	23.3	..	34.0	43.1	38.3	58.7	68	102	85	112	أ	فلسطين
	B	335.4	..	513.0	558.4	518.4	575.5	719.6	782.4	1165.3	943.7	ب	
	C	7.0	..	6.6	7.7	7.4	10.2	9.4	13.0	7.3	11.8	ج	
Qatar	A	1 673.5	2 013.7	2 105.5	1 486.9	3 584.4	6 556.1	7 215.2	9 388.7	9 590.5	10 160.2	أ	قطر
	B	12 919.0	18 070.2	22 839.1	30 832.6	35 421.0	54 617.9	87 895.8	106 852.3	110 741.9	105 476.4	ب	
	C	13.0	11.1	9.2	4.8	10.1	12.0	8.2	8.8	8.7	9.6	ج	

الجدول 2-2- حصة الصادرات البينية من إجمالي قيمة الصادرات حسب البلدان

Table II.2. Intraregional exports as a share of the total value of exports by country 2005-2015

A: Intraregional exports exclu(
B: Total exports excluding crude oil
C: Percentage share A/B

أ- الصادرات البينية باستثناء النفط الخام
ب- مجموع الصادرات باستثناء النفط الخام
ج- النسبة المئوية أ/ب

(Millions of US dollars) (مليون دولار أمريكي)

Country		2005	2006	2007	2008 (1)	2009 (1)	2010 (1)	2011 (1)	2012 (2)	2013 (2)	2014 (2)		البلد
Saudi Arabia	A	..	9 571.5 (3)	12 877.3 (3)	..	..	..	..	..	..	..	أ	المملكة العربية السعودية
	B	..	22 837.9 (3)	27 832.7 (3)	66 387.4	50 121.9	61 710.9	79 723.7	83 163.7	81 876.6	48 439.0	ب	
	C	..	41.9	46.3	..	..	..	..	..	..	..	ج	
Sudan	A	..	..	..	550.9	981.6	1 535.3	1 360.7	1 883.0	..	..	أ	السودان
	B	..	..	..	815.9	2 128.0	1 839.4	1 781.2	3 238.7	3 175.7	..	ب	
	C	..	..	..	67.5	46.1	83.5	76.4	58.1	..	..	ج	
Syrian Arab Republic[5]	A	1 211.2	3 272.1	3 699.1	6 974.0	5 010.4	4 479.1	3 778.4	..	..	..	أ	الجمهورية العربية السورية[5]
	B	4 911.6	6 708.7	6 992.6	10 542.4	7 633.7	7 935.4	10 393.9	..	..	..	ب	
	C	24.7	48.8	52.9	66.2	65.6	56.4	36.4	..	..	..	ج	
Tunisia	A	..	..	..	..	..	..	..	1 314.2	1 307.6	..	أ	تونس
	B	..	..	..	..	..	..	..	15 131.6	13 564.2	..	ب	
	C	..	..	..	..	..	..	..	8.7	9.6	..	ج	
United Arab Emirates[3]	A	8 273.0	8 635.6	10 782.7	14 405.6	15 540.6	15 558.4	15 204.3	21 798.9	26 191.7	30 406.8	أ	الإمارات العربية المتحدة[3]
	B	30 907.0	33 985.7	44 819.8	60 777.0	57 991.1	73 231.0	88 463.2	105 741.4	103 575.7	102 439.6	ب	
	C	26.8	25.4	25.4	23.7	26.8	21.2	17.2	20.6	25.3	29.7	ج	
Yemen	A	437.8	719.7	848.9	1 004.8	680.4	817.3	811.9	420.8	1 144.6	798.0	أ	اليمن
	B	706.7	1 041.0	1 342.0	1 722.0	1 198.5	1 919.5	2 436.5	1 730.0	3 881.1	1 145.4	ب	
	C	62.0	69.1	63.3	58.4	56.8	42.6	33.3	24.3	29.5	69.7	ج	
Total intraregional exports		..	..	40 795.1	..	..	..	..	..	..	..		مجموع الصادرات البينية
Total exports		..	..	158 562.3	..	..	..	..	..	..	..		مجموع الصادرات
Percentage share		..	..	25.7	..	..	..	..	..	..	..		النسبة المئوية
Total intraregional trade		..	..	78 292.7	..	..	..	..	..	..	..		مجموع التجارة البينية
Total trade		..	..	494 170.7	..	..	..	..	..	..	..		مجموع التجارة
Percentage share		..	..	15.8	..	..	..	..	..	..	..		النسبة المئوية

(1) Including Sudan figures.
(2) Including Libya, Morocco,Sudan and Tunisia figures.
(3) Excluding oil.
(4) Preliminary data.
(5) Excluding re-exports.
(6) Inculding crude oil.
(7) Excluding crude oil only.

(1) بما في ذلك بيانات السودان.
(2) بما في ذلك بيانات تونس، والسودان، وليبيا، والمغرب.
(3) باستثناء النفط.
(4) بيانات أولية.
(5) باستثناء إعادة التصدير.
(6) بما في ذلك النفط الخام.
(7) باستثناء النفط الخام فقط.

الجدول 2-3- مصفوفة قيمة الواردات البينية للبلدان الأعضاء في الإسكوا

Table II.3. Matrix of intraregional import value of ESCWA member countries

2008

(Millions of US dollars) (مليون دولار أمريكي)

From / Importing country من / البلد المستورد	Bahrain البحرين	Egypt مصر	Iraq العراق	Jordan الأردن	Kuwait الكويت	Lebanon لبنان	Oman عُمان	Palestine فلسطين	Qatar قطر	Saudi Arabia المملكة العربية السعودية	Sudan السودان	Syrian Arab Republic الجمهورية العربية السورية	United Arab Emirates الإمارات العربية المتحدة	Yemen اليمن	Total (Arab region) القيمة الإجمالية (المنطقة العربية)	
Bahrain		42.5	—	14.2	191.2	16.0	52.9	0.1	89.0	780.4	0.3	12.9	499.5	0.6	1 699.5	البحرين
Egypt	169.0		23.9	110.6	54.4	175.4	25.1	0.7	57.6	3 177.0	49.9	313.5	900.2	22.6	5 080.0	مصر
Iraq	..	..		..	..	..	..	..	..	..	..	..	..	..	..	العراق
Jordan	147.3	729.9	3.5		115.0	119.4	20.7	34.7	9.5	956.5	3.5	344.5	306.2	48.3	2 839.0	الأردن
Kuwait	136.8	228.5	—	82.8		140.9	101.0	1.8	50.2	1 393.3	2.2	94.1	982.3	3.0	3 216.9	الكويت
Lebanon	47.8	458.2	14.3	108.5	488.7		7.1	—	17.2	289.9	20.3	270.9	326.4	6.7	2 056.1	لبنان
Oman	211.5	176.8	—	29.0	96.9	14.7		—	35.6	566.2	0.4	11.7	5 554.3	15.9	6 712.9	عُمان
Palestine	—	23.5	—	52.2	—	—	0.3		—	2.4	—	—	3.2	—	81.6	فلسطين
Qatar	355.8	168.6	0.1	63.7	149.4	168.6	281.2	0.4		1 361.1	1.1	46.3	1 848.3	1.9	4 446.3	قطر
Saudi Arabia	1 171.5	1 452.5	—	485.1	298.9	240.7	461.7	2.5	124.0		144.3	494.5	2 834.6	174.5	7 884.8	المملكة العربية السعودية
Sudan	1.6	422.7	—	126.2	3.7	12.1	5.9	—	13.4	4 096.6		32.5	498.8	1.3	5 214.9	السودان
Syrian Arab Republic	52.9	615.2	412.7	132.8	59.4	169.0	15.2	—	60.8	665.2	22.5		322.5	5.0	2 533.1	الجمهورية العربية السورية
United Arab Emirates	668.3	499.3	73.9	299.1	513.1	333.1	955.8	5.0	463.1	4 396.1	282.3	136.5		156.6	8 782.2	الإمارات العربية المتحدة
Yemen	10.5	138.5	0.9	44.9	659.6	13.1	58.9	0.1	9.3	449.6	5.6	67.4	1 880.2		3 338.6	اليمن

الجدول 2-3- مصفوفة قيمة الواردات البينية للبلدان الأعضاء في الإسكوا

Table II.3. Matrix of intraregional import value of ESCWA member countries

2009

(Millions of US dollars) (مليون دولار أمريكي)

From / Importing country من / البلد المستورد	Bahrain البحرين	Egypt مصر	Iraq العراق	Jordan الأردن	Kuwait الكويت	Lebanon لبنان	Oman عُمان	Palestine فلسطين	Qatar قطر	Saudi Arabia المملكة العربية السعودية	Sudan السودان	Syrian Arab Republic الجمهورية العربية السورية	United Arab Emirates الإمارات العربية المتحدة	Yemen اليمن	Total (Arab region) القيمة الإجمالية (المنطقة العربية)	
Bahrain		44.2	—	17.4	149.7	14.8	40.5	—	45.6	588.6	0.1	6.7	397.5	0.8	1 305.8	البحرين
Egypt	44.9		2.4	72.6	83.3	90.7	52.3	1.4	38.5	2 007.0	43.5	314.6	434.1	71.9	3 257.3	مصر
Iraq	..	..		..	..	..	..	..	..	..	..	..	..	..	..	العراق
Jordan	75.5	859.0	7.2		67.0	112.0	19.3	32.0	9.5	1 052.5	12.6	306.5	331.6	14.4	2 899.1	الأردن
Kuwait	100.3	223.2	—	69.7		125.9	74.7	1.0	32.9	1 205.2	2.4	112.3	867.5	3.2	2 818.3	الكويت
Lebanon	13.2	420.6	1.7	189.6	290.6		9.4	—	13.6	309.9	21.3	233.7	261.2	2.6	1 767.5	لبنان
Oman	109.6	113.7	—	26.9	215.4	13.8		—	134.6	623.0	—	14.4	3 902.4	15.7	5 169.5	عُمان
Palestine	0.1	35.3	—	48.1	—	—	0.8		—	3.0	—	—	4.5	—	91.8	فلسطين
Qatar	411.5	293.3	1.4	47.0	111.8	128.2	278.0	0.2		1 330.1	2.1	57.5	1 763.4	2.3	4 426.8	قطر
Saudi Arabia	932.4	1 388.9	—	515.3	282.8	238.6	378.6	2.6	174.6		162.6	409.8	2 830.2	191.8	7 508.2	المملكة العربية السعودية
Sudan	10.2	410.2	0.1	86.2	18.9	17.9	35.8	—	3.6	640.9		47.0	633.4	88.5	1 992.8	السودان
Syrian Arab Republic	41.5	865.7	78.3	177.4	64.2	154.3	18.8	—	48.1	617.6	19.3		204.2	7.0	2 296.3	الجمهورية العربية السورية
United Arab Emirates	624.4	532.3	777.8	307.0	445.7	316.5	1 038.3	3.4	439.7	3 316.3	635.6	121.4		516.9	9 075.4	الإمارات العربية المتحدة
Yemen	5.2	144.2	0.8	37.2	388.6	10.7	58.8	0.2	7.2	450.6	4.5	42.0	891.4		2 041.3	اليمن

الجدول 2-3- مصفوفة قيمة الواردات البينية للبلدان الأعضاء في الإسكوا

Table II.3. Matrix of intraregional import value of ESCWA member countries

2010

(Millions of US dollars) (مليون دولار أمريكي)

From / Importing country	Bahrain البحرين	Egypt مصر	Iraq العراق	Jordan الأردن	Kuwait الكويت	Lebanon لبنان	Oman عُمان	Palestine فلسطين	Qatar قطر	Saudi Arabia المملكة العربية السعودية	Sudan السودان	Syrian Arab Republic الجمهورية العربية السورية	United Arab Emirates الإمارات العربية المتحدة	Yemen اليمن	Total (Arab region) القيمة الإجمالية (المنطقة العربية)	من / البلد المستورد
Bahrain		44.8	—	16.6	89.3	13.1	39.8	—	58.1	483.6	0.2	7.3	374.6	0.2	1 127.7	البحرين
Egypt	96.5		2.6	122.5	202.3	100.0	64.6	0.9	59.1	2 114.2	41.3	361.8	728.2	106.3	4 000.5	مصر
Iraq(*)	2.6	77.3		193.2	642.6	452.7	21.6	0.2	8.0	297.8	0.1	307.5	673.2	6.3	2 683.1	العراق(*)
Jordan	257.0	693.0	16.3		123.8	107.5	20.7	36.9	14.2	1 329.1	30.8	375.6	405.0	12.6	3 422.7	الأردن
Kuwait	135.0	245.0	—	67.8		109.4	90.5	1.3	89.7	1 201.2	3.0	99.0	1 009.7	10.4	3 062.0	الكويت
Lebanon	8.0	430.0	3.2	227.5	356.1		10.6	—	23.4	406.6	25.6	339.4	369.6	1.7	2 201.6	لبنان
Oman	235.1	96.2	—	23.2	266.5	35.0		—	51.8	623.5	0.2	12.9	5 251.6	10.0	6 606.0	عُمان
Palestine	0.4	38.2	—	67.4	0.7	—	1.9		2.8	11.1	—	—	6.5	—	129.0	فلسطين
Qatar	545.8	287.0	0.1	58.4	141.0	103.7	234.2	0.9		1 220.1	3.6	64.6	1 592.2	3.0	4 254.4	قطر
Saudi Arabia	1 078.4	1 619.8	—	624.5	373.3	292.5	469.9	4.0	251.2		210.7	572.5	3 784.0	210.1	9 492.4	المملكة العربية السعودية
Sudan	14.8	610.7	0.6	87.6	19.3	35.9	19.8	—	22.0	644.8		150.2	1 369.1	175.7	3 150.6	السودان
Syrian Arab Republic	47.5	733.3	30.1	175.6	55.3	181.1	17.6	—	62.3	799.9	16.7		224.4	8.1	2 351.8	الجمهورية العربية السورية
United Arab Emirates	618.7	571.1	1 251.5	284.2	601.5	321.5	1 033.7	6.5	568.8	3 259.3	1 351.1	122.1		344.4	10 334.5	الإمارات العربية المتحدة
Yemen	26.8	196.4	0.2	54.0	376.5	10.9	207.2	0.2	26.0	759.8	6.3	62.8	1 636.7		3 363.8	اليمن

(*) Excluding oil products.

(*) باستثناء المنتجات النفطية.

الجدول 2-3- مصفوفة قيمة الواردات البينية للبلدان الأعضاء في الإسكوا

Table II.3. Matrix of intraregional import value of ESCWA member countries

2011

(Millions of US dollars) (مليون دولار أمريكي)

From / Importing country	Bahrain البحرين	Egypt مصر	Iraq العراق	Jordan الأردن	Kuwait الكويت	Lebanon لبنان	Oman عُمان	Palestine فلسطين	Qatar قطر	Saudi Arabia المملكة العربية السعودية	Sudan السودان	Syrian Arab Republic الجمهورية العربية السورية	United Arab Emirates الإمارات العربية المتحدة	Yemen اليمن	Total (Arab region) القيمة الإجمالية (المنطقة العربية)	من / البلد المستورد
Bahrain		46.2	0.1	16.7	90.6	14.0	41.4	—	87.6	619.0	0.8	7.4	574.9	0.3	1 499.1	البحرين
Egypt	54.2		2.9	136.3	1 091.9	81.6	105.6	0.4	110.3	2 542.6	26.8	364.0	771.1	91.0	5 378.7	مصر
Iraq(*)	8.3	186.1		484.7	410.0	83.9	20.4	—	3.5	656.9	0.2	623.3	470.6	7.5	2 955.4	العراق(*)
Jordan	154.5	753.5	38.2		132.0	114.4	75.3	38.3	22.6	1 838.3	39.6	378.0	711.1	24.9	4 320.6	الأردن
Kuwait	143.4	268.0	—	116.6		123.0	304.1	2.0	163.2	1 442.4	4.0	83.7	1 602.9	8.0	4 261.4	الكويت
Lebanon	12.1	942.4	4.4	361.8	302.6		12.0	—	33.0	531.6	23.5	310.1	594.1	2.0	3 129.7	لبنان
Oman	381.7	118.9	—	28.4	198.4	18.1		—	336.8	1 180.1	0.1	13.7	5 931.3	16.6	8 224.2	عُمان
Palestine	0.2	34.0	—	90.0	1.5	—	1.8		3.7	23.0	—	—	7.0	0.3	161.7	فلسطين
Qatar	493.5	265.8	0.2	68.7	208.8	92.2	165.7	2.9		1 169.4	6.6	47.2	1 790.1	1.9	4 313.2	قطر
Saudi Arabia	1 274.7	1 872.3	—	657.6	463.5	389.9	904.5	5.1	479.2		333.1	521.6	5 447.0	258.4	12 606.8	المملكة العربية السعودية
Sudan	25.1	489.6	—	75.0	12.2	21.2	51.8	—	49.0	761.4		36.5	818.6	109.3	2 449.8	السودان
Syrian Arab Republic	60.7	647.7	36.9	191.1	31.6	152.8	17.2	—	158.4	902.2	27.3		259.2	9.3	2 494.4	الجمهورية العربية السورية
United Arab Emirates	856.1	637.9	1 348.3	237.2	878.2	417.8	1 213.9	8.6	530.1	4 097.6	2 026.5	132.3		205.1	12 589.3	الإمارات العربية المتحدة
Yemen	14.1	187.9	0.6	40.1	401.2	19.2	174.1	0.3	31.7	1 019.6	18.2	45.1	1 563.5		3 515.6	اليمن

(*) Excluding oil products.

(*) باستثناء المنتجات النفطية.

الجدول 2-3- مصفوفة قيمة الواردات البينية في بلدان الإسكوا

Table II.3. Matrix of intraregional import value of ESCWA member countries

2012

(Millions of US dollars) (مليون دولار أمريكي)

Importing country / From	Bahrain البحرين	Egypt مصر	Iraq العراق	Jordan الأردن	Kuwait الكويت	Lebanon لبنان	Libya ليبيا	Morocco المغرب	Oman عُمان	Palestine فلسطين	Qatar قطر	Saudi Arabia المملكة العربية السعودية	Sudan السودان	Syrian Arab Republic الجمهورية العربية السورية	Tunisia تونس	United Arab Emirates الإمارات العربية المتحدة	Yemen اليمن	Total (Arab region) القيمة الإجمالية (المنطقة العربية)	البلد المستورد / من
Bahrain		48.9	0.2	20.1	141.4	15.5	—	5.0	74.6	—	84.7	730.5	1.1	5.3	2.3	921.9	0.8	2 052.3	البحرين
Egypt	52.0		6.2	101.4	1 015.7	118.0	142.4	105.9	75.4	0.7	90.1	2 752.7	23.2	252.4	308.2	825.6	53.4	5 923.4	مصر
Iraq [(1)]	17.2	115.8		287.4	228.9	86.4	—	0.2	45.5	—	22.1	268.6	0.1	281.0	2.0	544.0	2.6	1 901.7	العراق [(1)]
Jordan	43.6	789.4	93.8		164.1	136.0	6.5	17.3	26.9	51.8	36.5	2 360.1	42.2	241.2	12.9	589.8	32.7	4 644.9	الأردن
Kuwait	147.3	297.9	0.1	78.9		127.1	—	27.6	226.4	3.3	154.0	1 434.7	5.4	61.8	20.1	1 980.5	6.7	4 571.7	الكويت
Lebanon	8.6	840.7	5.8	269.0	630.4		63.3	70.2	14.5	—	24.4	423.6	26.4	266.2	39.9	416.3	1.7	3 100.9	لبنان
Libya	..	..	..	..	..	..		..	..	..	..	..	..	..	..	..	..	..	ليبيا
Morocco	49.4	416.3	4.3	15.0	45.3	25.5	23.5		36.9	0.1	141.0	761.6	—	18.8	241.0	369.9	0.2	2 148.7	المغرب
Oman	307.3	114.9	26.1	26.5	313.4	24.8	—	0.9		—	245.4	1 170.4	0.6	4.7	5.4	6 472.3	30.5	8 743.0	عُمان
Palestine	1.9	34.7	—	98.4	0.7	—	—	0.3	1.0		6.7	34.6	—	—	0.2	8.8	—	187.2	فلسطين
Qatar	445.2	303.0	0.7	73.4	211.3	102.7	—	13.4	166.7	9.4		1 219.0	9.3	32.7	10.6	2 035.7	5.9	4 639.0	قطر
Saudi Arabia	1 332.3	2 005.4	1.9	719.2	414.9	459.5	—	143.5	1 464.8	8.3	604.8		392.8	407.2	34.1	6 532.1	268.8	14 789.5	المملكة العربية السعودية
Sudan	46.6	482.3	0.1	74.9	15.5	9.7	0.1	3.4	8.2	—	19.0	531.0		21.7	1.3	349.9	28.3	1 592.1	السودان
Syrian Arab Republic	..	..	..	..	..	..	..	..	..	..	..	..	..		..	..	..	..	الجمهورية العربية السورية
Tunisia	9.2	254.0	—	22.4	32.7	12.8	59.0	129.7	10.5	—	15.9	216.5	15.8	7.5		119.2	1.0	906.0	تونس
United Arab Emirates	723.2	575.0	3 319.3	246.2	908.8	565.9	992.2	275.6	1 256.7	11.8	638.8	4 026.8	3 225.1	93.8	49.7		230.4	17 139.3	الإمارات العربية المتحدة
Yemen	14.7	211.9	1.1	42.1	337.9	12.6	—	8.8	64.9	0.8	16.2	646.7	7.6	51.0	5.8	1 067.1		2 489.1	اليمن

الجدول 2-3- مصفوفة قيمة الواردات البينية في بلدان الإسكوا

Table II.3. Matrix of intraregional import value of ESCWA member countries

2013

(Millions of US dollars) (مليون دولار امريكي)

Importing country / From	Bahrain البحرين	Egypt مصر	Iraq العراق	Jordan الأردن	Kuwait الكويت	Lebanon لبنان	Libya ليبيا	Morocco المغرب	Oman عُمان	Palestine فلسطين	Qatar قطر	Saudi Arabia المملكة العربية السعودية	Sudan السودان	Syrian Arab Republic الجمهورية العربية السورية	Tunisia تونس	United Arab Emirates الإمارات العربية المتحدة	Yemen اليمن	Total (Arab region) القيمة الإجمالية (المنطقة العربية)	البلد المستورد / من
Bahrain		59.2	—	22.1	119.0	20.1	—	5.3	161.3	0.1	93.6	681.9	4.1	3.0	2.4	1 051.0	2.5	2 225.6	البحرين
Egypt	212.6		3.4	122.7	882.4	113.4	99.7	67.1	127.4	2.0	41.1	3 039.3	73.8	307.8	66.1	1 113.3	44.8	6 317.0	مصر
Iraq [(1)]	..	..		..	..	..	..	..	..	..	..	..	..	..	..	..	..	..	العراق [(1)]
Jordan	50.6	704.5	33.1		168.2	162.7	1.3	20.2	31.0	49.8	37.1	1 762.7	47.3	259.8	77.0	732.7	56.5	4 194.5	الأردن
Kuwait	227.4	345.7	—	87.4		141.1	0.1	28.3	505.1	3.4	130.4	1 413.8	5.3	28.4	26.1	2 631.8	6.8	5 580.8	الكويت
Lebanon	13.9	644.3	2.4	145.4	451.3		54.2	72.4	22.4	—	32.2	440.1	41.3	181.3	25.4	379.6	1.4	2 507.7	لبنان
Libya	..	..	..	..	..	..		..	..	..	..	..	..	..	..	..	..	..	ليبيا
Morocco	64.0	439.1	2.1	11.6	39.5	27.0	15.4		20.6	0.3	102.5	667.8	—	13.1	221.9	305.1	—	1 930.0	المغرب
Oman	250.8	111.9	225.8	30.1	269.7	12.5	—	5.3		—	1 235.2	2 023.7	4.1	1.2	1.9	10 171.5	63.3	14 406.9	عُمان
Palestine	6.0	43.5	—	91.5	0.6	—	—	0.6	1.1		11.4	44.0	—	—	0.2	15.8	—	214.8	فلسطين
Qatar	256.2	234.3	0.5	89.4	225.3	120.4	—	19.8	335.5	5.3		1 216.4	17.2	27.9	10.8	1 974.5	12.7	4 546.3	قطر
Saudi Arabia	1 696.0	2 109.1	1.6	850.1	500.3	450.4	137.1	83.7	1 568.8	10.4	637.1		521.6	193.3	37.9	8 517.3	243.2	17 557.9	المملكة العربية السعودية
Sudan	..	..	..	..	..	..	..	..	..	..	..	..		..	..	..	..	..	السودان
Syrian Arab Republic	..	..	..	..	..	..	..	..	..	..	..	..	..		..	..	..	..	الجمهورية العربية السورية
Tunisia	9.9	236.2	0.1	19.7	22.5	11.3	225.9	95.9	4.8	—	19.3	262.7	18.1	2.9		119.5	0.8	1 049.5	تونس
United Arab Emirates	651.1	608.7	777.6	280.7	1 140.6	414.5	507.7	142.8	2 070.2	9.3	725.7	4 101.4	1 882.2	63.6	58.0		55.6	13 489.5	الإمارات العربية المتحدة
Yemen	17.8	210.6	0.3	55.7	631.9	17.1	0.1	8.2	73.9	0.8	12.5	843.6	8.2	26.9	3.6	2 216.6		4 128.0	اليمن

الجدول 2-3- مصفوفة قيمة الواردات البينية في بلدان الإسكوا

Table II.3. Matrix of intraregional import value of ESCWA member countries

2014

(Millions of US dollars) (مليون دولار أمريكي)

From → / Importing country ↓	Bahrain البحرين	Egypt مصر	Iraq العراق	Jordan الأردن	Kuwait الكويت	Lebanon لبنان	Libya ليبيا	Morocco المغرب	Oman عُمان	Palestine فلسطين	Qatar قطر	Saudi Arabia المملكة العربية السعودية	Sudan السودان	Syrian Arab Republic الجمهورية العربية السورية	Tunisia تونس	United Arab Emirates الإمارات العربية المتحدة	Yemen اليمن	Total (Arab region) القيمة الإجمالية (المنطقة العربية)	من / البلد المستورد
Bahrain		74.0	0.1	42.4	130.2	32.6	—	9.2	200.4	0.2	95.4	927.3	7.3	3.0	3.9	1 071.9	5.3	2 603.2	البحرين
Egypt	153.1		8.0	112.5	1 149.1	105.2	50.1	117.3	161.7	0.1	41.0	2 738.4	113.9	114.4	71.4	1 723.5	74.4	6 734.1	مصر
Iraq [(1)]	..	..		..	..	..	..	..	..	..	..	..	..	..	..	..	..	..	العراق [(1)]
Jordan	79.4	548.3	6.3		144.3	117.6	0.9	21.4	27.6	56.2	50.4	2 140.1	47.5	152.2	11.2	1 092.6	47.2	4 543.1	الأردن
Kuwait	269.2	378.4	—	122.3		181.0	—	34.4	494.6	6.2	113.7	1 570.3	14.1	23.2	17.7	2 952.6	5.4	6 183.1	الكويت
Lebanon	16.0	529.0	3.7	145.4	251.1		55.4	111.6	22.8	—	24.6	415.4	41.6	124.8	32.8	372.6	1.5	2 148.4	لبنان
Libya	..	..	..	..	..	..		..	..	..	..	..	..	..	..	..	..	..	ليبيا
Morocco	79.6	546.3	3.1	13.4	86.1	23.8	22.1		38.9	—	73.4	726.2	—	8.1	205.4	430.1	0.2	2 256.8	المغرب
Oman	200.3	99.3	73.1	51.2	158.4	40.7	—	9.5		—	441.8	1 201.4	2.7	6.1	3.3	9 509.2	29.6	11 826.6	عُمان
Palestine	3.4	55.0	—	101.8	1.1	—	—	0.6	1.9		12.5	64.8	—	—	0.6	32.6	—	274.3	فلسطين
Qatar	327.7	323.6	0.4	105.0	235.9	110.1	0.1	20.8	385.2	7.5		1 390.2	11.8	20.9	11.5	2 492.5	5.7	5 448.9	قطر
Saudi Arabia	1 937.6	2 243.8	1.3	929.9	524.0	394.9	0.5	169.9	1 449.4	11.2	562.4		580.8	117.6	47.7	8 271.8	269.1	17 512.0	المملكة العربية السعودية
Sudan	..	..	..	..	..	..	..	..	..	..	..	..		..	..	..	..	..	السودان
Syrian Arab Republic	..	..	..	..	..	..	..	..	..	..	..	..	..		..	..	..	..	الجمهورية العربية السورية
Tunisia	..	..	..	..	..	..	..	..	..	..	..	..	..	..		..	..	..	تونس
United Arab Emirates	763.0	827.8	1 037.2	281.0	962.1	364.3	758.2	109.3	1 745.8	10.6	844.2	3 966.4	1 911.6	55.8	76.2		41.0	13 754.6	الإمارات العربية المتحدة
Yemen	21.6	250.9	0.7	56.3	9.9	14.0	0.1	10.8	80.6	1.3	12.4	822.9	15.0	16.4	2.8	583.1		1 898.9	اليمن

الجدول 2-4- مصفوفة قيمة الصادرات البينية للبلدان الأعضاء في الإسكوا

Table II.4. Matrix of intraregional export value of ESCWA member countries

2008

(Millions of US dollars) (مليون دولار أمريكي)

Exporting country \ To	Bahrain البحرين	Egypt مصر	Iraq العراق	Jordan الأردن	Kuwait الكويت	Lebanon لبنان	Oman عُمان	Palestine فلسطين	Qatar قطر	Saudi Arabia المملكة العربية السعودية	Sudan السودان	Syrian Arab Republic الجمهورية العربية السورية	United Arab Emirates الإمارات العربية المتحدة	Yemen اليمن	Total (Arab region) القيمة الإجمالية (المنطقة العربية)	البلد المصدر / إلى
Bahrain		85.6	32.4	116.0	158.4	7.9	91.4	—	289.8	1 438.9	4.5	66.3	415.8	8.4	2 715.5	البحرين
Egypt	33.5		352.8	733.0	172.5	427.3	140.8	88.1	151.4	1 275.7	557.5	568.6	542.3	161.0	5 204.5	مصر
Iraq [(1)]	—	2.8		45.3	1.3	1.4	—	—	—	0.2	—	122.9	10.8	0.2	185.0	العراق [(1)]
Jordan	47.9	153.8	1 282.7		100.9	158.2	35.5	62.0	84.6	547.3	100.0	246.8	366.9	51.9	3 238.6	الأردن
Kuwait	168.6	76.1	160.4	216.6		51.6	59.8	—	208.4	425.6	15.5	93.3	691.2	8.3	2 175.6	الكويت
Lebanon	27.3	127.1	269.0	119.1	95.8		14.4	—	85.0	208.9	31.6	223.6	346.3	16.0	1 564.0	لبنان
Oman [(1) (2)]	46.0	21.8	182.4	23.2	69.7	9.1		2.4	255.0	426.4	36.6	21.2	1 653.4	67.4	2 814.7	عُمان [(1) (2)]
Palestine	0.1	1.0	0.6	34.1	1.4	—	—		0.3	3.6	—	—	3.7	0.2	45.0	فلسطين
Qatar	104.8	18.3	10.3	55.3	73.2	11.5	47.2	—		272.3	8.0	16.7	870.9	5.3	1 493.8	قطر
Saudi Arabia	..	..	..	..	..	..	..	..	..		..	..	..	..	..	المملكة العربية السعودية
Sudan	—	130.8	0.1	4.7	2.7	12.1	—	—	—	114.7		17.2	98.5	170.1	550.9	السودان
Syrian Arab Republic [(2)]	19.4	731.9	2 550.7	452.0	273.4	1 338.1	36.3	—	67.0	1 033.3	129.3		189.4	153.3	6 974.0	الجمهورية العربية السورية [(2)]
United Arab Emirates [(1)]	1 723.6	909.8	3 003.4	201.7	1 065.6	469.9	1 410.0	0.5	3049.8	1 481.9	414.9	247.7		426.8	14 405.6	الإمارات العربية المتحدة [(1)]
Yemen	0.5	34.4	18.2	13.6	188.1	1.5	12.5	—	2.6	146.9	1.9	5.5	573.4		999.2	اليمن

(1) Excluding oil. (1) باستثناء النفط.

(2) Excluding re-exports. (2) باستثناء إعادة التصدير.

الجدول 2-4- مصفوفة قيمة الصادرات البينية للبلدان الأعضاء في الإسكوا

Table II.4. Matrix of intraregional export value of ESCWA member countries

2009

(Millions of US dollars) (مليون دولار أمريكي)

Exporting country \ To	Bahrain البحرين	Egypt مصر	Iraq العراق	Jordan الأردن	Kuwait الكويت	Lebanon لبنان	Oman عُمان	Palestine فلسطين	Qatar قطر	Saudi Arabia المملكة العربية السعودية	Sudan السودان	Syrian Arab Republic الجمهورية العربية السورية	United Arab Emirates الإمارات العربية المتحدة	Yemen اليمن	Total (Arab region) القيمة الإجمالية (المنطقة العربية)	البلد المصدر / إلى
Bahrain		69.4	24.4	58.7	96.4	4.8	87.3	0.1	231.4	974.7	2.1	49.6	336.0	10.7	1 945.5	البحرين
Egypt	40.6		364.9	925.7	195.1	436.8	117.4	81.2	258.7	1 317.8	558.2	820.5	553.5	226.9	5 897.4	مصر
Iraq [(1)]	—	2.4		23.7	—	0.9	—	—	—	—	—	88.2	—	—	115.2	العراق [(1)]
Jordan	39.3	115.1	1 273.4		76.7	213.5	40.3	49.9	69.7	579.5	82.0	232.9	251.5	46.2	3 069.9	الأردن
Kuwait	143.4	80.9	131.1	225.3		46.7	65.6	—	147.1	441.7	14.9	91.3	585.9	6.4	1 980.1	الكويت
Lebanon	22.1	74.7	270.8	105.4	77.3		12.7	—	79.6	242.8	27.2	225.4	332.8	11.6	1 482.4	لبنان
Oman [(1) (2)]	36.9	45.8	107.5	28.8	37.7	9.3		1.0	187.4	339.6	27.0	29.8	1 263.7	72.1	2 186.5	عُمان [(1) (2)]
Palestine	0.2	2.9	0.9	28.9	0.9	—	0.1		0.2	4.2	—	—	—	0.1	38.3	فلسطين
Qatar	74.0	32.6	8.2	73.5	143.3	18.3	160.5	1.2		359.9	30.9	36.8	2 635.2	10.1	3 584.4	قطر
Saudi Arabia	..	..	..	..	..	..	..	..	..		..	..	..	..	..	المملكة العربية السعودية
Sudan	—	93.5	48.8	15.5	1.5	12.1	0.1	—	0.6	254.4		16.5	514.1	24.4	981.6	السودان
Syrian Arab Republic [(2)]	17.2	363.2	2 697.1	347.2	139.9	349.5	31.2	—	115.3	588.2	97.1		173.8	90.7	5 010.4	الجمهورية العربية السورية [(2)]
United Arab Emirates [(1)]	1 273.7	490.8	4 200.6	228.4	1 186.1	591.7	1 408.4	0.7	2677.2	2 525.0	454.5	200.6		302.8	15 540.6	الإمارات العربية المتحدة [(1)]
Yemen	0.4	22.6	13.0	8.8	94.7	2.5	10.6	—	1.5	159.2	7.0	6.1	354.1		680.4	اليمن

(1) Excluding oil. (1) باستثناء النفط.

(2) Excluding re-exports. (2) باستثناء إعادة التصدير.

الجدول 2-4- مصفوفة قيمة الصادرات البينية في بلدان الإسكوا

Table II.4. Matrix of intraregional export value of ESCWA member countries

2010

(Millions of US dollars) (مليون دولار أمريكي)

Exporting country / To	Bahrain البحرين	Egypt مصر	Iraq العراق	Jordan الأردن	Kuwait الكويت	Lebanon لبنان	Oman عُمان	Palestine فلسطين	Qatar قطر	Saudi Arabia المملكة العربية السعودية	Sudan السودان	Syrian Arab Republic الجمهورية العربية السورية	United Arab Emirates الإمارات العربية المتحدة	Yemen اليمن	Total (Arab region) القيمة الإجمالية (المنطقة العربية)	البلد المصدر / إلى
Bahrain		137.0	20.9	38.1	114.5	15.3	160.6	0.2	619.4	1 159.6	5.0	67.9	366.8	15.4	2 720.7	البحرين
Egypt	41.6		415.2	732.9	254.0	530.6	95.5	94.2	227.3	1 664.1	673.3	820.1	636.8	252.8	6 438.4	مصر
Iraq[1]	—	3.2		47.6	—	8.3	—	—	—	—	0.1	98.3	—	—	157.5	العراق[1]
Jordan	50.1	143.4	1 126.2		89.6	231.3	40.7	66.0	96.5	661.7	86.3	256.5	296.1	47.7	3 192.1	الأردن
Kuwait	103.7	67.4	84.1	175.8		47.7	84.1	0.1	126.0	490.6	18.0	78.5	607.5	11.0	1 894.4	الكويت
Lebanon	18.0	201.0	266.9	103.6	72.0		11.7	—	82.7	245.9	19.1	220.7	418.4	12.7	1 672.7	لبنان
Oman[1] [2]	30.8	55.5	104.8	33.6	63.5	9.9		1.5	156.6	474.7	30.8	25.0	1 491.9	68.2	2 546.9	عُمان[1] [2]
Palestine	0.2	4.3	0.8	31.2	2.8	—	0.5		1.0	5.7	—	—	11.7	0.4	58.7	فلسطين
Qatar	176.1	207.6	24.2	191.0	285.5	68.5	157.0	0.6		1 063.8	49.0	65.8	4 101.0	166.0	6 556.1	قطر
Saudi Arabia	..	..	..	..	..	..	..	..	..		..	..	..	..	..	المملكة العربية السعودية
Sudan	—	104.6	50.5	42.0	1.3	18.2	0.2	—	0.4	162.6		11.9	1 140.1	3.5	1 535.3	السودان
Syrian Arab Republic[2]	8.9	314.1	2 282.1	403.7	160.3	433.9	17.9	—	65.7	539.7	78.2		89.8	85.0	4 479.1	الجمهورية العربية السورية[2]
United Arab Emirates[1]	1 851.0	599.4	4 584.7	231.0	1 419.5	390.1	1 272.4	1.3	1776.1	2 493.8	463.1	133.8		342.1	15 558.4	الإمارات العربية المتحدة[1]
Yemen	0.6	42.9	15.7	9.6	72.8	1.8	10.8	—	6.6	243.3	7.7	6.7	398.9		817.3	اليمن

(1) Excluding oil. (1) باستثناء النفط

(2) Excluding re-exports. (2) باستثناء إعادة التصدير.

الجدول 2-4- مصفوفة قيمة الصادرات البينية للبلدان الأعضاء في الإسكوا

Table II.4. Matrix of intraregional export value of ESCWA member countries

2011

(Millions of US dollars) (مليون دولار أمريكي)

Exporting country / To	Bahrain البحرين	Egypt مصر	Iraq العراق	Jordan الأردن	Kuwait الكويت	Lebanon لبنان	Oman عُمان	Palestine فلسطين	Qatar قطر	Saudi Arabia المملكة العربية السعودية	Sudan السودان	Syrian Arab Republic الجمهورية العربية السورية	United Arab Emirates الإمارات العربية المتحدة	Yemen اليمن	Total (Arab region) القيمة الإجمالية (المنطقة العربية)	البلد المصدر / إلى
Bahrain		94.6	27.2	57.6	161.5	7.8	764.9	0.2	771.8	1 636.5	11.1	68.9	583.5	10.8	4 196.4	البحرين
Egypt	38.2		445.8	807.6	254.7	942.5	116.3	79.9	274.7	1 892.3	513.3	639.8	799.4	188.1	6 992.6	مصر
Iraq[1]	—	5.6		51.6	—	7.0	—	—	0.2	—	—	106.6	—	—	171.1	العراق[1]
Jordan	52.0	125.6	1 214.4		143.6	335.7	40.7	85.2	93.4	680.1	83.7	286.8	289.6	28.8	3 459.7	الأردن
Kuwait	83.0	59.9	57.4	114.0		49.6	82.8	0.1	142.6	688.5	8.9	42.3	686.1	5.4	2 020.5	الكويت
Lebanon	16.3	67.6	197.5	127.1	76.7		13.2	—	79.8	307.9	26.0	214.8	322.3	13.5	1 462.9	لبنان
Oman[1] [2]	25.8	101.3	147.6	33.4	283.6	12.9		1.4	119.5	621.3	24.9	30.5	1 167.7	58.2	2 627.9	عُمان[1] [2]
Palestine	0.1	1.0	0.2	38.9	5.6	—	0.1		2.7	9.7	—	—	8.8	0.4	67.5	فلسطين
Qatar	108.9	273.1	117.3	124.0	891.7	26.9	309.2	0.4		861.6	46.7	73.5	4 305.1	76.8	7 215.2	قطر
Saudi Arabia	..	..	..	..	..	..	..	..	..		..	..	..	..	..	المملكة العربية السعودية
Sudan	0.2	65.2	25.7	20.9	4.9	13.6	0.2	—	1.2	259.9		19.1	885.7	64.0	1 360.7	السودان
Syrian Arab Republic[2]	8.4	231.7	1 903.0	295.6	89.8	459.4	17.9	—	39.0	525.3	46.8		105.3	56.2	3 778.4	الجمهورية العربية السورية[2]
United Arab Emirates[1]	1 515.6	634.5	3 255.4	331.8	2 194.1	570.7	1 180.3	1.4	1565.2	3 170.9	414.9	116.1		253.3	15 204.3	الإمارات العربية المتحدة[1]
Yemen	0.3	69.4	11.2	13.2	21.1	2.1	27.1	—	15.1	392.1	10.6	7.5	242.2		811.9	اليمن

(1) Excluding oil. (1) باستثناء النفط

(2) Excluding re-exports. (2) باستثناء إعادة التصدير.

الجدول 2-4- مصفوفة قيمة الصادرات البينية للبلدان الأعضاء في الإسكوا

Table II.4. Matrix of intraregional export value of ESCWA member countries
2012

(Millions of US dollars) (مليون دولار أمريكي)

Exporting country / To	Bahrain البحرين	Egypt مصر	Iraq العراق	Jordan الأردن	Kuwait الكويت	Lebanon لبنان	Libya ليبيا	Morocco المغرب	Oman عُمان	Palestine فلسطين	Qatar قطر	Saudi Arabia المملكة العربية السعودية	Sudan السودان	Syrian Arab Republic الجمهورية العربية السورية	Tunisia تونس	United Arab Emirates الإمارات العربية المتحدة	Yemen اليمن	Total (Arab region) القيمة الإجمالية (المنطقة العربية)	البلد المصدر / إلى
Bahrain		78.0	30.5	59.5	176.1	11.5	13.8	120.1	309.3	0.4	660.9	1 894.3	10.3	29.4	13.3	656.3	20.4	4 084.1	البحرين
Egypt	41.2		576.5	755.5	236.0	838.1	1 485.0	402.9	97.0	54.3	262.3	1 957.6	479.7	397.8	278.6	722.9	260.1	8 845.5	مصر
Iraq(*)	—	4.9		94.2	—	3.7	—	3.9	—	—	—	17.3	—	92.8	—	10.3	—	227.0	العراق(*)
Jordan	52.3	131.9	1 223.0		105.5	293.8	77.7	12.4	43.6	98.9	116.6	771.8	64.7	219.9	19.7	315.4	42.7	3 589.8	الأردن
Kuwait	113.0	64.2	88.1	119.9		36.9	4.8	12.0	188.9	0.1	168.0	705.4	19.5	8.8	7.1	731.9	10.3	2 278.6	الكويت
Lebanon	12.0	88.1	211.3	142.2	68.1		22.0	15.4	14.7	—	85.5	358.9	25.0	294.3	8.2	352.0	14.0	1 711.8	لبنان
Libya	..	..	..	..	..	..		..	..	..	..	..	..	..	..	..	..	..	ليبيا
Morocco	2.5	138.9	8.7	42.3	6.2	53.5	81.2		11.0	0.8	5.5	104.8	50.7	40.9	121.6	56.7	16.8	742.1	المغرب
Oman	63.1	121.0	741.1	39.9	182.6	11.9	15.4	53.0		1.1	188.8	998.9	17.2	29.7	8.3	1 854.2	82.4	4 408.6	عُمان
Palestine	0.1	1.6	0.3	58.6	6.5	—	—	0.1	0.8		7.4	11.0	0.1	—	—	14.5	0.9	102.0	فلسطين
Qatar	164.6	189.7	183.7	172.3	844.8	38.6	6.4	117.9	378.8	—		1 337.7	59.7	7.2	27.8	5 809.3	50.2	9 388.7	قطر
Saudi Arabia	..	..	..	..	..	..	..	..	..	..	..		..	..	..	..	..	..	المملكة العربية السعودية
Sudan	0.1	53.8	0.1	30.6	1.7	12.9	0.9	—	—	—	1.1	71.4		10.6	6.2	1 689.0	4.6	1 883.0	السودان
Syrian Arab Republic	..	..	..	..	..	..	..	..	..	..	..	..	..		..	..	..	..	الجمهورية العربية السورية
Tunisia	0.9	85.0	11.9	16.2	6.0	12.4	828.5	213.3	1.6	—	4.9	19.7	0.5	20.9		85.3	7.2	1 314.2	تونس
United Arab Emirates	1 841.9	765.1	3 324.3	399.9	2 133.9	554.0	1 165.5	226.6	4 241.4	1.2	2072.6	4 121.9	402.4	51.0	87.0		410.0	21 798.9	الإمارات العربية المتحدة
Yemen	0.6	45.9	5.7	23.4	2.2	1.8	3.4	0.2	12.0	—	3.7	248.7	15.0	2.6	0.5	54.9		420.8	اليمن

(*) Excluding oil.

(*) باستثناء النفط.

الجدول 2-4- مصفوفة قيمة الصادرات البينية للبلدان الأعضاء في الإسكوا

Table II.4. Matrix of intraregional export value of ESCWA member countries
2013

(Millions of US dollars) (مليون دولار امريكي)

Exporting country / To	Bahrain البحرين	Egypt مصر	Iraq العراق	Jordan الأردن	Kuwait الكويت	Lebanon لبنان	Libya ليبيا	Morocco المغرب	Oman عُمان	Palestine فلسطين	Qatar قطر	Saudi Arabia المملكة العربية السعودية	Sudan السودان	Syrian Arab Republic الجمهورية العربية السورية	Tunisia تونس	United Arab Emirates الإمارات العربية المتحدة	Yemen اليمن	Total (Arab region) القيمة الإجمالية (المنطقة العربية)	البلد المصدر / إلى
Bahrain		121.9	40.6	127.2	242.6	18.3	41.0	157.4	558.8	4.6	280.9	3 786.4	3.9	0.8	23.7	1 654.4	23.5	7 086.0	البحرين
Egypt	48.5		736.5	851.8	277.5	707.7	1 277.1	405.7	102.2	85.2	218.7	1 975.2	533.4	376.4	225.8	764.9	243.5	8 830.0	مصر
Iraq	..	..		..	..	..	..	..	..	..	..	..	..	..	..	..	..	..	العراق
Jordan	50.6	133.6	1 390.3		138.8	154.0	68.8	9.5	52.9	116.4	133.9	963.8	82.5	152.4	17.6	317.4	55.7	3 838.3	الأردن
Kuwait	97.2	60.9	576.9	136.8		42.2	5.2	9.4	128.7	0.2	161.8	709.6	23.5	1.7	6.2	859.9	16.6	2 837.0	الكويت
Lebanon	19.9	73.2	272.3	141.8	73.4		23.7	13.3	18.4	—	93.9	346.8	25.5	523.6	7.3	331.7	17.9	1 982.6	لبنان
Libya	..	..	..	..	..	..		..	..	..	..	..	..	..	..	..	..	..	ليبيا
Morocco	2.6	166.7	12.2	26.3	6.3	71.5	87.2		6.9	2.6	8.3	64.3	8.6	35.0	86.9	50.1	23.4	658.8	المغرب
Oman	122.5	157.8	236.7	34.2	461.8	28.3	120.5	9.5		1.0	396.3	2 363.4	26.3	7.3	14.2	5 013.1	235.1	9 228.0	عُمان
Palestine	0.1	0.2	0.3	57.6	3.9	—	0.6	0.2	0.2		4.8	8.4	0.1	—	—	7.4	0.9	84.8	فلسطين
Qatar	200.5	56.9	180.8	234.8	1 141.8	42.5	15.4	119.5	562.9	—		1 133.8	38.5	0.4	20.5	5 824.6	17.5	9 590.4	قطر
Saudi Arabia	..	..	..	..	..	..	..	..	..	..	..		..	..	..	..	..	..	المملكة العربية السعودية
Sudan	..	..	..	..	..	..	..	..	..	..	..	..		..	..	..	..	..	السودان
Syrian Arab Republic	..	..	..	..	..	..	..	..	..	..	..	..	..		..	..	..	..	الجمهورية العربية السورية
Tunisia	0.6	67.2	12.0	13.1	7.0	11.3	869.0	192.2	3.9	—	4.7	38.1	1.4	13.1		67.9	6.3	1 307.6	تونس
United Arab Emirates	1 823.6	1 499.3	3 502.3	484.1	2 664.9	704.1	1 086.2	199.2	4 993.0	5.4	2395.9	5 687.5	384.9	95.6	74.8		590.7	26 191.7	الإمارات العربية المتحدة
Yemen	352.9	41.7	5.3	50.7	125.3	1.7	0.5	0.2	12.2	—	9.8	219.6	1.7	2.1	0.6	320.2		1 144.6	اليمن

الجدول 2-4- مصفوفة قيمة الصادرات البينية في بلدان الإسكوا

Table II.4. Matrix of intraregional export value of ESCWA member countries
2014

(Millions of US dollars) (مليون دولار أمريكي)

Exporting country / To	Bahrain البحرين	Egypt مصر	Iraq العراق	Jordan الأردن	Kuwait الكويت	Lebanon لبنان	Libya ليبيا	Morocco المغرب	Oman عُمان	Palestine فلسطين	Qatar قطر	Saudi Arabia المملكة العربية السعودية	Sudan السودان	Syrian Arab Republic الجمهورية العربية السورية	Tunisia تونس	United Arab Emirates الإمارات العربية المتحدة	Yemen اليمن	Total (Arab region) القيمة الإجمالية (المنطقة العربية)	البلد المصدر / إلى
Bahrain		246.2	99.1	67.1	219.5	56.3	12.3	178.4	298.3	6.0	553.0	3 073.3	21.8	4.4	20.7	1 401.9	26.5	6 284.9	البحرين
Egypt	42.2		781.8	347.7	580.8	599.1	990.3	487.9	128.0	141.5	301.1	1 981.7	394.0	351.8	197.8	993.8	241.8	8 561.3	مصر
Iraq	..	..		..	..	..	..	..	..	..	..	..	..	..	..	..	..	..	العراق
Jordan	62.0	136.7	1 284.3		179.5	142.7	44.8	12.8	65.4	124.9	150.4	1 039.3	74.0	223.7	20.2	332.1	58.6	3 951.3	الأردن
Kuwait	97.5	72.3	683.0	123.4		45.7	2.4	6.1	107.8	0.2	197.9	745.8	15.0	2.5	5.8	839.2	14.5	2 959.2	الكويت
Lebanon	33.6	83.8	255.9	129.8	73.6		17.0	12.3	22.6	—	93.5	377.5	15.3	242.0	8.4	320.0	12.3	1 697.6	لبنان
Libya	..	..	..	..	..	..		..	..	..	..	..	..	..	..	..	..	..	ليبيا
Morocco	2.8	132.2	9.8	26.5	12.8	82.4	36.4		6.2	2.0	7.9	109.7	36.3	45.4	96.4	70.1	16.8	693.7	المغرب
Oman	106.4	201.8	131.2	31.9	446.1	18.3	11.4	18.0		1.4	250.6	1 135.6	26.6	12.0	6.1	2 018.3	99.0	4 514.6	عُمان
Palestine	0.3	0.3	0.5	66.3	9.0	—	—	—	0.2		8.1	11.1	0.2	—	—	14.2	1.5	111.6	فلسطين
Qatar	365.1	82.3	167.9	311.3	772.7	35.3	7.8	73.3	475.3	0.8		1 160.1	39.7	3.5	24.9	6 626.2	14.3	10 160.2	قطر
Saudi Arabia	..	..	..	..	..	..	..	..	..	..	..		..	..	..	..	..	..	المملكة العربية السعودية
Sudan	..	..	..	..	..	..	..	..	..	..	..	..		..	..	..	..	..	السودان
Syrian Arab Republic	..	..	..	..	..	..	..	..	..	..	..	..	..		..	..	..	..	الجمهورية العربية السورية
Tunisia	..	..	..	..	..	..	..	..	..	..	..	..	..	..		..	..	..	تونس
United Arab Emirates	1 643.1	1 755.7	6 674.4	543.1	2 954.5	769.5	879.4	268.3	5 318.7	6.8	2675.1	5 599.3	512.7	211.3	170.7		424.2	30 406.8	الإمارات العربية المتحدة
Yemen	0.9	46.5	2.0	33.3	3.2	1.3	0.8	0.2	72.7	—	7.5	507.3	21.0	0.3	0.2	100.7		798.0	اليمن

الجدول 2-5- النسبة المئوية للواردات البينية من إجمالي قيمة الواردات في البلدان الأعضاء في الإسكوا، حسب أقسام النظام المنسّق

Table II.5. Percentage share of intraregional value of imports in total imports of ESCWA member countries by HS section

2010

(Percentage) (نسبة مئوية)

Section / Country	Bahrain البحرين	Egypt مصر	Iraq(*) العراق(*)	Jordan الأردن	Kuwait الكويت	Lebanon لبنان	Oman عُمان	Palestine فلسطين	Qatar قطر	Saudi Arabia المملكة العربية السعودية	Sudan السودان	Syrian Arab Republic الجمهورية العربية السورية	United Arab Emirates الإمارات العربية المتحدة	Yemen اليمن	القسم / البلد
1. Live animals, animal products.	5.8	0.9	4.9	3.5	7.9	4.1	2.6	—	7.7	7.8	1.2	1.2	4.7	2.8	1. حيوانات حية ومنتجات حيوانية.
2. Vegetable products.	4.3	3.4	5.5	5.4	10.5	6.5	3.4	3.8	3.4	6.8	1.4	11.6	4.9	2.4	2. منتجات نباتية.
3. Animal or vegetable fats and oils.	1.6	0.3	3.3	2.4	1.3	2.4	0.4	2.1	1.3	2.0	0.2	1.6	0.8	0.6	3. شحوم ودهون وزيوت حيوانية أو نباتية.
4. Prepared foodstuffs, beverages, spirits, vinegar, tobacco…etc.	12.7	2.8	13.8	11.2	11.2	8.2	10.2	28.4	5.4	4.4	7.2	7.1	3.5	7.7	4. منتجات صناعة الأغذية، مشروبات، مشروبات روحية، خل، تبغ ... الخ.
5. Mineral products.	16.4	37.6	13.0	33.3	8.6	23.3	18.9	15.0	13.7	0.2	23.3	9.6	7.3	39.8	5. منتجات معدنية.
6. Chemical industry products.	11.5	7.1	5.0	9.6	14.3	11.3	7.8	9.4	8.1	5.8	12.4	12.2	6.2	6.8	6. منتجات الصناعات الكيميائية.
7. Plastics, rubber and related items.	5.9	18.0	2.5	9.6	6.0	9.1	5.3	11.9	4.5	1.9	8.1	27.9	8.1	5.4	7. اللدائن والمطاط ومصنوعاتها.
8. Raw hides and skins, leather…etc.	—	0.2	—	—	0.1	0.1	0.3	0.1	—	—	—	0.3	—	—	8. جلود خام ومدبوغة ...الخ.
9. Wood and wood products.	0.5	0.1	0.2	0.2	0.2	0.1	1.5	0.2	0.6	—	0.2	0.2	0.1	0.1	9. خشب ومصنوعات خشبية.
10. Pulp of wood or of other fibrous cellulosic material.	3.7	6.9	1.3	3.2	5.8	2.9	1.8	4.3	2.2	1.3	2.8	3.8	2.3	3.7	10. عجينة الخشب أو غيرها من عجائن المواد الليفية السليلوزية.
11. Textiles and textile articles.	1.3	7.6	1.9	2.7	2.1	1.1	3.2	2.9	1.0	0.3	5.2	2.2	1.0	0.9	11. مواد نسجية ومصنوعاتها.
12. Footwear, headgear and umbrellas.	0.1	0.1	0.3	0.3	0.1	0.2	0.6	0.1	0.5	—	0.2	—	0.1	0.1	12. أحذية، أغطية للرأس، مظلات للمطر.
13. Articles of stones, plaster, cement...etc.	4.0	0.5	2.2	3.1	2.0	5.2	1.9	1.6	6.2	3.0	4.0	3.6	2.3	0.9	13. مصنوعات من حجر أو جص أو إسمنت ...الخ.
14. Authentic and artificial peals, precious stones… etc.	3.2	0.4	—	0.7	5.6	13.0	2.8	—	3.2	4.0	—	—	38.8	0.4	14. لؤلؤ طبيعي أو مستنبت، أحجار كريمة ...الخ.
15. Base metals and related articles.	15.7	7.8	12.3	11.1	15.2	10.0	18.1	4.1	20.1	19.2	6.3	14.3	11.2	5.2	15. معادن متبلورة (فلزات) ومصنوعاتها.
16. Electrical machines and mechanical appliances.	10.7	4.6	11.8	2.7	6.8	1.2	18.6	12.4	17.9	3.3	19.7	3.8	7.7	8.7	16. آلات وأجهزة، معدات كهربائية.
17. Transportation vehicles.	0.7	1.1	19.1	0.2	1.2	0.1	0.3	0.8	1.5	0.4	3.7	0.1	0.3	13.8	17. مركبات النقل.
18. Optical, photographic, cinematographic…etc.	0.2	0.1	—	—	0.1	0.2	0.7	1.2	0.5	—	1.2	—	0.1	0.5	18. أدوات وأجهزة للبصريات أو التصوير الفوتوغرافي ...الخ.
19. Arms and ammunition: parts and accessories.	0.1	—	—	—	—	—	—	—	—	—	—	—	—	—	19. أسلحة وذخائر: أجزاؤها ولوازمها.
20. Miscellaneous manufactured articles.	1.5	0.3	3.1	0.6	1.1	0.7	1.6	1.7	2.1	0.4	2.3	0.5	0.7	0.3	20. سلع ومنتجات مصنعة أخرى.
21. Works of art, collectors' pieces.	0.1	—	—	0.2	—	0.1	—	—	—	—	0.5	—	—	—	21. تحف فنية وقطع أثرية.
Unspecified.	—	—	—	—	—	—	—	—	—	38.9	—	—	—	—	غير محدد.
Total (millions of US dollars)	1 128	4 000	2 683	3 423	3 062	2 202	6 606	129	4 254	9 492	3 151	2 352	10 334	3 364	المجموع (مليون دولار أمريكي)

(*) Excluding oil products.

(*) باستثناء المنتجات النفطية.

الجدول 2-5- النسبة المئوية للواردات البينية من إجمالي قيمة الواردات في البلدان الأعضاء في الإسكوا، حسب أقسام النظام المنسّق

Table II.5. Percentage share of intraregional value of imports in total imports of ESCWA member countries by HS section

2011

(*Percentage*) (نسبة مئوية)

Country / Section	Bahrain البحرين	Egypt مصر	Iraq(*) العراق(*)	Jordan الأردن	Kuwait الكويت	Lebanon لبنان	Oman عُمان	Palestine فلسطين	Qatar قطر	Saudi Arabia المملكة العربية السعودية	Sudan السودان	Syrian Arab Republic الجمهورية العربية السورية	United Arab Emirates الإمارات العربية المتحدة	Yemen اليمن	البلد / القسم
1. Live animals, animal products.	6.5	0.8	10.4	3.5	7.6	2.6	2.5	0.1	9.2	8.5	0.6	1.3	4.2	2.5	1. حيوانات حية ومنتجات حيوانية.
2. Vegetable products.	2.5	2.5	9.3	4.8	6.2	4.2	2.6	2.1	3.8	7.0	1.6	7.9	4.4	4.3	2. منتجات نباتية.
3. Animal or vegetable fats and oils.	1.8	0.2	0.6	2.9	1.2	2.1	0.4	1.5	1.9	3.2	0.3	2.7	0.8	0.9	3. شحوم ودهون وزيوت حيوانية أو نباتية.
4. Prepared foodstuffs, beverages, spirits, vinegar, tobacco...etc.	10.7	4.0	17.4	9.2	9.7	6.1	6.2	22.2	6.0	7.8	4.6	7.1	3.2	7.8	4. منتجات صناعة الأغذية، مشروبات، مشروبات روحية، خل، تبغ ... الخ.
5. Mineral products.	12.8	48.8	13.6	39.4	8.1	17.9	27.3	15.8	16.3	3.4	26.7	6.9	10.7	47.5	5. منتجات معدنية.
6. Chemical industry products.	11.4	6.6	8.0	8.9	11.6	8.4	7.1	7.8	8.6	10.3	13.2	11.6	7.0	5.3	6. منتجات الصناعات الكيميائية.
7. Plastics, rubber and related items.	7.0	19.2	5.5	9.0	5.8	7.3	4.8	16.5	4.9	4.8	15.6	32.2	7.7	5.1	7. اللدائن والمطاط ومصنوعاتها.
8. Raw hides and skins, leather...etc.	0.1	0.1	—	—	—	—	0.2	0.1	—	—	—	0.3	—	—	8. جلود خام ومدبوغة ...الخ.
9. Wood and wood products.	0.3	—	0.3	0.2	0.2	0.1	1.2	0.3	0.5	0.1	0.2	0.1	0.1	—	9. خشب ومصنوعات خشبية.
10. Pulp of wood or of other fibrous cellulosic material.	3.6	3.6	2.8	2.9	4.9	2.7	1.9	3.9	2.1	2.3	3.1	4.2	2.2	3.8	10. عجينة الخشب أو غيرها من عجائن المواد الليفية السليلوزية.
11. Textiles and textile articles.	1.5	3.4	1.4	1.9	1.7	0.6	3.1	2.1	1.1	2.0	3.0	1.7	0.8	0.5	11. مواد نسجية ومصنوعاتها.
12. Footwear, headgear and umbrellas.	0.2	—	0.2	0.2	0.1	0.1	0.5	0.1	0.1	0.1	0.2	—	—	0.1	12. أحذية، أغطية للرأس، مظلات للمطر.
13. Articles of stones, plaster, cement...etc.	3.3	0.3	4.9	2.5	1.9	4.1	1.9	1.8	4.3	4.1	1.6	2.5	2.1	0.6	13. مصنوعات من حجر أو جص أو إسمنت ...الخ.
14. Authentic and artificial peals, precious stones... etc.	3.2	0.5	—	1.0	12.9	32.4	2.6	—	2.8	4.6	—	—	37.4	—	14. لؤلؤ طبيعي أو مستنبت، أحجار كريمة ...الخ.
15. Base metals and related articles.	20.0	5.9	7.6	10.6	18.0	10.0	17.5	4.4	17.3	28.8	6.5	17.5	10.9	2.9	15. معادن متبلورة (فلزات) ومصنوعاتها.
16. Electrical machines and mechanical appliances.	11.2	3.6	9.7	2.1	8.2	0.8	17.6	19.0	16.1	6.1	16.9	2.6	7.4	6.1	16. آلات وأجهزة، معدات كهربائية.
17. Transportation vehicles.	1.7	0.3	4.5	0.1	0.8	—	0.3	0.4	1.6	3.4	2.6	0.3	0.3	11.7	17. مركبات النقل.
18. Optical, photographic, cinematographic...etc.	0.7	0.1	0.2	—	0.1	—	0.9	0.2	0.3	0.1	0.8	0.1	0.1	0.4	18. أدوات وأجهزة للبصريات أو التصوير الفوتوغرافي ...الخ.
19. Arms and ammunition: parts and accessories.	—	—	—	—	—	—	—	—	0.3	—	—	—	—	—	19. أسلحة وذخائر: أجزاؤها ولوازمها.
20. Miscellaneous manufactured articles.	1.6	0.2	3.6	0.6	1.1	0.4	1.5	1.8	2.6	1.5	1.8	0.1	0.7	0.3	20. سلع ومنتجات مصنعة أخرى.
21. Works of art, collectors' pieces.	—	—	—	0.2	—	0.1	—	—	0.1	—	—	0.9	0.1	—	21. تحف فنية وقطع أثرية.
Unspecified.	—	—	—	—	—	—	—	—	—	1.8	0.6	—	—	—	غير محدد.
Total (millions of US dollars)	1 500	5 379	2 955	4 321	4 261	3 130	8 224	162	4 313	12 707	2 450	2 494	12 589	3 516	المجموع (مليون دولار أمريكي)

(*) Excluding oil products.

(*) باستثناء المنتجات النفطية.

الجدول 2-5- النسبة المئوية للواردات البينية من إجمالي قيمة الواردات في البلدان الأعضاء في الإسكوا، حسب أقسام النظام المنسّق

Table II.5. Percentage share of intraregional value of imports in total imports of ESCWA member countries by HS section
2012
(Percentage) (نسبة مئوية)

Section / Country	Bahrain البحرين	Egypt مصر	Iraq(*) العراق(*)	Jordan الأردن	Kuwait الكويت	Lebanon لبنان	Libya ليبيا	Morocco المغرب	Oman عُمان	Palestine فلسطين	Qatar قطر	Saudi Arabia المملكة العربية السعودية	Sudan السودان	Syrian Arab Republic الجمهورية العربية السورية	Tunisia تونس	United Arab Emirates الإمارات العربية المتحدة	Yemen اليمن	القسم / البلد
1. Live animals, animal products.	6.9	1.0	9.1	3.7	6.6	3.2	..	0.3	3.1	—	9.8	8.3	0.4	..	1.2	3.3	4.4	1. حيوانات حية ومنتجات حيوانية.
2. Vegetable products.	3.3	3.0	6.8	4.8	6.0	4.4	..	5.3	2.8	2.4	4.2	6.2	2.1	..	3.1	3.0	1.6	2. منتجات نباتية.
3. Animal or vegetable fats and oils.	1.4	0.2	1.3	2.7	1.4	2.0	..	2.6	0.4	1.1	1.6	2.2	0.4	..	0.1	0.7	1.0	3. شحوم ودهون وزيوت حيوانية أو نباتية.
4. Prepared foodstuffs, beverages, spirits, vinegar, tobacco…etc.	10.8	5.0	21.0	8.2	7.9	5.4	..	3.2	6.5	19.6	6.8	7.7	3.2	..	6.9	2.6	11.6	4. منتجات صناعة الأغذية، مشروبات، مشروبات روحية، خل، تبغ ... الخ.
5. Mineral products.	15.7	46.8	15.3	40.6	9.4	28.4	..	22.7	18.6	15.9	15.7	5.1	31.9	..	21.7	7.6	51.6	5. منتجات معدنية.
6. Chemical industry products.	8.1	6.8	9.4	8.6	10.8	8.4	..	9.4	10.0	6.4	8.4	10.2	15.1	..	9.9	5.8	9.6	6. منتجات الصناعات الكيميائية.
7. Plastics, rubber and related items.	7.0	17.9	5.0	9.8	5.4	8.2	..	26.7	5.2	21.6	4.7	4.6	14.2	..	21.7	5.6	8.1	7. اللدائن والمطاط ومصنوعاتها.
8. Raw hides and skins, leather…etc.	—	0.1	—	—	0.1	—	..	—	0.3	0.1	—	—	—	..	0.4	—	—	8. جلود خام ومدبوغة ...الخ.
9. Wood and wood products.	0.3	—	0.2	0.2	0.2	0.1	..	0.2	1.7	0.9	0.5	0.2	0.2	..	0.1	0.1	—	9. خشب ومصنوعات خشبية.
10. Pulp of wood or of other fibrous cellulosic material.	3.4	4.2	2.7	1.9	4.4	1.8	..	7.7	2.4	2.3	1.8	2.3	2.8	..	3.8	1.4	3.1	10. عجينة الخشب أو غيرها من عجائن المواد الليفية السليلوزية.
11. Textiles and textile articles.	0.9	2.9	1.0	1.5	2.1	1.5	..	1.8	2.5	1.6	1.4	1.7	3.0	..	4.1	1.1	0.7	11. مواد نسجية ومصنوعاتها.
12. Footwear, headgear and umbrellas.	0.1	—	0.1	0.1	0.1	0.1	..	0.2	0.5	0.1	0.1	0.1	0.3	..	—	0.1	0.3	12. أحذية، أغطية للرأس، مظلات للمطر.
13. Articles of stones, plaster, cement...etc.	3.3	0.4	4.9	2.8	2.1	4.0	..	4.1	2.6	1.5	4.1	3.4	2.2	..	2.2	1.4	1.6	13. مصنوعات من حجر أو جص أو إسمنت ...الخ.
14. Authentic and artificial peals, precious stones… etc.	10.5	0.6	—	1.4	13.4	21.3	..	—	3.6	—	0.7	4.6	—	..	—	53.0	0.3	14. لؤلؤ طبيعي أو مستنبت، أحجار كريمة ...الخ.
15. Base metals and related articles.	15.6	5.7	7.3	9.4	16.9	8.5	..	10.6	18.2	5.7	20.6	31.2	8.1	..	11.1	8.6	3.4	15. معادن متبلورة (فلزات) ومصنوعاتها.
16. Electrical machines and mechanical appliances.	10.7	3.4	10.8	2.5	11.0	1.1	..	4.6	18.1	17.7	14.1	6.3	9.7	..	4.7	4.9	0.9	16. آلات وأجهزة، معدات كهربائية.
17. Transportation vehicles.	0.5	1.6	4.0	0.1	0.8	—	..	0.3	0.4	0.1	1.5	2.4	3.1	..	7.7	0.1	0.3	17. مركبات النقل.
18. Optical, photographic, cinematographic…etc.	0.1	—	0.2	0.1	0.1	—	..	0.1	1.3	0.2	0.4	0.1	0.7	..	0.1	0.1	0.1	18. أدوات وأجهزة للبصريات أو التصوير الفوتوغرافي ...الخ.
19. Arms and ammunition: parts and accessories.	—	—	—	—	—	—	..	—	—	—	—	—	—	..	—	—	—	19. أسلحة وذخائر: أجزاؤها ولوازمها.
20. Miscellaneous manufactured articles.	1.4	0.2	0.7	1.3	1.3	1.2	..	0.4	1.7	1.5	3.2	1.7	2.4	..	1.1	0.4	1.3	20. سلع ومنتجات مصنّعة أخرى.
21. Works of art, collectors' pieces.	—	—	—	0.2	—	0.1	..	—	0.1	—	0.4	—	—	..	—	—	—	21. تحف فنية وقطع أثرية.
Unspecified.	—	—	—	—	—	—	..	—	—	1.0	—	1.7	0.1	..	—	—	—	غير محدد.
Total (millions of US dollars)	2 052	5 923	1 902	4 645	4 572	3 101	..	2 149	8 743	187	4 639	14 790	1 592	..	906	17 139	2 489	المجموع (مليون دولار أمريكي)

(*) Excluding oil products.

(*) باستثناء المنتجات النفطية.

الجدول 2-5- النسبة المئوية للواردات البينية من إجمالي قيمة الواردات في البلدان الأعضاء في الإسكوا، حسب أقسام النظام المنسّق

Table II.5. Percentage share of intraregional value of imports in total imports of ESCWA member countries by HS section

2013

(Percentage) (نسبة مئوية)

Section / Country	Bahrain البحرين	Egypt مصر	Iraq العراق	Jordan الأردن	Kuwait الكويت	Lebanon لبنان	Libya ليبيا	Morocco المغرب	Oman عُمان	Palestine فلسطين	Qatar قطر	Saudi Arabia المملكة العربية السعودية	Sudan السودان	Syrian Arab Republic الجمهورية العربية السورية	Tunisia تونس	United Arab Emirates الإمارات العربية المتحدة	Yemen اليمن	القسم / البلد
1. Live animals, animal products.	5.9	0.9	..	4.1	5.4	4.1	..	0.6	3.0	—	9.5	7.6	..	..	1.3	4.7	2.6	1. حيوانات حية ومنتجات حيوانية.
2. Vegetable products.	3.2	3.5	..	6.8	4.8	6.9	..	5.3	2.0	2.4	4.8	5.4	..	..	2.5	3.6	1.1	2. منتجات نباتية.
3. Animal or vegetable fats and oils.	1.4	0.2	..	2.7	1.1	2.7	..	3.0	0.3	1.0	1.8	1.5	..	..	0.1	1.0	0.6	3. شحوم ودهون وزيوت حيوانية أو نباتية.
4. Prepared foodstuffs, beverages, spirits, vinegar, tobacco…etc.	12.2	4.1	..	9.6	6.6	7.3	..	5.8	4.6	23.6	8.0	7.5	..	..	5.9	3.9	8.1	4. منتجات صناعة الأغذية، مشروبات، مشروبات روحية، خل، تبغ ... الخ.
5. Mineral products.	11.1	43.6	..	25.0	7.2	25.8	..	12.6	32.0	16.8	15.8	7.3	..	..	34.1	16.2	5.0	5. منتجات معدنية.
6. Chemical industry products.	8.6	7.3	..	10.1	11.9	11.3	..	8.0	8.9	7.5	10.7	8.5	..	..	9.2	8.2	6.4	6. منتجات الصناعات الكيميائية.
7. Plastics, rubber and related items.	6.4	16.7	..	11.5	4.3	11.4	..	32.8	3.9	20.5	6.5	4.7	..	..	25.1	8.0	6.0	7. اللدائن والمطاط ومصنوعاتها.
8. Raw hides and skins, leather…etc.	—	—	..	—	0.1	0.1	..	—	0.2	0.1	—	—	..	..	0.3	0.1	—	8. جلود خام ومدبوغة ...الخ.
9. Wood and wood products.	0.3	—	..	0.3	0.3	0.3	..	0.3	0.9	0.8	0.5	0.2	..	..	—	0.1	—	9. خشب ومصنوعات خشبية.
10. Pulp of wood or of other fibrous cellulosic material.	3.0	3.5	..	2.3	3.1	2.2	..	7.1	1.1	2.6	1.9	2.0	..	..	2.1	1.4	2.6	10. عجينة الخشب أو غيرها من عجائن المواد الليفية السليلوزية.
11. Textiles and textile articles.	0.9	2.5	..	1.9	2.9	2.1	..	2.0	1.8	1.5	1.6	1.2	..	..	3.5	1.5	0.4	11. مواد نسجية ومصنوعاتها.
12. Footwear, headgear and umbrellas.	0.1	—	..	0.2	0.1	0.1	..	0.2	0.3	—	0.1	—	..	..	—	0.1	0.1	12. أحذية، أغطية للرأس، مظلات للمطر.
13. Articles of stones, plaster, cement...etc.	2.9	0.5	..	2.9	2.7	5.2	..	3.7	1.7	1.8	4.6	3.7	..	..	1.8	1.8	1.0	13. مصنوعات من حجر أو جص أو إسمنت ...الخ.
14. Authentic and artificial peals, precious stones… etc.	14.9	4.6	..	4.2	20.1	5.5	..	—	4.2	—	0.8	7.1	..	..	—	31.9	1.1	14. لؤلؤ طبيعي أو مستنبت، أحجار كريمة ...الخ.
15. Base metals and related articles.	19.9	7.1	..	14.0	15.9	11.8	..	13.9	12.9	11.0	16.7	31.4	..	..	8.8	11.1	2.9	15. معادن متبلورة (فلزات) ومصنوعاتها.
16. Electrical machines and mechanical appliances.	7.2	4.2	..	2.4	10.4	1.1	..	3.2	13.4	9.1	11.6	7.0	..	..	2.3	5.3	0.8	16. آلات وأجهزة، معدات كهربائية.
17. Transportation vehicles.	0.4	1.0	..	0.1	0.8	0.2	..	0.6	6.1	0.2	1.7	1.3	..	..	2.5	0.1	0.1	17. مركبات النقل.
18. Optical, photographic, cinematographic…etc.	0.1	—	..	0.1	0.5	—	..	0.2	1.1	0.2	0.2	0.2	..	..	0.1	—	—	18. أدوات وأجهزة للبصريات أو التصوير الفوتوغرافي ...الخ.
19. Arms and ammunition: parts and accessories.	—	—	..	—	—	—	..	—	—	—	—	—	..	..	—	—	—	19. أسلحة وذخائر: أجزاؤها ولوازمها.
20. Miscellaneous manufactured articles.	1.3	0.3	..	1.7	1.8	1.7	..	0.6	1.6	0.9	3.1	1.9	..	..	0.3	1.0	0.1	20. سلع ومنتجات مصنعة أخرى.
21. Works of art, collectors' pieces.	0.1	—	..	—	—	0.1	..	—	—	—	0.1	—	..	..	—	0.1	—	21. تحف فنية وقطع أثرية.
Unspecified.	—	—	..	0.3	—	—	..	—	0.1	—	—	1.3	..	..	—	—	61.1	غير محدد.
Total (millions of US dollars)	2 226	6 317	..	4 194	5 551	2 508	..	1 930	14 407	215	4 546	17 558	..	..	1 049	13 490	4 128	المجموع (مليون دولار أمريكي)

الجدول 2-5- نسبة الواردات البينية من إجمالي قيمة واردات بلدان الإسكوا، حسب أقسام النظام المنسّق لتوصيف وترميز السلع

Table II.5. Percentage share of intraregional value of imports in total imports of ESCWA member countries, by HS sections

2014

(*Percentage*) (نسبة مئوية)

Section \ Country	Bahrain البحرين	Egypt مصر	Iraq العراق	Jordan الأردن	Kuwait الكويت	Lebanon لبنان	Libya ليبيا	Morocco المغرب	Oman عُمان	Palestine فلسطين	Qatar قطر	Saudi Arabia المملكة العربية السعودية	Sudan السودان	Syrian Arab Republic الجمهورية العربية السورية	Tunisia تونس	United Arab Emirates الإمارات العربية المتحدة	Yemen اليمن	القسم \ البلد
1. Live animals, animal products.	6.9	0.9	..	4.0	5.9	5.4	..	0.3	3.4	0.1	9.8	7.0	..	..	..	5.1	6.2	1. حيوانات حية ومنتجات حيوانية.
2. Vegetable products.	3.8	2.1	..	6.0	5.9	7.4	..	5.5	3.2	3.4	4.2	3.7	..	..	..	3.8	3.2	2. منتجات نباتية.
3. Animal or vegetable fats and oils.	1.2	0.1	..	2.1	1.2	2.7	..	2.7	0.5	0.5	1.3	0.8	..	..	..	1.0	1.1	3. شحوم ودهون وزيوت حيوانية أو نباتية.
4. Prepared foodstuffs, beverages, spirits, vinegar, tobacco...etc.	8.8	3.9	..	9.4	6.9	9.4	..	6.2	6.0	22.5	6.9	3.1	..	..	..	4.3	20.2	4. منتجات صناعة الأغذية، مشروبات، مشروبات روحية، خل، تبغ ... الخ.
5. Mineral products.	27.9	45.6	..	32.4	6.9	20.3	..	17.5	12.9	16.9	15.5	4.6	..	..	..	9.5	12.0	5. منتجات معدنية.
6. Chemical industry products.	7.6	5.8	..	8.5	12.8	13.2	..	7.3	10.7	8.8	10.1	5.1	..	..	..	9.5	13.2	6. منتجات الصناعات الكيميائية.
7. Plastics, rubber and related items.	6.7	16.1	..	11.6	4.5	13.1	..	28.4	5.0	23.0	5.2	1.7	..	..	..	9.2	14.1	7. اللدائن والمطاط ومصنوعاتها.
8. Raw hides and skins, leather…etc.	0.1	0.1	..	—	0.2	0.1	..	—	0.2	0.1	—	—	..	..	..	0.1	—	8. جلود خام ومدبوغة ...الخ.
9. Wood and wood products.	0.3	—	..	0.1	0.2	0.2	..	0.2	1.0	0.6	0.5	—	..	..	..	0.1	—	9. خشب ومصنوعات خشبية.
10. Pulp of wood or of other fibrous cellulosic material.	2.4	3.1	..	3.2	3.0	2.1	..	5.9	1.7	2.3	1.7	0.7	..	..	..	1.3	4.6	10. عجينة الخشب أو غيرها من عجائن المواد الليفية السليلوزية.
11. Textiles and textile articles.	0.8	1.7	..	1.6	2.6	2.3	..	1.9	2.3	1.8	1.5	0.3	..	..	..	1.6	0.8	11. مواد نسجية ومصنوعاتها.
12. Footwear, headgear and umbrellas.	0.1	0.1	..	0.2	0.1	0.2	..	0.1	0.5	—	0.1	—	..	..	..	0.1	0.1	12. أحذية، أغطية للرأس، مظلات للمطر.
13. Articles of stones, plaster, cement...etc.	2.1	0.4	..	2.8	2.6	6.0	..	3.8	4.0	1.6	5.0	1.6	..	..	..	1.7	2.4	13. مصنوعات من حجر أو جص أو إسمنت ...الخ.
14. Authentic and artificial peals, precious stones… etc.	13.4	8.3	..	3.7	18.5	3.8	..	0.4	3.6	—	0.7	7.8	..	..	..	34.6	10.4	14. لؤلؤ طبيعي أو مستنبت، أحجار كريمة ...الخ.
15. Base metals and related articles.	11.0	6.8	..	10.9	15.9	9.8	..	14.3	14.8	10.0	17.5	18.5	..	..	..	10.8	6.1	15. معادن متبلورة (فلزات) ومصنوعاتها.
16. Electrical machines and mechanical appliances.	5.0	2.7	..	2.5	9.0	2.2	..	4.4	16.9	6.4	12.5	5.1	..	..	..	6.2	3.2	16. آلات وأجهزة، معدات كهربائية.
17. Transportation vehicles.	0.4	2.0	..	0.1	0.9	0.2	..	0.4	8.0	0.2	3.9	0.6	..	..	..	0.2	0.4	17. مركبات النقل.
18. Optical, photographic, cinematographic…etc.	0.1	0.1	..	—	1.0	—	..	0.1	1.4	0.3	0.2	—	..	..	..	0.1	0.1	18. أدوات وأجهزة للبصريات أو التصوير الفوتوغرافي ...الخ.
19. Arms and ammunition: parts and accessories.	—	—	..	—	—	—	..	—	—	—	—	—	..	..	..	—	—	19. أسلحة وذخائر: أجزاؤها ولوازمها.
20. Miscellaneous manufactured articles.	1.6	0.2	..	0.4	1.9	1.4	..	0.6	3.9	1.4	2.6	0.6	..	..	..	0.9	1.7	20. سلع ومنتجات مصنعة أخرى.
21. Works of art, collectors' pieces.	0.1	—	..	—	—	0.2	..	—	—	—	0.7	—	..	..	..	0.1	—	21. تحف فنية وقطع أثرية.
Unspecified.	—	—	..	0.3	—	—	..	—	—	—	—	38.9	..	..	..	—	—	غير محدد.
Total (millions of US dollars)	2 603	6 734	..	4 543	6 183	2 148	..	2 257	11 827	274	5 449	17 512	..	..	..	13 755	1 899	المجموع (مليون دولار أمريكي)

الجدول 2-6- النسبة المئوية للصادرات البينية من إجمالي قيمة الصادرات في البلدان الأعضاء في الإسكوا حسب أقسام النظام المنسق[(1)]

Table II.6. Percentage share of intraregional export value in total exports of ESCWA member countries by HS section[(1)]

2010

(Percentage) (نسبة مئوية)

Section / Country	Bahrain[(2)] البحرين	Egypt مصر	Iraq[(2)] العراق	Jordan الأردن	Kuwait الكويت	Lebanon لبنان	Oman[(2)(3)] عُمان	Palestine فلسطين	Qatar قطر	Saudi Arabia المملكة العربية السعودية	Sudan السودان	Syrian Arab Republic[(3)] الجمهورية العربية السورية	United Arab Emirates[(2)] الإمارات العربية المتحدة	Yemen اليمن	البلد / القسم
1. Live animals, animal products.	4.7	6.7	1.1	4.4	3.3	0.7	13.6	11.2	0.6	..	11.5	11.2	1.7	14.9	1. حيوانات حية ومنتجات حيوانية.
2. Vegetable products.	0.2	16.8	6.1	14.9	0.9	7.5	1.6	5.8	0.2	..	8.9	20.5	1.8	11.3	2. منتجات نباتية.
3. Animal or vegetable fats and oils.	—	1.1	—	0.3	0.2	0.8	5.3	16.6	—	..	—	1.6	0.4	0.3	3. شحوم ودهون وزيوت حيوانية أو نباتية.
4. Prepared foodstuffs, beverages, spirits, vinegar, tobacco…etc.	5.5	10.8	0.2	8.8	5.6	11.7	4.9	6.1	0.2	..	—	16.7	7.6	5.1	4. منتجات صناعة الأغذية، مشروبات، مشروبات روحية، خل، تبغ ... الخ.
5. Mineral products.	30.3	10.5	31.4	1.1	1.0	2.6	32.5	14.6	54.7	..	6.4	5.0	3.7	47.5	5. منتجات معدنية.
6. Chemical industry products.	1.9	8.2	52.3	25.5	5.3	7.3	7.9	3.7	3.5	..	—	10.6	4.8	0.6	6. منتجات الصناعات الكيميائية.
7. Plastics, rubber and related items.	2.9	3.3	—	4.5	21.1	3.7	6.3	2.2	6.0	..	—	7.3	5.3	0.2	7. اللدائن والمطاط ومصنوعاتها.
8. Raw hides and skins, leather…etc.	—	—	8.5	0.2	0.1	0.4	—	—	—	..	1.2	0.2	0.2	0.2	8. جلود خام ومدبوغة ...الخ.
9. Wood and wood products.	0.4	0.2	—	0.8	0.4	1.1	—	0.2	0.1	..	—	0.4	0.4	—	9. خشب ومصنوعات خشبية.
10. Pulp of wood or of other fibrous cellulosic material.	1.3	1.9	—	7.2	2.3	9.5	0.9	4.2	0.2	..	—	2.1	1.5	0.4	10. عجينة الخشب أو غيرها من عجائن المواد الليفية السليلوزية.
11. Textiles and textile articles.	0.3	2.9	0.2	1.9	2.5	4.0	0.1	0.3	0.1	..	0.9	12.6	7.7	0.1	11. مواد نسجية ومصنوعاتها.
12. Footwear, headgear and umbrellas.	—	—	—	0.1	0.1	1.1	—	6.9	—	..	—	1.4	0.6	—	12. أحذية، أغطية للرأس، مظلات للمطر.
13. Articles of stones, plaster, cement...etc.	0.7	5.3	—	1.3	5.5	1.8	4.6	18.0	0.4	..	—	1.2	1.9	0.1	13. مصنوعات من حجر أو جص أو إسمنت ...الخ.
14. Authentic and artificial peals, precious	0.6	3.6	—	3.7	5.0	9.9	1.6	—	0.1	..	70.6	—	15.5	3.5	14. لؤلؤ طبيعي أو مستنبت، أحجار كريمة ...الخ.
15. Base metals and related articles.	34.2	18.5	—	10.9	10.1	3.4	8.9	3.7	14.5	..	0.3	4.8	5.8	3.0	15. معادن متبلورة (فلزات) ومصنوعاتها.
16. Electrical machines and mechanical appliances.	9.7	7.2	—	11.0	16.1	28.8	10.4	2.6	8.4	..	0.1	3.2	27.0	8.3	16. آلات وأجهزة، معدات كهربائية.
17. Transportation vehicles.	6.0	0.3	—	1.0	18.3	1.0	—	1.4	10.3	..	—	0.4	11.6	4.2	17. مركبات النقل.
18. Optical, photographic, cinematographic…etc.	0.3	0.2	—	0.5	0.3	0.5	—	0.9	0.3	..	—	—	1.1	0.3	18. أدوات وأجهزة للبصريات أو التصوير الفوتوغرافي ...الخ.
19. Arms and ammunition: parts and accessories.	—	—	—	—	—	—	—	—	—	..	—	—	0.1	—	19. أسلحة وذخائر: أجزاؤها ولوازمها.
20. Miscellaneous manufactured articles.	0.9	2.5	—	1.9	1.9	4.0	1.2	1.3	0.4	..	—	0.6	1.3	0.1	20. سلع ومنتجات مصنعة أخرى.
21. Works of art, collectors' pieces.	0.1	—	—	0.1	—	0.1	—	0.2	—	..	—	—	0.1	—	21. تحف فنية وقطع أثرية.
Unspecified.	—	—	0.1	—	—	—	—	—	—	..	—	—	—	—	غير محدد.
Total (millions of US dollars)	2 721	6 438	157	3 192	1 894	1 673	2 547	59	6 556	..	1 535	4 479	15 558	817	المجموع (مليون دولار أمريكي)

(1) Excluding crude oil.
(2) Excluding oil.
(3) Excluding re-exports.

(1) باستثناء النفط الخام.
(2) باستثناء النفط.
(3) باستثناء إعادة التصدير.

الجدول 2-6- النسبة المئوية للصادرات البينية من إجمالي قيمة الصادرات في البلدان الأعضاء في الإسكوا حسب أقسام النظام المنسق[1]

Table II.6. Percentage share of intraregional export value in total exports of ESCWA member countries by HS section[1]

2011

(Percentage) (نسبة مئوية)

Section \ Country	Bahrain[2] البحرين[2]	Egypt مصر	Iraq[2] العراق[2]	Jordan الأردن	Kuwait الكويت	Lebanon لبنان	Oman[2][3] عُمان[2][3]	Palestine فلسطين	Qatar قطر	Saudi Arabia المملكة العربية السعودية	Sudan السودان	Syrian Arab Republic الجمهورية العربية السورية	United Arab Emirates[2] الإمارات العربية المتحدة[2]	Yemen اليمن	القسم \ البلد
1. Live animals, animal products.	4.4	6.4	1.7	5.4	..	0.6	12.5	0.2	0.5	..	18.5	8.8	2.0	17.8	1. حيوانات حية ومنتجات حيوانية.
2. Vegetable products.	0.2	13.5	8.1	15.5	..	9.1	2.3	7.0	0.1	..	9.6	19.7	2.5	16.6	2. منتجات نباتية.
3. Animal or vegetable fats and oils.	—	1.6	—	0.5	..	1.0	7.0	12.8	—	..	—	2.0	0.5	0.5	3. شحوم ودهون وزيوت حيوانية أو نباتية.
4. Prepared foodstuffs, beverages, spirits, vinegar, tobacco…etc.	5.2	8.3	0.3	8.9	..	15.4	5.4	10.1	0.1	..	0.3	10.3	9.1	6.6	4. منتجات صناعة الأغذية، مشروبات، مشروبات روحية، خل، تبغ ... الخ.
5. Mineral products.	44.0	8.8	15.1	1.6	..	1.4	19.2	0.9	61.3	..	12.7	7.1	4.5	36.1	5. منتجات معدنية.
6. Chemical industry products.	1.4	7.6	54.5	21.7	..	9.4	10.4	3.2	5.2	..	—	13.6	5.3	0.7	6. منتجات الصناعات الكيميائية.
7. Plastics, rubber and related items.	2.4	3.4	9.8	4.9	..	4.3	6.6	1.6	6.7	..	—	6.4	5.5	0.1	7. اللدائن والمطاط ومصنوعاتها.
8. Raw hides and skins, leather…etc.	—	—	10.1	0.4	..	0.4	—	—	—	..	1.4	0.1	0.1	0.2	8. جلود خام ومدبوغة ...الخ.
9. Wood and wood products.	0.3	0.5	—	0.9	..	0.8	0.1	0.1	0.1	..	—	0.3	0.4	—	9. خشب ومصنوعات خشبية.
10. Pulp of wood or of other fibrous cellulosic material.	1.4	1.7	—	6.3	..	9.8	1.1	1.4	0.2	..	—	1.9	1.5	0.1	10. عجينة الخشب أو غيرها من عجائن المواد الليفية السليلوزية.
11. Textiles and textile articles.	0.2	2.7	0.2	1.5	..	5.0	0.2	0.2	0.1	..	0.5	10.1	7.7	0.2	11. مواد نسجية ومصنوعاتها.
12. Footwear, headgear and umbrellas.	—	—	—	0.4	..	1.4	—	6.0	—	..	—	8.5	0.7	—	12. أحذية، أغطية للرأس، مظلات للمطر.
13. Articles of stones, plaster, cement...etc.	0.5	5.2	—	1.1	..	1.6	3.9	32.2	0.2	..	—	2.0	1.2	0.1	13. مصنوعات من حجر أو جص أو إسمنت ...الخ.
14. Authentic and artificial peals, precious	—	7.8	—	5.7	..	12.0	0.3	—	0.1	..	56.7	—	14.2	0.7	14. لؤلؤ طبيعي أو مستنبت، أحجار كريمة ...الخ.
15. Base metals and related articles.	24.4	18.9	—	10.1	..	4.0	19.0	20.1	13.0	..	0.2	4.8	7.7	6.0	15. معادن متبلورة (فلزات) ومصنوعاتها.
16. Electrical machines and mechanical appliances.	9.8	9.9	0.1	11.0	..	17.8	10.9	2.6	5.4	..	0.1	2.4	22.4	5.7	16. آلات وأجهزة، معدات كهربائية.
17. Transportation vehicles.	4.8	0.5	—	1.8	..	1.6	—	0.4	6.4	..	—	0.5	12.3	7.6	17. مركبات النقل.
18. Optical, photographic, cinematographic…etc.	0.1	0.2	—	0.5	..	0.7	—	—	0.6	..	—	—	0.9	0.7	18. أدوات وأجهزة للبصريات أو التصوير الفوتوغرافي ...الخ.
19. Arms and ammunition: parts and accessories.	—	—	—	—	..	—	—	—	—	..	—	—	—	—	19. أسلحة وذخائر: أجزاؤها ولوازمها.
20. Miscellaneous manufactured articles.	0.9	2.9	—	1.7	..	3.7	1.2	1.2	0.2	..	—	0.5	1.3	0.2	20. سلع ومنتجات مصنعة أخرى.
21. Works of art, collectors' pieces.	—	0.2	—	0.1	..	0.1	—	—	—	..	—	0.9	0.1	—	21. تحف فنية وقطع أثرية.
Unspecified.	—	—	—	—	..	—	—	—	—	..	—	—	—	—	غير محدد.
Total (millions of US dollars)	4 196	6 993	171	3 460	..	1 463	2 628	68	7 215	..	1 361	3 778	15 204	812	المجموع (مليون دولار أمريكي)

(1) Excluding crude oil. — (1) باستثناء النفط الخام.

(2) Excluding oil. — (2) باستثناء النفط.

(3) Excluding re-exports. — (3) باستثناء إعادة التصدير.

الجدول 2-6- النسبة المئوية للصادرات البينية من إجمالي قيمة الصادرات في البلدان الأعضاء في الإسكوا حسب أقسام النظام المنسق[1]

Table II.6. Percentage share of intraregional export value in total exports of ESCWA member countries by HS section[1]

2012

(Percentage) (نسبة مئوية)

Section / Country	Bahrain البحرين	Egypt مصر	Iraq[2] العراق[2]	Jordan الأردن	Kuwait الكويت	Lebanon لبنان	Libya ليبيا	Morocco المغرب	Oman[2] عُمان[2]	Palestine فلسطين	Qatar قطر	Saudi Arabia المملكة العربية السعودية	Sudan السودان	Syrian Arab Republic الجمهورية العربية السورية	Tunisia تونس	United Arab Emirates[2] الإمارات العربية المتحدة[2]	Yemen اليمن	القسم / البلد
1. Live animals, animal products.	4.5	4.7	2.0	5.6	3.7	0.8	..	12.6	7.5	1.0	0.4	..	3.5	..	3.7	1.6	32.2	1. حيوانات حية ومنتجات حيوانية.
2. Vegetable products.	0.3	12.6	5.4	16.2	1.7	8.4	..	1.2	2.3	9.3	0.2	..	6.2	..	7.8	2.3	30.4	2. منتجات نباتية.
3. Animal or vegetable fats and oils.	—	2.9	—	0.6	0.1	1.2	..	0.3	3.0	18.4	—	..	—	..	13.6	0.5	1.4	3. شحوم ودهون وزيوت حيوانية أو نباتية.
4. Prepared foodstuffs, beverages, spirits, vinegar, tobacco…etc.	6.3	7.9	0.9	8.7	5.9	13.9	..	16.0	4.3	11.8	0.1	..	0.2	..	12.6	7.3	8.2	4. منتجات صناعة الأغذية، مشروبات، مشروبات روحية، خل، تبغ ... الخ.
5. Mineral products.	22.4	9.2	19.9	1.7	0.8	5.6	..	3.4	38.6	11.6	50.8	..	—	..	2.7	5.5	16.4	5. منتجات معدنية.
6. Chemical industry products.	2.2	9.1	61.2	23.5	12.3	10.0	..	17.6	8.7	1.0	5.0	..	3.7	..	15.2	5.3	1.1	6. منتجات الصناعات الكيميائية.
7. Plastics, rubber and related items.	3.4	5.1	3.6	6.3	16.1	4.6	..	0.7	4.6	1.8	7.0	..	—	..	4.6	6.4	0.1	7. اللدائن والمطاط ومصنوعاتها.
8. Raw hides and skins, leather…etc.	0.1	0.1	6.8	0.3	0.1	0.4	..	0.2	—	—	—	..	1.3	..	0.1	0.2	0.2	8. جلود خام ومدبوغة ...الخ.
9. Wood and wood products.	0.4	0.2	—	2.2	0.1	1.0	..	0.1	0.2	0.2	0.1	..	0.1	..	0.3	0.5	—	9. خشب ومصنوعات خشبية.
10. Pulp of wood or of other fibrous cellulosic material.	2.6	2.6	0.1	5.9	2.6	7.7	..	4.4	0.9	1.6	0.1	..	—	..	5.1	2.3	0.3	10. عجينة الخشب أو غيرها من عجائن المواد الليفية السليلوزية.
11. Textiles and textile articles.	1.3	3.1	0.1	1.7	1.6	4.3	..	4.7	0.3	0.4	0.1	..	—	..	1.6	5.5	0.1	11. مواد نسجية ومصنوعاتها.
12. Footwear, headgear and umbrellas.	—	—	—	0.7	0.1	1.3	..	0.1	—	2.2	—	..	—	..	0.7	0.6	—	12. أحذية، أغطية للرأس، مظلات للمطر.
13. Articles of stones, plaster, cement...etc.	0.7	8.3	—	1.1	3.9	1.7	..	0.7	3.2	14.6	0.3	..	—	..	3.1	1.6	0.2	13. مصنوعات من حجر أو جص أو إسمنت ...الخ.
14. Authentic and artificial peals, precious	2.1	4.8	—	3.6	7.8	11.8	..	1.4	0.3	—	—	..	84.7	..	—	11.5	1.4	14. لؤلؤ طبيعي أو مستنبت، أحجار كريمة ...الخ.
15. Base metals and related articles.	30.0	16.5	—	7.2	8.0	4.0	..	9.9	12.5	14.1	28.8	..	0.2	..	8.3	11.9	7.2	15. معادن متبلورة (فلزات) ومصنوعاتها.
16. Electrical machines and mechanical appliances.	15.9	9.5	—	10.4	13.1	16.6	..	9.4	11.7	1.2	3.5	..	—	..	13.8	21.2	0.1	16. آلات وأجهزة، معدات كهربائية.
17. Transportation vehicles.	6.5	0.3	—	1.1	19.8	1.8	..	16.6	0.5	2.5	3.2	..	—	..	1.3	13.4	0.5	17. مركبات النقل.
18. Optical, photographic, cinematographic…etc.	0.5	0.1	—	0.5	0.6	0.5	..	0.2	0.2	—	0.1	..	—	..	0.7	0.9	—	18. أدوات وأجهزة للبصريات أو التصوير الفوتوغرافي ...الخ.
19. Arms and ammunition: parts and accessories.	—	—	—	—	—	—	..	—	—	—	—	..	—	..	—	—	—	19. أسلحة وذخائر: أجزاؤها ولوازمها.
20. Miscellaneous manufactured articles.	0.9	3.0	—	2.6	1.6	4.3	..	0.4	1.1	1.5	0.1	..	—	..	4.8	1.5	0.2	20. سلع ومنتجات مصنعة أخرى.
21. Works of art, collectors' pieces.	—	—	—	0.1	—	0.1	..	—	—	—	—	..	—	..	—	0.1	—	21. تحف فنية وقطع أثرية.
Unspecified.	—	—	—	—	—	—	..	—	0.1	6.8	—	..	—	..	—	—	—	غير محدد.
Total (millions of US dollars)	4 084	8 845	227	3 590	2 279	1 712	..	742	4 409	102	9 389	..	1 883	..	1 314	21 799	421	المجموع (مليون دولار أمريكي)

(1) Excluding crude oil. — (1) باستثناء النفط الخام.

(2) Excluding oil. — (2) باستثناء النفط.

الجدول 2-6- النسبة المئوية للصادرات البينية من إجمالي قيمة الصادرات في البلدان الأعضاء في الإسكوا حسب أقسام النظام المنسق[1]

Table II.6. Percentage share of intraregional export value in total exports of ESCWA member countries by HS section[1]

2013

(Percentage) (نسبة مئوية)

Section \ Country	البحرين Bahrain	مصر Egypt	العراق Iraq	الأردن Jordan	الكويت Kuwait	لبنان Lebanon	ليبيا Libya	المغرب Morocco	عُمان[2] Oman	فلسطين Palestine	قطر Qatar	المملكة العربية السعودية Saudi Arabia	السودان Sudan	الجمهورية العربية السورية Syrian Arab Republic	تونس Tunisia	الإمارات العربية المتحدة[2] United Arab Emirates	اليمن Yemen	البلد / القسم
1. Live animals, animal products.	3.9	4.9	..	7.8	5.6	0.9	..	16.7	3.8	0.1	0.4	..	..	..	4.4	1.5	13.3	1. حيوانات حية ومنتجات حيوانية.
2. Vegetable products.	0.1	14.7	..	16.8	2.6	8.8	..	3.2	1.0	23.0	0.2	..	..	..	9.8	2.4	10.8	2. منتجات نباتية.
3. Animal or vegetable fats and oils.	—	2.4	..	0.4	0.1	1.1	..	0.7	1.9	5.0	—	..	..	..	8.6	0.5	0.5	3. شحوم ودهون وزيوت حيوانية أو نباتية.
4. Prepared foodstuffs, beverages, spirits, vinegar, tobacco…etc.	7.5	9.9	..	9.5	8.1	14.6	..	16.2	2.0	8.2	0.1	..	..	..	10.8	6.2	2.2	4. منتجات صناعة الأغذية، مشروبات، مشروبات روحية، خل، تبغ ... الخ.
5. Mineral products.	12.3	8.4	..	1.4	0.8	16.7	..	4.8	30.6	23.7	49.1	..	..	..	3.8	5.2	30.8	5. منتجات معدنية.
6. Chemical industry products.	1.8	9.4	..	24.9	8.2	10.3	..	8.7	4.1	0.3	8.6	..	..	..	16.1	4.4	0.3	6. منتجات الصناعات الكيميائية.
7. Plastics, rubber and related items.	2.3	5.6	..	7.1	11.8	3.4	..	0.7	2.3	0.6	6.9	..	..	..	5.0	4.9	—	7. اللدائن والمطاط ومصنوعاتها.
8. Raw hides and skins, leather…etc.	0.1	0.1	..	0.1	0.1	0.2	..	0.1	—	0.1	—	..	..	..	0.1	0.3	0.2	8. جلود خام ومدبوغة ...الخ.
9. Wood and wood products.	0.6	0.3	..	1.1	0.2	0.8	..	0.1	0.1	0.1	0.1	..	..	..	0.2	0.4	—	9. خشب ومصنوعات خشبية.
10. Pulp of wood or of other fibrous cellulosic material.	1.6	2.3	..	4.9	2.3	5.9	..	1.5	0.3	0.2	0.1	..	..	..	10.4	2.8	0.1	10. عجينة الخشب أو غيرها من عجائن المواد الليفية السليلوزية.
11. Textiles and textile articles.	1.3	3.0	..	1.5	1.9	4.0	..	5.3	0.1	0.5	0.1	..	..	..	1.8	4.7	—	11. مواد نسجية ومصنوعاتها.
12. Footwear, headgear and umbrellas.	0.2	—	..	0.2	0.1	0.8	..	0.3	—	1.9	0.1	..	..	..	0.4	0.6	—	12. أحذية، أغطية للرأس، مظلات للمطر.
13. Articles of stones, plaster, cement...etc.	0.9	8.5	..	1.1	5.6	1.4	..	0.8	2.0	12.9	0.3	..	..	..	3.6	2.6	0.1	13. مصنوعات من حجر أو جص أو إسمنت ...الخ.
14. Authentic and artificial peals, precious	9.3	1.1	..	0.4	10.0	7.3	..	0.1	0.2	—	0.1	..	..	..	—	17.8	1.4	14. لؤلؤ طبيعي أو مستنبت، أحجار كريمة ...الخ.
15. Base metals and related articles.	31.0	16.4	..	8.0	8.4	4.3	..	6.2	9.2	16.0	26.8	..	..	..	8.2	13.2	3.9	15. معادن متبلورة (فلزات) ومصنوعاتها.
16. Electrical machines and mechanical appliances.	14.0	8.5	..	9.7	10.2	14.0	..	7.2	5.9	3.6	2.9	..	..	..	10.7	19.5	0.1	16. آلات وأجهزة، معدات كهربائية.
17. Transportation vehicles.	11.3	0.4	..	2.0	20.9	1.1	..	26.3	35.5	2.5	3.7	..	..	..	3.4	10.9	—	17. مركبات النقل.
18. Optical, photographic, cinematographic…etc.	0.4	0.1	..	0.3	0.7	0.5	..	0.1	0.2	—	0.2	..	..	..	0.8	0.8	—	18. أدوات وأجهزة للبصريات أو التصوير الفوتوغرافي ...الخ.
19. Arms and ammunition: parts and accessories.	—	—	..	—	—	—	..	—	—	—	0.1	..	..	..	—	—	—	19. أسلحة وذخائر: أجزاؤها ولوازمها.
20. Miscellaneous manufactured articles.	1.2	4.0	..	2.8	2.5	3.8	..	0.8	0.5	1.4	0.1	..	..	..	1.8	1.3	—	20. سلع ومنتجات مصنعة أخرى.
21. Works of art, collectors' pieces.	—	—	..	—	—	0.1	..	0.4	—	—	0.1	..	..	..	—	0.1	—	21. تحف فنية وقطع أثرية.
Unspecified.	—	—	..	—	—	—	..	—	—	—	—	..	..	..	—	—	36.3	غير محدد.
Total (millions of US dollars)	7 086	8 830	..	3 838	2 788	1 983	..	659	9 228	85	9 590	..	..	..	1 308	26 192	1 145	المجموع (مليون دولار أمريكي)

(1) Excluding crude oil.

(2) Excluding oil.

(1) لا تتضمن النفط الخام.

(2) لا تتضمن النفط.

الجدول 2-6- نسبة الصادرات البينية من إجمالي قيمة الصادرات، حسب أقسام النظام المنسق لبلدان الإسكوا[(1)]

Table II.6. Percentage share of intraregional export value in total exports of ESCWA member countries,[(1)] by HS sections 2014

(Percentage) (نسبة مئوية)

Section / Country	Bahrain البحرين	Egypt مصر	Iraq العراق	Jordan الأردن	Kuwait الكويت	Lebanon لبنان	Libya ليبيا	Morocco المغرب	Oman[(2)] عُمان[(2)]	Palestine فلسطين	Qatar قطر	Saudi Arabia المملكة العربية السعودية	Sudan السودان	Syrian Arab Republic الجمهورية العربية السورية	Tunisia تونس	United Arab Emirates[(2)] الإمارات العربية المتحدة[(2)]	Yemen اليمن	البلد / القسم
1. Live animals, animal products.	3.5	5.1	..	7.4	6.0	1.0	..	14.9	8.9	0.3	0.4	..	..	..	..	2.4	23.7	1. حيوانات حية ومنتجات حيوانية.
2. Vegetable products.	0.1	14.3	..	18.8	2.8	10.0	..	3.2	1.7	16.8	0.1	..	..	..	..	1.8	16.8	2. منتجات نباتية.
3. Animal or vegetable fats and oils.	—	1.4	..	0.2	0.2	1.3	..	0.2	4.5	8.9	—	..	..	..	..	0.4	1.0	3. شحوم ودهون وزيوت حيوانية أو نباتية.
4. Prepared foodstuffs, beverages, spirits, vinegar, tobacco…etc.	5.9	9.2	..	10.0	6.9	19.8	..	17.6	4.6	7.9	0.1	..	..	..	..	6.4	4.4	4. منتجات صناعة الأغذية، مشروبات، مشروبات روحية، خل، تبغ ... الخ.
5. Mineral products.	12.2	6.0	..	1.0	0.7	1.4	..	12.2	31.0	0.6	45.4	..	..	..	..	4.4	0.3	5. منتجات معدنية.
6. Chemical industry products.	4.3	9.6	..	24.7	7.3	12.8	..	13.5	8.5	3.0	9.8	..	..	..	..	4.1	0.6	6. منتجات الصناعات الكيميائية.
7. Plastics, rubber and related items.	2.7	5.1	..	6.9	9.4	4.1	..	1.0	6.1	1.4	6.7	..	..	..	..	4.3	0.1	7. اللدائن والمطاط ومصنوعاتها.
8. Raw hides and skins, leather…etc.	0.1	—	..	0.1	0.1	0.4	..	0.1	—	—	—	..	..	..	..	0.2	0.2	8. جلود خام ومدبوغة ...الخ.
9. Wood and wood products.	0.3	0.4	..	0.5	0.2	0.5	..	0.1	0.1	0.2	—	..	..	..	..	0.4	—	9. خشب ومصنوعات خشبية.
10. Pulp of wood or of other fibrous cellulosic material.	2.0	2.5	..	5.6	2.4	8.7	..	0.6	0.7	0.3	0.1	..	..	..	..	2.1	0.3	10. عجينة الخشب أو غيرها من عجائن المواد الليفية السليلوزية.
11. Textiles and textile articles.	1.9	3.1	..	1.4	3.0	4.7	..	4.6	0.3	0.1	0.3	..	..	..	..	4.2	0.2	11. مواد نسجية ومصنوعاتها.
12. Footwear, headgear and umbrellas.	0.2	—	..	0.1	0.3	1.4	..	0.2	—	2.5	—	..	..	..	..	0.5	—	12. أحذية، أغطية للرأس، مظلات للمطر.
13. Articles of stones, plaster, cement...etc.	0.9	7.4	..	1.7	5.1	1.3	..	0.6	5.0	39.0	0.2	..	..	..	..	1.7	0.2	13. مصنوعات من حجر أو جص أو إسمنت ...الخ.
14. Authentic and artificial peals, precious	4.5	1.7	..	0.4	7.4	6.7	..	0.3	0.2	—	0.1	..	..	..	..	24.0	2.2	14. لؤلؤ طبيعي أو مستنبت، أحجار كريمة ...الخ.
15. Base metals and related articles.	34.8	10.6	..	7.2	10.1	5.3	..	3.2	18.7	13.7	28.8	..	..	..	..	10.2	5.2	15. معادن متبلورة (فلزات) ومصنوعاتها.
16. Electrical machines and mechanical appliances.	13.9	17.4	..	10.5	11.1	14.4	..	6.8	8.5	0.8	2.8	..	..	..	..	19.7	6.9	16. آلات وأجهزة، معدات كهربائية.
17. Transportation vehicles.	9.9	0.4	..	0.7	22.6	1.1	..	19.8	—	2.6	4.8	..	..	..	..	10.8	37.8	17. مركبات النقل.
18. Optical, photographic, cinematographic…etc.	0.9	0.1	..	0.4	0.9	0.5	..	0.1	—	0.1	0.2	..	..	..	..	0.7	0.2	18. أدوات وأجهزة للبصريات أو التصوير الفوتوغرافي ...الخ.
19. Arms and ammunition: parts and accessories.	—	—	..	—	0.1	—	..	—	—	—	—	..	..	..	..	—	—	19. أسلحة وذخائر: أجزاؤها ولوازمها.
20. Miscellaneous manufactured articles.	1.3	3.7	..	—	3.4	4.5	..	0.7	1.3	1.8	0.1	..	..	..	..	1.1	0.1	20. سلع ومنتجات مصنعة أخرى.
21. Works of art, collectors' pieces.	0.8	—	..	—	—	0.2	..	0.3	—	—	—	..	..	..	..	0.4	—	21. تحف فنية وقطع أثرية.
Unspecified.	—	1.9	..	—	—	—	..	—	—	—	—	..	..	..	..	—	—	غير محدد.
Total (millions of US dollars)	6 285	8 561	..	3 951	2 959	1 698	..	694	4 515	112	10 160	..	..	..	..	30 407	798	**المجموع (مليون دولار أمريكي)**

(1) Excluding crude oil.
(2) Excluding oil.

(1) لا تتضمن النفط الخام.
(2) لا تتضمن النفط.

الجدول 2-7- مصفوفة قيمة الميزان التجاري البيني للبلدان الأعضاء في الإسكوا

Table II .7. Matrix of intraregional balance of trade of ESCWA member countries

2008

(Millions of US dollars) (مليون دولار أمريكي)

Between	Bahrain البحرين	Egypt مصر	Iraq العراق	Jordan الأردن	Kuwait الكويت	Lebanon لبنان	Oman عُمان	Palestine فلسطين	Qatar قطر	Saudi Arabia المملكة العربية السعودية	Sudan السودان	Syrian Arab Republic الجمهورية العربية السورية	United Arab Emirates الإمارات العربية المتحدة	Yemen اليمن	Total مجموع	بين
Bahrain		43.1	32.4	101.8	- 32.7	- 8.1	38.6	- 0.1	200.8	658.5	4.2	53.4	- 83.7	7.8	1 016.0	البحرين
Egypt	- 135.5		328.9	622.4	118.1	251.9	115.7	87.5	93.9	-1 901.4	507.6	255.0	- 358.0	138.4	124.6	مصر
Iraq	..	..		..	..	..	..	..	..	..	..	..	..	..	..	العراق
Jordan	- 99.4	- 576.1	1 279.2		- 14.1	38.8	14.8	27.3	75.1	- 409.2	96.6	- 97.6	60.6	3.6	399.6	الأردن
Kuwait	31.8	- 152.4	160.4	133.8		- 89.2	- 41.2	- 1.8	158.2	- 967.6	13.3	- 0.7	- 291.1	5.4	-1 041.3	الكويت
Lebanon	- 20.5	- 331.1	254.7	10.6	- 392.9		7.3	—	67.7	- 81.0	11.3	- 47.3	19.8	9.3	- 492.0	لبنان
Oman[(1) (2)]	- 165.5	- 155.0	182.4	- 5.7	- 27.2	- 5.6		2.4	219.4	- 139.7	36.2	9.6	-3 900.9	51.5	-3 898.2	عُمان[(1)(2)]
Palestine	0.1	- 22.6	0.6	- 18.1	1.4	—	- 0.3		0.3	1.2	—	—	0.5	0.2	- 36.6	فلسطين
Qatar	- 251.0	- 150.2	10.2	- 8.3	- 76.2	- 157.0	- 234.0	- 0.4		-1 088.8	6.9	- 29.6	- 977.4	3.3	-2 952.5	قطر
Saudi Arabia	..	..	..	..	..	..	..	..	..		..	..	..	..	..	المملكة العربية السعودية
Sudan	- 1.6	- 291.9	0.1	- 121.6	- 1.1	—	- 5.9	—	- 13.4	-3 981.9		- 15.2	- 400.3	168.8	-4 664.0	السودان
Syrian Arab Republic[(2)]	- 33.5	116.6	2 138.0	319.2	214.0	1 169.0	21.1	—	6.3	368.2	106.8		- 133.1	148.3	4 440.9	الجمهورية العربية السورية[(2)]
United Arab Emirates[(1)]	1 055.3	410.5	2 929.4	- 97.4	552.6	136.8	454.2	- 4.5	2586.7	-2 914.2	132.6	111.2		270.2	5 623.4	الإمارات العربية المتحدة[(1)]
Yemen	- 10.0	- 104.1	17.2	- 31.2	- 471.5	- 11.6	- 46.4	- 0.1	- 6.6	- 302.7	- 3.7	- 61.9	-1 306.7		-2 339.4	اليمن

(1) Excluding oil. (1) باستثناء النفط

(2) Excluding re-exports. (2) باستثناء إعادة التصدير.

الجدول 2-7- مصفوفة قيمة الميزان التجاري البيني للبلدان الأعضاء في الإسكوا

Table II .7. Matrix of intraregional balance of trade of ESCWA member countries

2009

(Millions of US dollars) (مليون دولار أمريكي)

Between	Bahrain البحرين	Egypt مصر	Iraq العراق	Jordan الأردن	Kuwait الكويت	Lebanon لبنان	Oman عُمان	Palestine فلسطين	Qatar قطر	Saudi Arabia المملكة العربية السعودية	Sudan السودان	Syrian Arab Republic الجمهورية العربية السورية	United Arab Emirates الإمارات العربية المتحدة	Yemen اليمن	Total مجموع	بين
Bahrain		25.1	24.4	41.3	- 53.3	- 10.0	46.7	0.1	185.8	386.1	2.1	42.9	- 61.5	10.0	639.7	البحرين
Egypt	- 4.3		362.5	853.2	111.8	346.1	65.1	79.9	220.2	- 689.2	514.7	505.9	119.3	155.0	2 640.1	مصر
Iraq	..	..		..	..	..	..	..	..	..	..	..	..	..	..	العراق
Jordan	- 36.2	- 743.9	1 266.1		9.7	101.5	21.0	17.9	60.1	- 473.0	69.5	- 73.6	- 80.1	31.9	170.8	الأردن
Kuwait	43.0	- 142.3	131.1	155.6		- 79.2	- 9.1	- 1.0	114.2	- 763.5	12.5	- 21.0	- 281.6	3.2	- 838.1	الكويت
Lebanon	8.9	- 346.0	269.1	- 84.2	- 213.3		3.2	—	66.0	- 67.1	5.9	- 8.2	71.6	9.0	- 285.2	لبنان
Oman[(1) (2)]	- 72.7	- 67.9	107.5	1.9	- 177.7	- 4.6		1.0	52.8	- 283.4	27.0	15.4	-2 638.7	56.4	-2 983.0	عُمان[(1)(2)]
Palestine	0.1	- 32.4	0.9	- 19.3	0.9	—	- 0.7		0.2	1.2	—	—	- 4.5	0.1	- 53.5	فلسطين
Qatar	- 337.5	- 260.7	6.8	26.5	31.5	- 109.9	- 117.6	1.0		- 970.2	28.8	- 20.7	871.8	7.8	- 842.4	قطر
Saudi Arabia	..	..	..	..	..	..	..	..	..		..	..	..	..	..	المملكة العربية السعودية
Sudan	- 10.2	- 316.7	48.8	- 70.7	- 17.4	- 5.8	- 35.7	—	- 3.0	- 386.5		- 30.6	- 119.3	- 64.1	-1 011.2	السودان
Syrian Arab Republic[(2)]	- 24.3	- 502.5	2 618.8	169.7	75.7	195.3	12.4	—	67.1	- 29.3	77.9		- 30.4	83.7	2 714.1	الجمهورية العربية السورية[(2)]
United Arab Emirates[(1)]	649.3	- 41.5	3 422.9	- 78.6	740.4	275.2	370.1	- 2.7	2237.5	- 791.4	- 181.1	79.2		- 214.2	6 465.2	الإمارات العربية المتحدة[(1)]
Yemen	- 4.8	- 121.6	12.2	- 28.4	- 293.9	- 8.2	- 48.2	- 0.2	- 5.6	- 291.4	2.6	- 35.9	- 537.3		-1 360.9	اليمن

(1) Excluding oil. (1) باستثناء النفط

(2) Excluding re-exports. (2) باستثناء إعادة التصدير.

الجدول 2-7- مصفوفة قيمة الميزان التجاري البيني للبلدان الأعضاء في الإسكوا

(Millions of US dollars) (مليون دولار أمريكي)

Between	Bahrain البحرين	Egypt مصر	Iraq العراق	Jordan الأردن	Kuwait الكويت	Lebanon لبنان	Oman عُمان	Palestine فلسطين	Qatar قطر	Saudi Arabia المملكة العربية السعودية	Sudan السودان	Syrian Arab Republic الجمهورية العربية السورية	United Arab Emirates الإمارات العربية المتحدة	Yemen اليمن	Total مجموع	بين
Bahrain		92.2	20.9	21.5	25.2	2.2	120.8	0.2	561.3	676.0	4.8	60.6	- 7.8	15.1	1 593.0	البحرين
Egypt	- 54.9		412.5	610.4	51.6	430.6	30.9	93.3	168.2	- 450.1	632.0	458.3	- 91.4	146.6	2 437.9	مصر
Iraq [(1)]	- 2.6	- 74.1		- 145.5	- 642.6	- 444.4	- 21.6	- 0.2	- 8.0	- 297.8	- 0.1	- 209.2	- 673.2	- 6.3	-2 525.7	العراق [(1)]
Jordan	- 206.8	- 549.6	1 109.9		- 34.2	123.7	20.0	29.1	82.3	- 667.4	55.4	- 119.2	- 109.0	35.0	- 230.6	الأردن
Kuwait	- 31.3	- 177.6	84.1	108.0		- 61.7	- 6.5	- 1.3	36.3	- 710.6	15.1	- 20.4	- 402.3	0.6	-1 167.7	الكويت
Lebanon	10.0	- 229.0	263.7	- 123.9	- 284.0		1.0	—	59.3	- 160.7	- 6.5	- 118.6	48.8	10.9	- 528.9	لبنان
Oman [(1) (2)]	- 204.3	- 40.6	104.8	10.4	- 203.1	- 25.1		1.5	104.8	- 148.8	30.6	12.1	-3 759.7	58.2	-4 059.1	عُمان [(1) (2)]
Palestine	- 0.2	- 33.8	0.8	- 36.2	2.0	—	- 1.4		- 1.8	- 5.5	—	—	5.2	0.4	- 70.3	فلسطين
Qatar	- 369.7	- 79.3	24.2	132.6	144.5	- 35.2	- 77.2	- 0.3		- 156.3	45.5	1.2	2 508.8	163.0	2 301.8	قطر
Saudi Arabia	..	..	..	..	..	..	..	..	..		..	..	..	..	..	المملكة العربية السعودية
Sudan	- 14.8	- 506.1	49.9	- 45.6	- 18.0	- 17.7	- 19.6	—	- 21.6	- 482.1		- 138.3	- 229.0	- 172.3	-1 615.3	السودان
Syrian Arab Republic [(2)]	- 38.6	- 419.2	2 252.1	228.1	105.0	252.8	0.2	—	3.3	- 260.2	61.5		- 134.6	76.9	2 127.3	الجمهورية العربية السورية [(2)]
United Arab Emirates [(1)]	1 232.3	28.2	3 333.3	- 53.2	818.0	68.5	238.7	- 5.2	1207.3	- 765.5	- 888.0	11.7		- 2.3	5 223.9	الإمارات العربية المتحدة [(1)]
Yemen	- 26.2	- 153.5	15.6	- 44.4	- 303.7	- 9.1	- 196.4	- 0.2	- 19.5	- 516.5	1.4	- 56.1	-1 237.8		-2 546.5	اليمن

(1) Excluding oil. (1) باستثناء النفط.

(2) Excluding re-exports. (2) باستثناء إعادة التصدير.

الجدول 2-7- مصفوفة قيمة الميزان التجاري البيني للبلدان الأعضاء في الإسكوا

Table II .7. Matrix of intraregional balance of trade of ESCWA member countries 2011

(Millions of US dollars) (مليون دولار أمريكي)

Between	Bahrain البحرين	Egypt مصر	Iraq العراق	Jordan الأردن	Kuwait الكويت	Lebanon لبنان	Oman عُمان	Palestine فلسطين	Qatar قطر	Saudi Arabia المملكة العربية السعودية	Sudan السودان	Syrian Arab Republic الجمهورية العربية السورية	United Arab Emirates الإمارات العربية المتحدة	Yemen اليمن	Total مجموع	بين
Bahrain		48.3	27.2	40.9	70.9	- 6.1	723.4	0.2	684.2	1 017.5	10.3	61.4	8.5	10.5	2 697.3	البحرين
Egypt	- 15.9		442.9	671.4	- 837.2	860.9	10.6	79.5	164.4	- 650.3	486.5	275.8	28.3	97.1	1 613.9	مصر
Iraq [(1)]	- 8.3	- 180.5		- 433.1	- 410.0	- 76.9	- 20.4	—	- 3.3	- 656.9	- 0.2	- 516.6	- 470.6	- 7.5	-2 784.3	العراق [(1)]
Jordan	- 102.5	- 627.8	1 176.2		11.6	221.3	- 34.6	47.0	70.8	-1 158.2	44.1	- 91.2	- 421.5	3.9	- 861.0	الأردن
Kuwait	- 60.4	- 208.1	57.4	- 2.6		- 73.4	- 221.3	- 1.9	- 20.6	- 753.9	4.9	- 41.4	- 916.8	- 2.7	-2 240.9	الكويت
Lebanon	4.2	- 874.8	193.2	- 234.7	- 225.9		1.2	—	46.8	- 223.7	2.5	- 95.3	- 271.8	11.5	-1 666.8	لبنان
Oman [(1) (2)]	- 355.9	- 17.6	147.6	5.0	85.2	- 5.2		1.4	- 217.4	- 558.9	24.8	16.8	-4 763.7	41.7	-5 596.2	عُمان [(1) (2)]
Palestine	- 0.2	- 33.0	0.2	- 51.1	4.1	—	- 1.7		- 1.1	- 13.4	—	—	1.8	0.1	- 94.2	فلسطين
Qatar	- 384.6	7.3	117.1	55.4	682.8	- 65.3	143.4	- 2.5		- 307.9	40.2	26.3	2 514.9	74.9	2 902.0	قطر
Saudi Arabia	..	..	..	..	..	..	..	..	..		..	..	..	..	..	المملكة العربية السعودية
Sudan	- 25.0	- 424.4	25.7	- 54.1	- 7.3	- 7.6	- 51.6	—	- 47.8	- 501.5		- 17.4	67.1	- 45.3	-1 089.1	السودان
Syrian Arab Republic [(2)]	- 52.3	- 415.9	1 866.1	104.5	58.2	306.6	0.7	—	- 119.3	- 376.9	19.5		- 153.9	46.9	1 284.0	الجمهورية العربية السورية [(2)]
United Arab Emirates [(1)]	659.5	- 3.4	1 907.2	94.5	1 316.0	153.0	- 33.5	- 7.3	1035.2	- 926.6	-1 611.6	- 16.2		48.2	2 615.0	الإمارات العربية المتحدة [(1)]
Yemen	- 13.8	- 118.5	10.6	- 26.9	- 380.1	- 17.2	- 147.0	- 0.3	- 16.6	- 627.5	- 7.5	- 37.6	-1 321.3		-2 703.7	اليمن

(1) Excluding oil. (1) باستثناء النفط.

(2) Excluding re-exports. (2) باستثناء إعادة التصدير.

الجدول 2-7- مصفوفة قيمة الميزان التجاري البيني للبلدان الأعضاء في الإسكوا

Table II .7. Matrix of intraregional balance of trade of ESCWA member countries
2012

(Millions of US dollars) (مليون دولار أمريكي)

Between	Bahrain البحرين	Egypt مصر	Iraq العراق	Jordan الأردن	Kuwait الكويت	Lebanon لبنان	Libya ليبيا	Morocco المغرب	Oman عُمان	Palestine فلسطين	Qatar قطر	Saudi Arabia المملكة العربية السعودية	Sudan السودان	Syrian Arab Republic الجمهورية العربية السورية	Tunisia تونس	United Arab Emirates الإمارات العربية المتحدة	Yemen اليمن	Total (Arab region) القيمة الإجمالية (المنطقة العربية)	بين
Bahrain		29.1	30.4	39.4	34.7	- 4.0	13.8	115.1	234.7	0.4	576.2	1 163.8	9.2	24.1	11.0	- 265.6	19.6	2 031.8	البحرين
Egypt	- 10.8		570.4	654.1	- 779.7	720.1	1 342.6	297.0	21.5	53.6	172.1	- 795.2	456.6	145.3	- 29.6	- 102.7	206.7	2 922.1	مصر
Iraq(*)	- 17.2	- 110.9		- 193.3	- 228.9	- 82.7	—	3.7	- 45.5	—	- 22.1	- 251.3	- 0.1	- 188.2	- 2.0	- 533.7	- 2.6	-1 674.7	العراق(*)
Jordan	8.6	- 657.6	1 129.2		- 58.6	157.7	71.2	- 5.0	16.7	47.1	80.1	-1 588.4	22.5	- 21.3	6.9	- 274.4	10.0	-1 055.1	الأردن
Kuwait	- 34.3	- 233.7	88.0	41.0		- 90.1	4.8	- 15.6	- 37.5	- 3.2	14.0	- 729.3	14.1	- 53.1	- 13.1	-1 248.6	3.6	-2 293.1	الكويت
Lebanon	3.3	- 752.6	205.6	- 126.8	- 562.3		- 41.3	- 54.8	0.2	—	61.0	- 64.6	- 1.4	28.1	- 31.7	- 64.3	12.3	-1 389.1	لبنان
Libya	..	..	..	..	..	..		..	..	..	..	..	..	..	..	..	..	..	ليبيا
Morocco	- 46.8	- 277.3	4.4	27.2	- 39.1	28.0	57.7		- 25.9	0.7	- 135.6	- 656.7	50.7	22.1	- 119.4	- 313.2	16.5	-1 406.6	المغرب
Oman	- 244.2	6.1	715.0	13.4	- 130.8	- 12.8	15.4	52.1		1.1	- 56.6	- 171.5	16.6	25.0	2.9	-4 618.2	52.0	-4 334.5	عُمان
Palestine	- 1.7	- 33.1	0.3	- 39.9	5.8	—	—	- 0.1	- 0.2		0.8	- 23.6	0.1	—	- 0.2	5.7	0.9	- 85.2	فلسطين
Qatar	- 280.6	- 113.3	183.0	98.9	633.6	- 64.1	6.4	104.6	212.1	- 9.4		118.8	50.4	- 25.5	17.2	3 773.6	44.3	4 749.7	قطر
Saudi Arabia	..	..	..	..	..	..	..	..	..	..	..		..	..	..	..	..	..	المملكة العربية السعودية
Sudan	- 46.5	- 428.6	—	- 44.3	- 13.8	3.1	0.9	- 3.4	- 8.2	—	- 17.8	- 459.6		- 11.2	4.9	1 339.1	- 23.7	291.0	السودان
Syrian Arab Republic	..	..	..	..	..	..	..	..	..	..	..	..	..		..	..	..	..	الجمهورية العربية السورية
Tunisia	- 8.3	- 169.0	11.9	- 6.2	- 26.7	- 0.5	769.5	83.7	- 8.9	—	- 11.0	- 196.8	- 15.3	13.4		- 33.9	6.2	408.2	تونس
United Arab Emirates	1 118.7	190.1	5.1	153.7	1 225.1	- 11.9	173.3	- 49.0	2 984.7	- 10.6	1433.9	95.1	-2 822.7	- 42.8	37.3		179.6	4 659.5	الإمارات العربية المتحدة
Yemen	- 14.1	- 166.0	4.7	- 18.7	- 335.7	- 10.8	3.4	- 8.6	- 52.9	- 0.8	- 12.5	- 398.0	7.5	- 48.3	- 5.3	-1 012.3		-2 068.3	اليمن

(*) Excluding oil.

(*) باستثناء النفط.

الجدول 2-7- مصفوفة قيمة الميزان التجاري البيني للبلدان الأعضاء في الإسكوا

Table II .7. Matrix of intraregional balance of trade of ESCWA member countries
2013

(Millions of US dollars) (مليون دولار أمريكي)

Between	Bahrain البحرين	Egypt مصر	Iraq العراق	Jordan الأردن	Kuwait الكويت	Lebanon لبنان	Libya ليبيا	Morocco المغرب	Oman عُمان	Palestine فلسطين	Qatar قطر	Saudi Arabia المملكة العربية السعودية	Sudan السودان	Syrian Arab Republic الجمهورية العربية السورية	Tunisia تونس	United Arab Emirates الإمارات العربية المتحدة	Yemen اليمن	Total (Arab region) القيمة الإجمالية (المنطقة العربية)	بين
Bahrain		62.7	40.6	105.1	123.7	- 1.8	41.0	152.1	397.4	4.5	187.2	3 104.6	- 0.2	- 2.2	21.2	603.4	21.0	4 860.3	البحرين
Egypt	- 164.1		733.1	729.1	- 604.9	594.2	1 177.4	338.5	- 25.1	83.1	177.6	-1 064.1	459.5	68.6	159.7	- 348.4	198.6	2 512.9	مصر
Iraq	..	..		..	..	..	..	..	..	..	..	..	..	..	..	..	..	..	العراق
Jordan	—	- 570.9	1 357.2		- 29.4	- 8.7	67.5	- 10.7	21.9	66.7	96.8	- 798.9	35.2	- 107.4	- 59.3	- 415.3	- 0.9	- 356.2	الأردن
Kuwait	- 130.2	- 284.7	576.9	49.4	0.0	- 98.8	5.2	- 18.9	- 376.4	- 3.2	31.4	- 704.2	18.2	- 26.6	- 19.9	-1 771.9	9.8	-2 743.9	الكويت
Lebanon	6.0	- 571.1	269.9	- 3.6	- 377.9		- 30.5	- 59.1	- 4.0	—	61.6	- 93.2	- 15.9	342.3	- 18.1	- 48.0	16.5	- 525.1	لبنان
Libya	..	..	..	..	..	..		..	..	..	..	..	..	..	..	..	..	..	ليبيا
Morocco	- 61.5	- 272.4	10.2	14.7	- 33.2	44.5	71.8	0.0	- 13.6	2.3	- 94.2	- 603.6	8.5	21.9	- 135.0	- 255.0	23.4	-1 271.2	المغرب
Oman	- 128.2	45.9	10.9	4.1	192.1	15.8	120.5	4.2		1.0	- 838.9	339.7	22.3	6.1	12.3	-5 158.4	171.8	-5 179.0	عُمان
Palestine	- 5.9	- 43.3	0.3	- 33.9	3.3	—	0.6	- 0.5	- 0.9		- 6.6	- 35.6	0.1	—	- 0.2	- 8.4	0.9	- 129.9	فلسطين
Qatar	- 55.7	- 177.4	180.3	145.4	916.6	- 77.9	15.4	99.7	227.4	- 5.3		- 82.7	21.2	- 27.5	9.7	3 850.1	4.7	5 044.1	قطر
Saudi Arabia	..	..	..	..	..	..	..	..	..	..	..		..	..	..	..	..	..	المملكة العربية السعودية
Sudan	..	..	..	..	..	..	..	..	..	..	..	..		..	..	..	..	..	السودان
Syrian Arab Republic	..	..	..	..	..	..	..	..	..	..	..	..	..		..	..	..	..	الجمهورية العربية السورية
Tunisia	- 9.4	- 169.0	11.9	- 6.6	- 15.5	—	643.1	96.3	- 0.9	—	- 14.6	- 224.6	- 16.7	10.2		- 51.5	5.5	258.2	تونس
United Arab Emirates	1 172.5	890.7	2 724.7	203.4	1 524.4	289.6	578.5	56.5	2 922.8	- 3.9	1670.2	1 586.1	-1 497.2	32.0	16.8		535.2	12 702.1	الإمارات العربية المتحدة
Yemen	335.1	- 168.9	5.0	- 5.0	- 506.7	- 15.3	0.4	- 8.0	- 61.7	- 0.8	- 2.7	- 624.0	- 6.5	- 24.9	- 3.0	-1 896.4	0.0	-2 983.4	اليمن

الجدول 2-7- مصفوفة قيمة الميزان التجاري البيني لبلدان الإسكوا

Table II .7. Matrix of intraregional balance of trade of ESCWA member countries
2014

(Millions of US dollars) (مليون دولار أمريكي)

Between	Bahrain البحرين	Egypt مصر	Iraq العراق	Jordan الأردن	Kuwait الكويت	Lebanon لبنان	Libya ليبيا	Morocco المغرب	Oman عُمان	Palestine فلسطين	Qatar قطر	Saudi Arabia المملكة العربية السعودية	Sudan السودان	Syrian Arab Republic الجمهورية العربية السورية	Tunisia تونس	United Arab Emirates الإمارات العربية المتحدة	Yemen اليمن	Total (Arab region) القيمة الإجمالية (المنطقة العربية)	بين
Bahrain		172.2	99.0	24.7	89.3	23.7	12.3	169.2	97.9	5.8	457.6	2 146.0	14.5	1.4	16.8	329.9	21.3	3 681.7	البحرين
Egypt	- 110.8		773.8	235.2	- 568.3	493.9	940.2	370.6	- 33.8	141.4	260.1	- 756.7	280.1	237.4	126.4	- 729.8	167.4	1 827.2	مصر
Iraq	..	..		..	..	..	..	..	..	..	..	..	..	..	..	..	..	..	العراق
Jordan	- 17.4	- 411.6	1 278.1		35.2	25.1	44.0	- 8.6	37.7	68.7	100.1	-1 100.9	26.5	71.5	9.1	- 760.5	11.3	- 591.8	الأردن
Kuwait	- 171.7	- 306.1	683.0	1.1		- 135.3	2.4	- 28.3	- 386.8	- 6.0	84.2	- 824.5	0.9	- 20.7	- 12.0	-2 113.4	9.1	-3 224.0	الكويت
Lebanon	17.6	- 445.2	252.3	- 15.6	- 177.5		- 38.4	- 99.3	- 0.3	—	68.9	- 38.0	- 26.3	117.2	- 24.4	- 52.6	10.8	- 450.8	لبنان
Libya	..	..	..	..	..	..		..	..	..	..	..	..	..	..	..	..	..	ليبيا
Morocco	- 76.8	- 414.1	6.7	13.0	- 73.3	58.6	14.3		- 32.7	1.9	- 65.6	- 616.5	36.3	37.3	- 109.0	- 360.0	16.5	-1 563.2	المغرب
Oman	- 93.9	102.5	58.1	- 19.4	287.7	- 22.4	11.3	8.5		1.4	- 191.2	- 65.8	24.0	5.9	2.8	-7 490.9	69.4	-7 312.0	عُمان
Palestine	- 3.1	- 54.7	0.5	- 35.5	7.9	—	—	- 0.6	- 1.7		- 4.4	- 53.8	0.2	—	- 0.5	- 18.4	1.5	- 162.5	فلسطين
Qatar	37.4	- 241.3	167.4	206.3	536.8	- 74.9	7.7	52.5	90.1	- 6.7		- 230.1	27.9	- 17.4	13.3	4 133.6	8.6	4 711.3	قطر
Saudi Arabia	-1 937.6	-2 243.8	- 1.3	- 929.9	- 524.0	- 394.9	- 0.5	- 169.9	-1 449.4	-11.2	- 562.4		- 580.8	- 117.6	- 47.7	-8 271.8	- 269.1	-17 512.0	المملكة العربية السعودية
Sudan	..	..	..	..	..	..	..	..	..	..	..	..		..	..	..	..	..	السودان
Syrian Arab Republic	..	..	..	..	..	..	..	..	..	..	..	..	..		..	..	..	..	الجمهورية العربية السورية
Tunisia	..	..	..	..	..	..	..	..	..	..	..	..	..	..		..	..	..	تونس
United Arab Emirates	880.1	927.8	5 637.2	262.1	1 992.3	405.2	121.2	159.0	3 573.0	- 3.8	1830.8	1 632.9	-1 398.9	155.6	94.5		383.2	16 652.2	الإمارات العربية المتحدة
Yemen	- 20.7	- 204.4	1.3	- 23.0	- 6.7	- 12.7	0.7	- 10.5	- 7.9	- 1.3	- 4.9	- 315.6	6.0	- 16.1	- 2.6	- 482.5		-1 100.9	اليمن

الجزء الثالث

اتجاه التجارة الخارجية للبلدان الأعضاء في الإسكوا

Part III

DIRECTION OF EXTERNAL TRADE OF ESCWA MEMBER COUNTRIES

الجدول 3-1- البحرين: الواردات والصادرات حسب أهم البلدان والكتل الاقتصادية

Table III.1. Bahrain: Imports and exports by main countries and economic groupings 2010-2014

(Millions of US dollars) (مليون دولار أمريكي)

	Imports					Exports[1]					
	2010	2011	2012	2013	2014	2010	2011	2012	2013	2014	
World	**16 002.2**	**17 573.2**	**19 822.2**	**18 584.0**	**20 044.2**	**16 059.2**	**22 416.7**	**21 928.2**	**25 500.1**	**23 404.6**	العالم
Developed countries	**4 349.1**	**4 144.7**	**4 504.1**	**4 187.8**	**5 315.5**	**767.5**	**1 009.9**	**1 032.1**	**1 552.4**	**1 449.4**	البلدان المتقدمة النمو
Developing countries and territories	**5 788.7**	**5 977.9**	**6 383.1**	**5 906.8**	**7 230.0**	**3 774.3**	**5 943.4**	**5 687.0**	**8 713.4**	**7 503.4**	البلدان والأقاليم النامية
Oil trade (2)	**5 858.8**	**7 439.7**	**8 930.9**	**8 452.5**	**7 410.5**	**11 504.8**	**15 429.1**	**15 194.0**	**15 231.2**	**14 443.4**	النفط[2]
Other countries[3]	**5.7**	**10.9**	**4.2**	**37.0**	**88.2**	**12.6**	**34.2**	**15.1**	**3.1**	**8.4**	بلدان أخرى[3]
Europe	**2 130.3**	**2 346.5**	**2 280.1**	**2 149.8**	**2 569.4**	**392.3**	**549.5**	**375.7**	**434.6**	**373.8**	أوروبا
Developed countries[4]	**2 051.3**	**2 082.0**	**2 111.6**	**2 020.7**	**2 383.4**	**386.4**	**514.6**	**362.4**	**414.7**	**350.8**	البلدان المتقدمة النمو[4]
European Union	**1 947.3**	**2 030.8**	**1 988.6**	**1 847.9**	**2 262.7**	**361.2**	**500.4**	**321.9**	**387.7**	**331.4**	الاتحاد الأوروبي
Developed countries	**1 876.0**	**1 903.6**	**1 866.4**	**1 748.8**	**2 096.9**	**358.4**	**490.7**	**320.0**	**382.6**	**323.9**	البلدان المتقدمة النمو
Austria	23.3	23.0	33.9	24.8	32.7	0.1	0.1	2.8	2.2	12.8	النمسا
Belgium	50.0	59.8	52.4	57.6	63.8	3.3	3.6	3.7	6.4	32.8	بلجيكا
Denmark	34.4	27.9	27.7	22.5	30.5	0.4	6.2	11.9	26.3	2.3	الدانمرك
Finland	11.6	11.9	10.4	9.1	17.5	21.9	10.3	5.2	1.8	1.2	فنلندا
France	270.6	240.9	179.8	222.1	255.2	49.2	42.0	22.0	30.6	23.3	فرنسا
Germany	538.7	498.0	559.3	508.0	580.0	51.7	45.6	24.6	21.8	27.7	المانيا
Greece	7.1	5.6	11.0	10.5	11.5	6.6	0.4	1.3	2.1	0.2	اليونان
Ireland	48.9	68.5	53.1	44.7	57.1	—	0.2	0.2	0.2	0.4	آيرلندا
Italy	240.6	311.9	321.7	293.4	343.9	103.4	158.3	43.5	114.0	75.6	ايطاليا
Luxembourg	1.1	1.2	2.8	2.6	1.1	—	0.1	0.7	0.8	—	لكسمبرغ
Netherlands	142.5	131.7	100.7	101.8	136.8	77.1	141.3	155.3	109.9	93.9	هولندا
Portugal	6.4	9.7	8.9	8.5	16.4	0.8	4.1	—	6.9	—	البرتغال
Spain	93.3	174.1	129.5	92.6	97.9	24.6	32.6	5.3	17.7	10.5	اسبانيا
Sweden	27.7	32.1	33.9	39.4	112.8	0.3	4.6	12.7	5.0	1.2	السويد
United Kingdom of Great Britain and Northern Ireland	379.7	307.4	341.2	311.0	339.7	19.0	41.4	30.7	36.8	42.0	المملكة المتحدة لبريطانيا العظمى وأيرلندا الشمالية
Developing countries	**71.3**	**127.2**	**122.2**	**99.1**	**165.8**	**2.8**	**9.7**	**1.9**	**5.1**	**7.5**	البلدان النامية
Bulgaria	0.6	1.8	3.0	2.6	4.8	0.3	—	0.2	—	—	بلغاريا
Cyprus	3.5	4.5	2.8	4.5	6.3	0.2	0.4	0.6	0.8	0.9	قبرص
Czech Republic	15.4	14.0	17.2	14.4	26.9	0.3	7.0	—	—	0.1	الجمهورية التشيكية
Hungary	14.6	55.3	32.0	15.2	12.7	0.5	0.5	0.1	0.1	—	هنغاريا
Poland	16.2	25.9	35.1	27.4	42.6	1.0	0.3	0.6	3.0	3.2	بولندا
Romania	9.6	10.9	8.6	10.0	33.7	0.1	0.4	0.3	0.7	1.4	رومانيا
Slovakia	6.5	10.3	14.3	14.3	13.7	—	—	—	—	—	سلوفاكيا
Others	4.8	4.6	9.4	10.7	25.1	0.3	1.2	0.1	0.5	1.9	غيرها
European Free Trade Association (EFTA)	**174.9**	**178.2**	**241.0**	**266.0**	**284.0**	**25.7**	**23.9**	**42.4**	**32.1**	**26.5**	الرابطة الأوروبية للتجارة الحرة
Norway	6.6	16.1	4.7	22.8	35.1	7.0	10.4	17.7	21.7	5.8	النرويج
Switzerland	167.6	161.8	236.0	243.1	248.5	18.3	13.6	24.6	10.4	20.7	سويسرا
Others	0.6	0.3	0.3	0.1	0.4	0.4	—	—	—	—	غيرها
Other developed countries	**0.4**	**0.2**	**4.2**	**5.8**	**2.5**	**2.3**	—	—	—	**0.3**	بلدان أوروبية متقدمة أخرى

الجدول 3-1- البحرين: الواردات والصادرات حسب أهم البلدان والكتل الاقتصادية

Table III.1. Bahrain: Imports and exports by main countries and economic groupings
2010-2014

(Millions of US dollars)	Imports					Exports[1]					(مليون دولار أمريكي)
	2010	2011	2012	2013	2014	2010	2011	2012	2013	2014	
Developing countries[5]	**79.0**	**264.5**	**168.5**	**129.2**	**185.9**	**5.9**	**34.8**	**13.4**	**19.9**	**23.0**	**البلدان النامية[5]**
Bosnia and Herzegovina	0.1	0.1	0.2	0.4	0.6	—	16.9	—	—	—	البوسنة والهرسك
Russian Federation	1.8	131.9	41.0	11.8	5.5	1.9	6.2	9.0	13.2	14.6	الاتحاد الروسي
Ukraine	5.5	4.1	2.7	15.5	10.2	1.0	1.8	0.3	0.3	0.1	أوكرانيا
Other developing countries	**0.4**	**1.2**	**2.4**	**2.4**	**3.9**	**0.3**	**0.1**	**2.2**	**1.3**	**0.9**	بلدان اوروبية نامية اخرى
America	**2 683.5**	**2 286.5**	**1 874.1**	**1 406.6**	**1 706.9**	**244.4**	**432.1**	**577.6**	**817.3**	**998.3**	**أمريكا**
Developed countries	**802.4**	**938.4**	**1 003.2**	**847.1**	**1 002.7**	**237.4**	**300.6**	**513.2**	**766.2**	**941.4**	**البلدان المتقدمة النمو**
Canada	85.1	106.9	106.5	68.9	55.9	1.1	0.7	13.3	67.9	29.2	كندا
United States of America	717.3	831.5	896.6	778.2	946.8	236.3	299.9	499.9	698.3	912.3	الولايات المتحدة الأمريكية
Developing countries	**1 881.1**	**1 348.1**	**871.0**	**559.5**	**704.2**	**7.0**	**131.5**	**64.3**	**51.2**	**56.8**	**البلدان النامية**
Latin American Integration Association (LAIA)	1 876.7	1 342.6	856.7	534.6	694.2	6.7	126.4	53.4	49.7	56.2	**رابطة التكامل لأمريكا اللاتينية**
Argentina	6.3	24.8	26.8	12.1	10.7	—	0.5	1.0	0.5	0.9	الأرجنتين
Bolivia	—	—	—	—	0.1	0.6	—	—	—	—	بوليفيا
Brazil	1 828.6	1 253.0	659.9	343.7	463.8	0.6	22.7	33.3	26.7	53.8	البرازيل
Chile	2.7	6.9	93.2	119.6	170.1	0.2	0.2	0.1	—	—	شيلي
Ecuador	0.7	0.9	1.2	1.5	1.6	0.4	—	—	—	—	اكوادور
Mexico	34.1	43.5	62.4	52.7	39.1	—	0.5	1.3	12.3	1.0	المكسيك
Others	4.4	13.6	13.2	5.0	8.8	4.8	102.5	17.7	10.1	0.6	غيرها
Other America	4.4	5.5	14.2	24.9	10.1	0.3	5.1	11.0	1.5	0.7	**بلدان أمريكية أخرى**
Oceania	**694.1**	**477.9**	**560.5**	**487.9**	**865.8**	**95.4**	**143.4**	**131.5**	**326.9**	**97.3**	**أوقيانوسيا**
Developed countries	**693.6**	**476.5**	**559.1**	**486.0**	**863.6**	**95.4**	**142.0**	**131.2**	**326.8**	**97.1**	**البلدان المتقدمة النمو**
Australia	626.1	420.3	507.8	453.5	806.5	76.1	108.9	104.9	108.9	93.9	استراليا
New Zealand	67.5	56.2	51.3	32.5	57.2	19.3	33.1	26.3	218.0	3.2	نيوزيلندا
Developing countries	**0.5**	**1.4**	**1.4**	**2.0**	**2.2**	**—**	**1.4**	**0.4**	**—**	**0.2**	**البلدان النامية**
Asia	**4 572.0**	**4 902.7**	**6 091.3**	**5 911.9**	**7 199.3**	**3 718.3**	**5 685.2**	**5 487.0**	**8 548.9**	**7 188.1**	**آسيا**
Developed countries: Japan	**753.9**	**586.9**	**784.8**	**785.7**	**1 035.1**	**25.1**	**22.7**	**19.7**	**33.7**	**31.9**	**البلدان المتقدمة النمو: اليابان**
Developing countries	**3 818.1**	**4 315.8**	**5 306.4**	**5 126.3**	**6 164.2**	**3 693.2**	**5 662.5**	**5 467.2**	**8 515.2**	**7 156.2**	**البلدان النامية**
ESCWA member countries	**1 137.9**	**1 505.5**	**2 052.3**	**2 225.7**	**2 603.3**	**2 844.6**	**4 325.2**	**4 084.1**	**7 086.0**	**6 284.9**	**البلدان الأعضاء في الإسكوا**
Asia Middle East (non ESCWA member countries)	**254.5**	**154.7**	**178.5**	**192.4**	**274.9**	**57.7**	**33.8**	**290.2**	**258.1**	**201.5**	**آسيا- الشرق الأوسط (ما عدا بلدان الإسكوا)**
Islamic Republic of Iran	43.6	7.9	25.3	15.6	18.3	30.3	9.5	89.1	5.3	5.8	جمهورية إيران الإسلامية
Turkey	210.9	146.8	153.3	176.9	256.6	27.5	24.3	201.1	252.8	195.7	تركيا

الجدول 3-1- البحرين: الواردات والصادرات حسب أهم البلدان والكتل الاقتصادية

Table III.1. Bahrain: Imports and exports by main countries and economic groupings
2010-2014

(Millions of US dollars)	Imports					Exports[1]					(مليون دولار أمريكي)
	2010	2011	2012	2013	2014	2010	2011	2012	2013	2014	
Association of Southeast Asian Nations (ASEAN)	**372.1**	**422.7**	**506.6**	**490.4**	**664.6**	**157.7**	**239.1**	**269.7**	**269.4**	**138.2**	**منظمة التجارة الحرة لرابطة أمم جنوب شرقي آسيا**
Indonesia	52.9	47.6	57.9	63.2	84.3	34.2	93.1	17.1	17.1	15.3	إندونيسيا
Malaysia	113.9	103.8	106.5	92.8	99.0	44.1	81.4	100.9	12.6	5.0	ماليزيا
Philippines	19.3	21.2	26.3	35.0	26.1	4.2	0.4	0.5	4.2	1.8	الفلبين
Singapore	49.1	44.2	36.8	39.1	101.5	42.1	40.3	84.3	130.8	79.9	سنغافورة
Thailand	125.8	185.7	185.0	223.5	250.0	30.8	22.4	54.0	96.4	32.8	تايلند
Others	11.1	20.1	94.0	36.7	103.6	2.3	1.4	13.0	8.3	3.4	غيرها
Other Asian countries	**2 053.6**	**2 232.9**	**2 569.0**	**2 217.8**	**2 621.5**	**633.1**	**1 064.4**	**823.3**	**901.7**	**531.5**	**بلدان آسيوية أخرى**
Afghanistan	0.1	0.1	—	0.1	0.2	3.0	—	0.5	0.6	0.2	أفغانستان
Bangladesh	3.7	6.9	10.8	14.9	23.1	1.9	4.0	3.2	12.0	60.9	بنغلاديش
China	1 178.0	1 361.6	1 360.0	1 336.0	1 615.9	173.2	383.1	369.3	509.3	145.8	الصين
Hong Kong	14.5	17.9	14.4	20.5	13.7	4.2	4.4	4.8	27.8	14.2	هونغ كونغ
India	345.9	394.9	622.0	395.5	504.4	402.9	487.3	324.0	229.2	167.2	الهند
Korea, Democratic People's Republic of	—	—	—	2.3	—	—	—	—	—	—	جمهورية كوريا الشعبية الديمقراطية
Korea, Republic of	363.7	263.5	371.5	241.3	247.8	23.0	26.2	22.1	80.9	63.0	جمهورية كوريا
Pakistan	85.4	88.2	80.9	102.1	115.6	18.2	68.1	74.8	18.7	16.5	باكستان
Sri Lanka	17.4	30.0	8.9	7.1	12.6	1.2	0.2	3.7	1.7	2.5	سري لانكا
Others	44.9	69.7	100.4	98.0	88.1	5.5	91.1	20.8	21.4	61.3	غيرها
Africa	**57.8**	**109.1**	**81.2**	**138.3**	**204.1**	**91.4**	**143.0**	**147.4**	**138.2**	**295.4**	**أفريقيا**
Developed countries: South Africa	**47.9**	**60.9**	**45.4**	**48.4**	**30.7**	**23.2**	**30.0**	**5.7**	**11.0**	**28.2**	**البلدان المتقدمة النمو: جنوب أفريقيا**
Developing countries	**9.9**	**48.2**	**35.8**	**89.9**	**173.4**	**68.2**	**113.0**	**141.7**	**127.1**	**267.2**	**البلدان النامية**
Arab countries[6]	**1.3**	**1.8**	**11.1**	**23.9**	**5.3**	**52.3**	**64.6**	**120.3**	**79.2**	**221.2**	**البلدان العربية[6]**
Algeria	1.0	0.1	0.2	0.1	1.0	51.6	63.1	120.1	78.6	220.8	الجزائر
Djibouti	—	—	0.8	4.7	0.2	0.5	0.6	0.2	0.5	0.4	جيبوتي
Somalia	0.2	1.6	9.8	18.9	4.0	—	—	—	0.1	0.1	الصومال
Others	—	0.1	0.3	0.2	0.1	0.2	0.9	—	—	—	غيرها
Central African Customs and Economic Union (CACEU)	2.0	2.7	1.2	4.7	4.8	2.0	—	0.8	1.1	0.2	الاتحاد الجمركي والاقتصادي لوسط أفريقيا
Economic Community of West African States (ECOWAS)	1.9	1.9	6.1	6.4	98.3	4.2	6.7	11.6	6.8	2.2	الجماعة الاقتصادية لدول غرب أفريقيا
Other Africa	4.8	41.8	17.4	55.0	65.0	9.7	41.7	9.0	40.0	43.5	**بلدان أفريقية أخرى**

(1) Export values include re-exports.
(2) Values are not disaggregated by crude oil imports or Oil trades.
(3) Including values of ship and aircraft supplies.
(4) Including EU developed countries, EFTA countries, and other developed countries.
(5) Including EU developing countries.
(6) Except Egypt, Libya, Morroco, Tunisia and Sudan, which are included under "ESCWA member countries",

(1) بما في ذلك قيم إعادة التصدير.
(2) لم تفصل قيم واردات النفط الخام وصادرات النفط.
(3) بما في ذلك قيم تموين السفن والطائرات.
(4) بما في ذلك البلدان المتقدمة في الاتحاد الأوروبي والرابطة الأوروبية للتجارة الحرة، والبلدان المتقدمة الأخرى.
(5) بما في ذلك البلدان النامية في الاتحاد الأوروبي.
(6) باستثناء تونس، والسودان، وليبيا، ومصر، والمغرب التي أدرجت في بند البلدان الأعضاء في الإسكوا.

الجدول 3-2- مصر: الواردات والصادرات حسب أهم البلدان والكتل الاقتصادية

Table III.2. Egypt: Imports and exports by main countries and economic groupings, 2010-2014

(Millions of US dollars) (مليون دولار أمريكي)

	Imports					Exports[1]					
	2010	2011	2012	2013	2014	2010	2011	2012	2013	2014	
World	52 871.0	59 269.0	71 469.2	66 397.1	71 337.7	27 120.6	30 782.0	30 777.7	28 788.9	26 812.2	العالم
Developed countries	23 232.0	25 928.8	28 328.1	27 784.6	27 919.1	10 492.5	12 272.8	11 913.1	9 824.2	9 200.3	البلدان المتقدمة النمو
Developing countries and territories	29 566.7	33 226.8	43 138.4	38 504.4	43 404.0	15 577.5	17 372.5	17 627.5	18 026.4	16 747.8	البلدان والأقاليم النامية
Oil trade	1 317.5	1 709.2	2 933.3	2 028.6	3 044.0	1 763.6	3 030.0	3 022.6	3 059.5	3 050.5	النفط
Other countries[2]	72.3	113.4	2.7	108.0	14.6	1 050.6	1 136.7	1 237.1	938.3	864.1	بلدان أخرى[2]
Europe	21 638.2	22 452.5	30 032.0	27 718.1	29 671.6	8 803.2	10 408.4	8 684.5	8 585.3	8 373.5	أوروبا
Developed countries[3]	15 556.9	16 974.0	20 000.0	19 968.7	20 022.2	8064.8	9192.4	7661.0	7296.4	7022.8	البلدان المتقدمة النمو[3]
European Union	17 076.0	17 411.1	20 874.0	21 159.6	22 357.7	8 064.1	9 624.7	7 985.4	8 092.9	7 882.9	الاتحاد الأوروبي
Developed countries	**14 719.3**	**16 061.8**	**19 098.9**	**18 550.8**	**18 887.3**	**7 647.6**	**8 905.9**	**7 302.7**	**7 174.1**	**6 969.4**	البلدان المتقدمة النمو
Austria	204.7	203.4	204.9	236.3	268.2	56.0	21.5	15.5	13.1	18.0	النمسا
Belgium	859.2	1 299.1	1 712.9	1 203.9	981.7	358.6	567.3	403.5	447.6	345.5	بلجيكا
Denmark	187.2	225.5	268.4	218.6	206.9	14.9	27.2	18.5	12.8	14.8	الدانمرك
Finland	350.0	357.6	502.7	402.6	469.0	30.6	23.2	17.5	13.3	13.5	فنلندا
France	1 880.7	1 969.2	2 354.4	2 116.8	2 135.0	923.0	1 289.7	1 074.6	964.5	834.4	فرنسا
Germany	4 012.8	3 755.7	4 772.3	5 210.0	5 540.1	579.8	774.2	658.6	638.6	670.4	ألمانيا
Greece	416.0	388.3	380.1	705.8	646.1	258.0	400.9	235.7	270.5	471.9	اليونان
Ireland	196.6	164.0	177.3	168.8	209.1	28.5	25.4	48.6	31.0	25.3	أيرلندا
Italy	2 954.3	3 017.5	3 528.8	3 541.3	3 265.4	2 217.1	2 682.3	2 366.9	2 702.8	2 454.5	ايطاليا
Luxembourg	4.6	7.0	5.9	7.6	6.4	0.1	0.3	0.7	2.3	0.8	لكسمبرغ
Netherlands	829.2	1 639.4	1 467.5	1 082.9	1 069.0	580.2	702.2	414.3	306.7	382.9	هولندا
Portugal	76.4	111.0	80.7	81.7	97.6	96.3	89.1	106.3	132.5	106.8	البرتغال
Spain	845.6	1 054.6	1 398.2	1 505.3	1 519.5	1 650.6	1 297.1	1 039.3	635.7	582.3	اسبانيا
Sweden	621.6	689.9	943.3	660.0	843.6	41.6	39.0	37.0	32.8	37.4	السويد
United Kingdom of Great Britain and Northern Ireland	1 280.4	1 179.6	1 301.4	1 409.2	1 629.9	812.4	966.4	865.8	969.9	1 011.0	المملكة المتحدة لبريطانيا العظمى وأيرلندا الشمالية
Developing countries	**2 356.7**	**1 349.3**	**1 775.1**	**2 608.9**	**3 470.4**	**416.5**	**718.7**	**682.6**	**918.8**	**913.5**	البلدان النامية
Bulgaria	111.8	186.8	171.4	311.3	249.2	32.9	27.1	85.6	94.8	42.6	بلغاريا
Cyprus	387.4	61.7	116.7	305.8	80.4	93.6	138.6	254.6	296.0	72.2	قبرص
Czech Republic	197.7	194.1	325.3	342.6	680.6	45.2	53.4	60.6	78.6	99.1	الجمهورية التشيكية
Hungary	119.8	94.2	102.8	127.6	222.4	9.9	13.0	8.5	10.9	18.0	هنغاريا
Poland	159.1	118.0	166.5	234.7	236.0	29.6	64.3	83.6	65.5	99.5	بولندا
Romania	176.1	308.6	425.6	697.8	805.7	85.8	62.2	74.8	104.8	107.1	رومانيا
Slovakia	—	—	—	—	—	22.6	0.3	1.5	7.3	9.5	سلوفاكيا
Others	1 204.9	385.9	466.9	589.1	1 196.1	97.0	359.9	113.5	260.8	465.4	غيرها
European Free Trade Association (EFTA)	**645.6**	**890.1**	**900.9**	**1 396.2**	**1 092.4**	**416.9**	**284.3**	**358.2**	**119.3**	**47.5**	الرابطة الأوروبية للتجارة الحرة
Norway	103.3	235.6	153.6	170.2	181.3	15.3	10.5	12.5	14.6	12.0	النرويج
Switzerland	540.9	643.9	738.7	1 213.2	903.9	401.5	273.7	345.6	104.7	35.5	سويسرا
Others	1.5	10.5	8.6	12.8	7.3	0.1	0.2	0.1	—	—	غيرها
Other developed countries	**192.0**	**22.2**	**0.2**	**21.7**	**42.5**	**0.4**	**2.1**	**—**	**3.1**	**5.9**	بلدان أوروبية متقدمة أخرى

الجدول 3-2- مصر: الواردات والصادرات حسب أهم البلدان والكتل الاقتصادية

Table III.2. Egypt: Imports and exports by main countries and economic groupings, 2010-2014

(Millions of US dollars)	Imports					Exports[1]					(مليون دولار أمريكي)
	2010	2011	2012	2013	2014	2010	2011	2012	2013	2014	
Developing countries[4]	**6 081.3**	**5 478.5**	**10 032.0**	**7 749.4**	**9 649.4**	**738.4**	**1 216.0**	**1 023.6**	**1 288.9**	**1 350.7**	**البلدان النامية[4]**
Bosnia and Herzegovina	18.0	14.5	14.1	16.3	20.6	1.1	1.1	1.6	2.5	1.5	البوسنة والهرسك
Russian Federation	1 830.0	2 161.8	4 058.1	1 846.6	2 935.9	215.8	353.4	224.6	266.6	354.0	الاتحاد الروسي
Ukraine	1 620.3	1 811.6	3 960.2	3 148.6	3 009.7	78.3	112.1	81.1	66.7	48.7	أوكرانيا
Other developing countries	**256.4**	**141.3**	**224.6**	**129.0**	**212.8**	**26.6**	**30.7**	**33.5**	**34.4**	**33.0**	**بلدان اوروبية نامية اخرى**
America	**8 224.7**	**10 837.1**	**10 240.7**	**9 843.7**	**9 297.4**	**2 242.4**	**2 072.6**	**2 984.7**	**2 130.4**	**1 897.6**	**أمريكا**
Developed countries	**5 394.3**	**6 852.2**	**5 784.4**	**5 557.0**	**5 506.5**	**1 821.3**	**1 665.4**	**2 623.1**	**1 729.5**	**1 644.1**	**البلدان المتقدمة النمو**
Canada	446.6	512.8	386.2	372.9	307.7	143.2	60.2	477.9	547.2	515.0	كندا
United States of America	4 947.7	6 339.4	5 398.2	5 184.1	5 198.8	1 678.2	1 605.2	2 145.2	1 182.3	1 129.1	الولايات المتحدة الأمريكية
Developing countries	**2 830.3**	**3 984.9**	**4 456.2**	**4 286.7**	**3 790.9**	**421.1**	**407.2**	**361.6**	**400.9**	**253.4**	**البلدان النامية**
Latin American Integration Association (LAIA)	2 804.9	3 924.9	4 374.1	4 254.7	3 749.5	399.9	378.6	341.0	381.9	229.1	**رابطة التكامل لأمريكا اللاتينية**
Argentina	885.8	1 582.4	1 182.0	1 569.5	1 175.1	24.8	7.6	5.9	51.1	8.4	الأرجنتين
Bolivia	0.3	0.2	0.1	0.6	2.0	0.1	0.1	0.2	—	0.1	بوليفيا
Brazil	1 731.3	2 160.3	2 936.1	2 276.9	2 192.0	209.1	272.3	246.7	203.6	172.1	البرازيل
Chile	13.7	30.2	20.8	28.0	10.6	70.9	39.9	25.8	67.3	7.9	شيلي
Ecuador	3.4	15.1	39.6	23.6	24.8	1.5	1.3	1.2	1.7	1.6	اكوادور
Mexico	83.3	65.9	51.7	52.9	49.6	35.8	25.2	19.2	22.1	21.8	المكسيك
Others	87.1	70.8	143.8	303.3	295.3	57.7	32.2	42.0	36.1	17.3	غيرها
Other America	25.4	60.0	82.2	32.0	41.5	21.2	28.6	20.5	18.9	24.3	**بلدان أمريكية أخرى**
Oceania	**685.1**	**708.9**	**799.1**	**732.4**	**763.5**	**21.3**	**52.8**	**69.1**	**27.4**	**24.7**	**أوقيانوسيا**
Developed countries	**684.9**	**708.7**	**799.1**	**732.1**	**763.4**	**21.0**	**52.6**	**68.7**	**26.8**	**24.3**	**البلدان المتقدمة النمو**
Australia	537.0	498.4	475.3	419.8	405.1	19.6	48.3	62.4	23.4	21.6	استراليا
New Zealand	147.9	210.3	323.8	312.3	358.4	1.3	4.3	6.3	3.3	2.7	نيوزيلندا
Developing countries	**0.2**	**0.2**	**—**	**0.3**	**—**	**0.3**	**0.2**	**0.4**	**0.6**	**0.4**	**البلدان النامية**
Asia	**21 054.8**	**23 581.7**	**28 443.3**	**26 882.4**	**30 704.0**	**13 280.0**	**14 616.2**	**15 718.3**	**15 186.8**	**13 817.4**	**أسيا**
Developed countries: Japan	**1 436.2**	**1 319.0**	**1 638.2**	**1 448.8**	**1 576.6**	**188.3**	**362.4**	**1 016.2**	**456.8**	**363.2**	**البلدان المتقدمة النمو: اليابان**
Developing countries	**19 618.7**	**22 262.7**	**26 805.1**	**25 433.6**	**29 127.4**	**13 091.7**	**14 253.8**	**14 702.1**	**14 730.0**	**13 454.3**	**البلدان النامية**
ESCWA member countries	**5 788.3**	**7 270.3**	**8 444.7**	**8 345.5**	**9 779.4**	**8 246.0**	**8 215.2**	**8 902.3**	**8 830.0**	**8 834.2**	**البلدان الأعضاء في الإسكوا**
Asia Middle East (non ESCWA member countries)	**1 918.2**	**2 631.9**	**3 575.4**	**2 659.2**	**2 918.6**	**1 135.9**	**1 614.4**	**1 674.9**	**1 776.7**	**1 472.4**	**أسيا- الشرق الأوسط (ما عدا بلدان الإسكوا)**
Islamic Republic of Iran	43.4	34.2	47.3	36.4	64.3	138.4	93.7	63.9	30.6	21.8	جمهورية إيران الإسلامية
Turkey	1 874.7	2 597.7	3 528.1	2 622.8	2 854.3	997.5	1 520.7	1 610.9	1 746.1	1 450.6	تركيا

الجدول 3-2- مصر: الواردات والصادرات حسب أهم البلدان والكتل الاقتصادية

Table III.2. Egypt: Imports and exports by main countries and economic groupings, 2010-2014

(Millions of US dollars) (مليون دولار أمريكي)

	Imports					Exports[1]					
	2010	2011	2012	2013	2014	2010	2011	2012	2013	2014	
Association of Southeast Asian Nations (ASEAN)	**2 543.0**	**2 659.9**	**2 770.0**	**2 670.6**	**2 785.4**	**479.8**	**379.7**	**423.8**	**283.2**	**237.3**	منظمة التجارة الحرة لرابطة أمم جنوب شرقي آسيا
Indonesia	531.1	855.4	789.2	914.4	773.0	106.3	92.6	166.9	94.2	61.9	إندونيسيا
Malaysia	782.4	747.2	569.5	552.0	447.8	206.1	124.5	162.4	136.6	88.5	ماليزيا
Philippines	22.4	31.1	24.4	20.4	13.3	12.6	40.0	24.7	6.7	3.9	الفلبين
Singapore	323.6	186.1	189.1	148.8	179.8	111.9	88.3	9.8	12.1	46.1	سنغافورة
Thailand	747.0	654.8	940.2	830.1	1 108.2	24.2	17.2	46.0	22.7	21.7	تايلند
Others	136.4	185.2	257.5	204.9	263.3	18.6	17.1	13.9	10.9	15.2	غيرها
Other Asian countries	**9 369.2**	**9 700.6**	**12 015.0**	**11 758.3**	**13 644.0**	**3 230.1**	**4 044.4**	**3 701.2**	**3 840.1**	**2 910.4**	بلدان آسيوية أخرى
Afghanistan	0.7	0.2	0.3	1.0	0.7	43.4	4.2	5.6	3.9	13.0	أفغانستان
Bangladesh	24.6	20.7	24.0	26.2	23.3	27.9	50.8	62.0	44.8	52.9	بنغلاديش
China	4 888.1	5 417.6	6 764.7	6 974.8	8 057.6	450.8	606.3	817.6	560.0	329.9	الصين
Hong Kong	126.2	88.8	104.0	84.5	112.6	23.1	25.4	30.1	31.3	28.6	هونغ كونغ
India	1 553.5	1 547.1	2 304.4	2 263.5	2 472.0	1 259.0	2 261.2	2 106.8	2 135.1	1 923.3	الهند
Korea, Democratic People's Republic o	66.0	23.0	22.3	20.1	15.8	267.8	7.8	1.4	0.7	1.7	جمهورية كوريا الشعبية الديمقراطية
Korea, Republic of	1 900.7	1 667.5	1 802.1	1 552.2	2 245.2	534.5	434.5	282.7	709.7	273.7	جمهورية كوريا
Pakistan	94.6	143.4	223.1	139.1	120.7	134.5	157.5	152.3	132.6	146.0	باكستان
Sri Lanka	15.0	20.5	41.6	37.9	36.2	15.6	13.1	36.0	19.5	23.2	سري لانكا
Others	699.7	771.7	728.5	659.2	559.8	473.5	483.7	206.8	202.4	117.9	غيرها
Africa	**1 195.8**	**1 575.4**	**1 951.5**	**1 112.4**	**886.7**	**1 723.1**	**2 495.3**	**2 084.0**	**1 920.7**	**1 834.9**	أفريقيا
Developed countries: South Africa	**159.7**	**75.0**	**106.4**	**78.0**	**50.4**	**397.1**	**1 000.1**	**544.2**	**314.7**	**145.9**	البلدان المتقدمة النمو: جنوب أفريقيا
Developing countries	**1 036.2**	**1 500.4**	**1 845.1**	**1 034.4**	**836.2**	**1 326.0**	**1 495.2**	**1 539.8**	**1 606.1**	**1 689.0**	البلدان النامية
Arab countries[5]	**458.9**	**722.2**	**983.3**	**422.0**	**197.9**	**360.4**	**511.5**	**477.1**	**561.3**	**648.3**	البلدان العربية[5]
Algeria	411.6	687.3	968.7	411.5	193.5	264.6	388.8	396.1	504.8	568.0	الجزائر
Djibouti	43.5	29.9	12.3	9.0	0.7	29.8	44.6	36.8	19.8	20.8	جيبوتي
Somalia	0.3	0.4	0.3	0.4	0.7	19.1	70.1	31.5	23.2	40.4	الصومال
Others	3.5	4.6	2.1	1.0	2.9	46.9	8.0	12.8	13.5	19.2	غيرها
Central African Customs and Economic Union (CACEU)	6.0	6.5	31.7	7.1	23.8	64.5	96.9	67.0	77.6	95.1	الاتحاد الجمركي والاقتصادي لوسط أفريقيا
Economic Community of West African States (ECOWAS)	22.5	47.9	56.7	57.4	63.8	346.9	302.4	314.3	338.0	291.8	الجماعة الاقتصادية لدول غرب أفريقيا
Other Africa	548.7	723.8	773.4	547.9	550.8	554.1	584.4	681.4	629.2	653.7	بلدان أفريقية أخرى

(1) Export values include re-exports.
(2) Including values of ship and aircraft supplies.
(3) Including EU developed countries, EFTA countries, and other developed countries.
(4) Including EU developing countries.
(5) Except Libya, Morroco, Tunisia and Sudan, which are included under "ESCWA member countries",

(1) بما في ذلك قيم إعادة التصدير.
(2) بما في ذلك قيم تموين السفن والطائرات.
(3) بما في ذلك البلدان المتقدمة النمو في الاتحاد الأوروبي والرابطة الأوروبية للتجارة الحرة، والبلدان المتقدمة النمو الأخرى.
(4) بما في ذلك البلدان النامية في الاتحاد الأوروبي.
(5) ما عدا وليبيا، والمغرب والسودان، وتونس وأدرجوا تحت بند البلدان الأعضاء في الإسكوا.

الجدول 3-3- العراق: الواردات والصادرات حسب أهم البلدان والكتل الاقتصادية

Table III.3. Iraq: Imports and exports by main countries and economic groupings, 2010-2014

(Millions of US dollars) (مليون دولار أمريكي)

	Imports 2010	Imports 2011	Imports 2012	Imports 2013	Imports 2014	Exports 2010	Exports 2011	Exports 2012	Exports 2013	Exports 2014	
World	**27 410.8**	**49 141.6**	**24 443.2**	..	..	**52 482.6**	**83 225.9**	**94 391.5**	..	..	**العالم**
Developed countries	**11 855.6**	**26 036.3**	**5 833.1**	..	..	**1.7**	**2.7**	**6.4**	..	..	**البلدان المتقدمة النمو**
Developing countries and territories	**13 627.8**	**19 680.3**	**13 290.5**	..	..	**199.2**	**221.1**	**287.6**	..	..	**البلدان والأقاليم النامية**
Oil trade (1)	**1 927.5**	**3 417.0**	**5 319.7**	..	..	**52 281.6**	**83 002.1**	**94 097.5**	..	..	**النفط[1]**
Other countries	—	**7.9**	—	..	..	—	—	—	..	..	**بلدان أخرى**
Europe	**5 833.8**	**17 771.9**	**4 710.0**	..	..	**1.7**	**2.6**	**6.4**	..	..	**أوروبا**
Developed countries[2]	**3 578.7**	**17 160.6**	**2 175.9**	..	..	**1.4**	**2.6**	**6.4**	..	..	**البلدان المتقدمة النمو[2]**
European Union	**3 516.4**	**3 783.7**	**3 555.1**	..	..	**1.4**	**2.6**	**6.4**	..	..	**الاتحاد الأوروبي**
Developed countries	**3 434.8**	**3 735.0**	**1 659.3**	..	..	**1.4**	**2.6**	**6.4**	..	..	**البلدان المتقدمة النمو**
Austria	62.2	241.2	43.0	..	..	—	—	—	..	..	النمسا
Belgium	191.4	25.1	20.5	..	..	—	—	—	..	..	بلجيكا
Denmark	3.8	19.8	29.0	..	..	—	—	—	..	..	الدانمرك
Finland	10.5	3.8	7.6	..	..	—	—	—	..	..	فنلندا
France	1 188.7	1 664.8	248.1	..	..	—	—	—	..	..	فرنسا
Germany	924.4	694.1	569.4	..	..	—	—	—	..	..	المانيا
Greece	4.3	6.5	4.6	..	..	—	—	—	..	..	اليونان
Ireland	7.1	19.7	12.4	..	..	—	—	—	..	..	آيرلندا
Italy	410.0	294.1	288.3	..	..	1.1	2.3	—	..	..	ايطاليا
Luxembourg	0.4	—	—	..	..	—	—	—	..	..	لكسمبرغ
Netherlands	13.0	95.7	58.3	..	..	—	—	—	..	..	هولندا
Portugal	—	1.8	0.7	..	..	—	—	—	..	..	البرتغال
Spain	28.2	87.0	82.2	..	..	—	—	0.1	..	..	اسبانيا
Sweden	136.2	115.9	79.2	..	..	0.1	—	—	..	..	السويد
United Kingdom of Great Britain and Northern Ireland	454.5	465.5	215.9	..	..	0.3	0.2	6.3	..	..	المملكة المتحدة لبريطانيا العظمى وآيرلندا الشمالية
Developing countries	**81.6**	**48.8**	**1 895.8**	..	..	—	—	—	..	..	**البلدان النامية**
Bulgaria	20.0	2.4	0.5	..	..	—	—	—	..	..	بلغاريا
Cyprus	0.3	2.0	2.0	..	..	—	—	—	..	..	قبرص
Czech Republic	22.1	2.4	6.6	..	..	—	—	—	..	..	الجمهورية التشيكية
Hungary	0.3	1.7	0.2	..	..	—	—	—	..	..	هنغاريا
Poland	4.6	8.7	15.6	..	..	—	—	—	..	..	بولندا
Romania	33.9	29.4	1 870.2	..	..	—	—	—	..	..	رومانيا
Slovakia	0.1	1.3	0.4	..	..	—	—	—	..	..	سلوفاكيا
Others	0.3	0.7	0.3	..	..	—	—	—	..	..	غيرها
European Free Trade Association (EFTA)	**20.2**	**107.3**	**77.2**	..	..	—	—	—	..	..	**الرابطة الأوروبية للتجارة الحرة**
Norway	6.4	16.4	2.3	..	..	—	—	—	..	..	النرويج
Switzerland	13.8	90.9	74.9	..	..	—	—	—	..	..	سويسرا
Others	—	—	—	..	..	—	—	—	..	..	غيرها
Other developed countries	**123.7**	**13 318.4**	**439.5**	..	..	—	—	—	..	..	**بلدان أوروبية متقدمة أخرى**

الجدول 3-3- العراق: الواردات والصادرات حسب أهم البلدان والكتل الاقتصادية

Table III.3. Iraq: Imports and exports by main countries and economic groupings, 2010-2014

(Millions of US dollars) (مليون دولار أمريكي)

	Imports					Exports					
	2010	2011	2012	2013	2014	2010	2011	2012	2013	2014	
Developing countries[3]	**2 255.1**	**611.3**	**2 534.1**	**..**	**..**	**0.3**	**—**	**—**	**..**	**..**	**البلدان النامية[3]**
Bosnia and Herzegovina	—	—	—	..	..	—	—	—	..	..	البوسنة والهرسك
Russian Federation	240.9	47.4	191.9	..	..	0.2	—	—	..	..	الاتحاد الروسي
Ukraine	1 926.4	513.3	443.8	..	..	—	—	—	..	..	أوكرانيا
Other developing countries	**6.2**	**1.7**	**2.6**	**..**	**..**	**—**	**—**	**—**	**..**	**..**	**بلدان اوروبية نامية اخرى**
America	**7 192.7**	**6 622.2**	**3 158.8**	**..**	**..**	**0.3**	**0.1**	**—**	**..**	**..**	**أمريكا**
Developed countries	**6 871.9**	**5 780.6**	**2 742.8**	**..**	**..**	**0.3**	**0.1**	**—**	**..**	**..**	**البلدان المتقدمة النمو**
Canada	569.3	156.9	500.6	..	..	0.2	0.1	—	..	..	كندا
United States of America	6 302.6	5 623.7	2 242.2	..	..	0.1	—	—	..	..	الولايات المتحدة الأمريكية
Developing countries	**320.9**	**841.6**	**416.0**	**..**	**..**	**—**	**—**	**—**	**..**	**..**	**البلدان النامية**
Latin American Integration Association (LAIA)	313.2	829.8	414.9	..	..	—	—	—	..	..	**رابطة التكامل لأمريكا اللاتينية**
Argentina	22.4	381.4	69.3	..	..	—	—	—	..	..	الأرجنتين
Bolivia	—	—	—	..	..	—	—	—	..	..	بوليفيا
Brazil	220.8	350.1	239.1	..	..	—	—	—	..	..	البرازيل
Chile	—	—	—	..	..	—	—	—	..	..	شيلي
Ecuador	21.3	38.2	7.5	..	..	—	—	—	..	..	اكوادور
Mexico	42.8	38.1	73.8	..	..	—	—	—	..	..	المكسيك
Others	5.8	22.1	25.3	..	..	—	—	—	..	..	غيرها
Other America	7.7	11.7	1.1	..	..	—	—	—	..	..	**بلدان أمريكية أخرى**
Oceania	**73.1**	**2 013.3**	**153.4**	**..**	**..**	**—**	**—**	**—**	**..**	**..**	**أوقيانوسيا**
Developed countries	**73.1**	**2 013.3**	**153.4**	**..**	**..**	**—**	**—**	**—**	**..**	**..**	**البلدان المتقدمة النمو**
Australia	60.9	2 003.0	146.8	..	..	—	—	—	..	..	استراليا
New Zealand	12.2	10.2	6.6	..	..	—	—	—	..	..	نيوزيلندا
Developing countries	**—**	**—**	**—**	**..**	**..**	**—**	**—**	**—**	**..**	**..**	**البلدان النامية**
Asia	**12 367.9**	**19 296.4**	**10 995.5**	**..**	**..**	**198.9**	**221.1**	**287.4**	**..**	**..**	**آسيا**
Developed countries: Japan	**1 331.7**	**1 080.0**	**757.0**	**..**	**..**	**—**	**—**	**—**	**..**	**..**	**البلدان المتقدمة النمو: اليابان**
Developing countries	**11 036.2**	**18 216.4**	**10 238.5**	**..**	**..**	**198.9**	**221.1**	**287.4**	**..**	**..**	**البلدان النامية**
ESCWA member countries	**2 684.8**	**2 956.9**	**1 901.7**	**..**	**..**	**162.0**	**175.0**	**227.0**	**..**	**..**	**البلدان الأعضاء في الإسكوا**
Asia Middle East (non ESCWA member countries)	**589.0**	**1 079.8**	**650.6**	**..**	**..**	**36.8**	**46.1**	**60.2**	**..**	**..**	**آسيا- الشرق الأوسط (ما عدا البلدان الأعضاء في الإس**
Islamic Republic of Iran	522.9	961.3	510.8	..	..	—	0.6	—	..	..	جمهورية إيران الإسلامية
Turkey	66.1	118.5	139.8	..	..	36.8	45.5	60.2	..	..	تركيا

الجدول 3-3- العراق: الواردات والصادرات حسب أهم البلدان والكتل الاقتصادية

Table III.3. Iraq: Imports and exports by main countries and economic groupings, 2010-2014

(Millions of US dollars) (مليون دولار أمريكي)

	Imports 2010	Imports 2011	Imports 2012	Imports 2013	Imports 2014	Exports 2010	Exports 2011	Exports 2012	Exports 2013	Exports 2014	
Association of Southeast Asian Nations (ASEAN)	**917.6**	**4 926.0**	**1 401.5**	**..**	**..**	**—**	**—**	**—**	**..**	**..**	**منظمة التجارة الحرة لرابطة أمم جنوب شرقي آسيا**
Indonesia	18.4	140.8	23.8	..	..	—	—	—	..	..	إندونيسيا
Malaysia	78.0	108.0	59.2	..	..	—	—	—	..	..	ماليزيا
Philippines	4.6	3.1	12.9	..	..	—	—	—	..	..	الفلبين
Singapore	387.6	80.5	28.9	..	..	—	—	—	..	..	سنغافورة
Thailand	328.1	4 464.1	1 207.2	..	..	—	—	—	..	..	تايلند
Others	100.9	129.5	69.4	..	..	—	—	—	..	..	غيرها
Other Asian countries	**6 844.7**	**9 253.7**	**6 284.7**	**..**	**..**	**0.1**	**—**	**0.3**	**..**	**..**	**بلدان آسيوية أخرى**
Afghanistan	—	—	—	..	..	—	—	—	..	..	أفغانستان
Bangladesh	—	0.1	0.1	..	..	—	—	—	..	..	بنغلاديش
China	3 580.9	6 793.7	3 551.5	..	..	—	—	—	..	..	الصين
Hong Kong	—	—	—	..	..	—	—	—	..	..	هونغ كونغ
India	1 444.7	596.0	945.1	..	..	—	—	0.3	..	..	الهند
Korea, Democratic People's Republic of	—	0.1	—	..	..	—	—	—	..	..	جمهورية كوريا الشعبية الديمقراطية
Korea, Republic of	1 736.3	1 676.6	1 709.1	..	..	0.1	—	—	..	..	جمهورية كوريا
Pakistan	56.3	102.4	27.8	..	..	—	—	—	..	..	باكستان
Sri Lanka	20.5	70.4	40.6	..	..	—	—	—	..	..	سري لانكا
Others	5.9	14.4	10.6	..	..	—	—	—	..	..	غيرها
Africa	**15.8**	**12.9**	**105.8**	**..**	**..**	**—**	**—**	**0.1**	**..**	**..**	**أفريقيا**
Developed countries: South Africa	**0.2**	**1.8**	**3.9**	**..**	**..**	**—**	**—**	**—**	**..**	**..**	**البلدان المتقدمة النمو: جنوب أفريقيا**
Developing countries	**15.6**	**11.1**	**101.8**	**..**	**..**	**—**	**—**	**0.1**	**..**	**..**	**البلدان النامية**
Arab countries[(4)]	**14.6**	**10.3**	**101.8**	**..**	**..**	**—**	**—**	**0.1**	**..**	**..**	**البلدان العربية[(4)]**
Algeria	12.0	4.3	98.4	..	..	—	—	—	..	..	الجزائر
Djibouti	—	—	—	..	..	—	—	0.1	..	..	جيبوتي
Somalia	2.6	6.0	3.5	..	..	—	—	—	..	..	الصومال
Others	—	—	—	..	..	—	—	—	..	..	غيرها
Central African Customs and Economic Union (CACEU)	0.1	—	—	..	..	—	—	—	..	..	الاتحاد الجمركي والاقتصادي لوسط أفريقيا
Economic Community of West African States (ECOWAS)	0.2	0.3	—	..	..	—	—	—	..	..	الجماعة الاقتصادية لدول غرب أفريقيا
Other Africa	**0.8**	**0.5**	**—**	**..**	**..**	**—**	**—**	**—**	**..**	**..**	**بلدان أفريقية أخرى**

(1) Values are not disaggregated by oil product imports or Oil trades.
(2) Including EU developed countries, EFTA countries, and other developed countries.
(3) Including EU developing countries.
(4) Except Egypt, Libya, Morroco, Tunisia and Sudan, which are included under "ESCWA member countries",

(1) لم تفصّل قيم واردات مشتقات النفط وصادرات النفط
(2) بما في ذلك البلدان المتقدمة النمو في الاتحاد الأوروبي والرابطة الأوروبية للتجارة الحرة والبلدان المتقدمة النمو الأخرى.
(3) بما في ذلك البلدان النامية في الاتحاد الأوروبي.
(4) ما عدا مصر، وليبيا، والمغرب والسودان، وتونس وأدرجوا تحت بند البلدان الأعضاء في الإسكوا،

الجدول 3-3- الأردن: الواردات والصادرات حسب أهم البلدان والكتل الاقتصادية

Table III.3. Jordan: Imports and exports by main countries and economic groupings, 2010-2014

(Millions of US dollars) (مليون دولار أمريكي)

	Imports 2010	Imports 2011	Imports 2012	Imports 2013	Imports 2014	Exports[1] 2010	Exports[1] 2011	Exports[1] 2012	Exports[1] 2013	Exports[1] 2014	
World	**15 262.3**	**18 929.9**	**20 751.7**	**22 067.6**	**22 740.3**	**7 023.1**	**8 006.4**	**7 886.6**	**7 912.7**	**8 385.3**	**العالم**
Developed countries	**4 542.8**	**5 567.2**	**5 597.5**	**6 926.4**	**6 693.5**	**1 359.8**	**1 480.3**	**1 482.8**	**1 536.5**	**1 759.2**	**البلدان المتقدمة النمو**
Developing countries and territories	**10 691.6**	**13 312.4**	**15 089.6**	**15 038.3**	**15 938.4**	**5 054.1**	**5 834.6**	**5 626.2**	**5 476.0**	**5 804.2**	**البلدان والأقاليم النامية**
Oil trade	**1 866.1**	**2 614.6**	**2 758.0**	**2 575.0**	**2 313.6**	—	—	—	—	—	**النفط**
Other countries	**27.9**	**50.3**	**64.6**	**102.9**	**108.3**	**609.2**	**691.5**	**777.6**	**900.2**	**821.9**	**بلدان أخرى**
Europe	**3 687.8**	**4 972.0**	**5 286.3**	**5 980.0**	**6 077.9**	**410.8**	**462.9**	**406.6**	**309.2**	**383.9**	**أوروبا**
Developed countries[2]	**2 939.5**	**3 656.6**	**3 460.6**	**4 674.3**	**4 444.5**	**339.2**	**348.5**	**262.3**	**214.8**	**282.8**	**البلدان المتقدمة النمو[2]**
European Union	**3 036.2**	**3 863.2**	**3 632.2**	**4 788.0**	**4 479.3**	**237.4**	**340.2**	**339.2**	**272.1**	**344.7**	**الاتحاد الأوروبي**
Developed countries	**2 801.1**	**3 482.3**	**3 268.5**	**4 140.2**	**3 894.3**	**198.5**	**267.7**	**232.5**	**198.8**	**267.3**	**البلدان المتقدمة النمو**
Austria	54.4	80.3	82.7	77.5	81.5	7.5	6.2	4.3	1.6	1.4	النمسا
Belgium	97.4	128.5	110.7	389.9	271.6	15.5	21.7	10.0	16.9	29.9	بلجيكا
Denmark	48.9	61.6	57.7	73.9	180.9	1.1	1.1	0.8	1.6	1.1	الدانمرك
Finland	41.5	79.3	53.7	312.6	49.7	0.2	—	0.1	0.1	0.1	فنلندا
France	346.3	372.1	374.2	381.3	464.6	5.2	6.7	6.4	11.0	12.9	فرنسا
Germany	923.9	855.6	810.2	842.3	897.3	6.9	15.2	13.3	10.5	41.3	المانيا
Greece	17.3	27.7	22.2	43.5	45.2	7.6	17.6	22.6	15.8	10.7	اليونان
Ireland	90.9	87.7	79.7	82.2	109.9	0.8	0.9	0.8	1.1	6.4	آيرلندا
Italy	532.1	969.7	927.6	1 036.5	697.4	67.2	70.7	55.9	54.6	57.1	ايطاليا
Luxembourg	0.3	0.5	0.7	2.8	2.1	—	—	—	—	—	لكسمبرغ
Netherlands	145.1	177.8	162.9	203.2	272.7	36.8	38.2	34.7	14.5	24.0	هولندا
Portugal	17.7	21.1	20.6	50.9	33.2	0.4	3.2	8.7	2.5	1.8	البرتغال
Spain	119.7	230.3	193.0	232.1	337.5	25.2	39.7	32.5	35.1	42.6	اسبانيا
Sweden	99.1	90.3	114.6	136.0	94.3	0.8	8.9	1.1	1.5	1.8	السويد
United Kingdom of Great Britain and Northern Ireland	266.5	299.9	258.0	275.6	356.7	23.5	37.6	41.4	32.0	36.0	المملكة المتحدة لبريطانيا العظمى وآيرلندا الشمالية
Developing countries	**235.1**	**380.9**	**363.7**	**647.8**	**585.0**	**38.9**	**72.4**	**106.6**	**73.3**	**77.4**	**البلدان النامية**
Bulgaria	15.2	23.0	19.2	42.3	21.2	7.8	38.0	79.2	55.8	55.5	بلغاريا
Cyprus	13.4	10.5	12.7	48.4	17.5	2.7	1.7	3.7	2.1	2.4	قبرص
Czech Republic	51.5	32.1	39.4	35.7	34.5	0.7	1.0	0.3	0.4	0.1	الجمهورية التشيكية
Hungary	26.5	58.3	43.4	47.7	34.4	7.5	7.1	6.7	5.6	3.3	هنغاريا
Poland	38.9	45.0	57.8	75.6	74.5	0.8	1.0	0.5	0.3	0.5	بولندا
Romania	76.9	192.0	167.8	290.5	374.6	17.3	20.8	13.2	6.3	9.0	رومانيا
Slovakia	3.6	4.1	4.8	6.7	8.2	1.3	2.1	2.5	2.2	2.0	سلوفاكيا
Others	9.2	16.0	18.7	100.9	19.9	0.8	0.8	0.5	0.5	4.5	غيرها
European Free Trade Association (EFTA)	**138.4**	**174.3**	**171.3**	**525.1**	**543.2**	**140.7**	**80.7**	**29.6**	**13.0**	**11.2**	**الرابطة الأوروبية للتجارة الحرة**
Norway	6.0	6.6	15.2	8.1	8.0	—	—	—	2.7	8.7	النرويج
Switzerland	132.4	167.1	155.9	516.7	534.8	140.6	80.6	29.6	10.3	2.5	سويسرا
Others	—	0.6	0.2	0.3	0.4	—	0.1	—	—	—	غيرها
Other developed countries	—	—	**20.8**	**8.9**	**6.9**	—	—	**0.1**	**3.0**	**4.2**	**بلدان أوروبية متقدمة أخرى**

الجدول 3-3- الأردن: الواردات والصادرات حسب أهم البلدان والكتل الاقتصادية

Table III.3. Jordan: Imports and exports by main countries and economic groupings, 2010-2014

(Millions of US dollars) (مليون دولار أمريكي)

	Imports					Exports[1]					
	2010	2011	2012	2013	2014	2010	2011	2012	2013	2014	
Developing countries[3]	**748.3**	**1 315.5**	**1 825.7**	**1 305.7**	**1 633.4**	**71.6**	**114.5**	**144.3**	**94.3**	**101.1**	**البلدان النامية[3]**
Bosnia and Herzegovina	3.8	1.1	1.6	0.8	1.3	0.9	0.5	1.3	1.3	0.7	البوسنة والهرسك
Russian Federation	244.2	722.6	634.2	331.5	663.5	16.1	23.1	21.9	6.9	6.8	الاتحاد الروسي
Ukraine	248.9	205.9	502.6	324.3	378.8	14.7	17.3	13.7	11.8	14.8	أوكرانيا
Other developing countries	**16.3**	**4.8**	**323.6**	**1.3**	**4.9**	**1.1**	**1.2**	**0.9**	**1.1**	**1.5**	**بلدان اوروبية نامية اخرى**
America	**1 363.2**	**1 817.8**	**2 116.7**	**2 229.3**	**2 113.0**	**960.4**	**1 090.8**	**1 158.9**	**1 269.0**	**1 401.2**	**أمريكا**
Developed countries	**935.6**	**1 298.7**	**1 439.5**	**1 445.3**	**1 380.2**	**941.9**	**1 054.1**	**1 139.8**	**1 240.1**	**1 372.9**	**البلدان المتقدمة النمو**
Canada	75.9	85.5	62.7	80.1	60.4	13.5	13.7	14.5	34.3	49.6	كندا
United States of America	859.6	1 213.2	1 376.8	1 365.2	1 319.8	928.4	1 040.5	1 125.4	1 205.8	1 323.3	الولايات المتحدة الأمريكية
Developing countries	**427.7**	**519.1**	**677.3**	**784.0**	**732.8**	**18.5**	**36.6**	**19.1**	**28.9**	**28.3**	**البلدان النامية**
Latin American Integration Association (LAIA)	421.5	512.8	661.2	757.7	711.2	14.9	31.9	15.8	26.3	24.9	**رابطة التكامل لأمريكا اللاتينية**
Argentina	164.8	244.7	328.6	303.4	323.4	0.1	0.4	0.4	6.2	6.3	الأرجنتين
Bolivia	—	—	—	—	—	0.1	0.1	0.1	0.1	0.2	بوليفيا
Brazil	184.9	207.5	254.1	346.1	270.6	1.1	1.6	5.0	6.5	7.0	البرازيل
Chile	5.6	6.8	5.5	5.6	6.8	0.2	0.4	0.5	0.5	0.5	شيلي
Ecuador	1.1	8.0	3.9	3.4	3.7	1.8	1.2	0.8	0.4	1.2	اكوادور
Mexico	25.4	26.3	30.5	41.1	54.3	9.1	25.2	5.6	8.7	4.6	المكسيك
Others	39.7	19.6	38.6	58.1	52.4	2.5	3.0	3.5	3.8	5.0	غيرها
Other America	6.2	6.3	16.1	26.3	21.6	3.6	4.7	3.3	2.6	3.4	**بلدان أمريكية أخرى**
Oceania	**165.1**	**219.9**	**274.1**	**304.2**	**281.5**	**4.0**	**7.3**	**15.5**	**8.7**	**28.3**	**أوقيانوسيا**
Developed countries	**165.1**	**219.8**	**274.1**	**304.2**	**281.4**	**4.0**	**7.3**	**15.4**	**8.7**	**28.3**	**البلدان المتقدمة النمو**
Australia	118.5	167.3	207.3	241.0	198.8	3.9	7.0	14.7	8.4	20.0	استراليا
New Zealand	46.6	52.6	66.8	63.2	82.5	—	0.3	0.7	0.2	8.3	نيوزيلندا
Developing countries	—	—	—	—	**0.2**	—	—	—	—	—	**البلدان النامية**
Asia	**9 933.4**	**11 796.1**	**12 929.5**	**13 360.4**	**14 049.2**	**4 757.3**	**5 462.3**	**5 281.1**	**5 161.1**	**5 473.9**	**آسيا**
Developed countries: Japan	**482.0**	**364.8**	**390.9**	**481.2**	**555.0**	**57.3**	**47.3**	**40.5**	**40.6**	**32.6**	**البلدان المتقدمة النمو: اليابان**
Developing countries	**9 451.4**	**11 431.4**	**12 538.6**	**12 879.3**	**13 494.2**	**4 699.9**	**5 415.1**	**5 240.6**	**5 120.5**	**5 441.3**	**البلدان النامية**
ESCWA member countries	**5 334.4**	**6 962.6**	**7 402.9**	**6 769.4**	**6 856.7**	**3 284.2**	**3 523.0**	**3 589.8**	**3 838.3**	**3 951.3**	**البلدان الأعضاء في الإسكوا**
Asia Middle East (non ESCWA member countries)	**565.2**	**564.7**	**817.2**	**779.0**	**866.4**	**68.2**	**115.3**	**142.9**	**115.9**	**189.8**	**آسيا- الشرق الأوسط (ما عدا البلدان الأعضاء في الإسـ**
Islamic Republic of Iran	6.8	10.5	15.9	20.5	17.2	7.4	17.1	10.6	12.7	19.3	جمهورية إيران الإسلامية
Turkey	558.4	554.2	801.3	758.5	849.2	60.8	98.1	132.3	103.2	170.5	تركيا

الجدول 3-3- الأردن: الواردات والصادرات حسب أهم البلدان والكتل الاقتصادية

Table III.3. Jordan: Imports and exports by main countries and economic groupings, 2010-2014

(Millions of US dollars) (مليون دولار أمريكي)

	Imports 2010	Imports 2011	Imports 2012	Imports 2013	Imports 2014	Exports[1] 2010	Exports[1] 2011	Exports[1] 2012	Exports[1] 2013	Exports[1] 2014	
Association of Southeast Asian Nations (ASEAN)	**512.4**	**486.1**	**534.8**	**785.0**	**810.4**	**267.2**	**423.1**	**373.8**	**377.3**	**243.2**	**منظمة التجارة الحرة لرابطة أمم جنوب شرقي آسيا**
Indonesia	110.7	124.3	109.5	120.5	124.4	149.1	221.2	271.4	227.7	121.3	إندونيسيا
Malaysia	173.2	147.3	148.9	113.9	225.6	71.4	112.6	65.8	94.9	56.0	ماليزيا
Philippines	6.2	12.3	6.3	5.3	6.5	17.7	44.7	11.0	11.5	7.8	الفلبين
Singapore	52.7	25.3	25.4	212.2	92.4	15.0	7.1	1.8	5.3	22.7	سنغافورة
Thailand	140.9	143.8	180.5	219.6	234.5	10.6	32.2	19.8	28.1	21.6	تايلند
Others	28.8	33.0	64.3	113.4	127.1	3.4	5.3	3.9	9.7	13.8	غيرها
Other Asian countries	**3 039.4**	**3 418.0**	**3 783.7**	**4 545.9**	**4 960.6**	**1 080.3**	**1 353.6**	**1 134.2**	**789.1**	**1 057.0**	**بلدان آسيوية أخرى**
Afghanistan	1.9	2.8	1.8	2.9	2.7	1.2	1.9	2.0	1.7	1.3	أفغانستان
Bangladesh	4.5	7.3	10.9	14.4	20.7	9.6	9.6	2.2	9.8	3.7	بنغلاديش
China	1 655.7	1 855.5	1 995.0	2 281.9	2 392.1	113.0	203.5	188.9	105.8	186.3	الصين
Hong Kong	20.1	13.6	11.4	12.8	10.1	3.8	13.9	2.6	3.9	7.4	هونغ كونغ
India	379.6	507.3	713.8	1 112.5	1 243.8	783.0	914.1	725.8	495.7	650.8	الهند
Korea, Democratic People's Republic of	—	—	—	—	—	—	—	—	—	—	جمهورية كوريا الشعبية الديمقراطية
Korea, Republic of	648.6	614.0	572.2	553.6	763.4	24.6	33.0	20.1	18.4	26.2	جمهورية كوريا
Pakistan	31.8	36.4	55.4	69.7	50.4	12.5	20.1	13.7	15.0	23.3	باكستان
Sri Lanka	25.6	27.6	27.0	29.6	35.3	1.4	6.0	2.3	1.3	1.3	سري لانكا
Others	271.6	353.6	396.1	468.4	442.2	131.3	151.4	176.6	137.4	156.6	غيرها
Africa	**84.8**	**73.7**	**80.5**	**90.7**	**110.4**	**281.3**	**291.7**	**246.9**	**264.6**	**276.2**	**أفريقيا**
Developed countries: South Africa	**20.6**	**27.3**	**32.4**	**21.4**	**32.5**	**17.3**	**23.2**	**24.8**	**32.3**	**42.7**	**البلدان المتقدمة النمو: جنوب أفريقيا**
Developing countries	**64.2**	**46.4**	**48.1**	**69.3**	**77.9**	**264.0**	**268.5**	**222.1**	**232.3**	**233.4**	**البلدان النامية**
Arab countries[4]	**18.4**	**6.0**	**6.9**	**4.3**	**7.6**	**129.9**	**129.8**	**136.0**	**142.6**	**127.3**	**البلدان العربية[4]**
Algeria	17.2	3.2	5.5	3.8	7.3	127.8	126.9	131.7	139.6	122.9	الجزائر
Djibouti	0.1	—	—	0.3	0.1	1.6	1.8	2.2	0.9	2.2	جيبوتي
Somalia	1.0	2.8	1.3	0.2	0.1	0.4	0.5	1.0	1.4	1.2	الصومال
Others	—	—	—	—	—	0.2	0.5	1.2	0.7	1.0	غيرها
Central African Customs and Economic Union (CACEU)	0.5	0.9	0.9	1.4	1.3	1.3	2.2	5.4	2.5	2.8	الاتحاد الجمركي والاقتصادي لوسط أفريقيا
Economic Community of West African States (ECOWAS)	2.5	2.0	2.8	2.8	5.6	6.6	13.1	20.0	16.5	10.2	الجماعة الاقتصادية لدول غرب أفريقيا
Other Africa	42.8	37.6	37.5	60.8	63.4	126.2	123.4	60.7	70.7	93.1	**بلدان أفريقية أخرى**

(1) Export values include re-exports.
(2) Including EU developed countries, EFTA countries, and other developed countries.
(3) Including EU developing countries.
(4) Except Egypt, Libya, Morroco, Tunisia and Sudan, which are included under "ESCWA member countries",

(1) بما في ذلك قيم إعادة التصدير.
(2) بما في ذلك البلدان المتقدمة النمو في الاتحاد الأوروبي والرابطة الأوروبية للتجارة الحرة والبلدان المتقدمة النمو الأخرى.
(3) بما في ذلك البلدان النامية في الاتحاد الأوروبي.
(4) ما عدا مصر، وليبيا، والمغرب والسودان، وتونس وأدرجوا تحت بند البلدان الأعضاء في الإسكوا،

الجدول 3-4- الكويت: الواردات والصادرات حسب أهم البلدان والكتل الاقتصادية

Table III.4. Kuwait: Imports and exports by main countries and economic groupings, 2010-2014

(Millions of US dollars)	Imports					Exports[1]					(مليون دولار أمريكي)
	2010	2011	2012	2013	2014	2010	2011	2012	2013	2014	
World	**22 670.5**	**25 143.6**	**27 267.4**	**29 645.6**	**31 488.7**	**62 749.4**	**102 703.7**	**114 516.3**	**114 404.1**	**101 132.0**	العالم
Developed countries	**11 205.4**	**11 137.0**	**12 530.0**	**13 426.3**	**13 662.0**	**343.2**	**343.5**	**492.4**	**528.8**	**401.4**	البلدان المتقدمة النمو
Developing countries and territories	**11 448.3**	**13 993.4**	**14 723.6**	**16 200.1**	**17 808.9**	**4 221.5**	**4 982.5**	**5 460.0**	**6 094.9**	**6 193.1**	البلدان والأقاليم النامية
Oil trade (2)	—	—	—	—	—	**36 883.0**	**68 816.2**	**78 408.9**	**79 040.9**	**69 298.2**	النفط(2)
Other countries	**16.8**	**13.2**	**13.7**	**19.1**	**17.8**	**21 301.7 (3)**	**28 561.5 (3)**	**30 155.0 (3)**	**28 739.5 (3)**	**25 239.2 (3)**	بلدان أخرى
Europe	**6 413.4**	**6 372.1**	**7 403.9**	**7 945.0**	**8 048.3**	**125.4**	**106.6**	**124.5**	**238.5**	**205.3**	أوروبا
Developed countries[4]	**5 837.9**	**5 665.9**	**6 618.9**	**7 136.0**	**7 228.5**	**103.8**	**94.4**	**109.2**	**222.6**	**196.3**	البلدان المتقدمة النمو(4)
European Union	**5 762.3**	**5 798.3**	**6 686.0**	**7 075.0**	**7 184.7**	**100.6**	**91.2**	**110.8**	**202.9**	**176.9**	الاتحاد الأوروبي
Developed countries	**5 319.6**	**5 243.7**	**6 142.5**	**6 526.6**	**6 600.1**	**92.3**	**86.8**	**105.5**	**195.8**	**171.6**	البلدان المتقدمة النمو
Austria	163.4	133.2	179.5	172.7	173.3	0.2	1.2	0.1	0.8	1.1	النمسا
Belgium	153.5	159.8	168.2	154.1	153.0	12.7	53.8	16.0	81.9	68.1	بلجيكا
Denmark	75.0	78.8	79.3	74.7	99.9	0.1	0.4	0.6	0.3	0.2	الدانمرك
Finland	49.7	55.3	59.3	37.3	47.7	1.3	0.9	0.3	1.3	1.5	فنلندا
France	534.1	555.6	637.8	844.4	815.8	8.3	4.1	3.3	16.9	9.3	فرنسا
Germany	1 657.1	1 658.3	1 743.6	1 987.0	2 099.4	6.9	9.7	8.8	12.5	16.7	ألمانيا
Greece	15.8	14.7	21.5	28.0	26.1	0.5	1.2	2.4	2.9	1.6	اليونان
Ireland	161.2	185.1	289.2	178.8	195.5	—	—	—	0.9	0.1	آيرلندا
Italy	1 071.2	963.8	1 296.8	1 213.4	1 171.4	9.7	1.7	4.2	6.1	24.9	ايطاليا
Luxembourg	6.5	9.3	8.0	4.4	10.4	0.1	—	—	0.1	0.1	لكسمبرغ
Netherlands	297.3	333.1	345.2	445.3	494.1	17.0	5.6	16.0	6.9	16.6	هولندا
Portugal	45.8	50.9	76.0	74.8	71.7	3.0	1.8	1.3	3.7	3.8	البرتغال
Spain	231.9	231.7	274.7	309.6	309.3	26.9	2.5	43.1	15.3	17.3	اسبانيا
Sweden	159.5	137.9	121.1	170.5	116.6	0.1	0.1	0.2	0.2	1.5	السويد
United Kingdom of Great Britain and Northern Ireland	697.8	676.2	842.2	831.7	816.0	5.4	3.8	9.1	45.7	8.7	المملكة المتحدة لبريطانيا العظمى وآيرلندا الشمالية
Developing countries	**442.7**	**554.6**	**543.4**	**548.4**	**584.7**	**8.4**	**4.3**	**5.2**	**7.1**	**5.4**	البلدان النامية
Bulgaria	11.8	8.8	16.6	18.2	24.4	0.3	0.3	0.3	0.7	1.0	بلغاريا
Cyprus	20.3	18.4	18.6	22.8	26.2	4.4	3.1	3.2	3.3	2.9	قبرص
Czech Republic	82.7	78.7	87.0	86.2	94.7	0.1	—	—	1.2	0.2	الجمهورية التشيكية
Hungary	112.7	186.0	133.7	95.7	89.9	0.5	0.1	0.5	0.5	0.4	هنغاريا
Poland	95.2	95.1	116.1	128.6	139.4	0.2	0.4	0.2	0.1	—	بولندا
Romania	38.3	84.7	63.9	71.4	94.3	1.1	0.2	0.1	0.1	0.6	رومانيا
Slovakia	56.9	58.6	81.3	81.2	71.3	—	—	—	—	—	سلوفاكيا
Others	24.7	24.4	26.3	44.2	44.4	1.7	0.2	0.9	1.1	0.3	غيرها
European Free Trade Association (EFTA)	**516.9**	**421.0**	**475.0**	**606.3**	**625.1**	**11.5**	**7.6**	**3.7**	**26.7**	**24.8**	الرابطة الأوروبية للتجارة الحرة
Norway	15.3	21.8	19.8	21.2	18.7	—	0.1	0.4	0.4	0.4	النرويج
Switzerland	501.0	398.5	454.4	584.8	606.2	11.5	7.5	3.2	26.2	24.4	سويسرا
Others	0.7	0.8	0.9	0.2	0.1	—	—	—	—	—	غيرها
Other developed countries	**1.4**	**1.2**	**1.3**	**3.1**	**3.4**	—	—	—	—	—	بلدان أوروبية متقدمة أخرى

الجدول 3-4- الكويت: الواردات والصادرات حسب أهم البلدان والكتل الاقتصادية

Table III.4. Kuwait: Imports and exports by main countries and economic groupings, 2010-2014

(Millions of US dollars) (مليون دولار أمريكي)

	Imports					Exports[1]					
	2010	2011	2012	2013	2014	2010	2011	2012	2013	2014	
Developing countries[5]	**575.5**	**706.2**	**785.0**	**809.0**	**819.8**	**21.6**	**12.2**	**15.3**	**15.9**	**9.0**	البلدان النامية[5]
Bosnia and Herzegovina	5.0	10.3	5.2	10.2	5.7	—	0.1	—	0.1	0.1	البوسنة والهرسك
Russian Federation	83.6	126.5	206.0	186.0	189.7	7.9	3.7	9.1	7.4	1.3	الاتحاد الروسي
Ukraine	39.1	7.6	21.5	50.6	29.6	1.0	0.9	0.6	1.1	2.1	أوكرانيا
Other developing countries	**5.2**	**7.2**	**9.0**	**13.9**	**10.1**	**4.3**	**3.2**	**0.4**	**0.2**	**0.1**	بلدان اوروبية نامية اخرى
America	**3 367.2**	**3 540.1**	**3 693.2**	**4 055.5**	**3 958.3**	**209.2**	**271.4**	**341.9**	**262.8**	**334.6**	أمريكا
Developed countries	**2 867.6**	**2 950.3**	**3 018.9**	**3 279.3**	**3 343.4**	**173.2**	**188.9**	**296.6**	**217.0**	**174.3**	البلدان المتقدمة النمو
Canada	273.7	262.6	293.6	348.7	266.6	0.7	1.3	7.6	12.7	20.5	كندا
United States of America	2 593.9	2 687.8	2 725.3	2 930.6	3 076.8	172.5	187.6	289.0	204.4	153.8	الولايات المتحدة الأمريكية
Developing countries	**499.7**	**589.7**	**674.2**	**776.2**	**614.8**	**35.9**	**82.5**	**45.3**	**45.8**	**160.3**	البلدان النامية
Latin American Integration Association (LAIA)	477.7	565.5	652.7	753.5	588.5	35.9	82.1	26.6	45.5	160.0	رابطة التكامل لأمريكا اللاتينية
Argentina	54.1	38.3	53.3	77.1	58.8	0.1	10.5	13.6	0.1	—	الأرجنتين
Bolivia	0.1	0.2	—	0.1	0.4	—	—	—	—	—	بوليفيا
Brazil	258.4	365.7	365.0	411.3	305.1	35.8	70.7	12.3	44.9	159.0	البرازيل
Chile	15.0	15.3	12.9	14.2	11.2	—	—	—	—	—	شيلي
Ecuador	1.5	1.9	2.2	4.0	5.8	—	0.1	0.1	0.1	0.1	اكوادور
Mexico	137.7	134.6	194.1	222.1	171.4	—	—	0.1	0.1	—	المكسيك
Others	10.8	9.5	25.1	24.6	35.8	—	0.8	0.4	0.3	0.9	غيرها
Other America	21.9	24.2	21.5	22.6	26.3	—	0.4	18.7	0.3	0.3	بلدان أمريكية أخرى
Oceania	**593.5**	**750.6**	**643.5**	**643.3**	**715.6**	**44.4**	**43.8**	**51.5**	**60.2**	**16.9**	أوقيانوسيا
Developed countries	**593.2**	**750.4**	**643.1**	**642.3**	**714.4**	**44.4**	**43.8**	**51.5**	**59.9**	**16.9**	البلدان المتقدمة النمو
Australia	532.7	664.8	571.8	571.6	651.8	44.2	43.6	51.5	59.0	16.8	استراليا
New Zealand	60.6	85.5	71.2	70.7	62.6	0.1	0.1	—	0.9	0.1	نيوزيلندا
Developing countries	**0.2**	**0.2**	**0.4**	**1.0**	**1.2**	**—**	**0.1**	**—**	**0.3**	**—**	البلدان النامية
Asia	**12 073.9**	**14 238.1**	**15 303.8**	**16 788.6**	**18 548.2**	**4 110.9**	**4 832.7**	**5 354.6**	**5 993.3**	**6 001.9**	آسيا
Developed countries: Japan	**1 803.7**	**1 661.2**	**2 140.0**	**2 225.1**	**2 235.6**	**5.5**	**5.6**	**6.9**	**9.4**	**11.1**	البلدان المتقدمة النمو: اليابان
Developing countries	**10 270.2**	**12 576.9**	**13 163.8**	**14 563.5**	**16 312.6**	**4 105.4**	**4 827.1**	**5 347.8**	**5 983.9**	**5 990.8**	البلدان النامية
ESCWA member countries	**3 096.9**	**4 295.4**	**4 571.7**	**5 580.9**	**6 183.2**	**1 924.9**	**2 044.5**	**2 278.6**	**2 837.0**	**2 959.2**	البلدان الأعضاء في الإسكوا
Asia Middle East (non ESCWA member countries)	**586.7**	**524.0**	**556.0**	**651.2**	**798.3**	**243.1**	**310.5**	**330.9**	**371.0**	**288.5**	آسيا- الشرق الأوسط (ما عدا البلدان الأعضاء في الإسكوا)
Islamic Republic of Iran	108.8	105.0	166.2	190.0	238.4	112.5	82.4	89.1	73.9	88.1	جمهورية إيران الإسلامية
Turkey	477.9	419.0	389.8	461.2	559.9	130.6	228.1	241.8	297.1	200.4	تركيا

الجدول 3-4- الكويت: الواردات والصادرات حسب أهم البلدان والكتل الاقتصادية

Table III.4. Kuwait: Imports and exports by main countries and economic groupings, 2010-2014

(Millions of US dollars) (مليون دولار أمريكي)

	Imports					Exports[1]					
	2010	2011	2012	2013	2014	2010	2011	2012	2013	2014	
Association of Southeast Asian Nations (ASEAN)	**1 004.4**	**1 144.0**	**1 439.9**	**1 437.9**	**1 708.3**	**456.6**	**436.0**	**593.5**	**436.7**	**410.5**	**منظمة التجارة الحرة لرابطة أمم جنوب شرقي آسيا**
Indonesia	141.9	167.5	184.9	213.9	235.7	203.1	127.7	336.9	185.2	180.6	إندونيسيا
Malaysia	246.0	293.6	289.7	263.5	261.4	133.1	106.6	102.2	100.0	77.3	ماليزيا
Philippines	92.4	122.5	123.2	124.4	127.3	10.2	10.0	10.1	13.9	10.8	الفلبين
Singapore	106.2	80.2	155.8	114.4	92.9	29.6	33.3	45.5	41.6	75.0	سنغافورة
Thailand	355.2	395.9	477.0	461.8	566.6	70.8	146.4	81.1	62.2	38.6	تايلند
Others	62.7	84.3	209.3	259.8	424.4	9.7	12.0	17.7	33.8	28.2	غيرها
Other Asian countries	**5 582.2**	**6 613.5**	**6 596.2**	**6 893.5**	**7 622.8**	**1 480.8**	**2 036.1**	**2 144.7**	**2 339.2**	**2 332.6**	**بلدان آسيوية أخرى**
Afghanistan	—	0.1	—	0.2	0.1	7.9	8.7	12.7	20.9	9.0	أفغانستان
Bangladesh	75.6	48.6	50.8	72.8	70.1	5.8	3.5	5.0	5.6	5.1	بنغلاديش
China	2 833.3	3 713.6	3 601.0	4 011.8	4 452.2	679.4	829.8	839.5	1 035.8	1 038.8	الصين
Hong Kong	25.7	17.6	15.4	13.6	24.1	80.1	91.2	102.6	83.4	64.4	هونغ كونغ
India	1 287.8	1 493.9	1 303.0	1 162.3	1 307.8	413.9	639.0	650.9	722.4	890.8	الهند
Korea, Democratic People's Republic of	0.3	0.7	0.3	0.1	0.1	0.1	1.4	—	0.4	—	جمهورية كوريا الشعبية الديمقراطية
Korea, Republic of	1 022.9	955.8	1 225.0	1 141.7	1 288.0	88.9	188.8	62.8	34.1	25.8	جمهورية كوريا
Pakistan	113.5	127.8	126.7	154.2	171.2	155.9	247.1	227.7	221.7	202.2	باكستان
Sri Lanka	27.7	32.8	30.5	37.3	41.5	12.7	15.3	14.1	17.7	18.7	سري لانكا
Others	195.4	222.7	243.5	299.5	267.8	36.0	11.3	229.4	197.4	77.7	غيرها
Africa	**205.7**	**229.5**	**209.3**	**194.1**	**200.5**	**74.8**	**71.5**	**79.8**	**68.9**	**35.8**	**أفريقيا**
Developed countries: South Africa	**102.9**	**109.1**	**109.1**	**143.7**	**140.1**	**16.3**	**10.8**	**28.2**	**19.8**	**2.8**	**البلدان المتقدمة النمو: جنوب أفريقيا**
Developing countries	**102.7**	**120.4**	**100.2**	**50.5**	**60.4**	**58.5**	**60.7**	**51.6**	**49.1**	**33.0**	**البلدان النامية**
Arab countries[6]	**13.9**	**18.5**	**22.9**	**15.1**	**3.5**	**32.2**	**31.4**	**18.4**	**18.6**	**14.2**	**البلدان العربية[6]**
Algeria	0.5	0.8	5.0	12.3	0.1	28.8	28.5	12.3	16.1	10.6	الجزائر
Djibouti	—	0.4	1.8	2.0	2.9	1.5	2.0	3.4	2.0	1.8	جيبوتي
Somalia	13.3	17.3	16.0	0.6	0.3	0.1	0.9	0.3	0.1	0.2	الصومال
Others	0.1	—	0.1	0.3	0.2	1.9	0.1	2.4	0.3	1.7	غيرها
Central African Customs and Economic Union (CACEU)	0.6	2.6	4.6	5.7	2.5	0.8	0.5	1.4	1.2	0.6	الاتحاد الجمركي والاقتصادي لوسط أفريقيا
Economic Community of West African States (ECOWAS)	1.6	2.0	3.1	4.4	6.3	10.1	11.7	16.2	6.7	7.6	الجماعة الاقتصادية لدول غرب أفريقيا
Other Africa	86.5	97.2	69.7	25.3	48.2	15.4	17.1	15.5	22.6	10.6	**بلدان أفريقية أخرى**

(1) Including re-exports.
(2) Crude oil values are not distributed.
(3) Including the values of oil products.
(4) Including EU developed countries, EFTA countries, and other developed countries.
(5) Including EU developing countries.
(6) Except Egypt, Libya, Morroco, Tunisia and Sudan, which are included under "ESCWA member countries",

(1) بما في ذلك قيم إعادة التصدير.
(2) قيم النفط الخام غير موزعة.
(3) بما في ذلك قيم مشتقات النفط.
(4) بما في ذلك البلدان المتقدمة النمو في الاتحاد الأوروبي والرابطة الأوروبية للتجارة الحرة والبلدان المتقدمة النمو الأخرى.
(5) بما في ذلك البلدان النامية في الاتحاد الأوروبي.
(6) ما عدا مصر، وليبيا، والمغرب والسودان، وتونس وأدرجوا تحت بند البلدان الأعضاء في الإسكوا،

الجدول 3-5- لبنان: الواردات والصادرات حسب أهم البلدان والكتل الاقتصادية

Table III.5. Lebanon: Imports and exports by main countries and economic groupings, 2010-2014

(Millions of US dollars) (مليون دولار أمريكي)

	Imports					Exports[1]					
	2010	2011	2012	2013	2014	2010	2011	2012	2013	2014	
World	17 963.8	20 158.3	21 279.8	21 228.5	20 493.7	4 252.9	4 265.4	4 483.1	3 936.0	3 312.9	العالم
Developed countries	9 082.8	10 278.3	11 041.4	10 158.4	9 969.8	1 681.9	1 759.5	1 934.2	1 012.0	817.3	البلدان المتقدمة النمو
Developing countries and territories	8 597.9	9 773.2	10 168.0	11 025.8	10 430.2	2 531.6	2 477.2	2 490.9	2 879.1	2 454.3	البلدان والأقاليم النامية
Oil trade	0.1	—	—	—	—	—	0.1	—	—	—	النفط
Other countries[2]	283.1	106.7	70.4	44.3	93.7	39.3	28.7	58.1	44.8	41.3	بلدان أخرى[2]
Europe	8 047.9	9 360.0	9 775.6	10 525.9	10 504.7	1 275.0	1 036.4	1 001.8	538.9	464.7	أوروبا
Developed countries[3]	6 422.0	7 745.4	8 130.9	8 109.4	8 194.9	1231.8	970.0	948.7	489.5	412.6	البلدان المتقدمة النمو[3]
European Union	6 430.8	7 275.8	8 250.2	8 324.7	8 687.1	766.5	505.1	444.1	353.8	367.0	الاتحاد الأوروبي
Developed countries	5 847.7	6 724.7	7 600.3	7 437.8	7 632.0	728.6	454.3	400.2	313.5	324.7	البلدان المتقدمة النمو
Austria	82.8	79.9	75.5	85.7	85.5	0.7	1.5	4.5	2.7	3.7	النمسا
Belgium	246.3	250.1	279.4	300.8	604.2	101.8	130.5	111.5	45.7	29.1	بلجيكا
Denmark	92.1	104.0	117.2	146.6	172.3	3.9	4.8	4.6	3.3	4.0	الدانمرك
Finland	43.3	37.4	40.4	119.7	43.5	0.4	0.5	0.4	0.5	0.9	فنلندا
France	1 195.6	1 510.0	1 540.9	1 534.6	1 274.9	347.7	57.4	59.7	49.2	61.7	فرنسا
Germany	1 259.4	1 140.0	1 201.7	1 241.9	1 256.7	48.9	45.3	34.5	45.4	53.8	ألمانيا
Greece	248.2	303.4	890.7	607.4	816.3	33.1	27.7	29.3	31.0	17.6	اليونان
Ireland	59.7	62.8	100.7	112.1	118.6	1.5	1.2	2.4	0.8	1.3	آيرلندا
Italy	1 393.8	1 867.8	1 829.7	1 789.4	1 644.7	30.7	36.8	36.7	38.0	40.7	ايطاليا
Luxembourg	7.6	4.8	4.3	10.7	5.1	—	1.1	0.1	—	—	لكسمبرغ
Netherlands	240.8	344.7	406.7	309.4	439.3	36.6	26.4	19.1	15.7	19.8	هولندا
Portugal	59.3	62.1	64.4	74.3	77.2	1.2	1.3	0.4	0.8	1.1	البرتغال
Spain	306.9	338.3	426.0	376.3	470.8	63.1	48.9	44.0	32.0	37.2	اسبانيا
Sweden	85.1	98.2	104.1	97.0	85.6	10.3	9.8	8.5	10.9	15.5	السويد
United Kingdom of Great Britain and Northern Ireland	526.7	521.2	518.6	632.0	537.4	48.7	61.2	44.6	37.5	38.3	المملكة المتحدة لبريطانيا العظمى وآيرلندا الشمالية
Developing countries	**583.1**	**551.1**	**650.0**	**886.9**	**1 055.2**	**37.9**	**50.8**	**43.9**	**40.3**	**42.3**	البلدان النامية
Bulgaria	109.6	48.1	77.9	237.7	149.1	8.8	8.4	11.6	10.8	11.4	بلغاريا
Cyprus	15.4	31.8	69.8	54.8	23.7	16.9	23.8	17.1	18.7	14.0	قبرص
Czech Republic	63.0	78.5	73.2	80.1	90.5	0.7	0.8	1.0	1.8	1.7	الجمهورية التشيكية
Hungary	52.5	45.0	56.4	95.4	115.5	0.4	0.5	0.2	0.5	0.5	هنغاريا
Poland	59.1	64.5	98.7	106.4	113.0	2.9	3.9	3.6	2.2	3.3	بولندا
Romania	232.5	208.8	194.9	238.9	452.3	2.7	7.6	3.3	3.3	2.2	رومانيا
Slovakia	16.4	27.1	17.7	31.3	28.5	0.1	0.1	0.2	0.1	—	سلوفاكيا
Others	34.7	47.3	61.2	42.2	82.7	5.5	5.8	6.9	2.9	9.2	غيرها
European Free Trade Association (EFTA)	569.5	1 007.5	520.8	652.5	551.1	502.9	515.4	548.0	175.3	87.0	الرابطة الأوروبية للتجارة الحرة
Norway	10.1	13.1	12.8	12.0	16.9	0.5	0.7	0.7	0.6	0.3	النرويج
Switzerland	559.0	994.1	507.7	640.2	534.0	502.4	514.7	547.3	174.7	86.6	سويسرا
Others	0.5	0.2	0.2	0.4	0.2	—	—	—	—	0.1	غيرها
Other developed countries	4.8	13.2	9.8	19.1	11.8	0.3	0.2	0.4	0.7	1.0	بلدان أوروبية متقدمة أخرى

الجدول 3-5- لبنان: الواردات والصادرات حسب أهم البلدان والكتل الاقتصادية

Table III.5. Lebanon: Imports and exports by main countries and economic groupings, 2010-2014

(Millions of US dollars) (مليون دولار أمريكي)

	Imports					Exports[1]					
	2010	2011	2012	2013	2014	2010	2011	2012	2013	2014	
Developing countries[4]	**1 626.0**	**1 614.6**	**1 644.8**	**2 416.4**	**2 309.8**	**43.2**	**66.4**	**53.1**	**49.4**	**52.1**	**البلدان النامية[4]**
Bosnia and Herzegovina	6.4	2.9	3.1	3.2	1.6	0.1	—	0.3	—	—	البوسنة والهرسك
Russian Federation	507.0	514.3	423.0	900.7	887.3	3.4	13.5	7.2	7.1	7.6	الاتحاد الروسي
Ukraine	338.2	384.8	423.6	553.7	260.5	1.1	1.1	1.0	0.8	0.7	أوكرانيا
Other developing countries	**191.3**	**161.5**	**145.1**	**71.9**	**105.2**	**0.7**	**1.0**	**0.8**	**1.1**	**1.5**	**بلدان اوروبية نامية اخرى**
America	**2 469.7**	**2 634.7**	**3 017.1**	**2 169.9**	**1 976.0**	**90.4**	**95.7**	**105.8**	**120.5**	**108.4**	**أمريكا**
Developed countries	**1 966.6**	**2 058.1**	**2 482.4**	**1 582.3**	**1 303.4**	**76.6**	**79.4**	**82.0**	**80.2**	**78.5**	**البلدان المتقدمة النمو**
Canada	57.6	67.9	106.9	81.9	76.6	15.2	15.2	17.5	16.4	19.9	كندا
United States of America	1 909.0	1 990.2	2 375.5	1 500.4	1 226.8	61.5	64.2	64.6	63.9	58.6	الولايات المتحدة الأمريكية
Developing countries	**503.1**	**576.6**	**534.7**	**587.6**	**672.6**	**13.8**	**16.3**	**23.7**	**40.2**	**29.9**	**البلدان النامية**
Latin American Integration Association (LAIA)	480.0	556.7	519.6	566.8	641.0	8.2	10.6	21.2	38.1	27.5	**رابطة التكامل لأمريكا اللاتينية**
Argentina	96.5	105.2	98.0	105.1	143.6	0.5	1.0	0.2	2.7	0.3	الأرجنتين
Bolivia	0.3	0.5	0.3	0.4	0.5	—	0.1	—	0.1	0.1	بوليفيا
Brazil	267.1	304.6	302.0	367.0	387.7	2.1	2.6	11.2	26.7	15.4	البرازيل
Chile	3.4	6.0	5.0	5.9	5.2	—	0.5	0.2	0.2	0.4	شيلي
Ecuador	0.6	1.2	1.3	1.1	1.3	1.4	—	0.2	0.1	—	اكوادور
Mexico	27.1	41.9	42.7	41.2	54.8	0.4	0.5	0.4	0.2	0.4	المكسيك
Others	85.0	97.3	70.3	46.1	48.0	3.8	6.0	8.9	8.1	11.0	غيرها
Other America	23.2	19.9	15.1	20.8	31.5	5.6	5.7	2.5	2.1	2.4	**بلدان أمريكية أخرى**
Oceania	**62.1**	**62.0**	**54.2**	**71.1**	**61.5**	**15.6**	**15.2**	**13.6**	**14.8**	**14.9**	**أوقيانوسيا**
Developed countries	**61.5**	**61.8**	**53.9**	**70.9**	**61.3**	**15.6**	**15.1**	**13.2**	**14.7**	**14.9**	**البلدان المتقدمة النمو**
Australia	52.7	53.4	43.8	49.1	49.4	15.0	14.5	12.7	14.0	14.0	استراليا
New Zealand	8.8	8.4	10.2	21.8	11.9	0.6	0.6	0.5	0.7	0.9	نيوزيلندا
Developing countries	**0.6**	**0.2**	**0.2**	**0.2**	**0.2**	**0.1**	**—**	**0.4**	**0.1**	**—**	**البلدان النامية**
Asia	**6 857.5**	**7 663.9**	**7 878.4**	**7 978.1**	**7 403.4**	**2 161.4**	**2 045.7**	**2 074.9**	**2 394.5**	**1 997.9**	**آسيا**
Developed countries: Japan	**622.1**	**403.9**	**363.7**	**373.8**	**358.7**	**13.6**	**21.9**	**25.9**	**29.7**	**14.2**	**البلدان المتقدمة النمو: اليابان**
Developing countries	**6 235.4**	**7 260.0**	**7 514.7**	**7 604.4**	**7 044.7**	**2 147.9**	**2 023.8**	**2 049.0**	**2 364.9**	**1 983.7**	**البلدان النامية**
ESCWA member countries	**2 326.3**	**3 273.7**	**3 100.9**	**2 507.7**	**2 148.4**	**1 710.8**	**1 491.8**	**1 711.8**	**1 982.6**	**1 697.6**	**البلدان الأعضاء في الإسكوا**
Asia Middle East (non ESCWA member countries)	**722.1**	**882.1**	**1 003.9**	**1 176.1**	**755.7**	**270.6**	**289.2**	**162.2**	**186.7**	**148.1**	**آسيا- الشرق الأوسط (ما عدا البلدان الأعضاء في الإسكوا)**
Islamic Republic of Iran	38.4	41.8	38.4	42.0	50.1	40.0	13.2	5.0	3.9	3.2	جمهورية إيران الإسلامية
Turkey	683.8	840.3	965.5	1 134.1	705.6	230.6	276.0	157.2	182.8	144.9	تركيا

الجدول 3-5- لبنان: الواردات والصادرات حسب أهم البلدان والكتل الاقتصادية

Table III.5. Lebanon: Imports and exports by main countries and economic groupings, 2010-2014

(Millions of US dollars) (مليون دولار أمريكي)

	Imports					Exports[1]					
	2010	2011	2012	2013	2014	2010	2011	2012	2013	2014	
Association of Southeast Asian Nations (ASEAN)	**524.4**	**543.3**	**602.3**	**658.7**	**624.3**	**15.3**	**12.9**	**8.5**	**7.9**	**9.3**	منظمة التجارة الحرة لرابطة أمم جنوب شرقي آسيا
Indonesia	75.0	82.0	85.5	92.3	98.5	5.5	5.5	2.3	1.1	1.7	إندونيسيا
Malaysia	154.1	144.8	147.1	128.4	100.0	1.9	1.7	1.7	2.3	2.2	ماليزيا
Philippines	10.3	12.2	11.5	10.3	9.7	1.4	1.4	0.6	0.5	0.2	الفلبين
Singapore	30.8	30.0	32.7	33.7	34.0	2.8	1.8	2.1	0.8	0.9	سنغافورة
Thailand	193.4	203.1	237.5	260.6	258.1	3.5	2.2	1.6	2.5	3.6	تايلند
Others	60.7	71.2	88.1	133.4	124.1	0.3	0.3	0.3	0.6	0.6	غيرها
Other Asian countries	**2 662.5**	**2 560.9**	**2 807.6**	**3 261.9**	**3 516.4**	**151.2**	**229.9**	**166.5**	**187.7**	**128.7**	بلدان آسيوية أخرى
Afghanistan	0.1	—	0.1	0.7	1.2	2.6	5.5	1.0	0.8	0.2	أفغانستان
Bangladesh	14.7	18.8	26.1	32.9	38.7	20.9	93.3	34.7	17.8	26.9	بنغلاديش
China	1 637.9	1 624.1	1 772.2	2 282.6	2 483.9	50.0	43.6	31.3	29.0	12.4	الصين
Hong Kong	9.0	10.9	10.1	7.1	11.0	5.6	7.8	6.9	10.6	8.3	هونغ كونغ
India	296.4	354.4	348.5	407.8	406.1	23.1	18.9	21.1	25.5	23.7	الهند
Korea, Democratic People's Republic of	4.4	3.6	1.5	0.5	0.7	0.2	0.1	—	0.5	—	جمهورية كوريا الشعبية الديمقراطية
Korea, Republic of	295.8	262.7	307.2	339.3	275.3	24.8	26.7	56.7	88.5	45.6	جمهورية كوريا
Pakistan	20.6	21.2	22.8	28.6	33.5	8.1	13.5	2.9	3.1	4.3	باكستان
Sri Lanka	15.1	17.8	21.2	26.2	30.9	0.5	0.4	0.3	0.3	0.3	سري لانكا
Others	368.6	247.5	297.8	136.2	235.0	15.4	20.0	11.6	11.6	7.0	غيرها
Africa	**243.5**	**330.9**	**484.2**	**439.2**	**454.5**	**671.0**	**1 043.8**	**1 229.0**	**822.4**	**685.6**	أفريقيا
Developed countries: South Africa	**10.6**	**9.0**	**10.5**	**22.0**	**51.5**	**344.3**	**673.1**	**864.4**	**397.9**	**297.0**	البلدان المتقدمة النمو: جنوب أفريقيا
Developing countries	**232.9**	**321.9**	**473.7**	**417.2**	**402.9**	**326.7**	**370.7**	**364.7**	**424.5**	**388.6**	البلدان النامية
Arab countries[5]	**31.3**	**30.3**	**21.5**	**27.7**	**71.7**	**18.7**	**18.1**	**30.7**	**39.9**	**37.7**	البلدان العربية[5]
Algeria	24.7	20.7	14.3	25.1	69.0	14.7	14.5	26.9	37.1	31.0	الجزائر
Djibouti	—	—	—	0.3	0.8	1.9	1.6	2.2	1.6	4.8	جيبوتي
Somalia	4.5	7.3	5.1	0.7	0.3	0.3	—	—	—	0.2	الصومال
Others	2.1	2.3	2.2	1.7	1.5	1.8	2.0	1.6	1.3	1.6	غيرها
Central African Customs and Economic Union (CACEU)	19.5	23.4	15.3	7.0	6.0	63.2	75.5	74.6	91.0	86.4	الاتحاد الجمركي والاقتصادي لوسط أفريقيا
Economic Community of West African States (ECOWAS)	172.3	251.3	424.3	371.1	310.7	177.1	206.7	184.3	222.3	204.3	الجماعة الاقتصادية لدول غرب أفريقيا
Other Africa	9.8	17.0	12.5	11.4	14.6	67.6	70.4	75.1	71.2	60.2	بلدان أفريقية أخرى

(1) Export values include re-exports.
(2) Including values of ship and aircraft supplies.
(3) Including EU developed countries, EFTA countries, and other developed countries.
(4) Including EU developing countries.
(5) Except Egypt, Libya, Morroco, Tunisia and Sudan, which are included under "ESCWA member countries",

(1) بما في ذلك قيم إعادة التصدير.
(2) بما في ذلك قيم تموين السفن والطائرات.
(3) بما في ذلك البلدان المتقدمة النمو في الاتحاد الأوروبي والرابطة الأوروبية للتجارة الحرة والبلدان المتقدمة النمو الأخرى.
(4) بما في ذلك البلدان النامية في الاتحاد الأوروبي.
(5) ما عدا مصر، وليبيا، والمغرب والسودان، وتونس وأدرجوا تحت بند البلدان الأعضاء في الإسكوا،

الجدول 3-6- ليبيا: الواردات والصادرات حسب أهم البلدان والكتل الاقتصادية

Table III.6. Libya: Imports and exports by main countries and economic groupings, 2010-2014

(Millions of US dollars) (مليون دولار أمريكي)

	Imports					Exports					
	2010	2011	2012	2013	2014	2010	2011	2012	2013	2014	
World	**17 674.4**	..	..	..	..	**36 440.4**	..	..	..	..	العالم
Developed countries	**7 377.1**	..	..	..	..	**30 809.7**	..	..	..	..	البلدان المتقدمة النمو
Developing countries and territories	**10 297.3**	..	..	..	..	**5 630.7**	..	..	..	..	البلدان والأقاليم النامية
Oil trade	—	..	..	..	..	**30 544.9**	..	..	..	..	النفط
Other countries	—	..	..	..	..	—	..	..	..	..	بلدان أخرى
Europe	**7 899.8**	..	..	..	..	**29 897.3**	..	..	..	..	أوروبا
Developed countries[1]	**5 464.9**	..	..	..	..	**29666.6**	..	..	..	..	البلدان المتقدمة النمو[1]
European Union	**5 556.7**	..	..	..	..	**29 790.0**	..	..	..	..	الاتحاد الأوروبي
Developed countries	**5 405.3**	..	..	..	..	**29 666.6**	..	..	..	..	البلدان المتقدمة النمو
Austria	146.8	..	..	..	..	42.0	..	..	..	..	النمسا
Belgium	108.1	..	..	..	..	24.8	..	..	..	..	بلجيكا
Denmark	32.2	..	..	..	..	52.2	..	..	..	..	الدانمرك
Finland	21.6	..	..	..	..	—	..	..	..	..	فنلندا
France	882.5	..	..	..	..	5 662.6	..	..	..	..	فرنسا
Germany	1 203.2	..	..	..	..	932.7	..	..	..	..	المانيا
Greece	74.4	..	..	..	..	1 624.8	..	..	..	..	اليونان
Ireland	41.5	..	..	..	..	327.9	..	..	..	..	آيرلندا
Italy	1 663.9	..	..	..	..	15 404.0	..	..	..	..	ايطاليا
Luxembourg	1.2	..	..	..	..	—	..	..	..	..	لكسمبرغ
Netherlands	199.1	..	..	..	..	1 229.4	..	..	..	..	هولندا
Portugal	27.3	..	..	..	..	590.7	..	..	..	..	البرتغال
Spain	233.9	..	..	..	..	3 364.1	..	..	..	..	اسبانيا
Sweden	207.7	..	..	..	..	21.3	..	..	..	..	السويد
United Kingdom of Great Britain and Northern Ireland	561.9	..	..	..	..	390.3	..	..	..	..	المملكة المتحدة لبريطانيا العظمى وآيرلندا الشمالية
Developing countries	**151.4**	..	..	..	..	**123.4**	..	..	..	..	البلدان النامية
Bulgaria	27.0	..	..	..	..	9.1	..	..	..	..	بلغاريا
Cyprus	—	..	..	..	..	17.3	..	..	..	..	قبرص
Czech Republic	15.1	..	..	..	..	—	..	—	..	..	الجمهورية التشيكية
Hungary	8.6	..	..	..	..	—	..	..	..	..	هنغاريا
Poland	17.4	..	..	..	..	—	..	..	..	..	بولندا
Romania	39.7	..	..	..	..	40.7	..	..	..	..	رومانيا
Slovakia	2.3	..	..	..	..	—	..	..	..	..	سلوفاكيا
Others	41.3	..	..	..	..	56.3	..	..	..	..	غيرها
European Free Trade Association (EFTA)	**38.8**	..	..	..	..	—	..	..	..	..	الرابطة الأوروبية للتجارة الحرة
Norway	17.4	..	..	..	..	—	..	..	..	..	النرويج
Switzerland	21.3	..	..	..	..	—	..	..	..	..	سويسرا
Others	—	..	..	..	..	—	..	..	..	..	غيرها
Other developed countries	**20.8**	..	..	..	..	—	..	..	..	..	بلدان أوروبية متقدمة أخرى

الجدول 3-6- ليبيا: الواردات والصادرات حسب أهم البلدان والكتل الاقتصادية

Table III.6. Libya: Imports and exports by main countries and economic groupings, 2010-2014

(Millions of US dollars) (مليون دولار أمريكي)

	Imports					Exports					
	2010	2011	2012	2013	2014	2010	2011	2012	2013	2014	
Developing countries[2]	**2 434.9**	..	..	..	..	**230.7**	..	..	..	..	البلدان النامية[2]
Bosnia and Herzegovina	14.5	..	..	..	..	—	..	..	..	..	البوسنة والهرسك
Russian Federation	229.7	..	..	..	..	—	..	..	..	..	الاتحاد الروسي
Ukraine	245.8	..	..	..	..	—	..	..	..	..	أوكرانيا
Other developing countries	**1 793.5**	..	..	..	..	**107.3**	..	..	..	..	بلدان اوروبية نامية اخرى
America	**1 760.4**	..	..	..	..	**1 350.5**	..	..	..	..	أمريكا
Developed countries	**1 087.0**	..	..	..	..	**1 143.1**	..	..	..	..	البلدان المتقدمة النمو
Canada	156.1	..	..	..	..	227.1	..	..	..	..	كندا
United States of America	930.9	..	..	..	..	916.0	..	..	..	..	الولايات المتحدة الأمريكية
Developing countries	**673.4**	..	..	..	..	**207.4**	..	..	..	..	البلدان النامية
Latin American Integration Association (LAIA)	664.9	..	..	..	..	207.4	..	..	..	..	رابطة التكامل لأمريكا اللاتينية
Argentina	174.3	..	..	..	..	5.5	..	..	..	..	الأرجنتين
Bolivia	—	..	..	..	..	—	..	..	..	..	بوليفيا
Brazil	427.7	..	..	..	..	197.1	..	..	..	..	البرازيل
Chile	1.7	..	..	..	..	—	..	..	..	..	شيلي
Ecuador	35.2	..	..	..	..	—	..	..	..	..	اكوادور
Mexico	15.1	..	..	..	..	4.7	..	..	..	..	المكسيك
Others	10.8	..	..	..	..	—	..	..	..	..	غيرها
Other America	8.5	..	..	..	..	—	..	..	..	..	بلدان أمريكية أخرى
Oceania	**86.0**	..	..	..	..	—	..	..	..	..	أوقيانوسيا
Developed countries	**86.0**	..	..	..	..	—	..	..	..	..	البلدان المتقدمة النمو
Australia	70.9	..	..	..	..	—	..	..	..	..	استراليا
New Zealand	15.1	..	..	..	..	—	..	..	..	..	نيوزيلندا
Developing countries	—	..	..	..	..	—	..	..	..	..	البلدان النامية
Asia	**7 854.3**	..	..	..	..	**5 182.9**	..	..	..	..	آسيا
Developed countries: Japan	**707.1**	..	..	..	..	—	..	..	..	..	البلدان المتقدمة النمو: اليابان
Developing countries	**7 147.2**	..	..	..	..	**5 182.9**	..	..	..	..	البلدان النامية
ESCWA member countries	**1 317.3**	..	..	..	..	**643.1**	..	..	..	..	البلدان الأعضاء في الإسكوا
Asia Middle East (non ESCWA member countries)	**1 875.1**	..	..	..	..	**192.9**	..	..	..	..	آسيا- الشرق الأوسط (ما عدا البلدان الأعضاء في الإس
Islamic Republic of Iran	3.1	..	..	..	..	—	..	..	..	..	جمهورية إيران الإسلامية
Turkey	1 872.1	..	..	..	..	192.9	..	..	..	..	تركيا

الجدول 3-6- ليبيا: الواردات والصادرات حسب أهم البلدان والكتل الاقتصادية

Table III.6. Libya: Imports and exports by main countries and economic groupings, 2010-2014

(Millions of US dollars) (مليون دولار أمريكي)

	Imports					Exports					
	2010	2011	2012	2013	2014	2010	2011	2012	2013	2014	
Association of Southeast Asian Nations (ASEAN)	**363.3**	..	..	..	..	**367.1**	..	..	..	..	منظمة التجارة الحرة لرابطة أمم جنوب شرقي آسيا
Indonesia	25.9	..	..	..	..	154.1	..	..	..	..	إندونيسيا
Malaysia	80.8	..	..	..	..	116.3	..	..	..	..	ماليزيا
Philippines	0.2	..	..	..	..	—	..	..	..	..	الفلبين
Singapore	34.0	..	..	..	..	81.0	..	..	..	..	سنغافورة
Thailand	218.2	..	..	..	..	15.7	..	..	..	..	تايلند
Others	4.2	..	..	..	..	—	..	..	..	..	غيرها
Other Asian countries	**3 591.4**	..	..	..	..	**3 979.7**	..	..	..	..	بلدان آسيوية أخرى
Afghanistan	—	..	..	..	..	—	..	..	..	..	أفغانستان
Bangladesh	1.5	..	..	..	..	—	..	..	..	..	بنغلاديش
China	1 724.6	..	..	..	..	3 407.2	..	..	..	..	الصين
Hong Kong	—	..	..	..	..	—	..	..	..	..	هونغ كونغ
India	176.7	..	..	..	..	503.9	..	..	..	..	الهند
Korea, Democratic People's Republic o	—	..	..	..	..	—	..	..	..	..	جمهورية كوريا الشعبية الديمقراطية
Korea, Republic of	1 627.7	..	..	..	..	51.5	..	..	..	..	جمهورية كوريا
Pakistan	3.8	..	..	..	..	—	..	..	..	..	باكستان
Sri Lanka	21.3	..	..	..	..	—	..	..	..	..	سري لانكا
Others	35.7	..	..	..	..	17.1	..	..	..	..	غيرها
Africa	**73.8**	..	..	..	..	**9.7**	..	..	..	..	أفريقيا
Developed countries: South Africa	**32.0**	..	..	..	..	—	..	..	..	..	البلدان المتقدمة النمو: جنوب أفريقيا
Developing countries	**41.8**	..	..	..	..	**9.7**	..	..	..	..	البلدان النامية
Arab countries[(3)]	**25.9**	..	..	..	..	**9.7**	..	..	..	..	البلدان العربية(3)
Algeria	25.5	..	..	..	..	9.7	..	..	..	..	الجزائر
Djibouti	—	..	..	..	..	—	..	..	..	..	جيبوتي
Somalia	—	..	..	..	..	—	..	..	..	..	الصومال
Others	0.5	..	..	..	..	—	..	..	..	..	غيرها
Central African Customs and Economic Union (CACEU)	5.7	..	..	..	..	—	..	..	..	..	الاتحاد الجمركي والاقتصادي لوسط أفريقيا
Economic Community of West African States (ECOWAS)	8.7	..	..	..	..	—	..	..	..	..	الجماعة الاقتصادية لدول غرب أفريقيا
Other Africa	1.5	..	..	..	..	—	..	..	..	..	بلدان أفريقية أخرى

(1) Including EU developed countries, EFTA countries, and other developed countries.

(2) Including EU developing countries.

(3) Except Egypt, Morroco, Tunisia and Sudan, which are included under "ESCWA member countries",

(1) بما في ذلك البلدان المتقدمة النمو في الاتحاد الأوروبي والرابطة الأوروبية للتجارة الحرة والبلدان المتقدمة النمو الأخرى.

(2) بما في ذلك البلدان النامية في الاتحاد الأوروبي.

(3) ما عدا مصر، والمغرب والسودان، وتونس وأدرجوا تحت بند البلدان الأعضاء في الإسكوا،

الجدول 3-7- المغرب: الواردات والصادرات حسب أهم البلدان والكتل الاقتصادية

Table III.7. Morocco: Imports and exports by main countries and economic groupings, 2010-2014

(Millions of US dollars) (مليون دولار أمريكي)

	Imports					Exports					
	2010	2011	2012	2013	2014	2010	2011	2012	2013	2014	
World	**35 378.9**	**44 262.9**	**44 789.8**	**45 186.4**	**46 191.7**	**17 764.8**	**21 649.9**	**21 417.2**	**21 965.4**	**23 815.8**	**العالم**
Developed countries	**20 392.4**	**24 878.0**	**24 635.3**	**25 962.1**	**26 618.1**	**11 619.6**	**13 992.9**	**13 540.7**	**14 550.4**	**16 071.6**	**البلدان المتقدمة النمو**
Developing countries and territories	**14 979.3**	**19 370.2**	**20 148.1**	**19 210.1**	**19 342.7**	**5 927.8**	**7 324.4**	**7 630.4**	**7 095.8**	**7 323.1**	**البلدان والأقاليم النامية**
Oil trade	**2 979.6**	**3 888.0**	**4 352.0**	**4 320.7**	**3 374.2**	—	—	—	**0.3**	—	**النفط**
Other countries	**7.2**	**14.7**	**6.5**	**14.2**	**230.9**	**217.4**	**332.6**	**246.1**	**319.3**	**421.1**	**بلدان أخرى**
Europe	**19 403.0**	**24 347.1**	**25 279.4**	**25 831.4**	**26 716.3**	**11 205.1**	**13 432.2**	**12 910.1**	**14 069.5**	**15 620.4**	**اوروبا**
Developed countries[1]	**16 996.6**	**20 355.8**	**20 537.9**	**21 633.2**	**22 457.4**	**10627.7**	**12639.7**	**12213.7**	**13202.1**	**14682.3**	**البلدان المتقدمة النمو[1]**
European Union	**17 411.8**	**21 054.9**	**21 220.8**	**22 618.5**	**23 616.1**	**10 613.0**	**12 713.0**	**12 171.0**	**13 298.2**	**15 132.1**	**الاتحاد الأوروبي**
Developed countries	**16 649.1**	**19 855.9**	**20 082.0**	**21 235.2**	**22 062.4**	**10 287.2**	**12 253.7**	**11 791.9**	**12 751.2**	**14 446.5**	**البلدان المتقدمة النمو**
Austria	147.7	186.5	134.9	172.9	221.0	69.2	84.0	108.0	138.6	190.1	النمسا
Belgium	508.6	843.2	737.7	808.5	980.6	473.3	433.1	402.6	565.7	436.9	بلجيكا
Denmark	82.0	76.5	183.0	249.7	200.2	18.6	23.6	42.6	21.1	19.1	الدانمرك
Finland	137.9	181.5	151.8	164.5	184.5	47.8	6.8	8.4	3.7	5.4	فنلندا
France	5 507.7	6 308.9	5 548.5	5 849.1	6 225.0	3 991.8	4 564.2	4 619.5	4 717.3	4 951.1	فرنسا
Germany	1 626.0	1 981.3	2 139.4	2 167.2	2 398.3	556.4	618.5	644.8	597.2	681.8	المانيا
Greece	221.4	88.7	51.9	115.7	46.6	21.7	18.5	13.5	19.1	14.9	اليونان
Ireland	159.3	146.6	141.9	120.9	258.1	29.7	45.7	106.4	103.9	111.1	آيرلندا
Italy	2 105.4	2 297.4	2 196.3	2 412.9	2 277.5	798.6	908.1	782.3	829.8	1 023.8	ايطاليا
Luxembourg	12.1	26.1	17.5	20.6	18.8	0.6	3.1	1.3	4.1	6.2	لكسمبرغ
Netherlands	617.0	729.1	666.8	717.6	935.7	501.0	673.7	621.4	654.1	662.2	هولندا
Portugal	571.3	754.0	730.7	1 041.0	917.8	213.4	283.4	261.5	285.2	297.1	البرتغال
Spain	3 753.1	4 858.6	5 901.4	6 119.8	6 161.2	3 004.3	3 953.8	3 540.9	4 142.1	5 206.0	اسبانيا
Sweden	449.0	491.8	497.5	422.3	405.8	45.0	32.3	41.6	75.6	126.1	السويد
United Kingdom of Great Britain and Northern Ireland	750.7	885.7	983.0	852.3	831.2	515.5	604.9	597.1	593.7	714.7	المملكة المتحدة لبريطانيا العظمى وآيرلندا الشمالية
Developing countries	**762.7**	**1 199.0**	**1 138.8**	**1 383.3**	**1 553.7**	**325.9**	**459.3**	**379.0**	**547.0**	**685.6**	**البلدان النامية**
Bulgaria	23.1	29.3	56.9	97.4	106.9	3.1	34.9	29.0	31.8	69.8	بلغاريا
Cyprus	1.3	2.9	1.3	0.5	2.0	71.0	0.8	17.8	0.6	1.8	قبرص
Czech Republic	102.8	129.0	124.4	176.5	207.9	5.9	5.8	12.3	26.8	57.3	الجمهورية التشيكية
Hungary	85.4	118.8	96.3	117.4	161.5	3.2	5.0	9.6	11.5	25.5	هنغاريا
Poland	151.6	202.3	254.8	339.6	500.5	47.1	113.8	106.9	124.7	152.8	بولندا
Romania	154.6	367.5	390.7	465.2	309.6	31.6	80.2	87.6	119.2	137.4	رومانيا
Slovakia	58.6	65.3	57.5	91.4	114.2	39.2	44.0	33.5	42.9	53.0	سلوفاكيا
Others	185.4	284.0	156.8	95.2	151.2	124.7	174.8	82.4	189.4	188.0	غيرها
European Free Trade Association (EFTA)	**317.9**	**434.3**	**453.6**	**379.4**	**355.6**	**336.7**	**341.4**	**322.7**	**284.8**	**226.2**	**الرابطة الأوروبية للتجارة الحرة**
Norway	64.6	124.6	214.2	125.6	51.9	60.1	84.7	93.9	83.3	80.8	النرويج
Switzerland	246.7	307.3	231.5	247.8	301.7	274.4	250.9	228.2	198.9	142.3	سويسرا
Others	6.7	2.4	7.9	6.0	2.0	2.2	5.8	0.6	2.6	3.1	غيرها
Other developed countries	**29.5**	**65.6**	**2.2**	**18.6**	**39.3**	**3.9**	**44.7**	**99.1**	**166.1**	**9.5**	**بلدان أوروبية متقدمة أخرى**

الجدول 3-7- المغرب: الواردات والصادرات حسب أهم البلدان والكتل الاقتصادية

Table III.7. Morocco: Imports and exports by main countries and economic groupings, 2010-2014

(Millions of US dollars)	Imports					Exports					(مليون دولار أمريكي)
	2010	2011	2012	2013	2014	2010	2011	2012	2013	2014	
Developing countries[2]	**2 406.4**	**3 991.3**	**4 741.5**	**4 198.2**	**4 258.9**	**577.3**	**792.4**	**696.4**	**867.4**	**938.2**	**البلدان النامية[2]**
Bosnia and Herzegovina	53.8	35.5	28.5	8.0	4.1	0.3	1.0	2.2	0.6	1.3	البوسنة والهرسك
Russian Federation	1 338.4	2 047.7	2 350.5	1 907.0	1 948.5	205.4	266.1	251.6	272.4	209.3	الاتحاد الروسي
Ukraine	190.0	676.8	751.9	582.6	650.4	3.3	34.4	44.4	31.7	19.6	أوكرانيا
Other developing countries	**61.5**	**32.2**	**471.8**	**317.3**	**102.2**	**42.5**	**31.6**	**19.2**	**15.7**	**22.4**	**بلدان اوروبية نامية اخرى**
America	**4 222.8**	**5 967.2**	**5 336.3**	**5 426.2**	**5 280.1**	**1 714.6**	**2 458.8**	**2 577.2**	**2 527.8**	**2 324.8**	**أمريكا**
Developed countries	**2 716.4**	**3 955.2**	**3 309.8**	**3 819.0**	**3 568.4**	**724.6**	**1 029.3**	**996.5**	**994.4**	**1 017.6**	**البلدان المتقدمة النمو**
Canada	221.7	363.9	450.8	422.1	348.6	54.7	45.6	66.7	67.8	160.7	كندا
United States of America	2 494.8	3 591.3	2 859.0	3 396.8	3 219.8	669.9	983.6	929.8	926.7	856.9	الولايات المتحدة الأمريكية
Developing countries	**1 506.4**	**2 012.0**	**2 026.5**	**1 607.3**	**1 711.7**	**990.0**	**1 429.6**	**1 580.7**	**1 533.3**	**1 307.2**	**البلدان النامية**
Latin American Integration Association (LAIA)	1 451.0	1 962.5	2 007.3	1 569.3	1 574.8	975.4	1 414.2	1 565.1	1 508.3	1 292.4	**رابطة التكامل لأمريكا اللاتينية**
Argentina	344.6	560.9	630.4	550.3	581.2	93.5	87.3	94.1	42.1	40.7	الأرجنتين
Bolivia	0.1	0.1	0.2	0.3	0.4	0.1	—	0.2	0.2	—	بوليفيا
Brazil	765.1	1 040.9	1 013.2	805.5	548.3	670.4	1 118.2	1 266.4	1 311.6	1 088.6	البرازيل
Chile	11.5	13.5	11.8	19.0	20.1	1.9	0.8	1.7	3.3	8.8	شيلي
Ecuador	6.6	5.2	5.1	6.2	6.1	—	0.1	0.4	0.8	1.4	اكوادور
Mexico	31.5	60.5	45.8	49.7	153.4	111.9	94.5	112.5	75.4	95.9	المكسيك
Others	291.6	281.4	300.9	138.3	265.3	97.5	113.3	89.8	74.9	57.0	غيرها
Other America	55.5	49.5	19.2	37.9	136.9	14.6	15.4	15.6	25.0	14.9	**بلدان أمريكية أخرى**
Oceania	**100.8**	**104.9**	**85.8**	**110.1**	**131.3**	**119.6**	**161.3**	**98.2**	**76.9**	**141.1**	**أوقيانوسيا**
Developed countries	**100.8**	**104.7**	**85.5**	**110.0**	**131.3**	**117.7**	**159.6**	**95.6**	**74.7**	**138.4**	**البلدان المتقدمة النمو**
Australia	47.7	24.8	27.4	42.0	57.4	34.4	46.1	31.8	12.1	67.0	استراليا
New Zealand	53.1	79.9	58.1	68.0	74.0	83.3	113.4	63.8	62.6	71.3	نيوزيلندا
Developing countries	**—**	**0.2**	**0.2**	**0.1**	**—**	**2.0**	**1.7**	**2.6**	**2.1**	**2.8**	**البلدان النامية**
Asia	**10 272.1**	**12 261.3**	**12 534.0**	**12 182.0**	**12 192.8**	**3 525.1**	**4 087.9**	**3 938.6**	**3 387.8**	**3 636.3**	**آسيا**
Developed countries: Japan	**447.2**	**416.1**	**653.2**	**321.5**	**345.7**	**132.5**	**153.8**	**204.5**	**261.6**	**218.1**	**البلدان المتقدمة النمو: اليابان**
Developing countries	**9 824.9**	**11 845.2**	**11 880.8**	**11 860.5**	**11 847.1**	**3 392.7**	**3 934.1**	**3 734.0**	**3 126.2**	**3 418.2**	**البلدان النامية**
ESCWA member countries	**3 998.4**	**5 665.8**	**5 583.2**	**5 454.9**	**4 902.2**	**668.8**	**527.2**	**742.1**	**658.8**	**693.7**	**البلدان الأعضاء في الإسكوا**
Asia Middle East (non ESCWA member countries)	**922.5**	**1 179.2**	**1 137.6**	**1 388.3**	**1 652.8**	**424.6**	**347.6**	**338.2**	**416.8**	**548.3**	**آسيا- الشرق الأوسط (ما عدا البلدان الأعضاء في الإسكوا)**
Islamic Republic of Iran	159.6	10.6	1.2	1.0	0.8	82.3	0.6	0.2	0.4	1.0	جمهورية إيران الإسلامية
Turkey	763.0	1 168.6	1 136.4	1 387.3	1 651.9	342.3	347.0	338.0	416.4	547.3	تركيا

الجدول 3-7- المغرب: الواردات والصادرات حسب أهم البلدان والكتل الاقتصادية

Table III.7. Morocco: Imports and exports by main countries and economic groupings, 2010-2014

(Millions of US dollars) (مليون دولار أمريكي)

	Imports					Exports					
	2010	2011	2012	2013	2014	2010	2011	2012	2013	2014	
Association of Southeast Asian Nations (ASEAN)	**639.7**	**743.5**	**706.1**	**668.4**	**687.7**	**483.7**	**561.0**	**495.6**	**429.8**	**451.4**	منظمة التجارة الحرة لرابطة أمم جنوب شرقي آسيا
Indonesia	70.1	136.5	135.8	91.7	111.7	76.2	77.3	117.1	56.8	109.0	إندونيسيا
Malaysia	105.3	118.1	91.8	93.2	102.6	3.0	6.2	5.7	8.4	4.8	ماليزيا
Philippines	7.9	6.1	8.1	11.2	15.9	1.8	0.8	26.2	29.2	2.6	الفلبين
Singapore	199.3	218.5	138.2	119.0	116.3	343.7	405.3	291.6	293.2	300.2	سنغافورة
Thailand	215.7	212.1	202.6	205.4	145.5	56.8	68.5	37.1	38.0	32.2	تايلند
Others	41.4	52.1	129.6	148.1	195.7	2.3	2.9	18.0	4.3	2.6	غيرها
Other Asian countries	**4 264.3**	**4 256.6**	**4 453.9**	**4 348.9**	**4 604.4**	**1 815.5**	**2 498.3**	**2 158.0**	**1 620.8**	**1 724.9**	بلدان آسيوية أخرى
Afghanistan	—	—	—	0.1	—	2.3	—	—	—	—	أفغانستان
Bangladesh	10.5	13.4	17.0	24.4	28.4	62.7	232.7	143.0	93.7	175.1	بنغلاديش
China	2 968.1	2 884.6	2 967.8	3 136.7	3 507.5	244.5	196.5	278.8	341.5	270.9	الصين
Hong Kong	26.1	46.8	28.1	24.7	27.6	10.0	32.5	33.2	19.7	8.0	هونغ كونغ
India	579.1	588.9	507.7	629.1	507.6	1 075.6	1 504.9	1 160.6	814.5	866.8	الهند
Korea, Democratic People's Republic o	—	—	2.6	1.4	1.4	—	—	0.8	3.9	1.5	جمهورية كوريا الشعبية الديمقراطية
Korea, Republic of	499.9	443.7	596.0	400.9	401.6	49.6	72.0	174.8	75.7	116.4	جمهورية كوريا
Pakistan	19.9	35.6	33.7	30.9	23.3	262.6	425.5	332.3	247.8	254.6	باكستان
Sri Lanka	4.1	6.4	3.5	5.7	7.0	1.2	0.8	0.3	2.6	1.8	سري لانكا
Others	156.8	237.2	297.5	94.9	99.9	106.9	33.4	34.2	21.3	29.7	غيرها
Africa	**1 372.9**	**1 567.8**	**1 547.9**	**1 622.5**	**1 640.3**	**983.0**	**1 177.1**	**1 647.0**	**1 584.2**	**1 672.0**	أفريقيا
Developed countries: South Africa	**131.4**	**46.3**	**48.8**	**78.4**	**115.2**	**17.2**	**10.5**	**30.4**	**17.5**	**15.3**	البلدان المتقدمة النمو: جنوب أفريقيا
Developing countries	**1 241.5**	**1 521.6**	**1 499.0**	**1 544.1**	**1 525.1**	**965.8**	**1 166.6**	**1 616.6**	**1 566.7**	**1 656.7**	البلدان النامية
Arab countries[(3)]	**839.1**	**1 075.9**	**1 128.3**	**1 285.8**	**1 332.6**	**215.0**	**352.9**	**464.7**	**351.9**	**396.6**	البلدان العربية[(3)]
Algeria	837.8	1 074.9	1 127.5	1 284.5	1 331.6	138.1	234.9	228.6	209.4	210.3	الجزائر
Djibouti	—	—	—	—	—	0.4	14.6	101.8	0.5	12.5	جيبوتي
Somalia	0.1	0.1	0.1	—	—	—	—	—	—	—	الصومال
Others	1.3	0.9	0.7	1.3	1.0	76.4	103.4	134.2	142.0	173.8	غيرها
Central African Customs and Economic Union (CACEU)	150.3	69.7	46.6	46.4	42.0	194.3	154.8	174.2	185.8	260.7	الاتحاد الجمركي والاقتصادي لوسط أفريقيا
Economic Community of West African States (ECOWAS)	223.7	333.8	281.9	157.5	94.9	457.8	520.5	848.0	874.7	790.3	الجماعة الاقتصادية لدول غرب أفريقيا
Other Africa	28.4	42.2	42.3	54.4	55.7	98.7	138.4	129.8	154.3	209.1	بلدان أفريقية أخرى

(1) Including EU developed countries, EFTA countries, and other developed countries.

(2) Including EU developing countries.

(3) Except Egypt, Libya, Morroco, Tunisia and Sudan, which are included under "ESCWA member countries",

(1) بما في ذلك البلدان المتقدمة النمو في الاتحاد الأوروبي والرابطة الأوروبية للتجارة الحرة والبلدان المتقدمة النمو الأخرى.

(2) بما في ذلك البلدان النامية في الاتحاد الأوروبي.

(3) ما عدا مصر، وليبيا، والمغرب والسودان، وتونس وأدرجوا تحت بند البلدان الأعضاء في الإسكوا،

الجدول 3-8- عُمان: الواردات والصادرات حسب أهم البلدان والكتل الاقتصادية

Table III.8. Oman: Imports and exports by main countries and economic groupings, 2010-2014

(Millions of US dollars)	Imports					Exports[1]					(مليون دولار أمريكي)
	2010	2011	2012	2013	2014	2010	2011	2012	2013	2014	
World	**19 777.8**	**23 619.9**	**28 117.6**	**34 331.2**	**29 303.1**	**31 603.6**	**41 246.4**	**52 138.2**	**55 497.1**	**50 718.3**	العالم
Developed countries	**4 352.3**	**5 051.7**	**5 887.5**	**9 453.3**	**9 158.5**	**797.7**	**902.0**	**1 235.7**	**4 095.3**	**4 955.6**	البلدان المتقدمة النمو
Developing countries and territories	**10 491.6**	**13 806.7**	**15 754.2**	**24 877.9**	**20 144.6**	**5 568.0**	**6 976.1**	**10 588.7**	**19 314.7**	**44 955.2**	البلدان والأقاليم النامية
Oil trade[2]	**0.3**	**0.2**	**3.8**	**15.9**	**4.3**	**25 236.2**	**33 357.7**	**30 676.6**	**32 087.1**	**34 834.5**	النفط[2]
Other countries	**4 933.8**	**4 761.5**	**6 475.9**	—	—	**1.7**	**10.7**	**9 637.2**	—	**807.5**	بلدان أخرى
Europe	**3 119.0**	**3 530.2**	**4 180.6**	**4 929.0**	**4 296.9**	**423.3**	**520.9**	**490.7**	**974.6**	**476.6**	أوروبا
Developed countries[3]	**2 809.7**	**2 981.8**	**3 527.3**	**4 081.9**	**3 763.1**	**371.0**	**470.4**	**433.1**	**905.0**	**406.0**	البلدان المتقدمة النمو[3]
European Union	**2 689.7**	**2 956.3**	**3 506.9**	**4 313.5**	**3 718.3**	**399.7**	**516.2**	**481.9**	**949.1**	**460.7**	الاتحاد الأوروبي
Developed countries	**2 588.1**	**2 775.0**	**3 266.9**	**3 875.0**	**3 578.7**	**354.9**	**470.0**	**429.6**	**898.4**	**403.4**	البلدان المتقدمة النمو
Austria	27.7	59.4	40.7	10.0	13.7	0.4	0.1	0.4	0.5	12.8	النمسا
Belgium	198.7	151.4	273.8	387.7	344.0	32.4	43.5	44.3	99.8	18.2	بلجيكا
Denmark	131.6	147.7	118.1	117.6	141.7	0.4	5.6	1.5	18.5	4.9	الدانمرك
Finland	35.8	28.8	29.2	19.6	19.4	2.0	2.0	1.6	13.4	—	فنلندا
France	434.0	367.6	390.4	346.8	258.9	31.4	16.7	44.7	50.7	8.2	فرنسا
Germany	596.6	633.9	689.3	938.5	863.4	32.4	27.2	49.8	76.4	41.0	المانيا
Greece	5.5	8.6	12.9	112.2	8.8	6.3	8.4	3.8	8.8	6.0	اليونان
Ireland	47.5	52.0	61.9	37.1	33.5	6.0	4.3	4.2	4.5	7.8	آيرلندا
Italy	306.8	418.0	530.2	638.1	572.9	49.0	93.7	53.3	102.0	36.5	ايطاليا
Luxembourg	1.3	1.1	4.3	6.5	3.9	—	—	—	—	—	لكسمبرغ
Netherlands	199.2	270.6	309.3	494.3	425.4	65.8	173.3	109.5	350.6	158.1	هولندا
Portugal	3.0	4.3	60.6	33.4	12.8	9.5	5.9	0.1	17.6	0.3	البرتغال
Spain	94.9	110.6	150.8	171.9	218.7	28.8	45.3	13.4	70.5	48.0	اسبانيا
Sweden	100.6	90.7	114.8	45.0	147.0	1.3	0.2	3.4	1.0	0.4	السويد
United Kingdom of Great Britain and Northern Ireland	405.0	430.5	480.5	516.2	514.5	89.3	43.7	99.8	84.0	61.3	المملكة المتحدة لبريطانيا العظمى وأيرلندا الشمالية
Developing countries	**101.5**	**181.4**	**240.0**	**438.5**	**139.7**	**44.8**	**46.1**	**52.2**	**50.8**	**57.3**	البلدان النامية
Bulgaria	24.5	31.6	18.8	53.7	23.4	6.0	1.4	3.4	12.3	2.9	بلغاريا
Cyprus	4.5	5.1	4.9	78.8	4.9	2.7	1.7	1.4	0.8	0.5	قبرص
Czech Republic	12.7	34.9	26.4	2.7	3.2	9.3	12.4	12.1	14.2	8.0	الجمهورية التشيكية
Hungary	17.0	35.3	33.4	3.4	4.4	0.1	0.2	4.3	3.8	1.9	هنغاريا
Poland	19.0	33.0	74.7	66.8	40.9	5.1	3.3	3.4	5.9	8.1	بولندا
Romania	13.0	24.5	47.8	63.4	32.1	12.7	12.5	7.8	8.6	14.5	رومانيا
Slovakia	2.6	7.2	5.2	0.3	0.6	—	—	—	—	—	سلوفاكيا
Others	8.2	9.8	28.8	169.5	30.1	8.9	14.7	19.7	5.0	21.4	غيرها
European Free Trade Association (EFTA)	**221.6**	**206.8**	**260.4**	**206.9**	**184.5**	**16.1**	**0.4**	**3.4**	**6.6**	**2.6**	الرابطة الأوروبية للتجارة الحرة
Norway	37.8	11.7	41.9	18.2	7.9	0.1	—	0.2	0.3	—	النرويج
Switzerland	183.8	195.1	218.4	188.7	176.3	16.0	0.4	3.2	6.3	2.5	سويسرا
Others	—	—	—	—	0.3	—	—	—	—	—	غيرها
Other developed countries	**0.1**	—	—	—	—	—	—	—	—	—	بلدان أوروبية متقدمة أخرى

الجدول 3-8- عُمان: الواردات والصادرات حسب أهم البلدان والكتل الاقتصادية

Table III.8. Oman: Imports and exports by main countries and economic groupings, 2010-2014

(Millions of US dollars) (مليون دولار أمريكي)

	Imports					Exports[1]					
	2010	2011	2012	2013	2014	2010	2011	2012	2013	2014	
Developing countries[4]	**309.3**	**548.4**	**653.3**	**847.1**	**533.7**	**52.2**	**50.5**	**57.6**	**69.6**	**70.6**	**البلدان النامية[4]**
Bosnia and Herzegovina	—	0.1	0.3	—	—	—	—	—	—	—	البوسنة والهرسك
Russian Federation	184.5	318.7	312.4	333.6	362.4	3.7	0.5	2.5	12.2	0.9	الاتحاد الروسي
Ukraine	19.3	45.5	83.3	72.5	30.5	0.6	0.4	0.7	3.2	3.8	أوكرانيا
Other developing countries	**3.9**	**2.7**	**17.3**	**2.4**	**1.2**	**3.2**	**3.4**	**2.1**	**3.5**	**8.6**	**بلدان اوروبية نامية اخرى**
America	**1 056.3**	**1 929.3**	**2 596.9**	**2 992.1**	**2 587.7**	**339.9**	**405.7**	**689.5**	**692.6**	**865.0**	**أمريكا**
Developed countries	**818.2**	**1 197.0**	**1 327.9**	**1 612.9**	**1 355.0**	**288.9**	**297.6**	**663.0**	**576.9**	**595.2**	**البلدان المتقدمة النمو**
Canada	95.1	85.2	168.3	98.2	90.3	3.9	7.5	31.9	19.5	13.1	كندا
United States of America	723.1	1 111.8	1 159.7	1 514.6	1 264.7	285.0	290.1	631.1	557.3	582.2	الولايات المتحدة الأمريكية
Developing countries	**238.1**	**732.3**	**1 269.0**	**1 379.2**	**1 232.7**	**51.0**	**108.0**	**26.5**	**115.7**	**269.8**	**البلدان النامية**
Latin American Integration Association (LAIA)	236.7	730.1	1 267.3	1 354.6	1 230.5	49.0	106.8	24.5	110.2	267.3	**رابطة التكامل لأمريكا اللاتينية**
Argentina	49.8	54.3	40.4	40.8	38.3	7.8	28.3	0.6	1.1	1.6	الأرجنتين
Bolivia	—	—	—	—	—	—	—	—	0.4	—	بوليفيا
Brazil	149.2	623.1	1 189.2	1 235.0	1 139.5	20.9	51.5	5.4	96.8	233.2	البرازيل
Chile	13.3	30.7	15.2	50.5	12.7	0.3	11.4	0.2	0.8	0.1	شيلي
Ecuador	0.4	0.2	0.6	0.4	0.2	2.0	1.3	0.4	1.1	8.1	اكوادور
Mexico	20.7	18.6	18.9	25.9	20.2	0.2	13.5	17.1	8.3	10.7	المكسيك
Others	3.4	3.1	3.1	1.9	19.5	17.7	0.8	0.9	1.7	13.5	غيرها
Other America	1.4	2.2	1.7	24.7	2.2	2.0	1.2	2.0	5.4	2.5	**بلدان أمريكية أخرى**
Oceania	**353.6**	**377.6**	**412.9**	**397.6**	**385.4**	**27.6**	**65.8**	**21.0**	**81.1**	**87.1**	**أوقيانوسيا**
Developed countries	**353.6**	**377.6**	**412.9**	**397.6**	**385.4**	**27.6**	**65.6**	**20.4**	**81.0**	**85.7**	**البلدان المتقدمة النمو**
Australia	316.8	326.5	325.4	332.6	319.4	27.1	40.6	20.0	80.6	63.6	استراليا
New Zealand	36.8	51.1	87.5	65.0	66.0	0.4	24.9	0.3	0.4	22.1	نيوزيلندا
Developing countries	**—**	**—**	**—**	**—**	**—**	**—**	**0.2**	**0.7**	**0.1**	**1.4**	**البلدان النامية**
Asia	**10 189.0**	**12 858.2**	**14 242.8**	**25 778.8**	**21 753.2**	**5 335.9**	**6 527.4**	**9 512.1**	**19 881.1**	**47 733.5**	**أسيا**
Developed countries: Japan	**337.2**	**432.8**	**564.2**	**3 323.0**	**3 579.2**	**32.0**	**11.5**	**44.2**	**2 175.2**	**3 652.4**	**البلدان المتقدمة النمو: اليابان**
Developing countries	**9 851.8**	**12 425.4**	**13 678.6**	**22 455.8**	**18 174.0**	**5 303.9**	**6 515.9**	**9 467.9**	**17 705.9**	**44 081.1**	**البلدان النامية**
ESCWA member countries	**6 609.0**	**8 226.3**	**8 747.0**	**14 406.9**	**11 830.9**	**2 564.6**	**2 662.4**	**4 408.6**	**9 233.3**	**4 514.6**	**البلدان الأعضاء في الإسكوا**
Asia Middle East (non ESCWA member countries)	**249.1**	**326.6**	**403.5**	**948.1**	**678.7**	**41.2**	**32.5**	**260.9**	**504.1**	**134.8**	**أسيا- الشرق الأوسط (ما عدا البلدان الأعضاء في الإس**
Islamic Republic of Iran	126.8	174.1	206.1	561.2	346.3	7.0	5.0	177.9	323.2	2.9	جمهورية إيران الإسلامية
Turkey	122.3	152.5	197.4	386.9	332.4	34.2	27.5	82.9	180.9	131.8	تركيا

الجدول 3-8- عُمان: الواردات والصادرات حسب أهم البلدان والكتل الاقتصادية

Table III.8. Oman: Imports and exports by main countries and economic groupings, 2010-2014

(Millions of US dollars) (مليون دولار أمريكي)

	Imports 2010	Imports 2011	Imports 2012	Imports 2013	Imports 2014	Exports[(1)] 2010	Exports 2011	Exports 2012	Exports 2013	Exports 2014	
Association of Southeast Asian Nations (ASEAN)	**612.0**	**873.1**	**872.4**	**1 471.5**	**1 480.1**	**636.7**	**871.9**	**931.9**	**939.5**	**2 462.1**	**منظمة التجارة الحرة لرابطة أمم جنوب شرقي آسيا**
Indonesia	86.9	161.7	171.3	214.7	233.2	154.2	300.4	235.9	100.3	69.4	إندونيسيا
Malaysia	228.2	283.7	276.3	267.5	248.5	134.4	203.7	234.4	248.8	225.2	ماليزيا
Philippines	6.6	4.9	6.7	6.7	6.6	2.8	9.9	55.7	137.0	8.3	الفلبين
Singapore	100.3	148.0	169.0	277.2	447.6	131.8	30.7	104.3	256.8	445.6	سنغافورة
Thailand	176.6	251.4	221.1	680.3	482.6	173.4	226.8	162.8	112.5	1 653.7	تايلند
Others	13.4	23.4	28.1	25.2	61.4	40.1	100.3	138.8	84.1	59.8	غيرها
Other Asian countries	**2 381.8**	**2 999.4**	**3 655.6**	**5 629.3**	**4 184.3**	**2 061.4**	**2 949.0**	**3 866.5**	**7 029.1**	**36 969.6**	**بلدان آسيوية أخرى**
Afghanistan	—	—	—	—	—	1.2	0.3	0.3	0.1	—	أفغانستان
Bangladesh	2.1	3.5	3.5	3.4	5.9	12.5	23.8	24.1	43.2	49.6	بنغلاديش
China	946.3	1 079.1	1 368.8	1 048.1	1 405.9	481.5	862.6	1 046.0	1 502.1	22 347.8	الصين
Hong Kong	48.1	12.9	23.4	68.5	78.5	7.5	25.9	32.3	120.5	12.1	هونغ كونغ
India	878.4	1 114.2	1 472.5	3 117.1	1 265.7	841.1	1 074.3	1 680.8	1 264.0	1 537.8	الهند
Korea, Democratic People's Republic o	—	—	—	—	—	—	—	—	—	—	جمهورية كوريا الشعبية الديمقراطية
Korea, Republic of	293.3	503.8	490.8	960.1	1 073.4	227.3	214.9	186.5	2 722.7	7 496.9	جمهورية كوريا
Pakistan	129.9	172.7	185.9	258.1	221.1	175.8	295.8	640.4	1 073.8	1 217.1	باكستان
Sri Lanka	8.1	9.5	7.8	12.6	10.1	52.7	25.8	55.1	160.7	488.3	سري لانكا
Others	75.6	103.6	102.9	161.3	123.7	261.7	425.6	201.0	141.9	3 820.1	غيرها
Africa	**126.0**	**163.1**	**208.4**	**233.6**	**279.9**	**239.1**	**358.3**	**1 111.2**	**1 780.7**	**748.7**	**أفريقيا**
Developed countries: South Africa	**33.5**	**62.5**	**55.2**	**37.9**	**75.8**	**78.3**	**56.9**	**75.1**	**357.2**	**216.3**	**البلدان المتقدمة النمو: جنوب أفريقيا**
Developing countries	**92.5**	**100.5**	**153.3**	**195.7**	**204.1**	**160.8**	**301.4**	**1 036.1**	**1 423.5**	**532.4**	**البلدان النامية**
Arab countries[(5)]	**75.8**	**75.5**	**90.0**	**115.3**	**138.2**	**91.4**	**145.9**	**236.9**	**383.2**	**212.7**	**البلدان العربية[(5)]**
Algeria	0.6	0.4	0.7	0.5	—	15.6	23.8	32.5	20.2	22.5	الجزائر
Djibouti	3.4	1.8	2.9	2.0	1.1	11.0	22.9	19.2	39.6	26.0	جيبوتي
Somalia	71.7	73.3	86.3	112.8	137.1	64.2	98.5	182.6	321.2	162.5	الصومال
Others	—	—	—	—	—	0.6	0.7	2.6	2.3	1.6	غيرها
Central African Customs and Economic Union (CACEU)	0.5	0.4	0.9	0.7	0.7	0.4	1.4	30.0	2.3	10.6	الاتحاد الجمركي والاقتصادي لوسط أفريقيا
Economic Community of West African States (ECOWAS)	1.8	0.1	0.4	0.3	0.3	27.2	25.1	25.3	29.4	41.7	الجماعة الاقتصادية لدول غرب أفريقيا
Other Africa	14.4	24.6	62.0	79.4	64.9	41.8	129.0	743.9	1 008.5	267.5	**بلدان أفريقية أخرى**

(1) Export values exclude re-exports.
(2) Values of Oil trades are not distributed, Year 2014 distributed.
(3) Including EU developed countries, EFTA countries, and other developed countries.
(4) Including EU developing countries.
(5) Except Egypt, Libya, Morroco, Tunisia and Sudan, which are included under "ESCWA member countries",

(1) باستثناء قيم إعادة التصدير.
(2) قيم صادرات النفط غير موزعة، باستثناء عام 2014
(3) بما في ذلك البلدان المتقدمة النمو في الاتحاد الأوروبي والرابطة الأوروبية للتجارة الحرة والبلدان المتقدمة النمو الأخرى.
(4) بما في ذلك البلدان النامية في الاتحاد الأوروبي.
(5) ما عدا مصر، وليبيا، والمغرب والسودان، وتونس وأدرجوا تحت بند البلدان الأعضاء في الإسكوا،

الجدول 3-9- فلسطين: الواردات والصادرات حسب أهم البلدان والكتل الاقتصادية

Table III.9. Palestine: Imports and exports by main countries and economic groupings, 2010-2014

(Millions of US dollars) (مليون دولار أمريكي)

	Imports					Exports[1]					
	2010	2011	2012	2013	2014	2010	2011	2012	2013	2014	
World	**3 958.5**	**4 221.1**	**4 697.4**	**5 163.9**	**5 683.2**	**575.5**	**719.6**	**782.4**	**1 165.3**	**943.7**	العالم
Developed countries	**445.0**	**507.4**	**524.6**	**489.8**	**565.2**	**19.2**	**22.9**	**28.0**	**22.9**	**33.1**	البلدان المتقدمة النمو
Developing countries and territories	**3 513.5**	**3 713.7**	**4 172.7**	**4 674.1**	**5 118.0**	**556.3**	**696.7**	**754.4**	**1 142.4**	**910.6**	البلدان والأقاليم النامية
Oil trade	—	—	—	—	—	—	—	—	—	—	النفط
Other countries	—	—	—	—	—	—	—	—	—	—	بلدان أخرى
Europe	**419.3**	**496.8**	**496.1**	**494.2**	**579.8**	**10.4**	**15.2**	**15.4**	**13.7**	**21.3**	أوروبا
Developed countries[2]	**370.0**	**444.2**	**449.5**	**426.4**	**477.2**	**9.5**	**12.2**	**11.0**	**11.0**	**19.9**	البلدان المتقدمة النمو[2]
European Union	**367.5**	**443.8**	**469.1**	**455.4**	**514.7**	**9.9**	**14.5**	**14.4**	**13.2**	**20.0**	الاتحاد الأوروبي
Developed countries	**332.6**	**403.4**	**435.3**	**416.1**	**454.5**	**9.0**	**11.7**	**10.6**	**10.6**	**19.5**	البلدان المتقدمة النمو
Austria	4.6	3.2	1.8	2.7	6.1	0.1	0.1	0.2	0.2	0.3	النمسا
Belgium	16.9	15.3	15.9	16.0	19.1	0.3	0.8	2.5	0.7	0.4	بلجيكا
Denmark	5.0	4.5	5.0	5.7	6.6	—	—	—	—	—	الدانمرك
Finland	1.0	3.8	2.0	1.4	1.0	—	—	—	—	—	فنلندا
France	43.4	48.2	62.4	51.6	53.6	0.5	1.4	1.0	0.5	0.6	فرنسا
Germany	82.9	100.3	114.0	124.2	138.4	2.7	1.1	0.8	1.8	2.3	ألمانيا
Greece	4.8	4.5	4.3	4.0	1.8	0.2	—	—	—	0.1	اليونان
Ireland	11.7	11.7	11.1	12.1	14.5	—	—	0.1	0.1	—	آيرلندا
Italy	49.0	61.8	64.9	61.2	62.0	1.0	1.4	1.1	1.2	0.6	ايطاليا
Luxembourg	0.1	0.3	0.7	1.1	0.1	—	—	—	—	—	لكسمبرغ
Netherlands	25.5	29.5	25.9	22.8	37.8	3.0	4.6	2.3	3.0	11.5	هولندا
Portugal	1.6	1.4	4.2	3.7	4.5	—	—	—	—	—	البرتغال
Spain	39.9	56.1	56.7	60.6	61.6	—	—	—	—	—	اسبانيا
Sweden	18.5	33.2	36.6	26.1	19.2	—	0.4	0.1	0.2	0.2	السويد
United Kingdom of Great Britain and Northern Ireland	27.7	29.5	29.8	22.9	28.3	1.1	1.8	2.6	2.9	3.4	المملكة المتحدة لبريطانيا العظمى وأيرلندا الشمالية
Developing countries	**34.9**	**40.5**	**33.8**	**39.3**	**60.1**	**0.8**	**2.8**	**3.8**	**2.6**	**0.5**	البلدان النامية
Bulgaria	1.8	1.0	0.8	1.8	1.9	—	—	—	—	—	بلغاريا
Cyprus	0.1	0.4	0.1	0.3	1.0	—	—	0.2	0.2	0.1	قبرص
Czech Republic	14.6	16.1	9.9	9.0	16.4	—	—	0.1	—	—	الجمهورية التشيكية
Hungary	4.2	3.6	6.4	5.8	11.5	—	—	—	—	—	هنغاريا
Poland	10.9	11.5	12.7	17.5	22.3	0.5	1.3	1.1	1.1	0.3	بولندا
Romania	1.9	3.7	2.1	3.2	3.9	—	—	—	—	—	رومانيا
Slovakia	0.7	1.5	0.8	0.5	0.7	—	—	1.3	1.1	—	سلوفاكيا
Others	0.7	2.4	0.9	1.2	2.4	0.3	1.5	1.2	0.2	0.1	غيرها
European Free Trade Association (EFTA)	**37.4**	**40.8**	**14.2**	**10.1**	**21.3**	**0.5**	**0.5**	**0.4**	**0.4**	**0.4**	الرابطة الأوروبية للتجارة الحرة
Norway	0.1	—	0.2	—	0.1	0.1	—	—	0.1	0.1	النرويج
Switzerland	37.3	40.4	13.8	10.0	21.1	0.4	0.4	0.4	0.3	0.3	سويسرا
Others	—	0.3	0.2	0.1	—	—	—	—	—	—	غيرها
Other developed countries	**0.1**	**0.1**	—	**0.2**	**1.3**	—	—	—	—	—	بلدان أوروبية متقدمة أخرى

الجدول 3-9- فلسطين: الواردات والصادرات حسب أهم البلدان والكتل الاقتصادية

Table III.9. Palestine: Imports and exports by main countries and economic groupings, 2010-2014

(Millions of US dollars)	Imports					Exports[1]					(مليون دولار أمريكي)
	2010	2011	2012	2013	2014	2010	2011	2012	2013	2014	
Developing countries[3]	**49.3**	**52.6**	**46.6**	**67.8**	**102.6**	**0.9**	**3.1**	**4.4**	**2.7**	**1.4**	**البلدان النامية[3]**
Bosnia and Herzegovina	—	—	—	—	0.4	—	—	—	—	—	البوسنة والهرسك
Russian Federation	—	8.5	4.0	6.2	2.0	—	0.3	0.6	0.2	0.8	الاتحاد الروسي
Ukraine	3.5	3.0	8.7	22.2	39.9	—	—	0.1	—	0.1	أوكرانيا
Other developing countries	**0.6**	**0.6**	**0.3**	**0.2**	**0.2**	—	—	—	—	—	**بلدان اوروبية نامية اخرى**
America	**67.2**	**76.5**	**81.3**	**88.1**	**95.2**	**9.5**	**10.6**	**17.1**	**11.2**	**13.1**	**أمريكا**
Developed countries	**50.1**	**42.3**	**46.8**	**45.1**	**54.6**	**9.3**	**10.5**	**16.8**	**11.2**	**12.5**	**البلدان المتقدمة النمو**
Canada	8.2	2.4	2.9	2.7	2.7	2.0	1.8	3.3	0.9	0.5	كندا
United States of America	41.9	39.9	43.9	42.4	51.9	7.3	8.7	13.6	10.3	12.0	الولايات المتحدة الأمريكية
Developing countries	**17.2**	**34.2**	**34.5**	**43.0**	**40.7**	**0.2**	**0.1**	**0.2**	—	**0.6**	**البلدان النامية**
Latin American Integration Association (LAIA)	14.8	27.4	30.5	35.0	36.4	0.2	0.1	0.2	—	0.5	**رابطة التكامل لأمريكا اللاتينية**
Argentina	1.7	1.8	3.3	4.6	3.2	—	—	—	—	—	الأرجنتين
Bolivia	—	—	—	—	0.1	—	—	—	—	—	بوليفيا
Brazil	9.2	18.9	19.3	20.0	23.4	0.2	0.1	0.1	—	0.1	البرازيل
Chile	0.3	0.6	0.1	0.4	0.3	—	—	—	—	—	شيلي
Ecuador	—	—	—	—	0.1	—	—	0.1	—	—	اكوادور
Mexico	1.7	3.2	1.8	3.3	3.6	—	—	—	—	—	المكسيك
Others	2.0	2.9	6.0	6.6	5.7	—	—	—	—	0.4	غيرها
Other America	2.3	6.8	4.0	8.0	4.3	—	—	—	—	0.1	**بلدان أمريكية أخرى**
Oceania	**4.4**	**4.0**	**12.8**	**5.3**	**5.3**	**0.1**	—	—	**0.2**	**0.4**	**أوقيانوسيا**
Developed countries	**4.2**	**3.6**	**12.7**	**5.2**	**5.3**	**0.1**	—	—	**0.2**	**0.4**	**البلدان المتقدمة النمو**
Australia	3.7	3.3	12.5	4.8	4.1	—	—	—	—	—	استراليا
New Zealand	0.5	0.3	0.2	0.4	1.2	0.1	—	—	0.1	0.4	نيوزيلندا
Developing countries	**0.2**	**0.3**	**0.1**	**0.1**	—	—	—	—	—	—	**البلدان النامية**
Asia	**3 461.5**	**3 635.7**	**4 097.9**	**4 565.6**	**4 988.4**	**548.4**	**687.3**	**742.6**	**1 138.2**	**907.7**	**آسيا**
Developed countries: Japan	**20.3**	**17.0**	**14.8**	**12.5**	**27.5**	**0.4**	**0.3**	**0.1**	**0.5**	**0.2**	**البلدان المتقدمة النمو: اليابان**
Developing countries	**3 441.2**	**3 618.7**	**4 083.1**	**4 553.1**	**4 960.9**	**548.0**	**687.0**	**742.6**	**1 137.7**	**907.5**	**البلدان النامية**
ESCWA member countries	**129.8**	**162.3**	**187.2**	**214.8**	**274.3**	**58.7**	**67.6**	**102.0**	**84.8**	**111.7**	**البلدان الأعضاء في الإسكوا**
Asia Middle East (non ESCWA member countries)	**179.1**	**214.7**	**233.1**	**289.2**	**325.9**	**0.5**	**0.4**	**0.9**	**3.0**	**3.0**	**آسيا- الشرق الأوسط (ما عدا البلدان الأعضاء في الإسكوا)**
Islamic Republic of Iran	—	—	—	—	—	—	—	—	—	—	جمهورية إيران الإسلامية
Turkey	179.1	214.7	233.1	289.2	325.9	0.5	0.4	0.9	3.0	3.0	تركيا

الجدول 3-9- فلسطين: الواردات والصادرات حسب أهم البلدان والكتل الاقتصادية

Table III.9. Palestine: Imports and exports by main countries and economic groupings, 2010-2014

(Millions of US dollars) (مليون دولار أمريكي)

	Imports					Exports[1]					
	2010	2011	2012	2013	2014	2010	2011	2012	2013	2014	
Association of Southeast Asian Nations (ASEAN)	**20.3**	**30.6**	**38.1**	**43.7**	**44.8**	**0.1**	**—**	**0.2**	**0.5**	**0.7**	منظمة التجارة الحرة لرابطة أمم جنوب شرقي آسيا
Indonesia	1.1	1.7	2.9	3.0	6.4	—	—	0.2	0.3	0.1	إندونيسيا
Malaysia	4.7	7.4	7.1	6.5	5.7	—	—	—	0.1	0.6	ماليزيا
Philippines	0.8	0.7	0.6	0.4	0.4	—	—	—	—	—	الفلبين
Singapore	1.4	3.5	3.8	4.4	3.2	—	—	—	0.1	—	سنغافورة
Thailand	9.1	12.9	16.9	23.4	21.9	—	—	—	—	—	تايلند
Others	3.2	4.5	6.8	6.1	7.2	0.1	—	—	—	—	غيرها
Other Asian countries	**3 112.0**	**3 211.0**	**3 624.6**	**4 005.4**	**4 315.9**	**488.7**	**619.0**	**639.5**	**1 049.4**	**792.1**	بلدان آسيوية أخرى
Afghanistan	—	—	—	—	—	—	—	—	—	—	أفغانستان
Bangladesh	—	—	—	0.1	0.2	—	—	—	—	—	بنغلاديش
China	181.3	194.1	197.3	236.6	281.8	—	—	—	—	—	الصين
Hong Kong	2.3	2.3	2.3	3.0	4.5	—	—	—	—	—	هونغ كونغ
India	17.1	21.5	22.7	23.5	27.6	—	0.5	—	—	0.1	الهند
Korea, Democratic People's Republic of	0.2	1.0	0.8	1.1	0.1	—	—	—	0.3	—	جمهورية كوريا الشعبية الديمقراطية
Korea, Republic of	29.7	46.9	42.4	38.4	33.5	0.3	0.7	0.2	0.3	0.4	جمهورية كوريا
Pakistan	0.1	0.1	0.1	0.3	0.4	—	—	—	—	—	باكستان
Sri Lanka	4.3	2.2	3.6	3.2	3.5	—	—	—	—	—	سري لانكا
Others	2 877.0	2 942.9	3 355.3	3 699.3	3 964.2	488.4	617.8	639.2	1 048.8	791.6	غيرها
Africa	**6.0**	**8.2**	**9.2**	**10.7**	**14.5**	**7.2**	**6.5**	**7.2**	**2.0**	**1.2**	أفريقيا
Developed countries: South Africa	**0.4**	**0.3**	**0.8**	**0.6**	**0.7**	**—**	**—**	**—**	**0.1**	**0.2**	البلدان المتقدمة النمو: جنوب أفريقيا
Developing countries	**5.6**	**7.9**	**8.4**	**10.2**	**13.8**	**7.2**	**6.5**	**7.2**	**1.9**	**1.1**	البلدان النامية
Arab countries[4]	**—**	**—**	**0.1**	**0.3**	**0.1**	**7.2**	**6.4**	**6.8**	**1.8**	**0.9**	البلدان العربية[4]
Algeria	—	—	—	—	—	7.2	6.4	6.8	1.7	0.8	الجزائر
Djibouti	—	—	—	—	—	—	—	—	—	—	جيبوتي
Somalia	—	—	0.1	0.2	0.1	—	—	—	—	—	الصومال
Others	—	—	—	0.1	—	—	—	0.1	0.1	0.1	غيرها
Central African Customs and Economic Union (CACEU)	0.4	0.2	0.4	0.4	0.3	—	—	0.3	0.2	—	الاتحاد الجمركي والاقتصادي لوسط أفريقيا
Economic Community of West African States (ECOWAS)	1.1	2.7	2.0	2.5	5.4	—	—	—	—	0.1	الجماعة الاقتصادية لدول غرب أفريقيا
Other Africa	4.1	5.0	6.0	6.9	8.0	—	—	0.1	—	—	بلدان أفريقية أخرى

(1) Export values include re-exports.

(2) Including EU developed countries, EFTA countries, and other developed countries.

(3) Including EU developing countries.

(1) بما في ذلك قيم إعادة التصدير.

(2) بما في ذلك البلدان المتقدمة النمو في الاتحاد الأوروبي والرابطة الأوروبية للتجارة الحرة والبلدان المتقدمة النمو الأخرى.

(3) تتضمن البلدان النامية في الاتحاد الأوروبي.

الجدول 3-10- قطر: الواردات والصادرات حسب أهم البلدان والكتل الاقتصادية

Table III.10. Qatar: Imports and exports by main countries and economic groupings, 2010-2014

(Millions of US dollars) (مليون دولار أمريكي)

	Imports					Exports[1]					
	2010	2011	2012	2013	2014	2010	2011	2012	2013	2014	
World	**23 240.2**	**22 329.6**	**26 082.6**	**27 038.3**	**30 442.7**	**74 811.6**	**114 300.6**	**132 967.6**	**136 857.6**	**131 591.7**	**العالم**
Developed countries	**12 595.0**	**11 505.2**	**13 753.2**	**14 014.2**	**15 448.3**	**33 408.8**	**51 328.3**	**53 619.2**	**55 712.8**	**45 700.2**	**البلدان المتقدمة النمو**
Developing countries and territories	**10 645.3**	**10 823.5**	**12 329.4**	**12 989.5**	**14 994.3**	**41 164.8**	**62 843.3**	**78 384.8**	**80 304.7**	**84 995.2**	**البلدان والأقاليم النامية**
Oil trade	—	0.9	—	—	—	**20 193.6**	**26 404.8**	**26 115.2**	**26 115.7**	**26 115.3**	**النفط**
Other countries	—	—	—	**34.6**	—	**238.1**	**128.9**	**963.6**	**840.1**	**896.3**	**بلدان أخرى**
Europe	**7 900.8**	**7 454.9**	**8 356.3**	**8 496.0**	**9 908.0**	**10 096.4**	**18 227.9**	**13 344.2**	**12 917.4**	**10 285.3**	**أوروبا**
Developed countries[2]	**7 480.2**	**6 924.1**	**7 760.3**	**7 942.7**	**9 201.1**	**10023.3**	**18132.8**	**13201.5**	**12780.7**	**10142.0**	**البلدان المتقدمة النمو[2]**
European Union	**7 344.1**	**6 669.7**	**6 984.2**	**7 322.8**	**8 615.3**	**10 054.0**	**18 183.6**	**13 062.4**	**12 740.4**	**9 994.7**	**الاتحاد الأوروبي**
Developed countries	**7 045.7**	**6 314.0**	**6 542.6**	**6 916.7**	**8 098.4**	**10 005.5**	**18 119.1**	**12 953.3**	**12 659.5**	**9 921.1**	**البلدان المتقدمة النمو**
Austria	136.6	143.1	238.0	192.9	182.8	2.5	9.3	14.0	27.9	33.9	النمسا
Belgium	269.3	193.2	189.1	183.8	246.7	1 334.0	1 975.0	1 703.0	1 701.7	1 329.7	بلجيكا
Denmark	103.9	80.0	73.9	74.7	123.5	6.2	86.1	10.3	14.7	47.7	الدانمرك
Finland	82.2	54.6	64.2	63.3	74.7	7.4	12.2	24.0	35.6	64.7	فنلندا
France	1 106.0	748.3	766.0	757.1	928.1	1 176.4	1 731.3	1 533.7	1 823.1	1 263.5	فرنسا
Germany	1 684.0	1 550.8	1 721.3	1 775.4	2 171.1	68.8	81.8	120.7	297.0	195.0	المانيا
Greece	19.7	12.6	20.0	48.8	41.4	20.9	120.6	68.3	54.8	50.0	اليونان
Ireland	76.5	93.1	97.4	105.1	122.5	3.6	6.8	10.5	7.7	9.9	آيرلندا
Italy	1 510.7	1 275.9	1 274.1	1 539.2	1 491.7	93.7	121.4	263.3	2 641.6	1 896.2	ايطاليا
Luxembourg	3.8	4.5	9.6	8.4	25.6	0.2	0.3	—	4.5	20.1	لكسمبرغ
Netherlands	364.4	333.5	377.7	292.9	347.7	509.3	1 432.1	124.0	739.8	433.9	هولندا
Portugal	24.9	35.4	29.2	36.9	59.9	3.7	167.2	56.5	156.4	150.3	البرتغال
Spain	254.8	299.2	304.0	306.0	349.7	3 225.2	4 340.8	4 437.7	1 276.5	1 372.8	اسبانيا
Sweden	225.2	384.1	202.9	182.7	274.5	18.0	25.9	16.0	22.4	25.6	السويد
United Kingdom of Great Britain and Northern Ireland	1 183.6	1 105.6	1 175.1	1 349.5	1 658.4	3 535.6	8 008.3	4 571.4	3 855.8	3 027.8	المملكة المتحدة لبريطانيا العظمى وآيرلندا الشمالية
Developing countries	**298.4**	**355.6**	**441.6**	**406.1**	**516.9**	**48.4**	**64.5**	**109.0**	**80.9**	**73.5**	**البلدان النامية**
Bulgaria	5.1	6.7	10.8	15.1	15.8	0.1	—	2.2	5.5	2.3	بلغاريا
Cyprus	11.4	4.5	8.3	6.1	8.5	20.9	0.4	27.6	1.9	1.8	قبرص
Czech Republic	89.5	86.8	97.8	101.2	129.2	0.3	1.0	3.1	1.3	9.8	الجمهورية التشيكية
Hungary	94.8	113.0	141.6	73.9	101.7	0.2	3.6	5.6	4.3	3.4	هنغاريا
—	54.0	64.3	81.2	88.2	106.2	1.7	14.4	15.5	27.0	20.3	بولندا
Romania	16.3	37.0	49.6	59.4	71.9	0.5	1.5	8.3	29.3	22.0	رومانيا
Slovakia	11.7	19.3	27.2	35.5	45.8	—	0.1	0.2	1.5	3.8	سلوفاكيا
Others	15.5	24.0	25.1	26.6	37.9	24.8	43.5	46.5	10.1	10.1	غيرها
European Free Trade Association (EFTA)	**434.1**	**610.1**	**1 217.7**	**1 026.0**	**1 102.7**	**17.8**	**13.7**	**248.1**	**99.3**	**143.7**	**الرابطة الأوروبية للتجارة الحرة**
Norway	52.4	79.6	207.4	167.3	148.9	0.9	4.8	218.0	1.8	6.0	النرويج
Switzerland	381.4	529.8	1 009.9	857.8	952.6	16.8	8.9	30.1	96.2	137.7	سويسرا
Others	0.4	0.6	0.3	0.9	1.2	—	—	—	1.4	—	غيرها
Other developed countries	**0.3**	—	—	—	—	—	—	—	**21.9**	**77.1**	**بلدان أوروبية متقدمة أخرى**

الجدول 3-10- قطر: الواردات والصادرات حسب أهم البلدان والكتل الاقتصادية

Table III.10. Qatar: Imports and exports by main countries and economic groupings, 2010-2014

(Millions of US dollars) (مليون دولار أمريكي)

	Imports					Exports[1]					
	2010	2011	2012	2013	2014	2010	2011	2012	2013	2014	
Developing countries[3]	**420.6**	**530.8**	**596.0**	**553.4**	**706.8**	**73.1**	**95.1**	**142.8**	**136.7**	**143.4**	**البلدان النامية[3]**
Bosnia and Herzegovina	1.1	1.3	1.2	0.8	1.8	—	—	—	—	7.4	البوسنة والهرسك
Russian Federation	17.9	65.2	109.2	116.2	117.9	0.6	5.5	13.1	16.3	18.4	الاتحاد الروسي
Ukraine	31.9	47.2	17.0	16.4	28.5	21.0	21.6	10.7	20.9	21.6	أوكرانيا
Other developing countries	**71.3**	**61.5**	**27.0**	**13.9**	**41.7**	**3.0**	**3.4**	**9.8**	**18.5**	**22.5**	**بلدان اوروبية نامية اخرى**
America	**3 505.3**	**3 462.1**	**3 745.1**	**4 101.1**	**4 329.0**	**1 366.1**	**2 592.4**	**2 771.5**	**2 285.3**	**2 085.2**	**أمريكا**
Developed countries	**2 901.9**	**2 744.2**	**3 043.0**	**3 458.6**	**3 663.4**	**866.1**	**1 449.3**	**1 273.1**	**940.6**	**564.3**	**البلدان المتقدمة النمو**
Canada	159.9	185.4	176.9	258.8	188.7	72.4	404.3	142.4	144.9	18.9	كندا
United States of America	2 741.9	2 558.8	2 866.2	3 199.8	3 474.7	793.7	1 045.0	1 130.7	795.7	545.4	الولايات المتحدة الأمريكية
Developing countries	**603.4**	**718.0**	**702.0**	**642.5**	**665.6**	**500.0**	**1 143.1**	**1 498.4**	**1 344.7**	**1 520.9**	**البلدان النامية**
Latin American Integration Association (LAIA)	543.6	691.6	683.9	618.7	641.8	354.3	1 134.8	1 392.8	1 328.5	1 477.2	**رابطة التكامل لأمريكا اللاتينية**
Argentina	30.7	19.3	19.0	13.6	20.5	38.1	304.7	17.3	313.5	539.9	الأرجنتين
Bolivia	0.2	0.1	0.1	0.1	0.2	0.3	0.1	0.2	0.1	0.1	بوليفيا
Brazil	396.6	535.6	417.8	366.2	423.8	66.7	188.3	936.6	417.8	309.7	البرازيل
Chile	8.0	10.4	14.3	14.6	11.6	19.5	224.9	0.4	65.8	6.4	شيلي
Ecuador	3.7	4.3	5.9	6.2	5.8	1.9	1.2	3.9	3.1	5.2	اكوادور
Mexico	100.0	118.0	221.4	213.8	175.5	190.7	401.6	299.7	482.6	561.3	المكسيك
Others	4.5	3.9	5.4	4.2	4.4	37.0	14.1	134.6	45.5	54.6	غيرها
Other America	59.8	26.4	18.1	23.8	23.8	145.7	8.3	105.6	16.2	43.7	**بلدان أمريكية أخرى**
Oceania	**386.1**	**534.0**	**758.0**	**619.1**	**554.8**	**848.0**	**1 209.2**	**1 185.9**	**1 201.5**	**1 116.7**	**أوقيانوسيا**
Developed countries	**385.6**	**533.5**	**757.6**	**618.9**	**554.6**	**847.6**	**1 208.9**	**1 185.1**	**1 200.8**	**1 115.2**	**البلدان المتقدمة النمو**
Australia	359.7	506.7	724.0	593.8	521.0	429.8	451.3	826.1	730.4	610.7	استراليا
New Zealand	25.9	26.8	33.6	25.1	33.6	417.8	757.6	359.0	470.4	504.5	نيوزيلندا
Developing countries	**0.5**	**0.5**	**0.4**	**0.2**	**0.2**	**0.4**	**0.3**	**0.8**	**0.7**	**1.6**	**البلدان النامية**
Asia	**11 343.7**	**10 800.3**	**13 137.4**	**13 648.1**	**15 540.3**	**61 730.3**	**91 104.9**	**113 334.1**	**118 319.7**	**116 186.5**	**أسيا**
Developed countries: Japan	**1 750.9**	**1 252.0**	**2 131.8**	**1 913.8**	**1 954.2**	**21 438.0**	**29 779.1**	**36 890.8**	**39 923.9**	**33 288.7**	**البلدان المتقدمة النمو: اليابان**
Developing countries	**9 592.8**	**9 548.2**	**11 005.6**	**11 734.3**	**13 586.0**	**40 292.3**	**61 325.8**	**76 443.3**	**78 395.8**	**82 897.8**	**البلدان النامية**
ESCWA member countries	**4 268.8**	**4 334.3**	**4 639.0**	**4 546.3**	**5 448.9**	**6 803.2**	**7 422.1**	**9 527.9**	**9 590.5**	**10 214.4**	**البلدان الأعضاء في الإسكوا**
Asia Middle East (non ESCWA member countries)	**335.5**	**304.6**	**407.8**	**371.6**	**506.8**	**812.0**	**757.1**	**1 201.2**	**800.7**	**1 396.5**	**أسيا- الشرق الأوسط (ما عدا البلدان الأعضاء في الإسكوا)**
Islamic Republic of Iran	66.1	63.8	39.5	52.1	50.8	38.9	19.6	13.4	15.2	7.3	جمهورية إيران الإسلامية
Turkey	269.3	240.8	368.4	319.6	456.0	773.1	737.5	1 187.8	785.4	1 389.2	تركيا

الجدول 3-10- قطر: الواردات والصادرات حسب أهم البلدان والكتل الاقتصادية

Table III.10. Qatar: Imports and exports by main countries and economic groupings, 2010-2014

(Millions of US dollars) (مليون دولار أمريكي)

	Imports					Exports[1]					
	2010	2011	2012	2013	2014	2010	2011	2012	2013	2014	
Association of Southeast Asian Nations (ASEAN)	**1 069.0**	**1 086.6**	**1 319.9**	**1 807.8**	**1 792.6**	**9 719.3**	**13 356.2**	**13 308.2**	**13 946.6**	**14 548.8**	**منظمة التجارة الحرة لرابطة أمم جنوب شرقي آسيا**
Indonesia	111.2	121.5	158.1	148.1	150.1	671.9	512.5	1 495.0	1 203.9	1 348.9	إندونيسيا
Malaysia	344.2	283.2	322.0	320.6	425.0	641.1	1 711.8	1 271.7	963.5	685.0	ماليزيا
Philippines	42.1	44.0	53.2	54.5	64.9	433.3	413.3	646.7	1 005.6	719.5	الفلبين
Singapore	165.4	206.8	136.7	595.0	359.7	5 749.5	8 154.8	7 037.4	6 963.2	8 093.9	سنغافورة
Thailand	370.9	377.9	527.8	483.1	523.5	2 174.9	2 413.5	2 630.3	3 568.3	3 430.9	تايلند
Others	35.2	53.2	122.2	206.4	269.5	48.7	150.2	227.1	242.0	270.6	غيرها
Other Asian countries	**3 919.5**	**3 822.7**	**4 638.8**	**5 008.6**	**5 837.7**	**22 957.8**	**39 790.5**	**52 406.0**	**54 058.0**	**56 738.1**	**بلدان آسيوية أخرى**
Afghanistan	—	—	—	0.5	0.1	0.8	0.3	—	—	0.7	أفغانستان
Bangladesh	12.4	15.9	27.8	43.5	42.2	127.0	160.7	305.0	249.2	325.7	بنغلاديش
China	2 103.9	2 154.5	2 547.9	2 659.8	3 212.1	2 225.3	4 495.0	6 814.0	8 864.7	10 109.2	الصين
Hong Kong	25.8	23.6	16.4	17.0	13.6	77.7	43.0	121.8	15.1	17.6	هونغ كونغ
India	701.4	734.2	936.4	895.4	1 168.3	6 397.8	10 817.6	14 629.7	14 303.5	16 739.8	الهند
Korea, Democratic People's Republic of	2.0	3.8	3.9	3.4	1.7	—	—	52.9	0.3	—	جمهورية كوريا الشعبية الديمقراطية
Korea, Republic of	725.9	562.8	797.0	1 080.3	1 031.0	12 030.5	20 136.2	24 675.7	24 551.1	24 722.7	جمهورية كوريا
Pakistan	141.9	170.3	113.7	104.6	104.5	124.7	164.7	392.1	220.7	244.3	باكستان
Sri Lanka	12.4	14.5	16.8	20.9	26.5	57.1	254.3	116.2	75.6	88.2	سري لانكا
Others	193.8	143.2	179.0	183.3	237.6	1 916.9	3 718.8	5 298.5	5 777.8	4 490.0	غيرها
Africa	**104.4**	**77.5**	**85.8**	**139.3**	**110.6**	**532.8**	**1 037.3**	**1 368.3**	**1 293.6**	**1 021.7**	**أفريقيا**
Developed countries: South Africa	**76.5**	**51.4**	**60.5**	**80.3**	**75.0**	**233.9**	**758.3**	**1 068.7**	**866.8**	**590.1**	**البلدان المتقدمة النمو: جنوب أفريقيا**
Developing countries	**27.9**	**26.1**	**25.3**	**59.1**	**35.6**	**298.9**	**279.0**	**299.5**	**426.8**	**431.5**	**البلدان النامية**
Arab countries[4]	**4.4**	**6.8**	**6.4**	**7.6**	**4.3**	**106.8**	**26.4**	**63.9**	**59.3**	**78.1**	**البلدان العربية[4]**
Algeria	0.6	1.4	2.8	4.9	0.6	44.3	24.0	55.3	55.8	75.6	الجزائر
Djibouti	—	0.1	0.3	2.3	2.6	61.5	1.0	1.7	1.8	0.3	جيبوتي
Somalia	3.6	5.2	3.0	0.3	0.8	0.8	0.7	0.9	0.7	1.4	الصومال
Others	0.1	0.1	0.3	0.1	0.3	0.3	0.8	6.1	1.1	0.9	غيرها
Central African Customs and Economic Union (CACEU)	0.9	1.1	1.9	3.0	1.0	2.6	20.6	5.5	9.9	6.7	الاتحاد الجمركي والاقتصادي لوسط أفريقيا
Economic Community of West African States (ECOWAS)	2.7	3.0	4.2	35.0	7.9	42.5	134.3	109.7	102.7	132.7	الجماعة الاقتصادية لدول غرب أفريقيا
Other Africa	20.0	15.2	12.9	13.5	22.4	147.0	97.7	120.4	254.8	213.9	**بلدان أفريقية أخرى**

(1) Export values include re-exports.

(2) Including EU developed countries, EFTA countries, and other developed countries.

(3) Including EU developing countries.

(4) Except Egypt, Libya, Morroco, Tunisia and Sudan, which are included under "ESCWA member countries",

(1) بما في ذلك قيم إعادة التصدير .

(2) بما في ذلك البلدان المتقدمة النمو في الاتحاد الأوروبي والرابطة الأوروبية للتجارة الحرة والبلدان المتقدمة النمو الأخرى.

(3) بما في ذلك البلدان النامية في الاتحاد الأوروبي.

(4) ما عدا مصر، وليبيا، والمغرب والسودان، وتونس وأدرجوا تحت بند البلدان الأعضاء في الإسكوا،

الجدول 3-11 - المملكة العربية السعودية: الواردات والصادرات حسب أهم البلدان والكتل الاقتصادية

Table III.11. Saudi Arabia: Imports and exports by main countries and economic groupings, 2010-2014

(Millions of US dollars) (مليون دولار أمريكي)

	Imports					Exports[1]					
	2010	2011	2012	2013	2014	2010	2011	2012	2013	2014	
World	**106 864.0**	**131 588.3**	**155 594.7**	**168 152.7**	**173 835.0**	**251 146.6**	**364 703.0**	**388 404.3**	**375 871.1**	**342 436.8**	العالم
Developed countries	**56 696.2**	**65 235.2**	**77 246.8**	**82 523.3**	**85 500.8**	**98 725.8**	**150 150.1**	**164 600.7**	**154 658.3**	**134 986.8**	البلدان المتقدمة النمو
Developing countries and territories	**50 162.2**	**66 347.2**	**78 344.7**	**85 628.6**	**88 332.0**	**152 375.8**	**214 528.8**	**223 802.5**	**221 212.5**	**207 449.0**	البلدان والأقاليم النامية
Oil trade (2)	—	—	—	—	—	**189 435.7**	**284 979.3**	**305 240.6**	**293 994.5**	**293 997.8**	النفط[2]
Other countries	**5.6**	**5.9**	**3.2**	**0.8**	**2.1**	**45.1**	**24.0**	**1.1**	**0.3**	**1.1**	بلدان أخرى
Europe	**34 758.0**	**41 387.2**	**46 268.0**	**50 775.0**	**53 587.6**	**24 121.1**	**44 087.0**	**47 463.3**	**43 914.2**	**41 940.8**	اوروبا
Developed countries[3]	**30 626.2**	**35 996.7**	**40 254.4**	**44 912.9**	**47 128.3**	**23850.2**	**43493.3**	**46534.7**	**42965.9**	**41120.8**	البلدان المتقدمة النمو[3]
European Union	**29 775.6**	**35 215.4**	**38 953.6**	**42 138.2**	**45 350.2**	**23 831.8**	**43 646.9**	**46 989.9**	**43 503.8**	**41 660.0**	الاتحاد الأوروبي
Developed countries	**27 607.0**	**32 274.5**	**36 000.2**	**39 070.7**	**42 154.7**	**23 560.8**	**43 093.6**	**46 144.0**	**42 810.7**	**41 001.6**	البلدان المتقدمة النمو
Austria	769.9	1 280.0	1 250.4	1 413.9	1 614.7	—	—	4.8	4.5	16.0	النمسا
Belgium	1 209.6	1 340.8	1 477.6	1 537.9	1 554.7	3 425.4	4 881.4	5 278.2	5 424.0	6 411.3	بلجيكا
Denmark	556.0	630.4	696.3	665.6	765.3	—	—	2.9	40.0	29.6	الدانمرك
Finland	445.6	610.9	671.5	690.1	915.5	—	—	4.5	5.9	21.9	فنلندا
France	4 372.1	4 847.5	4 960.9	5 243.5	5 901.9	4 197.1	6 581.1	6 934.0	8 584.3	8 443.3	فرنسا
Germany	8 275.3	9 057.2	11 031.3	11 949.9	12 558.3	253.9	416.0	367.5	418.7	273.6	ألمانيا
Greece	111.5	160.3	335.5	643.5	850.4	1 621.9	2 281.4	3 288.3	1 490.9	1 667.0	اليونان
Ireland	930.7	940.5	1 140.0	1 274.7	1 407.8	41.9	—	8.8	4.3	5.6	أيرلندا
Italy	3 381.9	4 610.7	4 662.5	5 433.1	5 847.8	4 141.1	10 296.4	10 487.1	9 097.3	6 816.1	ايطاليا
Luxembourg	55.5	65.1	70.1	55.2	48.8	—	—	0.8	0.8	0.5	لكسمبرغ
Netherlands	1 221.9	1 475.8	1 673.1	1 805.6	1 890.4	3 394.7	8 444.6	8 879.6	6 163.5	6 400.1	هولندا
Portugal	141.3	166.4	202.9	235.2	206.4	719.7	1 160.8	964.3	802.9	1 057.3	البرتغال
Spain	1 262.7	1 508.0	1 862.4	2 100.5	2 276.3	4 736.9	7 405.4	7 769.2	7 555.7	7 190.0	اسبانيا
Sweden	1 430.7	1 764.0	1 773.9	1 744.0	1 710.7	105.3	98.4	113.6	102.4	124.5	السويد
United Kingdom of Great Britain and Northern Ireland	3 442.4	3 816.8	4 191.8	4 278.1	4 605.7	922.9	1 528.0	2 040.6	3 115.5	2 544.8	المملكة المتحدة لبريطانيا العظمى وآيرلندا الشمالية
Developing countries	**2 168.6**	**2 940.8**	**2 953.4**	**3 067.5**	**3 195.5**	**270.9**	**553.3**	**845.9**	**693.1**	**658.4**	البلدان النامية
Bulgaria	91.7	214.7	178.9	200.8	179.2	—	—	14.7	11.5	40.0	بلغاريا
Cyprus	17.3	16.8	18.4	27.2	25.9	40.5	—	6.9	8.5	7.7	قبرص
Czech Republic	320.8	345.1	386.9	482.1	601.9	—	—	1.1	0.8	3.5	الجمهورية التشيكية
Hungary	672.3	1 027.2	750.9	470.1	377.9	—	—	3.7	11.5	2.4	هنغاريا
Poland	493.1	456.0	652.8	741.6	1 054.4	142.9	310.1	452.8	381.1	367.2	بولندا
Romania	297.3	511.2	448.3	513.6	426.4	—	—	20.8	4.8	13.9	رومانيا
Slovakia	62.9	99.7	118.7	124.5	168.3	—	—	—	2.1	1.6	سلوفاكيا
Others	213.1	270.1	398.4	507.5	361.6	87.5	243.2	345.9	272.8	222.1	غيرها
European Free Trade Association (EFTA)	**2 464.3**	**3 382.7**	**3 853.4**	**5 435.2**	**4 962.2**	**180.0**	**308.0**	**288.8**	**132.0**	**94.9**	الرابطة الأوروبية للتجارة الحرة
Norway	208.5	105.9	215.5	163.7	169.1	—	46.1	8.8	6.1	5.1	النرويج
Switzerland	2 249.9	3 270.4	3 632.0	5 264.0	4 787.5	180.0	261.9	279.2	124.5	88.5	سويسرا
Others	5.9	6.4	5.9	7.5	5.6	—	—	0.8	1.3	1.3	غيرها
Other developed countries	**554.9**	**339.5**	**400.8**	**406.9**	**11.5**	**109.3**	**91.7**	**101.9**	**23.2**	**24.3**	بلدان أوروبية متقدمة أخرى

الجدول 3-11- المملكة العربية السعودية: الواردات والصادرات حسب أهم البلدان والكتل الاقتصادية

Table III.11. Saudi Arabia: Imports and exports by main countries and economic groupings, 2010-2014

(Millions of US dollars) (مليون دولار أمريكي)

	Imports					Exports[1]					
	2010	2011	2012	2013	2014	2010	2011	2012	2013	2014	
Developing countries[4]	**4 131.8**	**5 390.5**	**6 013.7**	**5 862.1**	**6 459.3**	**270.9**	**593.6**	**928.5**	**948.3**	**820.0**	**البلدان النامية[4]**
Bosnia and Herzegovina	4.8	49.9	10.9	10.1	16.8	—	—	—	—	0.3	البوسنة والهرسك
Russian Federation	902.9	1 221.9	1 465.4	1 692.8	1 895.2	—	40.3	46.4	38.1	46.1	الاتحاد الروسي
Ukraine	1 018.9	1 131.7	1 539.2	998.9	1 232.8	—	—	34.9	211.7	45.6	أوكرانيا
Other developing countries	**36.5**	**46.1**	**44.8**	**92.8**	**118.9**	**—**	**—**	**1.3**	**5.3**	**69.6**	**بلدان اوروبية نامية اخرى**
America	**19 993.0**	**23 928.8**	**28 843.3**	**31 707.8**	**30 399.0**	**37 925.8**	**57 189.2**	**61 953.3**	**59 775.3**	**49 444.1**	**أمريكا**
Developed countries	**15 524.5**	**18 136.0**	**23 292.0**	**24 502.7**	**24 311.0**	**35 199.9**	**52 492.4**	**58 159.9**	**55 672.9**	**45 534.2**	**البلدان المتقدمة النمو**
Canada	1 457.9	1 617.6	2 286.4	1 735.7	1 716.0	1 952.8	2 485.9	2 602.2	2 590.1	2 211.0	كندا
United States of America	14 066.6	16 518.3	21 005.6	22 767.0	22 594.9	33 247.1	50 006.5	55 557.8	53 082.7	43 323.2	الولايات المتحدة الأمريكية
Developing countries	**4 468.6**	**5 792.9**	**5 551.3**	**7 205.1**	**6 088.1**	**2 725.9**	**4 696.9**	**3 793.4**	**4 102.4**	**3 909.9**	**البلدان النامية**
Latin American Integration Association (LAIA)	4 265.1	5 620.3	5 391.0	6 941.6	5 923.0	2 489.6	4 288.3	3 759.2	4 020.8	3 770.4	**رابطة التكامل لأمريكا اللاتينية**
Argentina	410.1	711.7	921.6	1 617.3	1 114.9	54.9	—	9.1	6.9	66.4	الأرجنتين
Bolivia	—	0.5	0.5	0.5	0.3	—	—	—	—	—	بوليفيا
Brazil	3 119.8	3 792.6	3 149.4	3 333.3	2 993.4	2 033.9	3 399.0	2 929.9	3 378.7	3 040.0	البرازيل
Chile	231.2	297.9	245.9	216.3	142.1	—	44.5	42.1	38.4	54.9	شيلي
Ecuador	20.8	18.1	26.1	36.0	47.7	—	31.5	17.6	37.1	36.0	اكوادور
Mexico	396.3	702.9	1 006.7	1 641.6	1 580.3	400.8	744.8	573.1	321.3	335.7	المكسيك
Others	86.9	96.5	40.8	96.5	44.3	—	68.5	187.5	238.4	237.3	غيرها
Other America	203.5	172.5	160.3	263.5	165.1	236.3	408.5	34.1	81.6	139.5	**بلدان أمريكية أخرى**
Oceania	**2 147.2**	**2 358.4**	**2 877.9**	**2 922.4**	**3 031.2**	**504.0**	**1 064.8**	**1 264.5**	**811.2**	**750.1**	**أوقيانوسيا**
Developed countries	**2 145.4**	**2 355.0**	**2 823.8**	**2 922.4**	**3 029.4**	**501.6**	**1 062.4**	**1 250.4**	**810.7**	**728.5**	**البلدان المتقدمة النمو**
Australia	1 657.6	1 751.2	2 186.4	2 387.2	2 318.4	258.7	402.7	430.9	327.2	481.1	استراليا
New Zealand	487.7	603.7	637.3	535.2	710.9	242.9	659.7	819.5	483.5	247.5	نيوزيلندا
Developing countries	**1.9**	**3.5**	**54.1**	**—**	**1.9**	**2.4**	**2.4**	**14.1**	**0.5**	**21.6**	**البلدان النامية**
Asia	**48 524.3**	**62 040.7**	**75 578.5**	**80 411.3**	**83 590.1**	**183 030.6**	**253 564.2**	**266 091.1**	**260 098.5**	**240 116.3**	**أسيا**
Developed countries: Japan	**7 988.6**	**8 284.1**	**10 397.2**	**9 374.1**	**9 948.4**	**36 169.5**	**48 221.4**	**51 254.2**	**47 953.4**	**41 819.5**	**البلدان المتقدمة النمو: اليابان**
Developing countries	**40 535.7**	**53 756.6**	**65 181.3**	**71 037.2**	**73 641.7**	**146 861.0**	**205 342.8**	**214 836.8**	**212 145.1**	**198 296.9**	**البلدان النامية**
ESCWA member countries	**9 596.7**	**12 706.8**	**14 789.5**	**17 557.9**	**17 512.0**	**32 513.7**	**39 620.5**	**40 396.2**	**39 328.0**	**40 472.2**	**البلدان الأعضاء في الإسكوا**
Asia Middle East (non ESCWA member countries)	**2 356.6**	**2 517.4**	**3 678.7**	**3 401.1**	**3 079.8**	**2 647.5**	**3 657.1**	**4 436.6**	**4 173.3**	**3 717.6**	**آسيا- الشرق الأوسط (ما عدا البلدان الأعضاء في الإسكوا)**
Islamic Republic of Iran	157.6	66.1	99.5	125.6	181.9	244.3	309.1	120.0	81.1	102.1	جمهورية إيران الإسلامية
Turkey	2 199.0	2 451.2	3 579.2	3 275.5	2 897.9	2 403.2	3 348.0	4 316.6	4 092.3	3 615.5	تركيا

الجدول 3-11- المملكة العربية السعودية: الواردات والصادرات حسب أهم البلدان والكتل الاقتصادية

Table III.11. Saudi Arabia: Imports and exports by main countries and economic groupings, 2010-2014

(Millions of US dollars) (مليون دولار أمريكي)

	Imports					Exports[1]					
	2010	2011	2012	2013	2014	2010	2011	2012	2013	2014	
Association of Southeast Asian Nations (ASEAN)	**5 641.4**	**7 111.8**	**9 627.1**	**11 015.2**	**11 930.8**	**23 229.6**	**33 963.6**	**33 229.7**	**29 537.1**	**31 161.2**	**منظمة التجارة الحرة لرابطة أمم جنوب شرقي آسيا**
Indonesia	1 144.3	1 441.9	1 947.0	1 977.9	2 433.6	3 836.8	4 759.3	5 263.8	5 497.3	5 586.5	إندونيسيا
Malaysia	1 183.7	1 634.4	1 557.4	1 289.1	1 400.0	1 718.4	2 525.6	2 487.5	2 198.1	2 877.1	ماليزيا
Philippines	200.0	259.2	274.7	255.5	245.9	2 460.3	3 483.8	3 432.0	2 618.1	3 213.4	الفلبين
Singapore	597.9	668.3	1 078.4	1 637.9	1 403.8	10 115.1	16 106.3	14 288.7	11 700.3	12 479.6	سنغافورة
Thailand	2 334.2	2 706.4	3 388.6	3 602.1	3 708.6	4 779.8	6 571.0	7 232.9	6 807.5	6 075.3	تايلند
Others	181.3	401.6	1 381.1	2 252.8	2 739.0	319.2	517.6	524.8	715.7	929.3	غيرها
Other Asian countries	**22 941.1**	**31 420.7**	**37 086.1**	**39 063.0**	**41 119.2**	**88 470.2**	**128 101.6**	**136 774.2**	**139 106.6**	**122 945.8**	**بلدان آسيوية أخرى**
Afghanistan	0.3	0.3	—	0.5	0.3	—	—	10.9	4.5	5.6	أفغانستان
Bangladesh	73.9	116.0	170.9	214.4	248.3	606.4	780.3	851.5	847.2	852.3	بنغلاديش
China	12 493.8	17 287.9	19 785.6	20 930.2	23 232.8	29 923.0	45 467.2	50 195.0	50 383.0	42 848.5	الصين
Hong Kong	70.1	73.9	59.5	55.7	40.5	414.9	505.9	465.9	231.5	276.5	هونغ كونغ
India	4 031.0	4 317.7	5 221.7	5 819.2	6 269.1	19 171.2	27 539.5	32 224.7	34 518.4	30 354.5	الهند
Korea, Democratic People's Republic of	29.3	41.1	25.9	13.6	7.5	—	—	1.1	5.1	2.4	جمهورية كوريا الشعبية الديمقراطية
Korea, Republic of	4 743.8	7 753.7	9 458.0	9 604.8	8 623.0	24 648.6	36 638.3	35 623.1	35 133.4	32 948.9	جمهورية كوريا
Pakistan	371.7	458.4	444.3	551.5	591.2	3 279.5	4 352.9	3 448.8	3 961.6	3 789.9	باكستان
Sri Lanka	42.9	68.8	72.5	77.1	90.1	192.8	193.1	508.3	111.5	120.0	سري لانكا
Others	1 084.3	1 302.9	1 847.8	1 796.0	2 016.3	10 233.7	12 624.4	13 445.0	13 910.4	11 747.1	غيرها
Africa	**1 435.8**	**1 867.2**	**2 023.8**	**2 335.5**	**3 224.8**	**5 520.1**	**8 773.7**	**11 631.1**	**11 271.7**	**10 184.4**	**أفريقيا**
Developed countries: South Africa	**411.5**	**463.5**	**479.5**	**811.2**	**1 083.7**	**3 004.6**	**4 880.6**	**7 401.4**	**7 255.5**	**5 783.8**	**البلدان المتقدمة النمو: جنوب أفريقيا**
Developing countries	**1 024.3**	**1 403.8**	**1 544.3**	**1 524.3**	**2 141.1**	**2 515.5**	**3 893.1**	**4 229.7**	**4 016.3**	**4 400.6**	**البلدان النامية**
Arab countries[5]	**162.4**	**249.1**	**267.5**	**358.1**	**326.4**	**1 230.7**	**1 861.6**	**1 663.0**	**1 877.3**	**2 004.6**	**البلدان العربية[5]**
Algeria	9.9	12.0	17.3	15.2	6.4	273.1	387.5	425.1	558.1	592.3	الجزائر
Djibouti	15.5	13.1	25.9	36.3	32.0	957.6	1 446.4	1 180.0	1 250.9	1 343.5	جيبوتي
Somalia	135.5	224.0	224.0	302.4	282.7	—	27.7	32.8	31.7	40.8	الصومال
Others	1.6	—	0.3	4.3	5.3	—	—	25.1	36.5	28.0	غيرها
Central African Customs and Economic Union (CACEU)	49.6	74.7	45.3	21.9	12.0	—	—	36.0	117.9	35.5	الاتحاد الجمركي والاقتصادي لوسط أفريقيا
Economic Community of West African States (ECOWAS)	9.1	6.9	15.5	26.9	65.6	325.6	514.7	490.1	722.1	630.9	الجماعة الاقتصادية لدول غرب أفريقيا
Other Africa	803.2	1 073.1	1 216.0	1 117.3	1 737.1	959.2	1 516.8	2 040.6	1 298.9	1 729.6	**بلدان أفريقية أخرى**

(1) Export values include re-exports.
(2) Crude oil values are not distributed.
(3) Including EU developed countries, EFTA countries, and other developed countries.
(4) Including EU developing countries.
(5) Except Egypt, Libya, Morroco, Tunisia and Sudan, which are included under "ESCWA member countries",

(1) بما في ذلك قيم إعادة التصدير .
(2) قيم النفط الخام غير موزعة.
(3) بما في ذلك البلدان المتقدمة النمو في الاتحاد الأوروبي والرابطة الأوروبية للتجارة الحرة والبلدان المتقدمة النمو الأخرى.
(4) بما في ذلك البلدان النامية في الاتحاد الأوروبي.
(5) ما عدا مصر، وليبيا، والمغرب والسودان، وتونس وأدرجوا تحت بند البلدان الأعضاء في الإسكوا،

الجدول 3-12- السودان: الواردات والصادرات حسب أهم البلدان والكتل الاقتصادية

Table III.12. Sudan: Imports and exports by main countries and economic groupings, 2010-2014

(Millions of US dollars) (مليون دولار أمريكي)

	Imports 2010	Imports 2011	Imports 2012	Imports 2013	Imports 2014	Exports[1] 2010	Exports[1] 2011	Exports[1] 2012	Exports[1] 2013	Exports[1] 2014	
World	11 855.1	9 546.3	6 580.6	9 918.1	..	11 283.8	8 981.7	3 383.9	7 086.2	..	العالم
Developed countries	3 687.0	2 275.7	1 474.1	2 068.7	..	427.5	607.2	170.4	291.5	..	البلدان المتقدمة النمو
Developing countries and territories	8 151.0	7 244.3	5 095.0	7 407.6	..	10 855.8	8 271.9	2 196.7	6 195.1	..	البلدان والأقاليم النامية
Oil trade	17.6	29.9	35.3	—	..	9 444.4	7 200.6	145.2	3 910.6	..	النفط
Other countries	17.0	26.3	11.6	441.7	..	0.4	102.7	1 016.8	599.7	..	بلدان أخرى
Europe	2 670.5	1 357.4	1 021.1	1 163.2	..	102.1	230.8	119.3	167.5	..	أوروبا
Developed countries[2]	2 349.7	1 065.2	823.3	1 027.4	..	101.0	229.4	81.3	154.1	..	البلدان المتقدمة النمو[2]
European Union	2 326.8	1 060.4	830.0	1 009.5	..	102.0	229.8	115.8	167.3	..	الاتحاد الأوروبي
Developed countries	2 287.2	1 029.3	777.1	992.3	..	101.0	229.3	81.2	153.9	..	البلدان المتقدمة النمو
Austria	40.5	13.5	7.7	5.1	..	0.1	—	—	—	..	النمسا
Belgium	35.2	29.2	33.8	30.8	..	1.0	1.9	0.6	1.5	..	بلجيكا
Denmark	8.9	1.7	5.8	7.0	..	0.3	—	—	0.1	..	الدانمرك
Finland	14.5	13.6	6.3	11.5	..	0.4	0.4	0.4	11.4	..	فنلندا
France	165.5	88.5	63.5	63.3	..	35.5	34.2	37.0	53.5	..	فرنسا
Germany	1 110.3	327.9	139.3	287.4	..	12.9	15.9	8.7	11.3	..	ألمانيا
Greece	3.0	4.6	4.0	7.2	..	5.9	6.0	5.2	6.2	..	اليونان
Ireland	23.1	16.1	8.4	13.5	..	—	—	—	0.3	..	آيرلندا
Italy	211.8	159.7	106.5	170.1	..	2.1	162.5	4.0	11.3	..	ايطاليا
Luxembourg	—	—	—	—	..	—	—	—	—	..	لكسمبرغ
Netherlands	101.3	173.6	82.7	97.2	..	3.6	0.1	6.3	20.0	..	هولندا
Portugal	1.8	1.6	8.6	5.6	..	—	—	0.1	11.6	..	البرتغال
Spain	28.5	21.0	25.1	28.3	..	0.9	0.4	8.8	7.8	..	اسبانيا
Sweden	92.0	46.1	82.3	79.7	..	2.0	1.1	1.7	1.0	..	السويد
United Kingdom of Great Britain and Northern Ireland	450.6	132.3	203.0	185.6	..	36.5	6.8	8.4	17.8	..	المملكة المتحدة لبريطانيا العظمى وآيرلندا الشمالية
Developing countries	39.7	31.2	52.9	17.2	..	1.0	0.5	34.7	13.4	..	البلدان النامية
Bulgaria	1.5	5.5	7.9	0.9	..	—	—	—	0.1	..	بلغاريا
Cyprus	11.0	5.1	9.6	8.7	..	—	—	0.1	—	..	قبرص
Czech Republic	4.6	4.0	2.7	—	..	—	—	—	—	..	الجمهورية التشيكية
Hungary	8.8	4.3	3.1	1.1	..	—	—	—	—	..	هنغاريا
Poland	5.6	4.2	7.3	6.1	..	1.0	0.3	17.9	13.3	..	بولندا
Romania	4.1	4.0	1.6	—	..	—	0.1	16.7	—	..	رومانيا
Slovakia	0.9	0.4	0.7	—	..	—	—	—	—	..	سلوفاكيا
Others	3.2	3.6	19.9	0.5	..	—	0.1	0.1	—	..	غيرها
European Free Trade Association (EFTA)	20.5	14.3	29.0	35.1	..	—	0.1	—	—	..	الرابطة الأوروبية للتجارة الحرة
Norway	2.4	1.6	2.0	4.1	..	—	0.1	—	—	..	النرويج
Switzerland	18.1	12.6	26.1	30.9	..	—	—	—	—	..	سويسرا
Others	0.1	—	0.9	—	..	—	—	—	—	..	غيرها
Other developed countries	42.0	21.7	17.1	0.1	..	—	—	0.1	0.2	..	بلدان أوروبية متقدمة أخرى

الجدول 3-12- السودان: الواردات والصادرات حسب أهم البلدان والكتل الاقتصادية

Table III.12. Sudan: Imports and exports by main countries and economic groupings, 2010-2014

(Millions of US dollars) (مليون دولار أمريكي)

	Imports					Exports[1]					
	2010	2011	2012	2013	2014	2010	2011	2012	2013	2014	
Developing countries[3]	**320.8**	**292.2**	**197.9**	**135.8**	..	**1.1**	**1.4**	**38.0**	**13.4**	..	**البلدان النامية[3]**
Bosnia and Herzegovina	2.2	1.2	0.5	—	..	—	—	—	—	..	البوسنة والهرسك
Russian Federation	170.2	107.3	63.1	—	..	0.1	0.9	3.3	—	..	الاتحاد الروسي
Ukraine	103.4	149.0	78.9	118.6	..	—	—	—	—	..	أوكرانيا
Other developing countries	**5.3**	**3.5**	**2.5**	—	..	—	—	—	—	..	**بلدان اوروبية نامية اخرى**
America	**630.0**	**520.6**	**287.3**	**554.5**	..	**69.2**	**85.9**	**97.4**	**147.2**	..	**أمريكا**
Developed countries	**331.0**	**242.2**	**79.3**	**251.4**	..	**57.1**	**62.3**	**83.9**	**131.1**	..	**البلدان المتقدمة النمو**
Canada	174.9	148.0	13.6	157.0	..	51.6	56.6	81.1	122.8	..	كندا
United States of America	156.1	94.2	65.7	94.4	..	5.5	5.7	2.8	8.3	..	الولايات المتحدة الأمريكية
Developing countries	**299.0**	**278.4**	**207.9**	**303.1**	..	**12.1**	**23.7**	**13.5**	**16.1**	..	**البلدان النامية**
Latin American Integration Association (LAIA)	217.0	166.4	139.0	142.6	..	3.6	7.7	5.0	4.8	..	**رابطة التكامل لأمريكا اللاتينية**
Argentina	26.3	6.5	16.3	6.5	..	—	0.1	0.1	—	..	الأرجنتين
Bolivia	0.1	—	4.6	—	..	—	—	—	—	..	بوليفيا
Brazil	111.9	119.9	88.8	93.1	..	—	—	0.1	0.1	..	البرازيل
Chile	4.5	4.7	1.2	—	..	—	—	—	—	..	شيلي
Ecuador	69.3	32.1	20.3	42.1	..	—	0.1	—	—	..	اكوادور
Mexico	1.7	2.1	1.8	0.8	..	3.6	7.3	4.8	4.7	..	المكسيك
Others	3.3	1.1	6.0	—	..	—	0.2	—	—	..	غيرها
Other America	82.0	112.0	68.9	160.6	..	8.5	16.0	8.5	11.3	..	**بلدان أمريكية أخرى**
Oceania	**257.6**	**316.3**	**255.4**	**448.7**	..	—	**0.1**	—	—	..	**أوقيانوسيا**
Developed countries	**256.2**	**315.6**	**254.6**	**448.7**	..	—	**0.1**	—	—	..	**البلدان المتقدمة النمو**
Australia	212.6	272.8	206.2	402.8	..	—	0.1	—	—	..	استراليا
New Zealand	43.6	42.8	48.4	45.8	..	—	—	—	—	..	نيوزيلندا
Developing countries	**1.4**	**0.7**	**0.8**	—	..	—	—	—	—	..	**البلدان النامية**
Asia	**8 040.9**	**7 080.4**	**4 827.2**	**7 069.5**	..	**11 109.2**	**8 254.4**	**2 133.2**	**5 870.9**	..	**آسيا**
Developed countries: Japan	**714.6**	**591.9**	**295.4**	**340.8**	..	**269.5**	**315.3**	**5.2**	**6.3**	..	**البلدان المتقدمة النمو: اليابان**
Developing countries	**7 326.4**	**6 488.6**	**4 531.9**	**6 728.7**	..	**10 839.8**	**7 939.1**	**2 128.1**	**5 864.6**	..	**البلدان النامية**
ESCWA member countries	**3 189.2**	**2 481.6**	**1 622.4**	**2 627.3**	..	**1 680.6**	**1 429.0**	**1 883.0**	**1 756.7**	..	**البلدان الأعضاء في الإسكوا**
Asia Middle East (non ESCWA member countries)	**253.5**	**645.0**	**247.0**	**360.8**	..	**2.6**	**5.2**	**8.6**	**18.4**	..	**آسيا- الشرق الأوسط (ما عدا البلدان الأعضاء في الإس**
Islamic Republic of Iran	41.3	407.2	20.2	53.8	..	—	—	0.1	—	..	جمهورية إيران الإسلامية
Turkey	212.2	237.7	226.8	307.0	..	2.6	5.2	8.6	18.4	..	تركيا

الجدول 3-12 - السودان: الواردات والصادرات حسب أهم البلدان والكتل الاقتصادية

Table III.12. Sudan: Imports and exports by main countries and economic groupings, 2010-2014

(Millions of US dollars) (مليون دولار أمريكي)

	Imports					Exports[1]					
	2010	2011	2012	2013	2014	2010	2011	2012	2013	2014	
Association of Southeast Asian Nations (ASEAN)	**766.5**	**344.4**	**275.6**	**572.2**	**..**	**45.8**	**149.7**	**10.3**	**8.4**	**..**	**منظمة التجارة الحرة لرابطة أمم جنوب شرقي آسيا**
Indonesia	41.8	33.3	36.7	78.1	..	0.3	56.9	2.5	1.9	..	إندونيسيا
Malaysia	544.0	120.0	102.4	267.7	..	40.0	—	0.6	0.6	..	ماليزيا
Philippines	1.0	0.7	0.5	—	..	—	—	—	—	..	الفلبين
Singapore	13.1	10.5	38.1	7.0	..	3.8	91.1	5.6	5.4	..	سنغافورة
Thailand	147.9	156.4	67.5	197.6	..	1.4	0.3	—	0.5	..	تايلند
Others	18.7	23.4	30.4	21.8	..	0.3	1.4	1.4	—	..	غيرها
Other Asian countries	**3 117.1**	**3 017.6**	**2 386.8**	**3 168.5**	**..**	**9 110.8**	**6 355.2**	**226.1**	**4 081.2**	**..**	**بلدان آسيوية أخرى**
Afghanistan	1.5	7.1	0.1	—	..	0.1	0.1	—	—	..	أفغانستان
Bangladesh	34.6	37.0	179.3	45.2	..	8.3	1.7	1.5	4.1	..	بنغلاديش
China	2 085.1	2 067.3	1 222.2	1 887.5	..	9 033.9	6 323.2	191.9	4 018.0	..	الصين
Hong Kong	4.3	3.4	8.6	5.8	..	0.1	0.1	—	—	..	هونغ كونغ
India	558.6	622.7	665.5	905.4	..	61.9	27.3	29.3	49.8	..	الهند
Korea, Democratic People's Republic of	0.2	0.1	—	—	..	—	—	—	—	..	جمهورية كوريا الشعبية الديمقراطية
Korea, Republic of	314.8	192.2	165.7	199.3	..	1.2	1.0	0.1	—	..	جمهورية كوريا
Pakistan	96.3	64.4	44.4	100.7	..	5.2	1.7	2.4	4.4	..	باكستان
Sri Lanka	0.4	0.6	2.2	1.7	..	—	—	—	—	..	سري لانكا
Others	21.1	22.7	98.7	23.0	..	0.1	0.1	1.0	4.8	..	غيرها
Africa	**239.0**	**245.2**	**178.0**	**240.4**	**..**	**2.8**	**307.8**	**17.1**	**300.9**	**..**	**أفريقيا**
Developed countries: South Africa	**35.6**	**60.8**	**21.5**	**0.4**	**..**	**—**	**0.1**	**—**	**—**	**..**	**البلدان المتقدمة النمو: جنوب أفريقيا**
Developing countries	**203.4**	**184.4**	**156.5**	**240.0**	**..**	**2.8**	**307.7**	**17.1**	**300.9**	**..**	**البلدان النامية**
Arab countries[4]	**29.4**	**47.8**	**19.2**	**28.1**	**..**	**0.4**	**1.6**	**0.3**	**1.7**	**..**	**البلدان العربية[4]**
Algeria	29.3	7.9	18.4	27.9	..	0.4	1.4	0.2	1.2	..	الجزائر
Djibouti	—	39.6	0.7	—	..	—	—	0.1	0.4	..	جيبوتي
Somalia	0.1	0.2	0.1	0.2	..	—	0.2	—	—	..	الصومال
Others	—	0.1	0.1	—	..	—	—	—	—	..	غيرها
Central African Customs and Economic Union (CACEU)	4.0	1.2	3.6	—	..	—	0.2	1.4	0.3	..	الاتحاد الجمركي والاقتصادي لوسط أفريقيا
Economic Community of West African States (ECOWAS)	23.8	2.7	2.9	0.5	..	0.3	0.3	1.0	2.9	..	الجماعة الاقتصادية لدول غرب أفريقيا
Other Africa	146.1	132.8	130.7	211.4	..	2.1	305.7	14.5	296.1	..	**بلدان أفريقية أخرى**

(1) Export values include re-exports.
(2) Including EU developed countries, EFTA countries, and other developed countries.
(3) Including EU developing countries.
(4) Except Egypt, Libya, Morroco, Tunisia and Sudan, which are included under "ESCWA member countries",

(1) بما في ذلك قيم إعادة التصدير.
(2) بما في ذلك البلدان المتقدمة النمو في الاتحاد الأوروبي والرابطة الأوروبية للتجارة الحرة والبلدان المتقدمة النمو الأخرى.
(3) بما في ذلك البلدان النامية في الاتحاد الأوروبي.
(4) ما عدا مصر، وليبيا، والمغرب والسودان، وتونس وأدرجوا تحت بند البلدان الأعضاء في الإسكوا،

الجدول 3-13- الجمهورية العربية السورية: الواردات والصادرات حسب أهم البلدان والكتل الاقتصادية

Table III.13. Syrian Arab Republic: Imports and exports by main countries and economic groupings, 2010-2014

(Millions of US dollars) (مليون دولار أمريكي)

	Imports					Exports[1]					
	2010	2011	2012	2013	2014	2010	2011	2012	2013	2014	
World	**17 392.0**	**19 870.8**	..	..	..	**12 237.9**	**10 501.2**	..	..	..	العالم
Developed countries	**5 029.5**	**5 386.6**	..	..	..	**4 943.8**	**4 438.6**	..	..	..	البلدان المتقدمة النمو
Developing countries and territories	**12 270.0**	**14 348.7**	..	..	..	**6 223.5**	**5 381.6**	..	..	..	البلدان والأقاليم النامية
Oil trade	—	—	..	..	..	**4 302.5**	**107.3**	..	..	..	النفط
Other countries	**92.6**	**135.6**	..	..	..	**1 070.6**	**681.0**	..	..	..	بلدان أخرى
Europe	**7 113.3**	**8 947.9**	..	..	..	**4 684.1**	**4 312.5**	..	..	..	أوروبا
Developed countries[2]	**4 073.1**	**4 445.7**	..	..	..	**4469.6**	**4078.8**	..	..	..	البلدان المتقدمة النمو[2]
European Union	**4 398.7**	**5 517.0**	..	..	..	**4 570.9**	**4 187.6**	..	..	..	الاتحاد الأوروبي
Developed countries	**3 659.4**	**4 125.6**	..	..	..	**4 465.5**	**4 077.7**	..	..	..	البلدان المتقدمة النمو
Austria	52.5	92.6	..	..	..	165.5	12.8	..	..	..	النمسا
Belgium	205.4	222.3	..	..	..	21.3	18.1	..	..	..	بلجيكا
Denmark	37.1	38.9	..	..	..	0.7	0.8	..	..	..	الدانمرك
Finland	55.5	52.5	..	..	..	1.5	1.0	..	..	..	فنلندا
France	346.2	520.1	..	..	..	482.3	605.8	..	..	..	فرنسا
Germany	731.5	820.3	..	..	..	1 469.1	1 162.1	..	..	..	المانيا
Greece	154.6	175.8	..	..	..	49.1	52.0	..	..	..	اليونان
Ireland	30.0	27.1	..	..	..	0.4	0.5	..	..	..	أيرلندا
Italy	1 280.2	1 341.5	..	..	..	1 512.0	1 315.7	..	..	..	ايطاليا
Luxembourg	0.3	0.3	..	..	..	—	0.1	..	..	..	لكسمبرغ
Netherlands	252.9	211.3	..	..	..	395.0	612.6	..	..	..	هولندا
Portugal	25.2	29.1	..	..	..	7.5	9.6	..	..	..	البرتغال
Spain	180.9	200.9	..	..	..	233.3	233.4	..	..	..	اسبانيا
Sweden	158.4	190.0	..	..	..	3.2	4.6	..	..	..	السويد
United Kingdom of Great Britain and Northern Ireland	148.6	202.9	..	..	..	124.5	48.8	..	..	..	المملكة المتحدة لبريطانيا العظمى وأيرلندا الشمالية
Developing countries	**739.3**	**1 391.4**	..	..	..	**105.5**	**109.9**	..	..	..	البلدان النامية
Bulgaria	107.1	40.8	..	..	..	35.2	38.4	..	..	..	بلغاريا
Cyprus	1.3	338.8	..	..	..	30.6	29.4	..	..	..	قبرص
Czech Republic	29.0	50.8	..	..	..	0.2	1.3	..	..	..	الجمهورية التشيكية
Hungary	34.5	105.2	..	..	..	1.3	1.1	..	..	..	هنغاريا
Poland	74.8	53.3	..	..	..	26.6	27.1	..	..	..	بولندا
Romania	171.7	215.5	..	..	..	9.3	8.6	..	..	..	رومانيا
Slovakia	7.5	23.5	..	..	..	0.4	0.2	..	..	..	سلوفاكيا
Others	313.4	563.5	..	..	..	2.0	3.8	..	..	..	غيرها
European Free Trade Association (EFTA)	**273.9**	**266.8**	..	..	..	**1.0**	**1.0**	..	..	..	الرابطة الأوروبية للتجارة الحرة
Norway	7.2	9.9	..	..	..	0.3	0.4	..	..	..	النرويج
Switzerland	266.6	256.0	..	..	..	0.7	0.7	..	..	..	سويسرا
Others	0.1	0.9	..	..	..	—	—	..	..	..	غيرها
Other developed countries	**139.8**	**53.3**	..	..	..	**3.1**	—	..	..	..	بلدان أوروبية متقدمة أخرى

الجدول 3-13 - الجمهورية العربية السورية: الواردات والصادرات حسب أهم البلدان والكتل الاقتصادية

Table III.13. Syrian Arab Republic: Imports and exports by main countries and economic groupings, 2010-2014

(Millions of US dollars) (مليون دولار أمريكي)

	Imports					Exports[1]					
	2010	2011	2012	2013	2014	2010	2011	2012	2013	2014	
Developing countries[3]	**3 040.3**	**4 502.2**	..	..	..	**214.5**	**233.8**	..	..	..	البلدان النامية[3]
Bosnia and Herzegovina	5.9	0.2	..	..	..	2.2	2.0	..	..	..	البوسنة والهرسك
Russian Federation	1 098.1	1 573.9	..	..	..	33.1	37.3	..	..	..	الاتحاد الروسي
Ukraine	1 122.9	1 445.6	..	..	..	63.1	66.2	..	..	..	أوكرانيا
Other developing countries	**74.0**	**91.2**	..	..	..	**10.5**	**18.4**	..	..	..	بلدان اوروبية نامية اخرى
America	**1 661.1**	**1 499.9**	..	..	..	**456.7**	**403.7**	..	..	..	أمريكا
Developed countries	**635.8**	**497.9**	..	..	..	**400.7**	**289.3**	..	..	..	البلدان المتقدمة النمو
Canada	69.6	62.7	..	..	..	3.3	3.0	..	..	..	كندا
United States of America	566.2	435.2	..	..	..	397.4	286.4	..	..	..	الولايات المتحدة الأمريكية
Developing countries	**1 025.4**	**1 002.0**	..	..	..	**56.0**	**114.4**	..	..	..	البلدان النامية
Latin American Integration Association (LAIA)	993.2	972.5	..	..	..	52.9	112.0	..	..	..	رابطة التكامل لأمريكا اللاتينية
Argentina	280.6	337.0	..	..	..	0.5	0.7	..	..	..	الأرجنتين
Bolivia	0.1	0.1	..	..	..	0.1	0.2	..	..	..	بوليفيا
Brazil	607.5	508.2	..	..	..	44.0	93.7	..	..	..	البرازيل
Chile	9.1	5.7	..	..	..	0.2	0.8	..	..	..	شيلي
Ecuador	41.7	46.1	..	..	..	0.4	1.1	..	..	..	اكوادور
Mexico	7.5	14.5	..	..	..	0.7	2.0	..	..	..	المكسيك
Others	46.7	60.8	..	..	..	6.9	13.6	..	..	..	غيرها
Other America	32.2	29.5	..	..	..	3.1	2.4	..	..	..	بلدان أمريكية أخرى
Oceania	**68.7**	**86.6**	..	..	..	**2.2**	**1.9**	..	..	..	أوقيانوسيا
Developed countries	**68.7**	**86.6**	..	..	..	**2.2**	**1.9**	..	..	..	البلدان المتقدمة النمو
Australia	8.5	14.3	..	..	..	2.1	1.8	..	..	..	استراليا
New Zealand	60.3	72.2	..	..	..	0.1	0.2	..	..	..	نيوزيلندا
Developing countries	—	—	..	..	..	—	—	..	..	..	البلدان النامية
Asia	**8 338.1**	**9 055.5**	..	..	..	**5 818.2**	**4 938.7**	..	..	..	آسيا
Developed countries: Japan	**228.2**	**301.8**	..	..	..	**69.3**	**63.4**	..	..	..	البلدان المتقدمة النمو: اليابان
Developing countries	**8 110.0**	**8 753.7**	..	..	..	**5 748.8**	**4 875.2**	..	..	..	البلدان النامية
ESCWA member countries	**2 524.0**	**2 641.8**	..	..	..	**4 736.0**	**4 030.2**	..	..	..	البلدان الأعضاء في الإسكوا
Asia Middle East (non ESCWA member countries)	**1 956.1**	**1 922.1**	..	..	..	**641.0**	**487.4**	..	..	..	آسيا- الشرق الأوسط (ما عدا البلدان الأعضاء في الإسكوا)
Islamic Republic of Iran	300.2	374.9	..	..	..	15.2	20.9	..	..	..	جمهورية إيران الإسلامية
Turkey	1 655.9	1 547.2	..	..	..	625.8	466.6	..	..	..	تركيا

الجدول 3-13- الجمهورية العربية السورية: الواردات والصادرات حسب أهم البلدان والكتل الاقتصادية

Table III.13. Syrian Arab Republic: Imports and exports by main countries and economic groupings, 2010-2014

(Millions of US dollars) (مليون دولار أمريكي)

	Imports					Exports[1]					
	2010	2011	2012	2013	2014	2010	2011	2012	2013	2014	
Association of Southeast Asian Nations (ASEAN)	**489.5**	**695.0**	**..**	**..**	**..**	**6.2**	**10.5**	**..**	**..**	**..**	**منظمة التجارة الحرة لرابطة أمم جنوب شرقي آسيا**
Indonesia	63.2	125.3	..	..	..	2.9	0.9	..	..	..	إندونيسيا
Malaysia	168.9	231.1	..	..	..	1.3	1.7	..	..	..	ماليزيا
Philippines	2.3	1.5	..	..	..	—	—	..	..	..	الفلبين
Singapore	8.4	14.0	..	..	..	0.3	1.1	..	..	..	سنغافورة
Thailand	227.7	294.1	..	..	..	0.2	1.0	..	..	..	تايلند
Others	19.0	29.1	..	..	..	1.4	5.9	..	..	..	غيرها
Other Asian countries	**3 140.4**	**3 494.7**	**..**	**..**	**..**	**365.6**	**347.1**	**..**	**..**	**..**	**بلدان آسيوية أخرى**
Afghanistan	1.6	0.4	..	..	..	1.2	0.8	..	..	..	أفغانستان
Bangladesh	24.4	22.5	..	..	..	16.1	3.1	..	..	..	بنغلاديش
China	1 531.0	1 877.4	..	..	..	81.0	107.6	..	..	..	الصين
Hong Kong	0.5	0.8	..	..	..	4.3	4.4	..	..	..	هونغ كونغ
India	417.2	581.0	..	..	..	12.0	15.5	..	..	..	الهند
Korea, Democratic People's Republic of	0.2	0.3	..	..	..	5.4	—	..	..	..	جمهورية كوريا الشعبية الديمقراطية
Korea, Republic of	915.9	679.3	..	..	..	140.2	51.4	..	..	..	جمهورية كوريا
Pakistan	17.7	23.2	..	..	..	2.3	1.7	..	..	..	باكستان
Sri Lanka	59.7	63.3	..	..	..	0.1	1.6	..	..	..	سري لانكا
Others	172.2	246.5	..	..	..	103.2	160.9	..	..	..	غيرها
Africa	**118.1**	**145.4**	**..**	**..**	**..**	**206.1**	**163.3**	**..**	**..**	**..**	**أفريقيا**
Developed countries: South Africa	**23.8**	**54.6**	**..**	**..**	**..**	**2.0**	**5.1**	**..**	**..**	**..**	**البلدان المتقدمة النمو: جنوب أفريقيا**
Developing countries	**94.4**	**90.8**	**..**	**..**	**..**	**204.1**	**158.2**	**..**	**..**	**..**	**البلدان النامية**
Arab countries[4]	**48.3**	**48.7**	**..**	**..**	**..**	**162.5**	**122.5**	**..**	**..**	**..**	**البلدان العربية[4]**
Algeria	47.5	47.1	..	..	..	156.8	113.4	..	..	..	الجزائر
Djibouti	—	—	..	..	..	2.2	2.6	..	..	..	جيبوتي
Somalia	0.7	1.3	..	..	..	0.8	2.1	..	..	..	الصومال
Others	0.1	0.2	..	..	..	2.7	4.4	..	..	..	غيرها
Central African Customs and Economic Union (CACEU)	0.6	1.8	..	..	..	3.8	3.9	..	..	..	الاتحاد الجمركي والاقتصادي لوسط أفريقيا
Economic Community of West African States (ECOWAS)	41.9	35.8	..	..	..	26.7	20.5	..	..	..	الجماعة الاقتصادية لدول غرب أفريقيا
Other Africa	3.6	4.5	..	..	..	11.0	11.3	..	..	..	**بلدان أفريقية أخرى**

(1) Export values excluded re-exports.
(2) Including EU developed countries, EFTA countries, and other developed countries.
(3) Including EU developing countries.
(4) Except Egypt, Libya, Morroco, Tunisia and Sudan, which are included under "ESCWA member countries", member countries"

(1) باستثناء قيم إعادة التصدير.
(2) تتضمن البلدان المتقدمة النمو في الاتحاد الأوروبي والرابطة الأوروبية للتجارة الحرة والبلدان المتقدمة النمو الأخرى.
(3) بما في ذلك البلدان النامية في الاتحاد الأوروبي.
(4) ما عدا مصر، وليبيا، والمغرب والسودان، وتونس وأدرجوا تحت بند البلدان الأعضاء في الإسكوا،

الجدول 3-14- تونس: الواردات والصادرات حسب أهم البلدان والكتل الاقتصادية

Table III-14. Tunisia: Imports and exports by main countries and economic groupings, 2010-2014

(Millions of US dollars) (مليون دولار أمريكي)

	Imports 2010	Imports 2011	Imports 2012	Imports 2013	Imports 2014	Exports 2010	Exports 2011	Exports 2012	Exports 2013	Exports 2014	
World	**22 215.4**	**23 952.1**	**24 475.6**	**24 266.4**	..	16 426.6	17 847.0	17 007.5	17 060.5	..	العالم
Developed countries	**14 481.0**	**14 610.3**	**13 764.9**	**14 073.0**	..	**12 461.9**	**13 851.3**	**12 805.6**	**12 987.9**	..	البلدان المتقدمة النمو
Developing countries and territories	**7 448.9**	**8 921.6**	**10 255.7**	**9 653.0**	..	**3 386.2**	**3 335.8**	**3 506.0**	**3 360.9**	..	البلدان والأقاليم النامية
Oil trade	**162.4**	**274.0**	**859.5**	**1 914.4**	..	**2 080.8**	**2 288.9**	**1 875.9**	**3 496.3**	..	النفط
Other countries	**285.5**	**420.3**	**455.1**	**540.4**	..	**578.4**	**659.9**	**695.9**	**711.7**	..	بلدان أخرى
Europe	**15 180.6**	**15 849.3**	**14 939.1**	**14 857.5**	..	**12 326.2**	**13 890.3**	**12 938.8**	**12 891.7**	..	اوروبا
Developed countries[1]	**13 126.6**	**13 302.2**	**12 417.9**	**12 864.4**	..	**11981.1**	**13428.3**	**12352.8**	**12484.4**	..	البلدان المتقدمة النمو [1]
European Union	**13 590.5**	**13 769.5**	**13 084.8**	**13 488.5**	..	**12 024.4**	**13 633.8**	**12 140.9**	**12 163.6**	..	الاتحاد الأوروبي
Developed countries	**12 889.4**	**12 997.9**	**12 157.7**	**12 558.9**	..	**11 705.4**	**13 196.9**	**11 586.8**	**11 797.2**	..	البلدان المتقدمة النمو
Austria	109.4	114.4	100.7	108.8	..	53.0	74.2	73.6	66.7	..	النمسا
Belgium	466.0	425.8	405.6	388.9	..	320.3	336.7	357.0	346.9	..	بلجيكا
Denmark	35.2	120.8	74.0	49.6	..	9.0	6.4	15.5	13.7	..	الدانمرك
Finland	98.0	90.3	76.6	86.2	..	1.0	1.2	0.6	—	..	فنلندا
France	4 203.2	4 380.9	4 022.3	4 436.7	..	4 717.3	5 476.8	4 583.5	4 502.9	..	فرنسا
Germany	1 696.6	1 768.5	1 684.4	1 739.8	..	1 388.1	1 615.6	1 398.4	1 533.4	..	المانيا
Greece	107.3	88.3	160.6	119.2	..	16.4	16.0	18.8	15.2	..	اليونان
Ireland	40.5	42.1	44.7	55.8	..	17.0	7.5	8.0	8.4	..	أيرلندا
Italy	3 907.3	3 790.3	3 467.2	3 521.6	..	3 264.9	3 863.8	3 211.8	3 151.3	..	ايطاليا
Luxembourg	4.2	5.3	6.0	7.0	..	0.3	0.5	0.4	0.2	..	لكسمبرغ
Netherlands	441.6	265.7	351.9	257.1	..	360.1	417.6	573.1	609.5	..	هولندا
Portugal	182.8	206.1	155.8	191.2	..	65.0	65.9	50.9	68.7	..	البرتغال
Spain	1 025.3	1 132.5	1 117.3	1 117.8	..	637.1	767.7	736.8	803.2	..	اسبانيا
Sweden	194.5	247.2	168.2	133.1	..	31.3	47.5	29.2	32.4	..	السويد
United Kingdom of Great Britain and Northern Ireland	377.3	319.8	322.6	346.1	..	824.8	499.5	529.1	644.7	..	المملكة المتحدة لبريطانيا العظمى وأيرلندا الشمالية
Developing countries	**701.1**	**771.5**	**927.1**	**929.6**	..	**319.0**	**436.8**	**554.1**	**366.4**	..	البلدان النامية
Bulgaria	49.3	60.8	125.3	247.1	..	17.0	14.1	12.3	11.3	..	بلغاريا
Cyprus	20.3	1.7	4.3	2.1	..	2.8	5.0	6.1	2.5	..	قبرص
Czech Republic	92.7	102.0	76.9	67.3	..	9.8	46.6	91.7	48.1	..	الجمهورية التشيكية
Hungary	69.8	86.4	71.1	89.4	..	12.6	17.8	21.1	32.2	..	هنغاريا
Poland	109.2	80.2	96.0	107.9	..	77.4	85.4	188.8	82.7	..	بولندا
Romania	88.8	85.8	116.1	120.7	..	86.4	121.7	115.7	129.5	..	رومانيا
Slovakia	40.2	26.8	35.2	58.2	..	76.7	93.9	71.6	42.8	..	سلوفاكيا
Others	230.9	327.7	402.3	237.0	..	36.4	52.3	46.6	17.3	..	غيرها
European Free Trade Association (EFTA)	**232.8**	**275.4**	**260.1**	**225.7**	..	**275.2**	**231.0**	**764.9**	**686.8**	..	الرابطة الأوروبية للتجارة الحرة
Norway	25.4	16.1	28.4	9.2	..	9.7	9.1	8.2	7.1	..	النرويج
Switzerland	207.2	258.2	231.0	216.4	..	263.7	219.2	748.8	678.5	..	سويسرا
Others	0.2	1.1	0.7	0.1	..	1.8	2.7	7.9	1.3	..	غيرها
Other developed countries	**4.4**	**28.9**	**0.1**	**79.8**	..	**0.4**	**0.4**	**1.1**	**0.3**	..	بلدان أوروبية متقدمة أخرى

الجدول 3-14- تونس: الواردات والصادرات حسب أهم البلدان والكتل الاقتصادية

Table III-14. Tunisia: Imports and exports by main countries and economic groupings, 2010-2014

(Millions of US dollars) (مليون دولار أمريكي)

	Imports					Exports					
	2010	2011	2012	2013	2014	2010	2011	2012	2013	2014	
Developing countries[2]	**2 054.0**	**2 547.1**	**2 521.2**	**1 993.1**	..	**345.2**	**462.0**	**586.0**	**407.4**	..	البلدان النامية[2]
Bosnia and Herzegovina	0.3	0.4	1.3	26.1	..	0.4	0.4	0.7	0.5	..	البوسنة والهرسك
Russian Federation	1 034.4	1 376.9	1 069.7	655.0	..	15.1	19.0	23.2	27.7	..	الاتحاد الروسي
Ukraine	303.0	333.2	382.0	306.9	..	0.8	1.0	1.7	3.1	..	أوكرانيا
Other developing countries	**15.2**	**65.0**	**141.0**	**75.6**	..	**9.8**	**4.7**	**6.4**	**9.6**	..	بلدان اوروبية نامية اخرى
America	**1 561.8**	**1 951.8**	**1 773.5**	**1 775.1**	..	**546.2**	**431.8**	**485.7**	**581.9**	..	أمريكا
Developed countries	**1 008.7**	**991.8**	**949.8**	**890.3**	..	**408.2**	**301.4**	**346.6**	**415.5**	..	البلدان المتقدمة النمو
Canada	103.4	110.0	157.5	92.0	..	19.6	24.8	20.4	18.1	..	كندا
United States of America	905.2	881.8	792.3	798.4	..	388.5	276.6	326.2	397.5	..	الولايات المتحدة الأمريكية
Developing countries	**553.2**	**960.0**	**823.7**	**884.8**	..	**138.0**	**130.4**	**139.1**	**166.4**	..	البلدان النامية
Latin American Integration Association (LAIA)	538.4	948.8	781.6	825.3	..	134.4	125.4	130.9	160.1	..	رابطة التكامل لأمريكا اللاتينية
Argentina	149.9	308.3	235.4	258.4	..	1.8	1.2	0.7	8.6	..	الأرجنتين
Bolivia	—	0.1	—	—	..	—	—	—	—	..	بوليفيا
Brazil	259.0	456.9	379.8	311.9	..	115.5	113.7	111.4	121.8	..	البرازيل
Chile	3.4	3.2	5.5	9.0	..	1.6	0.9	2.3	0.4	..	شيلي
Ecuador	3.7	10.7	2.0	4.5	..	0.3	2.1	0.2	0.1	..	اكوادور
Mexico	63.0	52.3	54.1	86.5	..	1.5	2.9	2.9	9.0	..	المكسيك
Others	59.5	117.3	104.8	155.0	..	13.7	4.6	13.4	20.2	..	غيرها
Other America	14.8	11.2	42.1	59.5	..	3.6	5.1	8.2	6.3	..	بلدان أمريكية أخرى
Oceania	**15.3**	**13.0**	**31.3**	**13.1**	..	**10.9**	**4.9**	**7.9**	**5.8**	..	أوقيانوسيا
Developed countries	**15.3**	**12.2**	**31.0**	**13.0**	..	**10.2**	**4.4**	**6.9**	**5.3**	..	البلدان المتقدمة النمو
Australia	10.3	8.3	23.6	7.7	..	3.9	4.2	5.2	4.2	..	استراليا
New Zealand	5.0	3.9	7.4	5.3	..	6.3	0.1	1.7	1.1	..	نيوزيلندا
Developing countries	**0.1**	**0.8**	**0.3**	**0.1**	..	**0.7**	**0.5**	**1.0**	**0.5**	..	البلدان النامية
Asia	**4 470.3**	**5 008.8**	**6 213.8**	**5 822.5**	..	**2 097.1**	**1 936.1**	**1 979.8**	**1 958.0**	..	آسيا
Developed countries: Japan	**312.6**	**293.5**	**341.8**	**293.4**	..	**59.8**	**106.7**	**90.2**	**72.9**	..	البلدان المتقدمة النمو: اليابان
Developing countries	**4 157.7**	**4 715.3**	**5 872.0**	**5 529.2**	..	**2 037.2**	**1 829.4**	**1 889.6**	**1 885.1**	..	البلدان النامية
ESCWA member countries	**943.1**	**777.0**	**1 162.4**	**1 232.6**	..	**1 245.1**	**1 299.1**	**1 314.2**	**1 307.6**	..	البلدان الأعضاء في الإسكوا
Asia Middle East (non ESCWA member countries)	**639.4**	**859.5**	**778.3**	**825.1**	..	**267.3**	**169.4**	**134.1**	**224.4**	..	آسيا- الشرق الأوسط (ما عدا البلدان الأعضاء في الإسكوا)
Islamic Republic of Iran	7.6	9.3	6.9	4.1	..	53.2	4.9	5.5	0.9	..	جمهورية إيران الإسلامية
Turkey	631.7	850.2	771.3	821.0	..	214.2	164.5	128.5	223.5	..	تركيا

الجدول 3-14- تونس: الواردات والصادرات حسب أهم البلدان والكتل الاقتصادية

Table III-14. Tunisia: Imports and exports by main countries and economic groupings, 2010-2014

(Millions of US dollars) (مليون دولار أمريكي)

	Imports					Exports					
	2010	2011	2012	2013	2014	2010	2011	2012	2013	2014	
Association of Southeast Asian Nations (ASEAN)	**346.6**	**391.1**	**456.9**	**397.8**	..	**25.3**	**26.6**	**37.9**	**41.1**	..	**منظمة التجارة الحرة لرابطة أمم جنوب شرقي آسيا**
Indonesia	71.6	97.3	115.5	97.0	..	9.0	8.9	12.8	16.6	..	إندونيسيا
Malaysia	74.4	94.8	73.7	80.7	..	12.7	12.8	17.7	16.7	..	ماليزيا
Philippines	9.2	7.7	22.3	14.4	..	0.3	0.2	0.2	0.6	..	الفلبين
Singapore	24.7	20.9	21.3	20.5	..	1.4	3.5	2.9	4.7	..	سنغافورة
Thailand	154.2	150.1	173.9	143.6	..	0.6	1.0	4.1	1.4	..	تايلند
Others	12.6	20.4	50.2	41.7	..	1.3	0.2	0.3	1.2	..	غيرها
Other Asian countries	**2 228.7**	**2 687.7**	**3 474.4**	**3 073.7**	..	**499.5**	**334.3**	**403.4**	**311.9**	..	**بلدان آسيوية أخرى**
Afghanistan	0.1	—	0.1	—	..	0.1	—	—	0.1	..	أفغانستان
Bangladesh	4.0	6.0	9.4	10.1	..	78.2	109.0	93.0	136.5	..	بنغلاديش
China	1 344.1	1 456.1	1 685.8	1 533.2	..	47.1	41.2	84.2	41.4	..	الصين
Hong Kong	40.1	41.2	33.3	25.4	..	14.0	15.8	13.8	27.1	..	هونغ كونغ
India	279.7	350.9	380.3	313.0	..	307.2	134.0	182.0	85.8	..	الهند
Korea, Democratic People's Republic o	2.1	1.2	1.8	1.3	..	—	—	0.1	—	..	جمهورية كوريا الشعبية الديمقراطية
Korea, Republic of	346.4	241.8	507.7	216.2	..	6.5	8.5	10.1	8.3	..	جمهورية كوريا
Pakistan	28.7	37.1	29.7	34.5	..	41.5	19.8	9.1	10.0	..	باكستان
Sri Lanka	3.9	1.2	2.0	1.1	..	—	—	—	—	..	سري لانكا
Others	179.5	552.2	824.2	938.8	..	4.8	6.0	11.0	2.8	..	غيرها
Africa	**701.8**	**709.0**	**1 062.9**	**1 257.8**	..	**867.8**	**923.9**	**899.3**	**911.2**	..	**أفريقيا**
Developed countries: South Africa	**17.9**	**10.6**	**24.4**	**11.9**	..	**2.6**	**10.5**	**9.0**	**9.7**	..	**البلدان المتقدمة النمو: جنوب أفريقيا**
Developing countries	**684.0**	**698.3**	**1 038.5**	**1 245.8**	..	**865.2**	**913.5**	**890.3**	**901.5**	..	**البلدان النامية**
Arab countries[(3)]	**623.5**	**638.3**	**984.3**	**1 186.4**	..	**502.3**	**493.1**	**506.4**	**520.4**	..	**البلدان العربية**[(3)]
Algeria	621.5	637.3	982.8	1 185.2	..	474.7	466.6	485.0	486.4	..	الجزائر
Djibouti	—	—	0.1	—	..	2.9	0.7	0.5	2.5	..	جيبوتي
Somalia	0.1	—	—	—	..	—	—	—	—	..	الصومال
Others	1.9	1.0	1.4	1.1	..	24.6	25.9	20.9	31.5	..	غيرها
Central African Customs and Economic Union (CACEU)	13.8	15.6	11.6	5.6	..	63.0	71.4	80.4	87.8	..	الاتحاد الجمركي والاقتصادي لوسط أفريقيا
Economic Community of West African States (ECOWAS)	39.2	29.4	31.5	24.4	..	176.4	176.2	183.2	195.0	..	الجماعة الاقتصادية لدول غرب أفريقيا
Other Africa	7.4	15.1	11.2	29.5	..	123.5	172.7	120.4	98.2	..	**بلدان أفريقية أخرى**

(1) Including EU developed countries, EFTA countries, and other developed countries.
(2) Including EU developing countries.
(3) Except Egypt, Libya, Morroco, Tunisia and Sudan, which are included under "ESCWA member countries",

(1) بما في ذلك البلدان المتقدمة النمو في الاتحاد الأوروبي والرابطة الأوروبية للتجارة الحرة والبلدان المتقدمة النمو الأخرى.
(2) بما في ذلك البلدان النامية في الاتحاد الأوروبي.
(3) ما عدا مصر، وليبيا، والمغرب والسودان، وتونس وأدرجوا تحت بند البلدان الأعضاء في الإسكوا،

الجدول 3-15 - الامارات العربية المتحدة: الواردات والصادرات حسب أهم البلدان والكتل الاقتصادية

Table III-15. United Arab Emirates: Imports and exports by main countries and economic groupings, 2010-2014

(Millions of US dollars) (مليون دولار أمريكي)

	Imports					Exports[1]					
	2010	2011	2012	2013	2014	2010	2011	2012	2013	2014	
World	**132 175.3**	**164 127.2**	**181 761.8**	**186 540.0**	**189 761.9**	**147 869.3**	**200 070.0**	**225 727.5**	**226 549.2**	**214 074.4**	العالم
Developed countries	**53 509.0**	**64 846.4**	**73 839.9**	**84 770.9**	**83 211.9**	**10 103.5**	**12 927.9**	**26 588.3**	**15 732.3**	**18 945.7**	البلدان المتقدمة النمو
Developing countries and territories	**76 714.2**	**97 044.9**	**105 732.0**	**99 148.4**	**103 599.2**	**62 449.6**	**73 220.9**	**75 579.5**	**82 646.9**	**79 513.9**	البلدان والأقاليم النامية
Oil trade [2]	—	—	—	—	—	**74 638.3**	**111 606.8**	**119 986.1**	**122 973.5**	**111 634.9**	النفط[2]
Other countries	**1 952.1**	**2 236.0**	**2 189.8**	**2 620.7**	**2 950.8**	**677.9**	**2 314.4**	**3 573.7**	**5 196.5**	**3 979.9**	بلدان أخرى
Europe	**33 029.7**	**39 818.6**	**44 074.0**	**54 355.6**	**52 323.3**	**9 387.0**	**11 052.6**	**24 955.3**	**13 374.6**	**16 727.0**	اوروبا
Developed countries[3]	**30 299.3**	**36 870.9**	**40 600.7**	**49 645.6**	**46 957.8**	**8677.2**	**10321.9**	**24286.1**	**12691.6**	**15651.5**	البلدان المتقدمة النمو[3]
European Union	**28 504.8**	**34 309.0**	**37 375.4**	**42 505.0**	**43 076.5**	**3 727.4**	**5 656.3**	**7 304.1**	**9 516.8**	**10 983.2**	الاتحاد الأوروبي
Developed countries	**26 957.6**	**32 488.8**	**35 198.2**	**40 142.7**	**40 240.0**	**3 525.1**	**5 407.8**	**7 086.9**	**9 252.7**	**10 679.8**	البلدان المتقدمة النمو
Austria	605.8	610.6	750.7	746.4	886.6	22.9	31.5	31.1	49.8	55.6	النمسا
Belgium	1 829.5	2 946.0	3 122.5	3 837.0	4 504.6	1 093.1	2 548.4	3 500.7	3 908.6	4 408.2	بلجيكا
Denmark	301.8	317.2	292.5	331.2	367.0	26.8	14.1	12.9	8.7	15.8	الدانمرك
Finland	249.4	352.4	322.2	438.3	277.3	81.2	99.6	92.8	137.9	118.8	فنلندا
France	3 479.7	4 352.1	4 000.1	4 167.6	4 823.5	411.8	485.6	358.1	387.3	546.3	فرنسا
Germany	8 081.5	8 347.5	9 971.8	10 325.0	11 554.5	318.3	417.2	438.4	617.8	699.3	المانيا
Greece	94.0	107.8	128.2	137.8	146.4	23.5	45.8	22.8	35.2	45.4	اليونان
Ireland	309.3	394.1	440.7	436.9	457.3	4.9	8.5	11.3	15.8	9.7	آيرلندا
Italy	4 125.5	5 436.9	6 398.7	5 487.9	5 869.8	348.8	520.0	455.3	368.3	732.8	ايطاليا
Luxembourg	67.3	99.8	84.6	56.2	59.5	6.8	1.3	2.3	13.7	36.3	لكسمبرغ
Netherlands	1 341.1	1 379.1	1 343.9	1 372.5	1 454.3	376.5	305.6	496.5	797.6	1 225.4	هولندا
Portugal	131.7	173.3	213.6	191.4	205.4	7.0	20.9	41.3	16.0	21.9	البرتغال
Spain	1 055.1	1 414.5	1 613.8	1 602.1	1 870.3	73.6	150.2	173.9	188.9	237.6	اسبانيا
Sweden	591.7	709.4	925.5	931.4	1 058.8	16.9	14.8	19.9	18.0	20.3	السويد
United Kingdom of Great Britain and Northern Ireland	4 694.0	5 848.2	5 589.4	10 081.0	6 704.6	712.9	744.4	1 429.5	2 689.1	2 506.6	المملكة المتحدة لبريطانيا العظمى وآيرلندا الشمالية
Developing countries	**1 547.2**	**1 820.1**	**2 177.1**	**2 362.3**	**2 836.5**	**202.3**	**248.5**	**217.2**	**264.1**	**303.4**	البلدان النامية
Bulgaria	37.4	81.9	310.0	208.0	428.6	11.1	18.1	16.7	17.0	17.5	بلغاريا
Cyprus	15.9	18.4	22.6	17.0	23.8	35.8	29.9	19.9	23.0	22.3	قبرص
Czech Republic	289.8	347.9	385.3	423.6	434.0	22.5	32.7	35.3	31.0	36.5	الجمهورية التشيكية
Hungary	531.9	510.2	483.8	677.5	516.8	21.3	11.0	10.3	43.4	20.6	هنغاريا
Poland	286.3	332.6	411.3	453.9	573.0	20.8	38.8	43.4	55.1	119.0	بولندا
Romania	223.0	267.1	235.9	260.9	402.9	48.6	48.0	26.7	28.7	21.0	رومانيا
Slovakia	63.8	154.2	201.1	200.6	221.1	0.8	0.3	1.4	1.5	1.1	سلوفاكيا
Others	99.1	107.7	127.2	120.9	236.2	41.3	69.6	63.6	64.4	65.3	غيرها
European Free Trade Association (EFTA)	**3 329.7**	**4 368.4**	**5 397.0**	**9 472.5**	**6 685.5**	**5 143.1**	**4 905.9**	**17 196.8**	**3 423.9**	**4 961.4**	الرابطة الأوروبية للتجارة الحرة
Norway	195.0	194.4	239.7	289.0	260.0	721.7	32.7	19.5	17.1	306.7	النرويج
Switzerland	3 128.2	4 163.3	5 145.1	9 173.5	6 416.8	4 420.2	4 872.6	17 176.8	3 404.8	4 654.4	سويسرا
Others	6.5	10.8	12.3	10.1	8.6	1.2	0.6	0.4	2.0	0.3	غيرها
Other developed countries	**12.0**	**13.7**	**5.5**	**30.4**	**32.4**	**9.0**	**8.2**	**2.4**	**15.0**	**10.3**	بلدان أوروبية متقدمة أخرى

الجدول 3-15- الامارات العربية المتحدة: الواردات والصادرات حسب أهم البلدان والكتل الاقتصادية

Table III-15. United Arab Emirates: Imports and exports by main countries and economic groupings, 2010-2014

(Millions of US dollars) (مليون دولار أمريكي)

	Imports 2010	Imports 2011	Imports 2012	Imports 2013	Imports 2014	Exports[1] 2010	Exports[1] 2011	Exports[1] 2012	Exports[1] 2013	Exports[1] 2014	
Developing countries[4]	**2 730.4**	**2 947.7**	**3 473.3**	**4 709.9**	**5 365.5**	**709.8**	**730.7**	**669.2**	**683.0**	**1 075.6**	**البلدان النامية[4]**
Bosnia and Herzegovina	6.9	4.0	7.8	8.0	11.8	1.3	1.6	0.7	1.2	3.7	البوسنة والهرسك
Russian Federation	676.6	818.4	841.2	1 941.2	2 059.0	372.3	357.4	362.2	315.2	674.3	الاتحاد الروسي
Ukraine	430.2	265.1	391.7	348.7	383.0	114.2	95.0	70.4	74.5	63.6	أوكرانيا
Other developing countries	**69.4**	**40.2**	**55.4**	**49.7**	**75.2**	**19.7**	**28.2**	**18.7**	**28.1**	**30.5**	**بلدان اوروبية نامية اخرى**
America	**14 656.0**	**19 520.2**	**24 494.6**	**25 734.0**	**25 517.0**	**1 994.1**	**2 625.2**	**1 647.2**	**2 364.6**	**2 537.6**	**أمريكا**
Developed countries	**12 206.6**	**15 986.4**	**19 992.4**	**21 127.7**	**20 962.2**	**960.8**	**1 914.4**	**1 433.9**	**2 118.5**	**2 195.9**	**البلدان المتقدمة النمو**
Canada	959.9	1 479.9	1 473.0	1 739.3	1 722.9	53.7	836.2	97.2	115.8	109.0	كندا
United States of America	11 246.7	14 506.4	18 519.4	19 388.4	19 239.3	907.1	1 078.2	1 336.8	2 002.7	2 086.9	الولايات المتحدة الأمريكية
Developing countries	**2 449.4**	**3 533.8**	**4 502.2**	**4 606.3**	**4 554.7**	**1 033.3**	**710.9**	**213.2**	**246.1**	**341.7**	**البلدان النامية**
Latin American Integration Association (LAIA)	2 021.6	2 611.4	3 236.5	3 356.3	3 700.0	923.6	687.3	167.4	207.1	280.1	**رابطة التكامل لأمريكا اللاتينية**
Argentina	238.5	334.4	376.0	372.3	262.4	10.4	6.0	5.2	7.7	7.0	الأرجنتين
Bolivia	0.4	0.4	0.7	1.3	2.6	3.4	5.6	1.8	0.7	3.2	بوليفيا
Brazil	1 217.5	1 572.0	1 842.9	1 619.9	2 121.6	838.5	567.1	46.1	88.0	97.8	البرازيل
Chile	103.1	146.2	152.3	184.8	179.4	15.6	30.8	39.2	49.3	62.0	شيلي
Ecuador	2.1	3.1	6.8	6.1	9.3	6.7	10.5	10.7	6.8	12.8	اكوادور
Mexico	412.8	480.5	704.8	988.2	1 009.6	13.3	19.4	13.3	12.0	56.1	المكسيك
Others	47.1	74.8	153.0	183.8	115.0	35.6	48.0	51.2	42.7	41.3	غيرها
Other America	427.8	922.4	1 265.8	1 249.9	854.8	109.7	23.6	45.8	39.0	61.6	**بلدان أمريكية أخرى**
Oceania	**2 343.2**	**2 860.7**	**2 660.2**	**3 082.9**	**3 031.7**	**299.4**	**360.6**	**327.0**	**305.4**	**301.6**	**أوقيانوسيا**
Developed countries	**2 342.4**	**2 859.2**	**2 657.6**	**3 080.7**	**3 028.7**	**209.5**	**314.9**	**310.9**	**296.7**	**290.6**	**البلدان المتقدمة النمو**
Australia	2 042.2	2 438.9	2 151.3	2 563.7	2 342.6	151.1	236.3	256.5	244.2	227.6	استراليا
New Zealand	300.2	420.4	506.3	517.0	686.1	58.4	78.6	54.4	52.6	63.0	نيوزيلندا
Developing countries	**0.7**	**1.4**	**2.6**	**2.2**	**3.0**	**89.9**	**45.6**	**16.2**	**8.7**	**11.0**	**البلدان النامية**
Asia	**75 402.0**	**91 490.6**	**97 271.3**	**87 851.1**	**92 565.2**	**56 379.2**	**66 194.8**	**68 989.0**	**76 330.1**	**71 414.2**	**آسيا**
Developed countries: Japan	**7 760.8**	**8 171.6**	**9 643.3**	**9 578.1**	**10 535.2**	**86.4**	**155.2**	**327.3**	**418.4**	**596.0**	**البلدان المتقدمة النمو: اليابان**
Developing countries	**67 641.2**	**83 319.0**	**87 628.0**	**78 273.0**	**82 030.0**	**56 292.8**	**66 039.6**	**68 661.8**	**75 911.7**	**70 818.1**	**البلدان النامية**
ESCWA member countries	**11 657.1**	**14 463.1**	**17 139.3**	**13 489.5**	**13 754.6**	**16 441.7**	**15 820.7**	**21 798.9**	**26 191.7**	**30 406.8**	**البلدان الأعضاء في الإسكوا**
Asia Middle East (non ESCWA member countries)	**3 602.8**	**3 754.5**	**10 725.0**	**5 714.7**	**4 796.9**	**9 623.0**	**15 404.9**	**15 328.9**	**17 650.0**	**14 289.9**	**آسيا- الشرق الأوسط (ما عدا البلدان الأعضاء في الإسكوا)**
Islamic Republic of Iran	1 122.5	1 314.1	1 856.0	1 354.6	1 229.6	9 320.3	14 219.2	12 078.8	12 238.8	11 489.5	جمهورية إيران الإسلامية
Turkey	2 480.3	2 440.4	8 869.0	4 360.1	3 567.4	302.7	1 185.7	3 250.1	5 411.2	2 800.4	تركيا

الجدول 3-15 - الامارات العربية المتحدة: الواردات والصادرات حسب أهم البلدان والكتل الاقتصادية

Table III-15. United Arab Emirates: Imports and exports by main countries and economic groupings, 2010-2014

(Millions of US dollars) (مليون دولار أمريكي)

	Imports					Exports[1]					
	2010	2011	2012	2013	2014	2010	2011	2012	2013	2014	
Association of Southeast Asian Nations (ASEAN)	**8 303.3**	**9 735.6**	**9 895.8**	**11 311.7**	**12 224.1**	**1 433.4**	**2 915.1**	**3 207.3**	**4 264.1**	**3 023.9**	**منظمة التجارة الحرة لرابطة أمم جنوب شرقي آسيا**
Indonesia	1 247.1	1 413.3	1 337.2	1 473.3	1 810.5	81.7	98.5	175.9	172.1	200.2	إندونيسيا
Malaysia	2 946.9	3 566.7	3 390.1	3 500.1	3 359.7	162.4	348.9	333.6	439.7	486.8	ماليزيا
Philippines	194.4	232.1	283.6	303.8	355.7	77.9	74.9	100.6	113.3	99.2	الفلبين
Singapore	1 381.3	1 555.6	1 729.1	1 801.5	1 783.5	578.6	1 306.5	1 749.3	2 672.7	1 375.0	سنغافورة
Thailand	2 119.9	2 443.9	2 385.1	2 967.7	2 934.6	335.3	809.1	589.4	604.3	589.0	تايلند
Others	413.7	523.9	770.7	1 265.3	1 980.1	197.4	277.1	258.5	261.8	273.7	غيرها
Other Asian countries	**44 078.1**	**55 365.9**	**49 867.9**	**47 757.0**	**51 254.3**	**28 794.7**	**31 898.9**	**28 326.7**	**27 806.0**	**23 097.6**	**بلدان آسيوية أخرى**
Afghanistan	21.5	50.3	185.2	37.8	25.4	2 238.4	1 713.4	1 781.9	2 138.7	1 830.4	أفغانستان
Bangladesh	88.3	117.6	191.9	213.5	239.6	90.7	116.7	140.9	150.4	639.2	بنغلاديش
China	13 588.9	14 965.3	15 945.8	17 470.0	22 165.0	619.3	678.6	1 956.3	1 766.9	2 478.2	الصين
Hong Kong	1 049.1	1 717.0	1 726.7	2 427.8	2 751.0	1 338.9	2 449.3	2 847.9	4 228.7	3 477.0	هونغ كونغ
India	22 651.4	28 626.9	20 492.4	19 898.1	17 441.0	21 842.9	24 236.5	18 633.5	16 347.5	11 147.5	الهند
Korea, Democratic People's Republic o	—	—	—	—	—	—	—	—	—	—	جمهورية كوريا الشعبية الديمقراطية
Korea, Republic of	3 305.7	6 240.8	6 683.3	4 433.9	5 594.6	126.3	215.7	177.3	340.5	585.7	جمهورية كوريا
Pakistan	1 782.9	1 961.0	3 154.1	1 204.3	896.3	1 083.1	761.8	733.4	663.8	685.0	باكستان
Sri Lanka	241.5	237.7	163.4	202.6	205.4	122.2	224.4	184.4	197.1	147.2	سري لانكا
Others	1 348.7	1 449.3	1 325.2	1 869.0	1 936.0	1 333.0	1 502.5	1 871.2	1 972.3	2 107.5	غيرها
Africa	**4 792.4**	**8 201.1**	**11 071.9**	**12 895.7**	**13 373.9**	**4 493.4**	**5 915.5**	**6 249.3**	**6 004.5**	**7 479.3**	**أفريقيا**
Developed countries: South Africa	**899.8**	**958.3**	**945.9**	**1 338.7**	**1 727.9**	**169.6**	**221.4**	**230.1**	**207.1**	**211.7**	**البلدان المتقدمة النمو: جنوب أفريقيا**
Developing countries	**3 892.5**	**7 242.8**	**10 126.0**	**11 557.0**	**11 646.0**	**4 323.8**	**5 694.1**	**6 019.2**	**5 797.4**	**7 267.5**	**البلدان النامية**
Arab countries[5]	**204.7**	**395.4**	**168.4**	**127.8**	**182.2**	**938.4**	**1 028.0**	**1 374.9**	**1 546.5**	**1 263.8**	**البلدان العربية[5]**
Algeria	45.7	202.8	16.1	6.3	12.9	304.0	371.9	373.9	417.7	480.8	الجزائر
Djibouti	21.8	14.9	29.7	31.7	66.8	231.6	188.7	222.5	280.8	231.8	جيبوتي
Somalia	80.9	71.9	78.0	73.0	86.8	288.3	365.1	663.0	745.7	432.0	الصومال
Others	56.3	105.9	44.6	16.8	15.7	114.6	102.3	115.6	102.3	119.3	غيرها
Central African Customs and Economic Union (CACEU)	208.4	454.3	690.1	1 292.7	1 480.7	260.6	282.6	331.3	371.3	447.4	الاتحاد الجمركي والاقتصادي لوسط أفريقيا
Economic Community of West African States (ECOWAS)	1 417.2	2 763.6	4 698.4	5 312.8	5 485.0	944.3	1 209.1	1 263.4	1 456.1	1 782.5	الجماعة الاقتصادية لدول غرب أفريقيا
Other Africa	2 062.3	3 629.5	4 569.2	4 823.7	4 498.0	2 180.5	3 174.4	3 049.6	2 423.5	3 773.9	**بلدان أفريقية أخرى**

(1) Export values include re-exports.
(2) Oil values not distributed.
(3) Including EU developed countries, EFTA countries, and other developed countries.
(4) Including EU developing countries.
(5) Except Egypt, Libya, Morroco, Tunisia and Sudan, which are included under "ESCWA member countries",

(1) بما في ذلك قيم إعادة التصدير.
(2) قيم النفط غير موزعة.
(3) بما في ذلك البلدان المتقدمة النمو في الاتحاد الأوروبي والرابطة الأوروبية للتجارة الحرة والبلدان المتقدمة النمو الأخرى.
(4) بما في ذلك البلدان النامية في الاتحاد الأوروبي.
(5) ما عدا مصر، وليبيا، والمغرب والسودان، وتونس وأدرجوا تحت بند البلدان الأعضاء في الإسكوا.

الجدول 3-16- اليمن: الواردات والصادرات حسب أهم البلدان والكتل الاقتصادية

Table III-16. Yemen: Imports and exports by main countries and economic groupings, 2010-2014

(Millions of US dollars) (مليون دولار أمريكي)

	Imports					Exports[1]					
	2010	2011	2012	2013	2014	2010	2011	2012	2013	2014	
World	**9 256.6**	**9 681.1**	**11 300.6**	**13 272.9**	**12 041.6**	**6 436.9**	**6 916.6**	**7 065.2**	**7 129.8**	**2 416.9**	العالم
Developed countries	**2 768.3**	**3 181.7**	**4 160.0**	**4 262.9**	**3 282.4**	**462.4**	**766.4**	**601.2**	**469.9**	**82.6**	البلدان المتقدمة النمو
Developing countries and territories	**6 360.2**	**6 363.0**	**6 866.6**	**8 548.6**	**8 178.3**	**5 958.2**	**6 140.6**	**6 378.9**	**6 628.4**	**2 333.2**	البلدان والأقاليم النامية
Oil trade	—	**0.1**	—	**0.1**	**0.2**	**4 517.4**	**4 480.1**	**5 335.2**	**3 248.7**	**1 271.5**	النفط
Other countries	**128.1**	**136.3**	**274.0**	**461.4**	**580.9**	**16.3**	**9.6**	**85.1**	**31.5**	**1.1**	بلدان أخرى
Europe	**1 930.4**	**2 456.3**	**2 981.1**	**3 109.6**	**1 963.7**	**294.0**	**413.1**	**195.4**	**119.6**	**67.0**	أوروبا
Developed countries[2]	**1 800.9**	**2 347.4**	**2 624.2**	**2 836.0**	**1 489.9**	**292.0**	**412.2**	**171.9**	**118.7**	**66.5**	البلدان المتقدمة النمو[2]
European Union	**1 482.1**	**1 523.7**	**1 673.0**	**2 041.5**	**1 336.7**	**292.1**	**386.5**	**95.6**	**75.7**	**66.1**	الاتحاد الأوروبي
Developed countries	**1 445.7**	**1 499.3**	**1 629.8**	**1 992.8**	**1 265.3**	**291.5**	**385.6**	**75.7**	**75.5**	**66.0**	البلدان المتقدمة النمو
Austria	26.8	21.1	23.9	35.0	35.9	0.3	0.4	0.2	1.8	—	النمسا
Belgium	69.1	56.2	26.7	36.8	51.1	5.7	96.1	4.6	3.4	2.6	بلجيكا
Denmark	37.3	66.7	59.8	66.4	87.3	0.2	—	—	—	—	الدانمرك
Finland	28.5	13.8	5.7	10.1	17.8	0.1	—	0.1	0.1	—	فنلندا
France	258.2	219.2	232.6	349.6	298.7	25.4	31.3	3.1	26.4	15.5	فرنسا
Germany	157.5	120.9	117.6	149.3	314.5	15.0	5.2	7.3	4.3	33.3	المانيا
Greece	1.8	9.0	13.8	3.0	4.1	124.6	65.3	0.3	0.2	—	اليونان
Ireland	12.4	29.9	17.6	14.9	16.8	—	—	0.7	—	0.2	أيرلندا
Italy	133.8	66.3	52.5	76.1	101.2	8.5	9.8	8.5	9.2	7.7	ايطاليا
Luxembourg	—	—	—	0.3	0.7	—	—	—	—	—	لكسمبرغ
Netherlands	533.4	738.5	890.2	1 022.8	58.8	24.2	37.0	36.7	22.0	1.4	هولندا
Portugal	0.3	0.1	0.5	0.8	1.3	0.2	0.5	0.2	0.1	—	البرتغال
Spain	23.5	18.5	42.0	44.9	55.4	38.2	9.0	4.1	2.4	3.1	اسبانيا
Sweden	37.3	27.0	91.8	98.7	113.5	0.1	0.4	0.6	—	—	السويد
United Kingdom of Great Britain and Northern Ireland	125.7	112.2	55.0	84.0	108.3	49.0	130.5	9.3	5.6	2.1	المملكة المتحدة لبريطانيا العظمى وأيرلندا الشمالية
Developing countries	**36.4**	**24.4**	**43.2**	**48.7**	**71.5**	**0.5**	**0.9**	**19.9**	**0.1**	—	البلدان النامية
Bulgaria	0.9	0.2	0.3	0.5	5.5	0.1	—	—	—	—	بلغاريا
Cyprus	3.3	3.4	1.0	1.4	1.0	—	—	—	—	—	قبرص
Czech Republic	0.9	1.8	1.8	9.1	18.6	—	—	—	—	—	الجمهورية التشيكية
Hungary	8.5	4.0	5.9	11.9	12.0	0.1	0.1	—	—	—	هنغاريا
Poland	10.1	3.5	15.1	11.9	8.8	0.2	0.8	0.5	—	—	بولندا
Romania	5.6	4.9	10.9	8.7	9.2	—	—	—	—	—	رومانيا
Slovakia	0.6	0.2	0.3	0.3	8.9	—	—	—	—	—	سلوفاكيا
Others	6.5	6.3	7.8	5.0	7.4	0.1	—	19.4	—	—	غيرها
European Free Trade Association (EFTA)	**305.6**	**820.0**	**993.7**	**681.3**	**25.4**	**0.4**	**26.6**	**96.2**	**41.7**	**0.5**	الرابطة الأوروبية للتجارة الحرة
Norway	1.0	3.3	3.2	0.8	0.9	—	—	—	—	—	النرويج
Switzerland	304.7	816.4	990.6	680.5	24.6	0.4	26.6	96.2	41.7	0.5	سويسرا
Others	—	0.3	—	—	—	—	—	—	—	—	غيرها
Other developed countries	**49.6**	**28.0**	**0.6**	**161.9**	**199.2**	**0.1**	**0.1**	—	**1.5**	—	بلدان أوروبية متقدمة أخرى

الجدول 3-16 - اليمن: الواردات والصادرات حسب أهم البلدان والكتل الاقتصادية

Table III-16. Yemen: Imports and exports by main countries and economic groupings, 2010-2014

(Millions of US dollars) (مليون دولار أمريكي)

	Imports					Exports[1]					
	2010	2011	2012	2013	2014	2010	2011	2012	2013	2014	
Developing countries[3]	**129.5**	**109.0**	**356.9**	**273.6**	**473.8**	**1.9**	**0.9**	**23.5**	**0.9**	**0.5**	**البلدان النامية[3]**
Bosnia and Herzegovina	—	0.1	0.7	0.3	0.2	—	—	—	—	—	البوسنة والهرسك
Russian Federation	73.6	73.3	265.1	209.6	317.6	1.3	—	3.1	0.2	0.4	الاتحاد الروسي
Ukraine	19.4	10.8	48.0	14.7	84.2	0.1	—	0.5	0.6	—	أوكرانيا
Other developing countries	**0.1**	**0.5**	**0.1**	**0.3**	**0.2**	—	—	—	—	—	**بلدان اوروبية نامية اخرى**
America	**1 109.8**	**1 052.3**	**1 128.6**	**1 155.5**	**1 886.2**	**169.3**	**321.2**	**112.6**	**315.2**	**6.4**	**أمريكا**
Developed countries	**539.5**	**487.0**	**447.3**	**470.4**	**723.6**	**126.2**	**277.0**	**57.7**	**58.1**	**5.5**	**البلدان المتقدمة النمو**
Canada	54.2	8.6	14.8	24.0	47.9	0.6	—	2.3	0.2	0.5	كندا
United States of America	485.3	478.4	432.5	446.4	675.8	125.6	277.0	55.3	57.9	5.0	الولايات المتحدة الأمريكية
Developing countries	**570.4**	**565.4**	**681.4**	**685.1**	**1 162.6**	**43.1**	**44.3**	**54.9**	**257.1**	**0.9**	**البلدان النامية**
Latin American Integration Association (LAIA)	527.4	532.2	436.9	672.7	1 160.6	42.5	44.0	53.3	230.9	0.8	**رابطة التكامل لأمريكا اللاتينية**
Argentina	134.0	158.3	—	195.3	408.6	—	0.1	—	—	0.6	الأرجنتين
Bolivia	0.6	—	—	—	—	—	—	—	—	—	بوليفيا
Brazil	381.7	361.5	417.3	468.2	741.6	1.3	—	1.1	0.5	0.2	البرازيل
Chile	0.8	0.1	0.8	1.2	0.7	34.5	29.3	48.1	95.6	—	شيلي
Ecuador	—	0.1	—	—	—	—	—	—	—	—	اكوادور
Mexico	5.1	0.2	1.3	5.2	6.9	6.7	14.6	4.1	32.6	—	المكسيك
Others	5.2	12.1	17.4	2.7	2.8	0.1	—	—	102.2	—	غيرها
Other America	43.0	33.1	244.5	12.4	2.0	0.6	0.2	1.6	26.1	0.1	**بلدان أمريكية أخرى**
Oceania	**218.5**	**202.7**	**592.0**	**362.3**	**467.0**	**1.5**	**—**	**156.7**	**0.1**	**0.2**	**أوقيانوسيا**
Developed countries	**217.9**	**202.4**	**591.7**	**362.0**	**466.8**	**0.1**	**—**	**156.7**	**0.1**	**0.2**	**البلدان المتقدمة النمو**
Australia	178.1	179.8	553.2	327.6	384.2	0.1	—	0.1	0.1	0.2	استراليا
New Zealand	39.8	22.6	38.4	34.3	82.6	—	—	156.6	—	—	نيوزيلندا
Developing countries	**0.7**	**0.3**	**0.3**	**0.3**	**0.2**	**1.4**	**—**	**—**	**—**	**—**	**البلدان النامية**
Asia	**5 753.2**	**5 687.7**	**6 130.0**	**7 965.4**	**6 872.3**	**5 818.5**	**6 050.8**	**6 281.6**	**6 503.6**	**2 227.7**	**أسيا**
Developed countries: Japan	**179.5**	**84.7**	**410.5**	**482.8**	**469.5**	**43.4**	**75.5**	**103.6**	**241.0**	**10.2**	**البلدان المتقدمة النمو: اليابان**
Developing countries	**5 573.7**	**5 603.0**	**5 719.5**	**7 482.6**	**6 402.8**	**5 775.1**	**5 975.3**	**6 178.0**	**6 262.6**	**2 217.5**	**البلدان النامية**
ESCWA member countries	**3 371.7**	**3 519.4**	**2 489.1**	**4 128.0**	**1 899.0**	**821.1**	**819.8**	**420.8**	**1 144.6**	**798.0**	**البلدان الأعضاء في الإسكوا**
Asia Middle East (non ESCWA member countries)	**311.9**	**243.1**	**402.1**	**477.9**	**875.9**	**5.2**	**0.6**	**1.0**	**26.9**	**17.1**	**أسيا- الشرق الأوسط (ما عدا البلدان الأعضاء في الإس**
Islamic Republic of Iran	21.3	12.5	21.7	18.0	27.0	0.9	—	0.5	0.2	—	جمهورية إيران الإسلامية
Turkey	290.6	230.6	380.4	459.8	848.9	4.3	0.6	0.5	26.7	17.1	تركيا

الجدول 3-16- اليمن: الواردات والصادرات حسب أهم البلدان والكتل الاقتصادية

Table III-16. Yemen: Imports and exports by main countries and economic groupings, 2010-2014

(Millions of US dollars) (مليون دولار أمريكي)

	Imports					Exports[1]					
	2010	2011	2012	2013	2014	2010	2011	2012	2013	2014	
Association of Southeast Asian Nations (ASEAN)	**722.5**	**596.8**	**740.8**	**785.2**	**970.9**	**1 068.4**	**1 357.6**	**1 720.1**	**1 890.9**	**481.1**	منظمة التجارة الحرة لرابطة أمم جنوب شرقي آسيا
Indonesia	86.1	48.6	123.2	168.3	271.6	1.4	2.2	0.9	1.2	10.7	إندونيسيا
Malaysia	341.3	221.3	282.6	226.3	321.9	160.1	3.6	126.7	142.1	120.8	ماليزيا
Philippines	0.5	2.0	13.1	21.3	6.5	0.1	—	—	119.8	0.4	الفلبين
Singapore	96.4	169.3	21.3	56.8	20.1	647.9	27.0	193.5	213.6	0.5	سنغافورة
Thailand	190.1	147.8	285.8	297.3	331.0	231.2	1 268.0	1 357.9	1 379.0	330.5	تايلند
Others	8.2	7.7	14.7	15.3	19.7	27.7	56.8	41.0	35.2	18.2	غيرها
Other Asian countries	**1 167.5**	**1 243.8**	**2 087.6**	**2 091.5**	**2 657.0**	**3 880.4**	**3 797.3**	**4 036.1**	**3 200.2**	**921.3**	بلدان أسيوية أخرى
Afghanistan	—	—	0.1	0.1	—	—	—	—	—	0.2	أفغانستان
Bangladesh	0.7	0.9	2.0	4.8	2.8	0.5	0.1	0.6	2.9	0.2	بنغلاديش
China	659.2	573.7	874.4	1 029.6	1 366.4	1 423.4	2 241.1	2 898.9	1 718.8	860.9	الصين
Hong Kong	9.9	6.9	0.4	0.3	0.5	8.3	3.7	2.1	2.3	2.7	هونغ كونغ
India	281.9	444.3	651.2	624.7	804.5	2 163.5	945.6	804.1	543.6	7.7	الهند
Korea, Democratic People's Republic of	0.3	0.6	0.5	0.4	0.8	—	—	—	—	—	جمهورية كوريا الشعبية الديمقراطية
Korea, Republic of	109.7	74.9	208.8	258.5	313.2	274.4	558.0	311.3	892.6	41.7	جمهورية كوريا
Pakistan	87.7	130.4	95.2	132.9	132.2	1.8	2.0	1.3	2.3	1.7	باكستان
Sri Lanka	0.6	0.6	1.6	3.2	3.9	5.7	3.9	4.7	4.4	1.1	سري لانكا
Others	17.4	11.3	253.3	37.0	32.5	2.7	42.9	13.0	33.2	5.1	غيرها
Africa	**116.5**	**145.7**	**195.0**	**218.7**	**271.5**	**137.3**	**121.8**	**233.8**	**159.9**	**114.5**	أفريقيا
Developed countries: South Africa	**30.6**	**60.2**	**86.4**	**111.6**	**132.6**	**0.7**	**1.7**	**111.3**	**51.9**	**0.2**	البلدان المتقدمة النمو: جنوب أفريقيا
Developing countries	**85.9**	**85.4**	**108.5**	**107.0**	**138.9**	**136.7**	**120.1**	**122.5**	**107.9**	**114.2**	البلدان النامية
Arab countries[4]	**51.5**	**43.4**	**48.0**	**50.5**	**24.2**	**110.6**	**89.8**	**70.0**	**84.6**	**94.6**	البلدان العربية[4]
Algeria	0.4	—	0.1	—	—	3.4	0.3	0.2	0.1	—	الجزائر
Djibouti	10.0	7.5	0.8	5.2	0.1	13.7	18.4	12.7	26.2	26.2	جيبوتي
Somalia	41.1	35.8	47.1	45.2	24.0	93.1	70.4	57.0	57.8	67.9	الصومال
Others	—	—	—	0.1	0.1	0.4	0.7	0.2	0.5	0.5	غيرها
Central African Customs and Economic Union (CACEU)	0.2	0.2	0.1	—	—	3.1	2.3	2.4	0.9	0.6	الاتحاد الجمركي والاقتصادي لوسط أفريقيا
Economic Community of West African States (ECOWAS)	0.1	0.6	0.4	0.6	2.0	2.3	4.4	31.9	1.7	0.5	الجماعة الاقتصادية لدول غرب أفريقيا
Other Africa	34.0	41.2	60.0	55.9	112.6	20.7	23.6	18.2	20.8	18.6	بلدان أفريقية أخرى

(1) Export values include re-exports.
(2) Including EU developed countries, EFTA countries, and other developed countries.
(3) Including EU developing countries.
(4) Except Egypt, Libya, Morroco, Tunisia and Sudan, which are included under "ESCWA member countries",

(1) بما في ذلك قيم إعادة التصدير .
(2) بما في ذلك البلدان المتقدمة النمو في الاتحاد الأوروبي والرابطة الأوروبية للتجارة الحرة والبلدان المتقدمة النمو الأخرى.
(3) بما في ذلك البلدان النامية في الاتحاد الأوروبي.
(4) ما عدا مصر، وليبيا، والمغرب والسودان، وتونس وأدرجوا تحت بند البلدان الأعضاء في الإسكوا،

Sources

Bahrain

Council of Ministers, Central Statistics Organization: Bahrain Government website: http://www.data.gov.bh/en/ResourceCenter; *Foreign Trade Statistics, on CD-Rom 2006-2007.*

Bahrain Monetary Agency: *Quarterly Statistical Bulletin (July 2011).*
Central Bank of Bahrain: *Economic Indicators (March 2012).*

Egypt

Central Agency for Public Mobilization and Statistics: *Annual Bulletin of Foreign Trade 2000, on CD-Rom 1999-2012.*

United Nations Statistics Division, Comtrade database: http://comtrade.un.org.

Iraq

Central Statistical Organization, http://cosit.gov.iq.
International Monetary Fund, www.imf.org.

Jordan

Department of Statistics: *External Trade Statistics, 2012* and previous issues;
Department of Statistics: http://www.dos.gov.jo. *External Trade Statistics, 1998-2013.*

United Nations Statistics Division, Comtrade database: http://comtrade.un.org.

المصادر

البحرين

مجلس الوزراء، الجهاز المركزي للإحصاء: صفحة حكومة البحرين على الإنترنت http://www.data.gov.bh/en/ResourceCenter؛ إحصاءات التجارة الخارجية، على أقراص ممغنطة ٢٠٠٦ و٢٠٠٧.

مؤسسة نقد البحرين: النشرة الإحصائية الفصلية (تموز/يوليو ٢٠١١).
مصرف البحرين المركزي: المؤشرات الاقتصادية (آذار/مارس ٢٠١٢).

مصر

الجهاز المركزي للتعبئة العامة والإحصاء؛ النشرة السنوية للتجارة الخارجية على أقراص ممغنطة ١٩٩٩-2012.
شعبة الإحصاءات في الأمم المتحدة، قاعدة بيانات الأمم المتحدة الإحصائية لتجارة السلع الأساسية: http://comtrade.un.org.

العراق

الجهاز المركزي للإحصاء: http://cosit.gov.iq.
صندوق النقد الدولي: www.imf.org.

الأردن

دائرة الإحصاءات العامة: الإحصاءات السنوية للتجارة الخارجية، 2012 وأعداد سابقة؛
دائرة الإحصاءات العامة: http://www.dos.gov.jo؛ الإحصاءات السنوية للتجارة الخارجية، ١٩٩٨-2013.

شعبة الإحصاءات في الأمم المتحدة، قاعدة بيانات الأمم المتحدة الإحصائية لتجارة السلع الأساسية: http://comtrade.un.org.

Kuwait

Ministry of Planning, Central Statistical Office; *Annual Bulletin of Foreign Trade, 2010.* Central Office of Statistics: http://www.mop.gov.kw.

United Nations Statistics Division, Comtrade database: http://comtrade.un.org.

Lebanon

Directorate General of the Customs: http://www.customs.gov.lb.

Libya

United Nations Statistics Division, Comtrade database: http://comtrade.un.org.

Morocco

United Nations Statistics Division, Comtrade database: http://comtrade.un.org.

Oman

Ministry of National Economy: *Foreign Trade Statistics, 2001-2005* and *2007-2011;* Ministry of National Economy.

United Nations Statistics Division, Comtrade database: http://comtrade.un.org.

الكويت

وزارة التخطيط، الإدارة المركزية للإحصاء: النشرة السنوية لإحصاءات التجارة الخارجية، ٢٠١٠، http://www.mop.gov.kw.

شعبة الإحصاءات في الأمم المتحدة، قاعدة بيانات الأمم المتحدة الإحصائية لتجارة السلع الأساسية: http://comtrade.un.org.

لبنان

المديرية العامة للجمارك، http://www.customs.gov.lb.

ليبيا

شعبة الإحصاءات في الأمم المتحدة، قاعدة بيانات إحصاءات تجارة السلع، http://comtrade.un.org

المغرب

شعبة الإحصاءات في الأمم المتحدة، قاعدة بيانات إحصاءات تجارة السلع، http://comtrade.un.org.

عُمان

وزارة الاقتصاد الوطني: إحصاءات التجارة الخارجية، ٢٠٠١-٢٠٠٥ و٢٠٠٧-٢٠١١؛ موقع وزارة الاقتصاد الوطني على الإنترنت.

شعبة الإحصاءات في الأمم المتحدة، قاعدة بيانات إحصاءات تجارة السلع، http://comtrade.un.org.

Palestine

Palestinian Central Bureau of Statistics, *Foreign Trade Statistics, 1998-2012.*

United Nations Statistics Division, Comtrade database: http://comtrade.un.org.

Qatar

The Planning Council: *Foreign Trade Statistics, 2000* (May 2001) and previous issues. *Foreign Trade Statistics, 1998- 2004* and *2007-2010.*

The Planning Council: http://www.gsdp.gov.qa.

Saudi Arabia

Central Department of Statistics: *External Trade Statistics, 1999-2011.* Central Department of Statistics: *Statistical Yearbook, 2003.*

Central Department of Statistics and Information: http://www.cdsi.gov.sa.

The Sudan

Central Bank of Sudan: Foreign Trade Statistical Digest, October-December 2013.

United Nations Statistics Division, Comtrade database: http://comtrade.un.org.

فلسطين

الجهاز المركزي للإحصاء الفلسطيني، إحصاءات التجارة الخارجية، ١٩٩٨-2012.

شعبة الإحصاءات في الأمم المتحدة: قاعدة بيانات إحصاءات تجارة السلع، http://comtrade.un.org.

قطر

مجلس التخطيط للإحصاءات: التجارة الخارجية، ٢٠٠٠ (أيار/مايو ٢٠٠١) وأعداد سابقة. إحصاءات التجارة الخارجية، ١٩٩٨-٢٠٠٤ و٢٠٠٧-٢٠١٠.

مجلس التخطيط، http://www.gsdp.gov.qa.

المملكة العربية السعودية

مصلحة الإحصاءات العامة؛ الإحصاءات السنوية للتجارة الخارجية، ١٩٩٩-٢٠١١. مصلحة الإحصاءات العامة: الكتاب الإحصائي السنوي، ٢٠٠٣.

مصلحة الإحصاءات العامة والمعلومات، http://www.cdsi.gov.sa.

السودان

بنك السودان المركزي، الموجز الإحصائي للتجارة الخارجية أكتوبر - ديسمبر ٢٠١٣.

شعبة الإحصاءات في الأمم المتحدة، قاعدة بيانات إحصاءات تجارة السلع، http://comtrade.un.org.

Syrian Arab Republic

Central Bureau of Statistics, *Statistical Abstract, 2001* and previous issues; *Foreign Trade Statistics, 2001* and previous issues; *Summary of foreign trade, 2003* and previous issues. Central Bureau of Statistics, *Foreign Trade Statistics 2006-2010*. Central Bank of Syria, Quarterly Bulletin, 2005, issues 1-2-3-4.

Central Bureau of Statistics: http://cbssyr.sy.

Tunisia

United Nations Statistics Division, Comtrade database: http://comtrade.un.org.

United Arab Emirates

Central Statistical Department, *Foreign Trade Statistics:* http://www.economy.gov.ae.

Foreign Trade Statistics, 2006-2011.

Central Bank of the United Arab Emirates: http://www.centralbank.ae.

Yemen

Central Statistical Organization, *Statistical Yearbook 2000* (Sana'a, June 2001) and previous issues; *Foreign Trade Statistics, 1998-2013.*

United Nations Statistics Division: Comtrade database: http://comtrade.un.org.

الجمهورية العربية السورية

المكتب المركزي للإحصاء، المجموعة الإحصائية، ٢٠٠١ وأعداد سابقة؛ إحصاءات التجارة الخارجية، ٢٠٠١ وأعداد سابقة؛ خلاصة التجارة الخارجية، ٢٠٠٣ وأعداد سابقة. المكتب المركزي للإحصاء، إحصاءات التجارة الخارجية ٢٠٠٦-٢٠١٠. مصرف سورية المركزي، النشرة الربعية، ٢٠٠٥، الأعداد ١-٢-٣-٤.

المكتب المركزي للإحصاء، http://cbssyr.sy.

تونس

شعبة الإحصاءات في الأمم المتحدة، قاعدة بيانات إحصاءات تجارة السلع، http://comtrade.un.org.

الإمارات العربية المتحدة

الإدارة المركزية للإحصاء، إحصاءات التجارة الخارجية على الإنترنت، http://www.economy.gov.ae.

إحصاءات التجارة الخارجية، ٢٠٠٦-٢٠١١.

المصرف المركزي للإمارات العربية المتحدة، http://www.centralbank.ae.

اليمن

الجهاز المركزي للإحصاء، الكتاب الإحصائي السنوي ٢٠٠٠ (صنعاء، حزيران/يونيو ٢٠٠١) وأعداد سابقة؛ إحصاءات التجارة الخارجية، ١٩٩٨-2013.

شعبة الإحصاءات في الأمم المتحدة، قاعدة بيانات إحصاءات تجارة السلع، http://comtrade.un.org.

Abstract

E/ESCWA/SD/2014/1

نشرة التجارة الخارجية للمنطقة العربية

العدد الرابع والعشرون

تقدم هذه النشرة بيانات ومؤشرات إحصائية عن التجارة الخارجية بالبضائع في البلدان الأعضاء في الإسكوا. وترد البيانات في سلاسل زمنية ممتدة حتى عام 2014، وهي مستمدة من مصادر وطنية بشكل رئيسي ومن مصادر ثانوية حسب الاقتضاء. ويؤمل أن تكون هذه النشرة، بما تقدمه من بيانات إجمالية وبيانات مفصلة عن التجارة البينية والتجارة الخارجية بالبضائع في البلدان الأعضاء، ذات فائدة لصانعي السياسات والمحللين والباحثين على الصعيد المحلي والإقليمي والدولي.

وتتألف النشرة من ثلاثة أجزاء، خُصّص الجزء الأول منها لإحصاءات التجارة الخارجية، ويتضمن جداول عن معدل النمو السنوي للتجارة في المنطقة وإجمالي قيمة الواردات والصادرات والنسبة المئوية لهذه الواردات والصادرات بحسب أقسام النظام المنسق لتوصيف السلع الأساسية وترقيمها. وخُصص الجزء الثاني للتجارة البينية ويتضمن جداول عن نسبة الواردات والصادرات البينية من إجمالي الواردات والصادرات بحسب البلدان وأقسام النظام المنسق. أما الجزء الثالث فيركّز على اتجاه التجارة الخارجية ويتضمن جداول عن واردات وصادرات كل من البلدان الأعضاء حسب أهم البلدان والكتل الاقتصادية في العالم.

This Bulletin presents data and statistical indicators on external and intraregional trade in goods in ESCWA member countries. Data are presented in time series until 2014 and were drawn primarily from national sources, and from secondary sources when needed. The Bulletin aims to assist policymakers, analysts, researchers and other users at the national, regional and international levels.

The Bulletin comprises three parts. Part I is on external trade and contains tables on annual trade growth rates in the region, the total values of imports and exports and the percentage of those values by section of the Harmonized Commodity Description and coding System (HS). Part II is on intraregional trade and contains tables on intraregional imports and exports as a share of total imports and exports by country and HS section. Part III is on the directions of trade and contains tables on the imports and exports of each member country with major countries and economic groupings in the world.

www.ingramcontent.com/pod-product-compliance
Lightning Source LLC
Chambersburg PA
CBHW080242270326
41926CB00020B/4338

* 9 7 8 9 2 1 1 2 8 3 8 4 6 *